Healing the Past,
Releasing Your Future

Healing the Past, Releasing Your Future

*Discover the roots of adult problems,
experience healing and
break through to your
God-given distiny*

Frank Fabiano
Catherine Cahill-Fabiano

Sovereign World

Sovereign World Ltd
PO Box 777
Tonbridge
Kent TN11 0ZS
England

Email: info@sovereign-world.com
Website: www.sovereign-world.com

Unless otherwise indicated, all scripture quotations are from the New International Version, inclusive language version, copyright the International Bible Society 1999; published by Hodder and Stoughton.

ISBN 1 85240 339 X

The publishers aim to produce books which will help to extend and build up the Kingdom of God. We do not necessarily agree with every view expressed by the authors, or with every interpretation of Scripture expressed. We expect readers to make their judgment in the light of their own understanding of God's Word and in an attitude of Christian love and fellowship.

Typeset by CRB Associates, Reepham, Norfolk
Cover design by CCD, www.ccdgroup.co.uk
Printed in the United States of America

Dedication

*To the Father ... the Son ... the Holy Spirit ...
who made this book possible*

If you enjoy this book and would like to help us to send
a copy of it and many other titles to needy pastors in the
Third World, please write for further information
or send your gift to:

Sovereign World Trust
PO Box 777, Tonbridge
Kent TN11 0ZS
United Kingdom

or to the **'Sovereign World'** distributor in your country.

Visit our website at **www.sovereign-world.org**
for a full range of Sovereign World books.

Contents

Acknowledgments

Healing the Past, Releasing Your Future is born out of many years of prayer ministry to those wounded on their journey through life. We can never find the words to fully express our thankfulness to the Lord for the wisdom and understanding He has revealed to us that He might heal and restore our own souls as well as the souls of countless others. We are in awe of the desire of the Lord to heal even the most wounded among us and restore to us our eternal destiny in His kingdom. Lord, we are eternally grateful.

This entire project has been an experience of God's grace from start to finish. Many have come alongside us to offer prayer support, encouragement and practical help.

We are thankful to so many friends who have been standing with us through these years. To those named and unnamed ... we thank you with all our heart.

To our grown "kids" Chris and Todd, and our families who have loved and inspired us over the years, we send our special thanks. To our pastors, C. Thomas and Maureen Anderson, you have been a major inspiration to us. Where we are today is in great part because you invested your lives into us and we are deeply grateful. We are also thankful to our church family, Living Word Bible, in Arizona, for all your love, prayers and encouragement from the beginning.

We want to thank Fraser and Puanana Haug, our long-standing friends with whom we have labored together side by side for the sake of the gospel for many years. It was through your influence that we first began to minister in YWAM internationally. Your faith in us and prayer support have been unfailing. You have been a significant part of this project from its conception.

The prayers of many have sustained us but there is one who has been our "anchor" in the spirit: Anne Marie Carlier. This project was born in prayer and sustained by prayer. Its success is in large part the fruit of her faithful intercession and the exact spiritual insights we needed at the perfect moment. We could not have done it without you. To Corrina Konkel, our long-standing "prayer warrior" who has also "labored in the spirit" to see this project birthed, we send a big hug! Corrina, as our research assistant, has found countless "hidden" treasures on the Internet that have been invaluable in this project, many thanks. Dear Corrina, you are a gift of God to us.

Our heartfelt thanks also to Albrecht and Barbara Fietz, our dear friends and committed promoters, who provided the graphic art photo in the book as a gift. Your prayer support and practical assistance also with quality graphic design is a great blessing.

We also want to thank our dear friends and ministry team, Geoff and Sonja Emerson, who have been such an encouragement and support for us over many years. Your faith in us and commitment to the ministry have contributed significantly to the success of this project.

To all our YWAM family in every corner of the world, you all have been a source of inspiration and insight from the Lord. Thanks ... Danke ... Gracias ... Dank ... Merci ... Gura maith agat ... Tapadh leat ... Diolch ... Tuck, etc. ...

Thanks to John and Paula Sandford, who have pioneered in this revelation of healing and have inspired us and personally heartened us to see this project birthed.

Our deep appreciation to Bernie Ogilvie who directed us to Sovereign World Publishing and provided the "word of the Lord" to point us in the right direction at just the right time. Bernie, you are always "spot on"!

A special word of thanks to Tim Pettingale who caught the vision and believed in the project. You are an answer to prayer and a partner from the Lord. We could not have asked for a better team to reach the world with the message God has revealed to us.

To Sovereign World Publishing your faith in and commitment

to the project have made it a reality and for this opportunity we are most grateful. You have made it possible for us to fulfill our mandate from the Lord:

> *"Write down the revelation*
> *and make it plain on tablets*
> *so that a herald may run with it."*   (Habakkuk 2:2)

Last but not least, we want to thank all those who have opened their hearts to receive the ministry and encouraged us to write the book. Without you there would be no ministry . . . no book.

Foreword

The first six years of life are the "incarnating" years. We are not speaking of physical incarnation. Our personal spirit resonates in every cell of our body, from conception to death. But sometimes we do not motivationally accept being who we are as spirit, soul and body, thus failing to incarnate fully into who we are meant to become. Traumas and our reactions may cause us to withdraw or rebel. When either happens, we bury a portion of who we are, until eventually, having failed to incarnate, we lose even what we think we have (Luke 19:24).

Many, even among born anew Christians, have persisted in thinking that the past is the past, having no effect upon us. Unfortunately, all too many people resist becoming aware that we have carried our *childish* reactions and coping mechanisms into the present, refusing to acknowledge that these afflict and inhibit our present relationships and activities. Some Christians especially do this, claiming that their conversion ended the process of healing when, in fact, it only began it.

Frank and Catherine Fabiano do a good job of cataloging for us how each developmental period of our life, from womb to adulthood, has become and remains a critical influence in all we think and do as adults. Psychologists have shown us how, in our infancy, nurture, or the lack of it, blesses or cripples us emotionally, and how that affects character development. The Fabianos reveal how our spiritual life is not something apart from and having little to do with all that psychology has revealed, but that we are one being, developing spiritually, emotionally and in every other way together. They show us how failing to develop has happened because we reacted and so failed to "incarnate" properly.

11

But they don't leave us there, as though we could be saved by right knowledge, if we just understood how we were formed – or malformed as the case may be. They know that *"You shall know the truth and the truth shall set you free"* means more than mere head knowledge. It means to know Jesus and He shall set you free. Throughout the book diagnosis is intertwined beautifully with resolution – redemptive healing love in our Lord Jesus Christ.

Too often in the past psychology and Christianity have appeared to be antagonistic to one another. Christians have reacted to what seems to them determinism, as though psychology is saying culture and society condition us, which of course does away with guilt, to us the necessary and blessed stepping stone to freedom in Christ. Whereas Christians say we have a personal spirit by which we choose how we will react to what forms us, thus guilt, leading to freedom in Christ (who did not come to save the righteous but the guilty). Psychologists have often felt that Christians load people with guilt (for many psychologists the *enemy* to freedom, since secular psychologists don't know Christ) and that Christians inhibit development of who we are through restrictive laws and fear.

The field of healing has greatly needed works that disparage neither side and show how psychological understanding and faith can work together to bring about healing and the full development of the Christ-like character God intends all of us to possess. In *Healing the Past, Releasing Your Future*, the Fabianos dance us joyfully beyond the warfare of history into harmony and saving action. They show us psychologically how we are to be developed, stage by stage, and how wounding inhibits or prevents altogether, and then how the merciful ministry of the Lord Jesus Christ is to be employed, not only to set us free, but to transform harmful events and their results into the blessing of a strong and helpful character.

Christians have sometimes been needlessly afraid of science, as though it would undo faith by its revelations. Frank and Catherine liberally quote from the latest scientific researches and turn those into blessings by showing how faith in our Lord Jesus Christ uses every truth, from whatever source, to set people free. Thus they dispel whatever remaining shrouds of fear clog the pathways of understanding and fullness of potential in maturation in Christ.

Look to enjoy as you read. This is not a dry tome of arcane knowledge. It is a lively testimony that employs real stories of real lives to move its revelations beyond our too analytical left brains into the right brain of revelation and emotion. Joy and freedom to breathe and enjoy life should be what results as you study its pages. If that isn't what happens to you, read it again, only this time with a light heart and a hope of freedom. That is the Fabianos' hope for you – and beyond theirs, our Lord's.

John Sandford

Introduction

Maturity does not happen in a "microwave moment." Nor is it an endowment bestowed on a person by virtue of growing old. Maturity is the quest of a lifetime. It is not a destination but rather a purposeful and deliberate journey, a process of transformation. It will not happen automatically with the accumulation of years but rather requires a conscious act of submitting our will to the will of God working in us. Many of us have heard people say, "Maturity comes with age," but it is a lie. *Old age* comes with age. We can grow "old in the Lord" and yet lack maturity. The mandate to mature is the highest calling for those who belong to Christ.

> *"It was he* [Christ] *who gave some to be apostles, some to be prophets, some to be evangelists and some to be pastors and teachers, to prepare God's people for works of service so that the Body of Christ may be built up until we all reach unity in the faith and in the knowledge of the Son of God and become* **mature, attaining to the whole measure of the fullness of Christ."** (Ephesians 4:11–13, our emphasis)

When we consider the standard of biblical maturity, none of us is completely mature. Yet, we are challenged to pursue maturity, to be transformed into the image of Christ, to open ourselves to the process of sanctification.

> *"Instead, speaking the truth in love, we will in all things* **grow up** *into him, who is the Head, that is Christ."* (Ephesians 4:15, our emphasis)

15

Hindrances to Maturity

The shortcomings of our natural human development affect our maturing process in the Lord.

> *"The spiritual did not come first, but the natural, and after that the spiritual."*   (1 Corinthians 15:46)

Just as we need to be "born again" (cf. John 3:7), so also we need to "grow up" again to become all that the Father created us to be.

> *"Like newborn babes, crave pure spiritual milk, so that by it you may **grow up*** in your salvation, now that you have tasted that the Lord is good."*   (1 Peter 2:2)

Our past is ever present. The whole of our life is influenced by what has gone before. We can no more detach the present from the past than a tree can walk away from its roots. To move forward on our quest to maturity, we must:

1. understand the process of human development as God intended it to be
2. recognize the "roots" of our adult problems in our infancy and childhood
3. experience the healing and restoration of the Lord as we relive the events of the past in His revealed presence.

Salvation

Jesus made provision for all of our needs through salvation. In the original Greek, the word used for "salvation" means healing, deliverance and eternal life. As Christians we often overemphasize eternal life and neglect to lay hold of the healing and deliverance so needed in this life. One practical aspect of this benefit of salvation is experiencing the healing the Lord provides to restore us to wholeness.

---

* **Note**: "grow up": According to a text note in the NIV Study Bible the Greek for this phrase is the standard term for the desirable growth of children.

God's Plan for Human Development

Father God has a plan for human development. Unfortunately, we human beings have not understood it. For generations we have *"leaned on our own understanding"* (Proverbs 3:5) and as a result have made grave errors that have caused serious deficits and wounding to generations of God's children, including ourselves. Many of us, troubled by our failures in life, wonder why we are the way we are. The truth is that we have unmet needs and emotional wounds from our early years which have a lingering impact on our lives. Father God knows each of us intimately and understands our need. He is the answer to every heart cry. He longs to heal us and redeem all that was lost. Whatever wounds we have suffered, or inflicted upon others, Father God will have the last word: *"He sent forth his word and healed them"* (Psalm 107:20).

Weeds and Roots

"And some [seed] *fell among thorns; and the thorns sprang up and choked them."*   (Matthew 13:7, NKJV)

*"Now he who received seed among the thorns is he who hears the word, and the **cares of this world** and the deceitfulness of riches choke the word, and he becomes unfruitful."*
(Matthew 13:22, NKJV, our emphasis)

There are two ways in which the experiences of our early life hinder us from becoming mature. The first is through unmet developmental needs. If, in our infancy and childhood, some of our needs remained unmet, we enter adulthood lacking in some of the resources we need to become a mature person. We cannot give what we have not received. Our neediness not only hinders us in our own life but it impoverishes our capacity to give to the next generation. The second way in which we are inhibited in our maturing process is by the wounds inflicted on us through parents, caretakers and other people who had a formative influence in our life. These negative influences, sown as seeds in our early months and years of life, come to harvest in our adult life as fears, pain, shame, insecurities, sin and cyclical problems. This harvest has a debilitating effect on our lives, frustrating us and often tripping us up in our quest for maturity. We get stuck and find ourselves confronting the same issues over and over again. This continues until we get to the "root cause." The Lord promises to rid us of these "roots" in our lives.

> *"Every plant that my heavenly Father has not planted will be pulled up by the roots."* (Matthew 15:13)

How Healing Can Happen

An unknown commentator once observed, "The past is not the past: it lives on in memory." Psychological studies of the brain have revealed that everything that has ever happened to us in our life remains a part of us. In 1951 Dr Wilder Penfield, a neurosurgeon at McGill University, made a startling discovery. He found that if he stimulated the temporal cortex of the brain (the frontal lobes of the brain near the temples) with an electric stimulation during surgery the patient would vividly recall a specific past event and experience it as if it were happening in the present moment with all the feelings that occurred when the original experience happened. Dr Penfield reported:

> "The subject feels again the emotion which the situation originally produced in him, and he is aware of the same interpretations, true or false, which he himself gave to the experience in the first place. This evoked recollection is not the exact photographic or phonographic reproduction of past scenes or events. It is a reproduction of what the patient saw and heard, felt and understood."[1]

He further demonstrated that a person can occupy two aspects of conscious awareness simultaneously. In one case, he described the patient crying out that he heard people laughing. The patient somehow had double consciousness of two simultaneous situations – one in the present, and the other forced into his conscious awareness from the past, by electrical stimulation. Dr Penfield writes: "when such a memory is forced into a patient's consciousness, it seems to him to be a present experience. Only when it is over does he recognize it is a vivid memory of the past. Such a memory is as clear as it would have been thirty seconds after the original experience."[2]

Penfield, Jasper and Roberts emphasize the difference between the re-experiencing of such complete memories and the isolated phenomena which occur on stimulation of the visual or auditory cortex or the memory for speech and words. They stress that the temporal recording carries with it important psychical elements, such as an understanding of the meaning of the experience and the emotion it may have aroused.[3]

Generally speaking, when the temporal cortex at either side of the brain is stimulated by electrical charge, the evoked memory becomes as imminent and vivid as the present. What is brought to life is a personal reliving of a specific experience.

In times of healing prayer, we have witnessed and personally experienced the Holy Spirit "stimulate" memory, although in a much less intrusive manner than that carried out by Penfield. A person touched in this way by the Holy Spirit re-experiences an actual event of the past in the present time. They are aware of the true present and yet simultaneously fully immersed in the living memory. The origins or "root cause" of adult problems are brought to light, but it does not end there. The Lord reveals His presence in the memory and changes the images and its effect for the good of the person concerned, releasing him or her from the trauma it carried. His presence renews and transforms everything. The old images give way to the new experience of Jesus reliving that time with us, our Healer, our Protector, our Savior.

Karen's story

Karen sat keeping watch through a crack in her bedroom door. Her father was an alcoholic and would often erupt in violent drunken rages. She feared for her mother's safety, so she kept vigil, naively believing if things got out of hand, she could save her.

Karen had all but forgotten that experience when, in a time of healing prayer, the Holy Spirit brought it back in vivid clarity. This time she asked the Lord to reveal His presence there. Suddenly, in her memory, as she kept her vigil the door opened – there stood

Jesus. He reached down, took her into His arms and carried her to bed. As He tucked her in, He comforted her and reassured her. She could not save her mom, but He could. He walked out the door and closed it, and as Karen closed her eyes to sleep, she heard something amazing . . . it was quiet.

That night the Lord lifted an immense burden from Karen's heart. Now, whenever she remembers that time, she never "sees" it the old way: she "sees" the new version. Jesus is there and His presence changes everything.

Father God's Intervention

God is ever present. We are not always aware of His presence, nevertheless He is present. He was there at the beginning of our life, in our infancy, as we learned to walk, in our childhood, through the teen years; He is there today. He is ever present watching over our lives.

> "When Israel was a child, I loved him,
>   and out of Egypt I called my son . . .
> It was I who taught Ephraim to walk,
>   taking them by the arms;
> but they did not realize
>   it was I who healed them.
> I led them with cords of human kindness,
>   with ties of love;
> I lifted the yoke from their neck
>   and bent down to feed them."   (Hosea 11:1, 3–4)

In the light of this truth, the inevitable question we are confronted with, is: "If God was really there, why did He allow bad things to happen to me?" A fair question that deserves a fair answer. The short answer is, free will. When He created us, God gave us free will and He will not take it back. It is what makes us unique, created in His image and likeness, and sets us apart in all of God's creation. The choices of our parents, caretakers and other authority figures in our life determined the good or evil that befell us. Wherever there is sin, someone gets hurt. Father

God knew this would happen, and so He planned a way of redemption.

> *"Our fathers disciplined us for a little while as they thought best;*
> *but God disciplines us for our good, that we may share in his*
> *holiness."*   (Hebrews 12:10)

Discipline in this context means to teach, train, nurture, correct, etc. The problem here is that our fathers did *"what they thought best"* rather than what God's word said was best. God makes a clear differentiation between our ways and His ways:

> *"As the heavens are higher than the earth,*
> *so are my ways higher than your ways*
> *and my thoughts than your thoughts."*   (Isaiah 55:9)

In Hebrews 12:10 there is also a "little hinge that swings a mighty door" the word "but." "But" functions like an eraser to wipe out all that went before and establish what comes after. This understanding helps us to hear what Father God is saying to us. In an updated paraphrase it might read: "Yes, yes, I know what happened. Your fathers did the best they knew how but I am going to take care of all that. I am going to 'father' you again. I am going to teach you, train you, correct you, nurture you, provide for all your needs, for your good, that you may share in my holiness." The Father wants to restore us because He loves us and wants us to share in His holiness, to be pure, blameless and sacred. If we are to be all that God intended us to be, we need Him to do a supernatural work in our lives. We were born to a destiny. That destiny can only be fulfilled as the Father redeems and restores us to be all that He created us to be in the first place.

Bryan Jones, a respected man of God from England, was speaking at a pastors' conference in Tucson, Arizona, some years ago and he shared this story. Bryan and his wife take delight in buying and restoring old English cottages to their original beauty. One day, as he was working on a piece of antique furniture, the Lord said to him, "Bryan, how do you restore furniture to its original condition?" Bryan replied and explained the process of restoration step by step to the Lord, as if He didn't know. The Lord then responded, "When I restore My children, I don't restore them to their original condition: I restore them to *My original intention.*"

Father God's Healing Process

"The Lord's desire is that we bear fruit and fulfill His destiny for our lives. This is possible only if we become desperate enough to stop covering up our fears, pains, insecurities and sin and allow Him to replace our compensatory facades with His healing virtue and power." (Doug Stringer)[4]

The Father loves each of us. It's true. He loves us with an everlasting love without any conditions. He loves us in our pain, in our immaturity, in our neediness. But He loves us all too much to leave us there. The Father knows the frailty of our human flesh; He knows we are not perfect. He also knew that we would be wounded in this life, so in His great love He has prepared a way to redeem what was lost to us; He has prepared a way for us to be healed and set free from bondages, a way for us to be restored to His original intention.

Truth: Facing the Pain

"Go to the place of your greatest fear, and there you will find your greatest strength."[5]

All of us have been wounded in our development. Our parents – even wonderful, loving, Christian parents – were not perfect and were not always able to meet all our needs. In many cases, they too suffered from emotional wounds and had unmet needs in their own lives. They could not give what they had not received. The Father wants to put an end to this inheritance of pain from generation to generation. But, in order to be free, we must face the truth. Jesus said,

"If you hold to my teaching, you are really my disciples. Then you will know the truth and the truth will set you free."
(John 8:31–32)

To be free we must be willing to look at the truth which the Lord will reveal to us. We all have a natural tendency to protect our family and those we love, sometimes to the extent of denying the truth. It is not always easy but, if we are willing, the Holy Spirit, the Spirit of Truth, will reveal the truth to us. Denial is not loyalty, it is deception. We do not dishonor our parents by being willing to see the truth as the Lord reveals it to us. It is the only way to freedom. Begin by facing the pain with Jesus. Acknowledge the hurts, fears, insecurities, problems, shame and need in your life. Focusing on each stage of your development, as you work your way through the book, the Lord will reveal what He intended for your life and begin a process of healing and restoration.

Revelation: Revisiting the Scene

The next step is identifying the specific adult problem in your life by asking the Holy Spirit to reveal the "root" of this pain or need. He may stimulate a memory, a picture, an impression, an awareness, or some other way of "knowing." Sometimes there is just a vague awareness that "something is there," that "something happened." The Lord knows each of us and He makes known the "root cause" of our pain or need in the way that is best for us. Not everyone "sees" pictures, and it is not necessary to "see" a picture to be healed. Some memories are too painful to be seen in sharp focus and the Lord shields us from anything that would be too much for us to endure. Ask the Lord to reveal His presence to you in the way that is best for you. Ask Him to show you what the Father intended for you in that experience. The presence of the Lord changes things. Leanne Payne has explained what happens like this: "In the Presence, listening, our souls are remythologized. The words and pictures that come from God replace the old negative, lying words and inner images that have their genesis in the world, the flesh and the devil – all that underlies our need for healing and salvation."[6]

Redemption: Healing and Deliverance

Often, we are not wounded by what actually happened, but by our "perception" of reality. As the Lord ministers to us, He removes the "sting of death" and gives us newness of life. The destruction is uprooted, the Lord heals us, sets us free from bondages and pulls down demonic strongholds. Jesus comes to reveal the Father to us in a very real way, by providing for all our needs, nurturing us, and restoring us supernaturally to His original intention.

Restoration: The Planting of the Lord

Through the process of restoration the Lord recalls to life what has been lost to us. He supernaturally "plants" in our lives what He intended for us from the beginning. Often what is planted by the Father is the exact opposite of what the enemy sowed into our life through the wounds of the past. The Lord gives us *"beauty instead of ashes, the oil of joy instead of mourning, a garment of praise instead of a spirit of despair."* His purpose is that, *"They will be called oaks of righteousness, a planting of the LORD for the display of His splendor"* (Isaiah 61:3).

In a meeting recently, I was sharing this revelation in a time of ministry when suddenly, at the back of the room, a woman exploded in an agonizing wail. The depth of her grief and piercing pitch sent a shudder over me as I moved toward her. The Lord said, "Tell her to call My name ... *Jesus.*" As I did as the Lord directed, in a desperate mournful cry she screamed, "Jeeeesus ... Jeeesus ... Jesus ..." A holy hush fell in the room and the strong presence of the Lord quieted her. Then suddenly, just as suddenly, she began to laugh. The more she laughed, the more she was filled with joy. The more she laughed, the more others caught the joy until we were all laughing, with tears running down our faces. As the Lord poured out His "oil of joy," sorrow and mourning fled away and many received healing just being in the presence of the Lord.

Reparenting: Father, "Father Me ... "

The Father longs to provide for our unmet needs and in a very *real* way "father" us again. Healing and deliverance are only the beginning of the process. As we seek the Father day by day, He will continue to nurture us and provide the love, guidance, direction, correction and instruction we need to mature in our newness of life. We are "born again" to "grow up" again into the fullness of all God created us to be. Setting our hearts on things above, we begin a journey to maturity led by the Holy Spirit through a process of transformations by the renewing of our minds – to become more and more like Jesus.

"God wants to turn crisis to victory, barrenness to greatness in our lives. Regardless of our circumstances the Lord wants to satisfy the longing in our souls. Though we may seem barren with great odds stacked against us, He has placed His seed of greatness in every one of us who has called on His name." (Doug Stringer)[7]

From the Father's Heart

Freedom and healing are Father God's gifts to us through His Son, Jesus. If you have never received the Father's free gift personally, please pray this simple prayer and invite Jesus into your life today and begin the most exciting adventure you have ever known:

"Father God, thank you for Jesus. Jesus, thank you for dying on the cross for me. Please forgive my sins. I receive the free gift of salvation you offer me. Jesus, come into my life and be my Lord and my Savior. Amen."

Welcome to the family of God!

Notes

1. W. Penfield, "Memory Mechanisms," *Arch. Neurol. & Psychiat.*, 67 (1952), 178–198, with discussion by L.S. Kubiem *et al.*
2. E. Berne MD, *Transactional Analysis in Psychotherapy* (Grove Press, 1961), pp. 17, 18, 178–198.
3. W. Penfield and H. Jasper, *Epilepsy and the Functional Anatomy of the Brain* (Boston: Little, Brown and Co., 1954), Chapter XI; W. Penfield and L. Roberts, *Speech and Brain Mechanisms* (Princeton: Princeton University Press, 1959).
4. Doug Stringer, *Charisma* magazine (March, 1999), 79.
5. Michael Rodgers and Marcus Losack, *Glendalough: A Celtic Pilgrimage* (Blackrock, C. Dublin: Columba Press, 1996), p. 112.
6. Leanne Payne, *The Healing Presence* (Grand Rapids, Michigan: Hamewith Books, 1995), p. 163.
7. Doug Stringer, *Pray Until Something Happens*, p. 80.

Chapter 1

In the Beginning

In Utero

Darkness ... impenetrable darkness enveloped Laura. So alone ... she longed for her mother. The loneliness closed around her. Laura kicked frantically to make her presence known. No response. An adrenaline rush shocked her. All around her a strange sound ... the sound of pain ... her mother crying. The words were imperceptible to the little one in the womb ... but the impression etched deep in her heart. Her dad was gone. When Laura was born she was told she was born face first ... her face bruised and battered ... she never understood ... she was looking for her father.

The journey of a lifetime does not begin at the moment of birth, but long before in the "secret place" under the comforting rhythm of a mother's heartbeat.

> "My frame was not hidden from you
>   when I was made in the secret place.
> When I was woven together in the depths of the earth ..."
>   (Psalm 139:15)

In the beginning God had a plan and purpose for your life – a divine destiny. That may be hard for you to believe given the present circumstances you may see, but nevertheless it is true. You were brought to life for an eternal purpose. If you are not in

touch with that destiny and clear about your purpose, something has gone wrong.

> *"Before I was born the* LORD *called me;*
> *from my birth he has made mention of my name."*
>
> (Isaiah 49:1)

Adult Problems

Some of our most perplexing personality problems in adult life
are deeply rooted in our impressions from the womb. Yet hidden
from conscious awareness, just beyond the grasp of cognitive
recall in that "gray space" referred to as "prememory impressions" or "memory traces," these "experiences" direct and
influence some of our most fundamental emotional responses,
thought processes, and behavior patterns.[1,2] They are existential
crises, very real, yet just out of memory's reach.

Laura's story continues ...

Shortly before her birth, Laura's dad returned to his wife and
daughter. He suffered from "post traumatic disorder" and could
not cope with impending fatherhood. He broke down and ran.
His return was a relief, but the damage of abandonment had
been done.

All through her life Laura had struggled with intermittent
anxiety attacks that came from "out of nowhere," without
warning, for no apparent reason. She was plagued with a fear of
abandonment and kept choosing men who did just that, validating the lie. Under extreme stress she would often hear the
"voice of death" – suicide – seducing her to give up on life.
Though she could admit it to no one, she felt very much alone
most of the time, as if there was a "glass wall" between her and
others, even her and God. At other times she wondered if she
should exist at all. Laura had serious problems in her life and she
knew it. Years of therapy and counseling had made her very
aware of every detail of her problems and trained her in excellent
coping strategies to be able to manage them. But she wasn't
free.

Laura's story is an all-too-familiar one. Long before we human beings are capable of cognitive thought, we are being impacted and impressed deeply in our "being" by the atmosphere and influences of the womb. In a very real sense, what happens in the womb establishes the foundation for our life.

At this earliest stage of development, the very serious impressions being made on our lives include: "I am to exist . . . I am not to exist . . . I do belong . . . I don't belong . . . I am accepted . . . I am rejected." Our experiences in the womb determine which of these impressions impact our life and subsequently affect us in later life. If we did not receive what the Lord intended for our development then we are hindered in our adult life.

Adult problems often found "rooted" in the womb are: existence issues, rejection issues, anxiety disorders, "autistic" behaviors and insecurity in belonging or having a place in this world. Each of these adult behavioral indicators helps us identify which impression may have been prevalent in the womb. In other words, our adult problems highlight the wounds of the past and bring the specific need for healing into the "light" where it can be seen. Recognizing our need is the first step in the healing process. The adult behavioral manifestations can be summarized like this:

- *Existence issues* are revealed in struggles with life and death, ranging from ambivalence about life to suicidal thoughts and compulsions.

- *Rejection* is revealed in a denial of acceptance, care, love, etc., and causes a person to feel worthless.

- *Anxiety disorders* range from chronic states of uneasiness, apprehension, restlessness to sudden, intermittent panic attacks.

- *Autistic behaviors* hinder the ability to establish or maintain close emotional relationship with others.

- *Insecurity* affects stability in life. This gives rise to questions and struggles with being and belonging, causing uncertainty.

In order to grasp how these problems take hold of a person, it is important to understand the process for healthy development in the womb.

Developmental Process

> *"For you created my inmost being;*
>   *you knit me together in my mother's womb.*
> *I praise you because I am fearfully and wonderfully made;*
>   *your works are wonderful,*
>   *I know that full well.*
> *My frame was not hidden from you,*
>   *when I was made in the secret place.*
> *When I was woven together in the depths of the earth,*
>   *your eyes saw my unformed body.*
> *All the days ordained for me*
>   *were written in your book*
>   *before one of them came to be."*   (Psalm 139:13–16)

From the moment of conception we begin growing – spirit, soul and body. Endowed with an innate personality and eternal destiny, the process of development will either enhance or diminish the person we are becoming. This time of development sets the foundation for our whole life and so is crucial to later development as well. No other stage of development so dramatically impacts the whole of our life as this stage. Acceptance or rejection, life or death are the realities confronting us in the womb. The result of this time of development can be positive or negative depending on what happens. A weak or faulty foundation affects stability in later life. Wherever the foundation is missing altogether, there is no platform on which to build.

New technology has made it possible to study the life of a child in the womb and amazing discoveries have been made in recent years. The child in the womb is very impressionable and far more alert and interactive than had been realized before.[3]

Researchers now believe that there is a degree of awareness even from the moment of conception.[4] The child is very sensitive to the atmosphere within the womb in the earliest weeks and months. In later months, particularly in the last trimester the child can be directly affected by external sounds as well.[5] The Bible affirms this truth in a familiar passage.

> *"When Elizabeth heard Mary's greeting, the baby leaped in her womb and Elizabeth was filled with the Holy Spirit. In a loud voice she exclaimed: 'Blessed are you among women and blessed is the*

child you will bear! . . . As soon as your greeting reached my ears,
the baby in my womb leaped for joy.'"   (Luke 1:41–42, 44)

Initially, the most direct impact on the child comes from the
mother, specifically the mother's thoughts and feelings.[6] However, it is important to recognize that the mother's thoughts and
feelings are most directly impacted by the father's thoughts
and feelings toward her and the child.[7] So both parents play an
important part in the child's life from the earliest moments.

During a seminar a few years ago, a first-time expectant mother
came up for prayer. Her due date was fast approaching but the
baby was in breach position.* The doctor had previously checked
the baby and the mom, and everything was normal for natural
birth. He had even turned the baby into position for birth, but
overnight the baby moved back into breach position. As we
prayed the Holy Spirit revealed that the baby was in emotional
distress. When we asked the woman if there had been any stress
between her and her husband she broke down in tears. Her
husband had lost his job just after she became pregnant and the
financial stress was causing tremendous pressure on their marriage. They would often have violent arguments. The baby had
been "listening" and was taking his "stand." He was not coming
out. Under the leading of the Holy Spirit she placed her hand on
her tummy and spoke to her baby. She told the little one what
had been happening and assured the baby that they loved and
wanted him and the stress was not his fault. We continued in
prayer and asked the Lord to remove the anxiety and release His
peace to the baby. That night her husband did the same and by
the next morning the baby had turned into position for birth on
his own. He was born naturally a few days later, a joyful, peaceful
baby. The Lord had healed him.

* **Note**: This is not always the reason for a baby to be breach: sometimes it is due
to threatening conditions such as the placenta blocking the birth canal or the
cord being wrapped around the baby's neck, to mention two possible causes. The
possible physical reasons should always be checked by your physician first. In
these cases the baby is right not to turn. However, if there is no medical or
physical reason, the cause may be stress.

Bonding: the Vital Connection

Bonding with our mother is critical for us in the womb. There is no more vital connection in this unfolding drama of life. Should this connection be hindered or missing in any way, the effects are dramatic. Bonding can be positive, negative or lacking because it does not happen automatically.

Dr Verny, a psychiatrist, pioneering research to understand the unborn child observes, "... intrauterine bonding does not happen automatically: Love for the child and understanding of one's own feelings are needed to make it work."[8]

Bonding was once believed to be initiated at birth, but research now indicates that it begins in the womb.[9] Bonding is achieved through a system of "communication" between mother and child.[10] According to Dr Verny, "Bonding occurs through three separate communication channels ... capable of carrying messages from baby to mother or from mother to baby." These three communications channels are *physiological*, *behavioral* and *sympathetic*.

Physiological Communication

The physiological connection with mom is essential and provides not only nourishment, but also transmits messages. If mom takes care to follow a healthy diet to provide everything needed for the baby to grow and develop properly, she sends a strong message: "Live, thrive, I love you, I want you to have all that you need to grow strong and healthy and I will make sure you get it." In this communiqué, a message of life, love and acceptance is communicated.

Behavioral Communication

The behavioral communication between mother and baby and vice versa is familiar and well documented. The baby kicks to communicate his or her need for attention, comfort, or when in distress. When mom responds by rubbing her tummy and speaking to the baby in reassuring comforting tones, mom and baby connect and the emotional bond between them is strengthened. This maternal response affirms the baby's existence and provides the needed nurturing for the baby. Studies have found the baby will kick when startled by loud noises and even to reassure mom when she is concerned about the baby.

Sympathetic Communication

Sympathetic communication is the least familiar and least understood in modern western cultures. It is an "intuitive" communication between mother and child that transcends physical and behavioral limitations and requires a willingness to trust our "senses."[11] This sensitivity of the baby to the thoughts and feelings of the mom and vice versa goes beyond behavioral communication.

Dr Verny observes, "Rationalization and mechanization of the kind that has spread across Europe and America over the past few centuries seems to have destroyed that trust. Nature's enigmas make us uncomfortable. If we cannot explain something we prefer to ignore it."[12]

Mom just seems to "know" what is needed. This intuitive knowledge is manifested in the maternal sensitivity, "knowing" the thoughts and feelings of the baby, and the baby's sensitivity, "knowing" the mother's thoughts and feelings.

Dr Emil Reinhold, an Austrian obstetrician, studied fetal reaction to maternal emotion. He demonstrated how the baby is an active participant in intrauterine bonding. In the study he got several mothers in their third trimester to lie down and be still for 20–30 minutes under ultra sound. The baby relaxes in this position and stops moving. The realization that the baby was not moving could cause panic in the mother. Seconds later, sensing the mother's distress, the baby started kicking intensely to reassure mom, "I'm OK." The baby reacted sympathetically to the mother's distress.

Emotional bonding that is forged through the behavioral and sympathetic communication between the mother and baby is not automatic, but is dependent upon the mother's ability to respond to "communication" received from the child. Even in the womb we are beginning to try to "reach out and touch someone." One clear mode of communication by the baby in the latter months is movement. When we move in our mother's womb and she responds by speaking to us, we emotionally bond with her. Moms who respond to their babies, connect and complete our initial attempts to be recognized, comforted in our need, and affirmed in our existence. In movement we are saying, "Mom ... Hey, Mom ... I'm here ... Do you know it? ... Is it OK???" Or "Mom ... what was that LOUD noise? I don't like it!!!" When mom responds, speaking to us in soothing, reassuring tones she affirms our existence. We are comforted and the emotional bond is complete.

To understand just a little of what this must be like from the child's perspective, let's consider this illustration: Let's say you are in your house locked in a closet. All your friends come over and bring your favorite pizza, turn on the music and are laughing and talking together, but you are locked in your closet. What would you do? Probably start pounding and kicking the door to get someone's attention so they respond to your need – in this case, to get out and join the party. In a similar way, the child needs to get mom's attention and so he or she begins to move and kick. Mom's response to that movement affirms his or her existence. Mom's willingness to respond to the child, and also to call dad's attention to the child's movement, establishes and strengthens the bonding not only with mom, but with dad also. It is possible for the in utero child to hear and respond to external sounds and stimuli in the last trimester.[13] So when the father speaks in loving tones and is attentive to the child, the child begins to bond with him as well, even before birth.[14]

The child in the womb has even been known to interact with older siblings.

> Jenna, pregnant with her second child Paul, was bathing her first born, Joseph. Joseph was just two years old. In the course of bathing, Joseph "accidentally" whacked his mom's tummy and also Paul's butt. Paul, not happy about the intrusion, started kicking back. Jenna pulled maternal rank on them both: "Hold it, I'm not getting in the middle of this. Paul, you have to wait until you come out to fight with your brother!"

Considering the biblical view of human beings as spirit, soul and body, we believe bonding through communication to the spirit of the baby is also essential to the healthy development of the whole person in the womb. As parents pray for the child and communicate the Scripture and prophetic words that God gives for the little one, the child's spirit is nurtured and strengthened even in the womb.[15] This bonding promotes the development of the child's spirit and builds a foundation for his or her spiritual destiny in God's plan.

When we receive what we need – physical nurture to grow and thrive, healthy bonding to establish a relationship with mom and dad, and spiritual sustenance to strengthen our eternal purpose and destiny – then a firm foundation is established for our life. But, if not, destruction takes root and destabilizes our development.

Weeds and Roots

> *"There is nothing concealed that will not be disclosed, or hidden that will not be made known."*   (Matthew 10:26)

The wounds inflicted in the womb have a dramatic effect even into adult life. Most of what we have learned about these wounds and the destruction that takes root as a result, has been through revelation by the Holy Spirit in over twenty-five years of counseling and prayer ministry. We have seen the Lord faithfully heal and set His people free as we have received and acted on the revelation He has given us. Also, each of these interventions has been repeated countless times by us and others, always resulting in life-changing healing and freedom. Over the years we have received countless testimonies of healing received directly from the Lord as individuals have applied the principles in the healing process and went to the Lord with open hearts. The healing process will be discussed in detail at the end of the chapter.

The Lord has been intimately involved with forming us in our mother's womb and so His revelation is the most reliable source of information. However, there has been significant confirming research in recent years, indicated previously, that has objectively supported what the Lord has revealed (see Bibliography).

Wounds at Conception

As early as conception, a person can be wounded in his or her being. We have found that insecurity in existence and shame are wounds often rooted in the circumstances of conception. Conception out of wedlock, conception through rape or incest, conception in an atmosphere of violence or perversion all inflict deep wounds. Individuals conceived in such circumstances often wonder if they should exist at all and their right to life is seriously undermined. The problem is often magnified when they are told they are an "accident," a "mistake," a "surprise," or "unplanned" by their parents. The truth is, our natural parents don't have the power to give us life. They cannot give us a spirit. It is our eternal Father who holds the power of life. When the Father breathes His breath of life into us and imparts His Spirit He says "Yes" to our life and only then do we become a living being. Why, you may wonder, would God give life to one who was conceived in horrifying circumstances? Because God loves to redeem. He knows He will redeem your life and restore you to be who He always meant you to be.

> *" . . . the LORD God formed the man from the dust of the ground and breathed into his nostrils the breath of life, and the man became a living being."*   (Genesis 2:7)

> *"The Spirit of God has made me;*
> * the breath of the Almighty gives me life."*   (Job 33:4)

> *"And he is not served by human hands, as if he needed anything, because he himself gives all men life and breath and everything else."*   (Acts 17:25)

The mother is often tormented by fear, guilt and shame and is under major stress in these cases. Whatever mom feels, the baby feels.[16] There is also an impression in the baby that says, "What mom feels is because of me," and so the baby takes on the shame. If you have been wounded in this way, you may struggle under a cloud of shame. You may not feel right about your existence and feel "driven" to earn the right to exist by performing to please others. Unconsciously, you are trying to earn your right to exist. You are trying to make up for your parents' choices, sin or shame and carry their responsibility. Wounding at conception can leave an emotional scar that overshadows your whole life.

Paula's story

Paula was an overachiever, committed to every endeavor 180 per cent and a driven perfectionist. She ran at only two speeds, turbo speed or dead stop. The latter only when she could not physically keep going. She never felt like she could rest unless she was sick or exhausted. Even flat on her back she felt guilty. Paula was a shining star, or maybe a better description would be a meteorite shooting brilliantly across the sky of life. She probably never would have noticed she had a problem until she physically collapsed and was not able to recover her strength. She came within a "hair's breath" of chronic fatigue syndrome when the Lord finally got her attention. In a desperate moment she asked the Lord what was happening. That was all He was waiting for.

Paula had been conceived before her parents were married. They were committed Christians so the shame was very intense. Her mother suffered under a heavy burden of internal guilt, condemnation and shame. No one knew except Paula. She felt responsible for her mother's pain and tried to help her carry it. Paula had a strong impression that she needed to be a very special person to earn the right to live. She loved her mom and was especially protective of her. When the Lord revealed His presence, she saw for the first time that she was in chains. She was enslaved by her perceived expectations from her parents. Paula was also burdened by the guilt and shame of her mom. Jesus lifted her burden and broke the chains of slavery. He breathed over her again the breath of life and she breathed deeply, as if for the first time. Once freed from the lies and bondages of the enemy, she was able to recover her strength and begin to learn to be really led by the Spirit.

Sometimes the effect is different on the child.

Al's story

Al was plagued by perverse thoughts and a deep sense of shame. He repented, fasted, prayed, but could not break through. When he came for ministry we asked the Lord to reveal the root cause of this recurring oppression in his life. The Holy Spirit gave Al a picture of a tiny cluster of cells overshadowed by a dark cloud.

The picture revealed the time of wounding and the Holy Spirit led us to understand that Al had been conceived in violence and perversion. This had been imparted into his life at conception. Al confirmed that his parents had had a horrifyingly violent life together. Sexual perversion and addiction to hardcore pornography was prevalent in his family. Being conceived in violence, compounded by the generational curse of sexual perversion and addiction to pornography, as well as being overshadowed by the shame of his parents' violent sexuality, had had a devastating effect on Al's life.* Al asked the Lord to reveal His presence to him in that picture and show him what the Father intended for his life. He heard the Father call his name and sensed a freshness all around him, in him – the "breath of life." The grayness that surrounded him at conception dissipated as the Lord revealed His presence in that moment.

Al saw the truth clearly for the first time – that the circumstances of his conception were *not* the will of God, but his life *was*. For God Himself, true to His word, had brought Al to life. Father God had breathed the breath of life and he had become a living being (Genesis 2:7). Al's life was not a mistake of nature, his life was planned by his eternal Father. The Father claimed him and took Al into His hands and suddenly the picture changed. Al saw himself coming to life in a burst of light, brilliant with color, in celebration and purity. From that moment on, he was free from the heavy oppression of perversion and shame and felt clean for the first time in his life. In closing Al asked the Lord to forgive the perversion of his forefathers and he forgave them. He was released from the inheritance of shame, perversion and addiction and received his inheritance of life through Christ according to Galatians 3:13. In the days that followed the enemy again tried to assault him with thoughts of perversion, but this time when Al resisted the enemy he did flee from him. The stronghold had been broken and Al knew he was free. The truth had set him free.

* **Note**: It is important to clarify that there can be other reasons for the oppression of perversion, including personal sin. Some other root causes that occur during development will be discussed in later chapters. However, the story here illustrates a cause not often considered and also a root cause for the oppression of perversion in some people.

*"Submit yourselves, then, to God. Resist the devil and he will flee
from you."*   (James 4:7)

Wounds in Bonding

The wounds that occur in the bonding process can cause serious
destruction to take root in a person's life. They include insecurity, rejection, existence issues, "autistic" behaviors and anxiety
disorders.

Insecurity in Existence

Insecurity in existence frequently comes from a mother's pervasive ambivalence about her pregnancy and, in effect, the baby's
life. This is not to say that every mother who has fleeting
misgivings about an unexpected pregnancy has wounded her
child. It is rather the impression imparted to the baby by an
extended or continuous ambivalence or rejection.[17] A mother
who is ambivalent about her pregnancy may send mixed
messages. The message "I'm not sure I want you. Sometimes I
do and sometimes I don't," is unsettling for the baby. If this
ambivalence continues for a long duration or is a consistent
pattern throughout the pregnancy, the child becomes ambivalent about his or her own existence and belonging. "If mom is
not too sure I should be here, I am not too sure I should be here."
The child in the womb is so sensitive that even the subtle
feelings of ambivalence in mom can leave an indelible impression on him or her.[18] The ambivalent mix of messages can rob us
of complete security in existence and certainty of belonging in
this world. If you struggle with existence, if you are never able to
really engage life fully, or if you don't even know what we are
talking about, then you may be existing tenuously on the surface
of life. In that case having a real impact in this world is very
difficult, as is feeling grounded and secure in life.

Mary's story

Mary was forever apologizing. It seemed she was sorry for
everything, even if it was not her fault. Her insecurity made it
difficult to be around her. Mary was the proverbial "wallflower"
hanging on the edges of a group, never really joining in. It was

impossible to do anything for her; she could not accept any care. She was skating on the surface of life and never really engaging it. Over the years she became more and more withdrawn until a good friend challenged her to ask the Lord what this behavior was about. When she did, He reminded her that she was a surprise to her parents conceived in their later years. She felt she was a burden to them even in the womb and tried to be as little trouble as possible. She never felt she had a right to ask for her needs to be met. In fact Mary never really received her "birthright." The Lord revealed that He gave her life and she was always planned by Him. He welcomed her to life and she heard Him proclaim her birthright. "You are to live and not die and proclaim the works of the Lord. You have a place; you do belong here."

The truth broke the power of the lie. Mary was able to embrace her life – the life her eternal Father had given her. She received her birthright from her eternal Father. No longer would Mary just exist, just going through life. Now she could begin to really *live* her life.

Insecurity in existence sometimes is the result of life circumstances. Before the introduction of ultra sound and the modern technologies we have today, some children in the womb went undetected before birth. In the case of twins there have been incidents of the second child being a surprise at birth. Even though the parents were loving, accepting and nurturing of the child in the womb, they were focused on one – the first born – and the second child, of whom they were unaware, felt abandoned and insecure.

Mike and Matt's story

Mike and Matt are twin brothers. Mike, the firstborn, is confident, secure and successful in whatever he does in life. Matt, the second born, is just the opposite. He is insecure, fears abandonment, suffers from anxiety attacks and feels like there is an invisible wall between him and others. For years Matt suffered, not understanding why there was such a huge difference between him and his twin brother. During a seminar as we were teaching about abandonment in the womb, Matt felt an ache inside. This was speaking to him somehow. During ministry the

Lord showed him that he had been hidden behind his brother in the womb; his parents had not known he existed. As he asked the Lord to reveal what the Father really wanted for that time of his life, he felt the Lord's presence and realized he was being cradled in the hands of Jesus. The tension of holding it all together on his own broke and he released the pain of a lifetime in gut-wrenching sobs. Matt became visibly relaxed as the Lord held him and spoke the love and acceptance over him he so desperately needed to hear.

Insecurity in Identity

Male/female identity is at the heart of who we are and is essential to our security as a person. "It's a boy" or "It's a girl" heralds our birth. Insecurity in identity is a reaction that comes from an initial rejection of our intrinsic identity as a boy or a girl from one or both parents. If your parents wanted a boy and you are a girl, or they wanted a girl and you are a boy, the rejection can cause insecurity in the essence of being either a girl or a boy. Somehow we don't feel quite right and no matter how much we may accomplish in life we never feel quite good enough. The experience of not being "good enough" or "not right" for our parents is seriously distressing. When our identity as a boy or girl is not right for our parents, insecurity destabilizes our true sense of who we are to be.

Rejection

Chronic rejection by others and toward others can have a debilitating effect on our relationships. Rejection is being denied acceptance, care, love, etc., and can cause a person to feel worthless. If you have known rejection "for as long as you can remember," then most likely it began in the womb. The child in the womb is aware of rejection in mom's thoughts and feelings and, in some cases, is aware of the father's rejection. Messages that say, "I don't want you ... you're an inconvenience ... you weren't planned ... you're not welcome," etc., rob a child of the security of acceptance and certainty of belonging. Children who are unwanted come to expect rejection and over the years build up defensive reactions and behaviors for self-protection. They will begin to reject others before others reject them. The related problem, fear of rejection, can complicate matters, causing individuals to give other people undue power over their life in an attempt to avoid being rejected.

When parents reject our existence or our identity we never feel right about ourselves. We can come under the influence of a "spirit of rejection" that makes sure rejection keeps coming and we may begin to take on a victim position in life. Encountering the presence of the Lord in the womb changes distorted, lying perceptions and brings the truth to light. Once a person is set free from the "spirit of rejection," dramatic changes take place. Tormenting rejection and fear of rejection give way to the loving acceptance and favor of the Lord. The truth of Father God's love becomes real to us. His perfect Love casts out all fear.

> *"Though my father and mother forsake me,*
> *the LORD will receive me."* (Psalm 27:10)

Existence Issues

Existence issues of a more severe nature are those associated with the oppression of death. We have encountered hundreds of people with this oppression over the years and in almost every case the oppression was rooted in the womb. This can happen in a number of ways. The most direct cause comes through abortion attempts against the child's life. A direct assault on the child's life gives the enemy permission to attack the child. If not successful in taking the life of the child in the womb, the "spirit of death" will continue to oppress the person pushing or seducing him or her toward death.

Another way this oppression can come on a person's life is through "death wishes" and "curses." If the mother or some other person speaks a curse or death wish over the child in the womb, again the enemy is given permission to "latch on" and attempt to fulfill the curse. It is especially strong if the mother or father releases the curse against their child.

Barbara's story

Barbara struggled to exist each day. Severely depressive, the desire to die was ever seducing her. Her waking moments were plagued with questions. "Why did God do this to me? Why do I have to live when most of life is so painful and disappointing?" Finally, wearied from this struggle she was ready to deal with the root of the problem. In prayer she asked the Lord where this was coming from. Barbara sensed herself in the womb and she "heard" her father's voice screaming, "I wish you would die – both of you!" Those words were a curse on Barbara, opening the door to the oppression of death against her life. Barbara felt the darkness closing in on her. She cried to the Lord and immediately He was present with her and she experienced the reality of His love surrounding her – His life shielding her from death. Barbara agreed with that life and told death to go in Jesus' name. She knew that Father God loved her, that He wanted her. She felt a big "YES!!!" planted in her heart, spoken over her life from her true Father, her eternal Father God. Now the troubling questions were gone and she had her answer. The depression was gone, the hopelessness was gone, the death was gone and the joy for life had come – a gift of life from her true Father.

Occultic rituals or curses over a child in the womb can also open the way for demonic oppression. A family history of witchcraft, sorcery, divination or other false spirituality such as Freemasonry can be an open door for the oppression of death.

Erika's story

Erika accepted Jesus as her Savior and Lord in her teen years. Before this time she had lived a fairly normal life. After her conversion she started experiencing bizarre nightmares – evil, dark beings chasing her trying to kill her. She would cry out "JESUS" and then they would be gone, but dreams with similar themes came night after night. After years of torment she came for prayer during a healing seminar. The Lord revealed that her life had been dedicated to serve false spirituality and Freemasonry by her grandfather even before she was born. A curse of death would come upon her if she did not serve Freemasonry. When Erika became a Christian, the curse kicked in. The enemy could not take her life outright, she was under the blood of Jesus, but he had legal right through the generational curse to torment her and punish her for committing her life to Christ. When this curse was exposed, Erika asked God to forgive her grandfather and her forefathers. She forgave them, recommitted her life to the Lord, and in the name and authority of Jesus she broke the dedication of her life to evil and the curse of death punishing her. She never had another tormenting dream. She was free.

Open assaults are easy to discern; however, there are other more subtle ways in which the oppression of death gains access. If death has taken a baby in the womb through abortion or miscarriage, the "spirit of death" may continue to oppress children conceived and born afterwards.

Nikki's story

All through her life Nikki had near brushes with death. Her life began in crisis. Taken from the womb by Cesarean section at eight months, a sudden hemorrhage nearly claimed her life and her mother's. Serious illnesses and accidents punctuated her life and posed threats to her well-being. She often dreamed of dying young and in her dreams everyone would be grieving her loss. Nikki had developed a romantic view of death that masked the oppression. Not until the generational curse of romanticizing tragedy was broken was she able to see her need. She had suffered a double hit: her mom's miscarriage of a child just before her birth and the attack of death against her own life. Death was unmasked and revealed for what it was: an evil attempt to rob her of her life. Truth revealed the lie and she chose life. She chose the Truth that set her free in Jesus.

Sometimes the child born *after* a child has died in the womb, feels guilty that he or she is alive and the other child has died. Often the surviving child will try to carry the life of the dead child and live life for them both.

Kara's story

Kara was thirty-five years old, totally exhausted, sick often, and beginning to look half dead. She was desperate for the Lord to do something. As we asked the Lord to reveal the root, I had a clear picture of Kara with a boy on her back with his arms around her neck. When asked about it, she told me it felt like that to her.

The boy was her brother who had died in the womb before she was conceived. Her mother never stopped grieving the loss of her son. Kara got the impression this brother's life was more valuable than her own and felt guilty that she was alive and he was dead. So she was somehow trying to carry his life and her own. Living for two people is exhausting and she had become so bonded to her dead brother that she had started to die a bit herself. The spirit of death was beginning to lure her into giving up on life. When the cause was clearly revealed, Kara needed to release her brother to the Lord and take authority over the spirit of death, breaking its grip on her life. It was time to be free to live her own life and to realize her life is a gift from God – a gift of great value.

People may be under the oppression of death and not even realize it because they have never known life without it. There are indicators in adult life that reveal this oppression. If there is an oppression of death in your life, you can look back over your life and see a pattern of "near death" accidents or illnesses. Another indicator is an obsession with death, i.e. frequent thoughts of death or dying or repeated nightmares about death or dying. It is also common with this oppression to hear the "voice of death" – suicide – under severe stress. This may manifest either as a fleeting thought or dream, or by a driving compulsion. Suicide can be active or passive. Active suicide is a conscious, premeditated attempt to take your own life by your own hands. Passive suicide is not caring if you live or die which can cause you to be careless and lose your life through an avoidable accident. The "voice of death" can be seductive, deceiving, even "religious."

A young woman I was counseling had endured a very hard life over a period of years. She was once again facing the pain of losing a man she had been sure she was to marry. This was only the most recent in a life-long series of abuses, heartaches and disappointments. In her brokenness she confessed she had had enough. "Life is too painful. I can't take any more. I just want to go home and be with the Lord." The only problem was that she would have to die to do it. The "voice of death" with a religious twist is the most dangerous deception. The enemy knows if he can get us to agree with death, he has an opportunity to bring it to pass.

People react differently to the oppression of death based on their personalities. Some are unaware of it and how it affects them. Others try to beat death by challenging it. When they feel threatened, they challenge death by running into risky, life-threatening situations and every time they survive it gives them a "rush." But no one can beat death by human strength. Even this reaction is an indication of bondage and oppression. There is only one way to deal with death – by enforcing the victory of the cross.

> *"Since the children have flesh and blood, he too shared in their humanity so that by his death he might destroy him who holds the power of death – that is the devil – and free those who all their lives were held in slavery by their fear of death."*
>
> (Hebrews 2:14–15)

If you find that this may be true in your life, remember that the Father car. and wants to set you free. His Spirit of Life swallows up death. Once the enemy is exposed and his works are brought into the light he has lost. He can only operate in darkness and hidden places. For those who belong to Father God through Jesus Christ there is the promise of freedom. What the Lord reveals, He heals.

Autism: the Bondage

Another wounding experience directly related to lack of emotional bonding in the womb is the bondage of "autism." This is not psychotic autism of a severe nature that often relates to neurological damage, but is rather an arresting of the normal developmental process. In the natural developmental process, the child grows from self-awareness to "other" awareness and from an exclusively internal focus to integration including an external focus. Communication in the womb works two ways, child to mom and mom to child.[19] When the child reaches out to mom and she responds and connects, there is no problem.

However, if the child reaches out repeatedly and there is no response, he or she is left with a sense of abandonment and isolation. In order to survive the child will close up, pull inside and try to make it on his/her own. For many different reasons, many of us have experienced abandonment in the womb. Life circumstances beyond our control, the realities of life in a fallen world, our mother's inability to form an emotional bond – all these can hinder the bonding between the mother and child. This happens when the child tries to "communicate" with mom and there is no response, no connection, and therefore no emotional bonding. Some hindrances on the mother's part may include the lack of a strong emotional bond with her own mother, trauma that distracts her attention from the child in the womb, or "frozen feelings" in her own life due to past wounds. We cannot give what we ourselves have not received. Often a mother who has suffered a miscarriage does not bond with the baby conceived afterwards in order to protect herself from the pain of loss again. This can be conscious or unconscious. So in a very real sense, for all these reasons, the child is abandoned in the womb, left in isolation, failing to make the first critical, emotional bond in life. To survive the child intuitively regresses back into natural autism, closes up inside and decides to focus inward instead of outward. In so doing the child is "locked into" a bondage of autism that continues into adult life. Those who suffer in this bondage often feel like they are on the "outside looking in," wanting to connect, yet totally at a loss to know how. They never seem to feel as though they belong or have a place. They have not been welcomed to life through the affirmation of their existence in the womb. Establishing or maintaining emotional or "heart" relationships is very difficult because they don't have that foundation of emotional bonding.

Nothing is more painful to live with than the feeling of isolation and loneliness. It is perplexing and frustrating to be able to function on the surface – to have amiable acquaintances and yet be totally unable to move into deeper levels of commitment and intimacy with those dear to us. This is the feeling of being alone in a crowd or the panic that erupts inside when someone wants to get closer to us. Running away or sabotaging the relationship are not uncommon responses to escape the pressure. Another related problem is the ability to initiate emotional relationships, but not to be able to maintain them over time. This often happens when a mom initially connected emotionally with her child, but trauma, tragedy or grief drew her attention away and the connection was broken.

The bondage of autism can also occur when the child blocks the bonding in self-defense. In some cases a child retreats into him/herself to escape a perverted bonding to mom. An emotionally needy mom who takes comfort from her in utero child is *pulling* life from the child instead of *giving* life to him/her. The child will block the bonding to survive. The Lord longs to restore this bonding and provide a firm foundation to build deep heart relationships. He still sets the captives free.

Peter's story

Peter could not let anyone get close to him. He had a wall all around him ten feet thick. His perception was that everyone was out to "suck him dry." Even his wife and kids could not reach him. When crisis hit his life an emotional breakdown followed. Now he had no choice. He had to deal with this irrational fear. In desperation he asked the Lord to reveal the root. He saw a picture of himself in the womb trying to pull out the cord connecting him to his mother. He felt life being pulled from him. His mother was very needy and he was the youngest child of five. She was drawing emotional comfort from him. He felt if he stayed connected he would be "sucked dry" and die. Jesus revealed His presence and took Peter in His arms shielding him from the neediness of his mother. Jesus touched the cord and the flow of life reversed. The life of God flowed into him, the walls of autism crumbled, and he fell into the arms of the Lord. He chose to give up his prison of autism and allow the Lord to bond with him and protect him. The foundation had been set. Now he is growing in emotional relationships and loving deeply from his heart, protected by the healthy boundaries the Lord has set for his protection.

Insecurity with Belonging

Belonging is very important. When you find yourself "on the outside looking in," trying to find your place and never really settling anywhere, it is an indication that you are insecure in your sense of belonging. A sense of belonging is not automatic.

It is the fruit of being accepted and welcomed to life. When you are not welcomed and affirmed in your existence, you can begin to feel like your life is an imposition on others and you don't belong here. The result is insecurity in your sense of belonging and inability to find where you "fit in."

Anxiety and Panic Attacks

Anxiety disorders can vary from chronic states of panic to being uneasy, apprehensive or worried about what might happen. If you cannot remember a time you did not feel this way, then usually the problem has its roots in the womb.[20] Panic attacks are sudden, intermittent, severe attacks of anxiety that occur for no apparent reason and can be quite disabling. The unpredictability of the attacks can significantly undermine confidence and security and give place to the ever pervasive fear of not knowing when the next one will strike.

Often chronic anxiety and panic attacks are rooted in trying to "carry" our mom's feelings and feeling that we have to help her. It is the sympathetic connection between mother and child that can allow this to happen. When a mother is struggling emotionally or physically during pregnancy, the baby may try to help her by "carrying" her feelings. The child senses that he or she must do this in order to survive. If you experienced this in the womb then you may feel burdened by anxiety, fear, grief, shame, or have a sense that you have unfairly carried depression with you your whole life. In many cases it is because, literally, *you have* – since the womb. You feel that you can never resolve these oppressive feelings because they are not your feelings, they belong to your mom. To be free, it is important to release those feelings to the Lord and also hand over the "care" of your mom to Jesus. Breaking this unhealthy bondage and giving her to Jesus along with her burdens is the way to freedom. Then the Lord can restore a healthy relationship between you and your mom.

Father God's Intervention

Laura's story continues . . .
The stress on Laura became unbearable. She was at her end. Something had to change. As she sought the Lord He revealed

the root cause of her pain. In a moment Laura was projected in her memory to the time in her mother's womb. The darkness, the smothering, the painful cries of her mother. The grief etched deep in her being resurfaced, but this time she was not alone. Jesus was there. Still the "glass wall" separated Laura from connecting with the Lord's presence and the prison of autism held her, so we began to pray. In desperation Laura cried to the Lord and immediately He turned to her and "the wall" melted away as He came near. Jesus cradled her and protected her. The darkness of death evaporated, the fear and grief gave way. Laura was experiencing the truth. It was the Lord who held her fast and shielded her life. It was the "everlasting arms beneath her" that secured her life. Now in the presence of Perfect Love all fear and anxiety was put away. Jesus revealed the Father's love and care for her and quieted her anxious heart. For the first time in her life, Laura felt the security of being "connected." The emotional bonding had been restored with the Lord and the abandonment and isolation plaguing her life were brought down. Jesus now was her protection. She took her stand in Jesus' name against the oppression of death, the fear of abandonment, and the bondage of autism, and she released the grief and anxiety she had carried for her mother to the Lord and was set free. Laura agreed with the truth and embraced the life and birthright Jesus had given her. She was to live and not die and proclaim what the Lord had done (Psalm 118:17). She had a place in her Father's Kingdom and she did belong. The Lord revealed that, in her desperation, Laura's mother had spoken curses and death wishes over her life. She broke those curses and forgave her mother. Finally she broke the power of shame and grief and the Lord released her from the lie that she was responsible for her mother's pain and her father's abandonment. Peace, security, life and belonging came to Laura – the planting of the Lord in her life for the display of His splendor.

"Who shall separate us from the love of Christ? Shall trouble or hardship or persecution or famine or nakedness or danger or sword? ... No in all these things we are more than conquerors through him who loved us." (Romans 8:35, 37)

Truth: Facing the Pain

Consider the adult problems identified in this chapter. Do you recognize any validating "indicators" in your thoughts, feelings or behavior? It is important to face the truth. Only by confronting the truth can you be healed and set free.

Revelation: Revisiting the Scene

The problems you have identified in your life did not start yesterday. Ask the Holy Spirit, the Spirit of Truth who leads us into all truth, to reveal the root cause of each one. He may give you a memory, an impression, a picture, an awareness, a word or some other way of "knowing." Ask Jesus to reveal Himself in the experience. Tell Jesus what you are feeling and thinking about the trauma brought into the light. Listen to what He says in response.

Redemption: Healing and Deliverance

The Father wants to heal you and restore you to His "original intention" for your life. Ask Jesus how the Father intended that time to be. The Lord will "uproot" the destruction that was planted. When we ask Him, He ministers healing and sets us free from bondages and demonic oppression supernaturally.

Restoration: The Planting of the Lord

Ask the Lord to provide for your emotional needs that went unmet during your development in the womb. He is able to restore to you all that you need and will supernaturally "plant" what He intended for your life from the beginning.

Re-parenting: Father God, "Father" Us

The Father by His Spirit will help you "work out your salvation." He will teach you day by day how to walk in His ways, the ways of life. Father God will set boundaries for your protection and discipline you for your good, and the Holy Spirit will be with you always ministering the heart of the Father. He is our Teacher and our Counselor (John 14:26). God's Word is God's way. If you proclaim His word as the final authority in every circumstance of your life, then you will be set free and will stay free.

Steps to Healing and Restoration

1. Identify the adult problems or manifestations that apply to you. (See Table 1 on page 174.)
2. Ask the Holy Spirit to reveal the "root cause" of each problem, i.e. whatever happened to you in the womb that caused a wounding in your life and allowed the problem to take root. The Holy Spirit may reveal this to you in the form of a memory, picture, impression, thought, awareness, or some other way of "knowing" (Luke 8:17).
3. Ask Jesus to reveal His presence there with you. The presence of the Lord changes everything (Hebrews 13:8; Psalm 31:14–16).
4. Tell Jesus what you are feeling and thinking in this time, place or experience. Listen to His response (Psalm 91:14–16).
5. Ask Jesus to reveal what the Father intended for this time of your life. Jesus comes to show us the Father. He comes to care for your developmental needs, to heal you, to redeem all that was lost to you and to restore you to be all He created you to be (Jeremiah 29:11; Matthew 15:13).
6. Forgive your parents and all those who wounded you. Break any generational curses if necessary (Matthew 6:14; Galatians 3:13; see also Appendix A, Generational Curses).
7. Take authority in Jesus' name over any demonic oppression or influences in your life that the Lord has revealed. Command them to leave in Jesus' name (Luke 10:19).
8. Break agreement with the lie planted in your heart and ask the Father to uproot it. Embrace the truth that has the power to set you free – the Word of God. Proclaim the promises in God's Word that are His answers to your need (John 8:31–32; Matthew 15:13).
9. Receive Father God as your eternal Father and receive your inheritance of life through Christ Jesus (1 John 1:2).

10. Seek the Father each day and ask Him to "father" you. Ask the Holy Spirit to teach you how to walk in your "newness of life" (Hebrews 12:10).

Notes

1. Thomas Verny, *The Secret Life of the Unborn Child* (New York: Dell Publishing Co., 1981), p. 23.
2. Ibid., pp. 15, 67.
3. Ibid., p. 12.
4. Ibid., p. 19.
5. Ibid., pp. 38–39.
6. Ibid., pp. 13, 16.
7. Ibid., pp. 13, 17, 49.
8. Ibid., pp. 78, 81, 95.
9. Ibid., pp. 16, 17, 27.
10. Ibid., pp. 74–76.
11. Ibid., pp. 87–90.
12. Ibid., p. 82.
13. Ibid., pp. 38–39.
14. Ibid., p. 30.
15. Frances MacNutt, *Praying for Your Unborn Child* (New York: Doubleday Publishing, 1988), pp. 1–3.
16. Verny, *The Secret Life of the Unborn Child,* pp. 76, 80.
17. Ibid., p. 13.
18. Ibid., pp. 16, 48, 50, 63, 89, 98.
19. Ibid., p. 81.
20. Ibid., pp. 55–58.

Chapter 2

Being

Birth to Six Months

Birth, for most of us, was the first trauma of life. Do you remember?

"For nine months – all my life – it has been so wonderful. Warm water cradles me in suspended peace. Mom's heartbeat comforts me and sometimes even excites me when it beats fast. I am upside down now. It is almost time to make my entry. It's getting a little cramped in here."

Suddenly, in an instant, swoosh – the water is gone.

"Yuck! I'm vacuum sealed! What is this sticky stuff? What's happening? I can feel pressure all around me. I'm being squeezed. The walls are closing in on me. This pressure is forcing me out. I'd better push too to get away from the squeezing. Oh no, I'm being squeezed through such a small opening, my head feels like it's going to be squished. PUSH!!! Here I come!!! ...

"Wow, it's bright out here! Oh, where is Mom's heartbeat? Hold me, Mom . . . (sigh). Hey, what are they doing? Oh no! My life line! Not my life line . . . Don't cut my life line! WWWAAAAAAAAAA!!!

"Now what's happening?! I'm being wrapped up in something . . . They think this is soft? It's the itchiest thing I ever felt . . . MOM!!!"

Voila! LIFE! How exciting, right? Hmm . . .

Each birth is a unique drama – mom and child working

together to bring the little one into the world. God provided these first months of life to establish what it means to exist, your identity and self-image, your security in life and feelings of basic trust. All these are essential in laying the foundations for effective thinking, problem solving and communication throughout life.

Adult Problems

Martha's story
Martha has difficulty speaking through her deep sobs. Finally, she is able to speak clearly as we sit and wait. "Suicide is my only option! So, I tried to kill myself. God's love is not real for me. All my life I have been experiencing deep bouts of severe depression and an overwhelming sense of hopelessness. I want to die because I just can't strive any longer."

When parents ignore God's way, when they impose their own needs, desires and expectations on a child, or when their care is marred by their own infant wounds, reacting to his or her demands for care with confusion, frustration or selfishness, the results are devastating.

Martha continues ...
"My father and mother have always expected me to perform for them and be perfect in order to receive their love. This has been for as long as I can remember. I want to die because I just can't strive any longer to reach this goal of expected perfection."

We will return to Martha later on in the chapter.

As a result of wounds suffered during the birth to six month period, a person is likely to advance into their adult years believing, as in Martha's case, that it would be better not to exist at all. These wounds can cause people to feel insecure within themselves and about their position in the world. If you have suffered in this way, then you may be overly dependent on others for care, and feel emotionally "shut down," ignoring your feelings and the feelings of others. You may find yourself falling in and out of relationships, always experiencing the same disappointments. Your needs and expectations are never satisfied or perhaps never even attended to. You may also find that you regularly experience difficulty in thinking effectively and solving problems. Perhaps you find yourself being confronted by others because you missed the signals that a problem existed, and therefore failed to deal with it effectively. You may be the type of person who periodically explodes in uncontrollable anger when confronted with the conflicts and frustrations of life.

All of these real-life conditions, although prevalent in the general population, are not God's plan for you. They are symptomatic of major wounds which occurred very early in your life, during the time between birth and six months old.

Developmental Process

A person's experiences during the period from birth through the first six months outside the womb, build on the foundations of life which began at conception. A child's responsibilities appear to be simple – just to *be* and to receive nurture and care. However, closer scrutiny of this time reveals much about what is being incorporated into the child's life. Unconditional nurturing is required and care for all the child's needs. The child's "survival" depends on being fed, and even on being held and caressed, because in this way the body's life support systems and functions are stimulated.

Because human beings are a spirit, have a soul and live in a body, the primary needs for survival are spiritual, psychological and physiological. Father God intends for all these to be attended to by newborn babies' caretakers in order to ensure that they grow and develop in the way He intended.

Ralph's story

For thirty years life for Ralph had been a burden. He found just living to be very difficult, always a struggle, with nothing coming easy. Constant high levels of energy were required just to get by each day. During prayer the Lord revealed something to Ralph he had long since forgotten. Family conversations had frequently focused on how Ralph was finally born after his "poor mother went through a marathon labor." His mother had been in labor for over twelve hours, struggling, pushing and squeezing before Ralph finally came out. The long struggle to be born and the energy he expended in this process established a foundational pattern of life for Ralph. Just to live required him to expend a great deal of effort. The prayer time was dramatic for Ralph. The Lord brought him back to his birth. Jesus revealed Himself in the memory (Psalm 22:9–10), calling Ralph forth, receiving him from his mother's womb and then receiving him into the world (Psalm 71:6). I prayed as the Lord encouraged Ralph to be born, that the Lord would make him easily delivered (Exodus 1:19). At that moment Ralph experienced an overwhelming sense of peace and security as he re-experienced his birth as the Lord had intended it to be. After this dramatic prayer time Ralph perceived the normal conflicts and struggles of life much differently. Gone was the enormous energy drain just to make it through the day. No longer did life present itself as a never-ending series of burdensome struggles. Ralph was free to live life as God had originally intended for him.

The circumstances surrounding birth can set a pattern which can influence the rest of life. Late births, premature births, cesarean births, instrument-assisted births all have their unique set of conditions and circumstances which are foundational and have a permanent influence throughout a person's life. They establish a foundation upon which the conditions of life are experienced and perceived. They can cause recurring patterns and struggles in life which are bondages to healthy growth and development.

Survival and Existence

During these first six months we are dependent on our primary needs being met for survival. We have *body* or physiological needs: food, water, shelter, air, hygiene, etc. We have *soul* or psychological needs: love, attention, to be held and caressed. We have *spiritual* needs: prayer, to have God's Word spoken to us, psalms and hymns sung to us, etc. We use each of these areas of nurturing to identify what it means to exist outside the womb. The establishment of a sense of self-worth, belonging and affirmation is dependent on the quality of these experiences.

We now learn about what internal and external existence means. Internal existence is self-concept learning. It is learning about our physiological, psychological and spiritual condition. For instance, we learn by being fed and the ensuing digestive process. If all is well we experience a sense of well-being and establish a healthy self-perception. This is an elemental building block to forming a good self-image.

External existence is learning about everything in the outside world. We discover that we have arms, legs, feet, etc., and we learn what the world is like. We find out if it is a good place or a hostile place. We learn this primarily by being held, touched and caressed. This is the foundation to later understanding and distinguishing the boundaries between ourselves and others. Being prayed over, having God's Word spoken to us, and being sung psalms and hymns nourishes our spirit and sets the foundation upon which we can later develop and mature into a close interactive relationship with Father God.

The Symbiotic Relationship

The key to healthy development is the symbiotic relationship between mother and child.[1]

Symbiosis is a biological term. Basically, it is an interdependency in which two dissimilar organisms live together in a mutually beneficial relationship. Within this relationship there is a merging and sharing of needs. The mother has maternal instincts and needs to provide nurturing for the infant. The infant needs to receive that nurturing. Thus, in a healthy and normal relationship the needs of both mother and infant are satisfied. The mother experiences joy and fulfillment in nurturing her baby; the baby experiences this nurturing as encouragement to survive, grow and be healthy. A strong foundation of basic trust is now being established. Symbiosis is the bonding necessary for the infant to survive. Thus, symbiosis ensures survival and must be maintained. As the child develops and matures, the need for the symbiosis breaks down to its final resolution at two years old. We will discuss this resolution in a later chapter. For our purposes here, we will focus on the symbiotic bond between mother and infant.

When a mother received what she needed from her own mother for healthy growth and development during her infancy, then she has within her the necessary resources to provide what her baby needs for healthy development.

Symbiosis is our first introduction to relationships. God provides this relationship so that we can learn about trust, what it means to exist in this world, who we are, what life is like and what it will take to survive. The quality of the care received within the symbiotic relationship imprints upon our life the significance and worth of our existence both internally and externally (1 Thessalonians 5:23).

The Feeding Process

It appears that the basic building blocks for all future adult thinking and problem solving are established during this time of life (for reference studies see note 2). A great deal of research on human thought and problem solving exists, and it is not our intention at all to seek to replace this research nor to propose a theory designed to refute these studies. What is presented here is intended to be considered as a functional, social-interactive understanding of the impact we have found the feeding process to have on a child and the results such influences have on adult life. For our purposes here we will break down all adult problem solving into three basic components: *feeling, thinking* and *doing*.

When all three components are appropriate to the situation and are accurately focused on, the result is that problems can be solved or situations handled effectively. (When we speak of the *feeling* component here, we mean this in a much broader sense than emotions such as happiness, sadness, anger, fear, etc. This feeling component in the *feel-think-do* process includes these emotions, but also anything within our environment which activates the nervous system signaling the need for attention and requiring a response.)

One of these basic building blocks is provided by the feeding process. As infants, when we are hungry we experience hunger pangs in the form of stomach contractions. These contractions cause pain. We cry to signal we hurt, we need help and need to be cared for. Mom's job is to figure out what we need, in this case food, and meet this need. Our part is to suck and take in nourishment to stop the contractions so the pain will cease. Thus, the need for food has been satisfied. We need to learn this connection between the discomfort of hunger pangs, crying, and sucking during the first three months of life. As we experience this process a number of times, we make the appropriate connection to satisfying our need. We learn to solve our first and most life-threatening problem. When mom allows us to feel the hunger before feeding us, she helps us become fully aware of our feelings which motivate us to perform an act which will resolve the problem. She has helped to put the foundation in place for us to develop effective thinking and problem solving.

These three aspects of the feeding process, hunger pangs, crying and sucking, are related to the three aspects of adult problem solving – feeling, thinking and doing. As we grow and mature, hunger pangs and our attention to them are transformed to a higher order. We develop an ability to recognize our feelings and do something effective about them. Crying transforms to a higher order called thinking. We can still cry about our problems, but hopefully this does not remain our primary response to them. Thinking replaces crying as the method of dealing with life's issues. Sucking is an action. We learn that we are able to perform an act which will be effective in dealing with the issues of life.

Why Crying?

Father God gives all children a gift at birth. This gift is called, *crying*. We believe all parents desire to reinforce and affirm the gifts given their children by God, and no matter what they may think about it, crying is not something meant to torment them. Crying is the foundation for learning how to communicate in this world. All mothers agree that babies have different cries for different needs. Crying signals to mom that there is a need to be met. Food, comfort, a diaper change, an emergency ("My head's stuck in my crib," etc.). When mom accurately discerns our cry and responds appropriately to the need, we learn that we are loved and cared for. Our existence is affirmed. We learn it is OK to have needs and get these needs met. This is our first experience of unconditional love.

Through this experience we learn about effectively communicating our needs in this world. If mom does not respond in an appropriate way to the cry or acts in a way to increase our discomfort, resulting in more crying, we learn the opposite. We incorporate the belief that we do not belong in this world and should not exist. Later in this chapter we will explore in detail problems that manifest in adult life when infant cries are handled inappropriately. The response of others to our crying signal tells us whether we are encouraged to be here, to exist and to be real.

Parents Count

Amongst all the things that parents need to do for their child at this time, one thing is imperative. It is crucial that parents take special care of their own needs for nurturing and being cared for, so they can provide the best possible environment for themselves, as well as for the child. This includes being healed of their own wounded past. Parents have a wonderful opportunity when their baby is this age to rethink, feel and experience their own being and dependency needs. Parents, like children, have developmental issues to work through. These issues will again resurface to be dealt with at each developmental stage you go through with your children. If as parents you do not allow the Lord to heal you of your childhood wounds, you will wound your children in the same way and at the same ages as you were wounded when you were a child.

The Significance of Father

In this chapter we have so far focused on the mother as the major care provider. Yet, it is important to add that the first representation of Father God for us is provided by our own natural father. We begin incorporating who Father God is as our own father relates and interacts with us, and cares for us during this time.

A study was conducted on the amount of time fathers spent per day verbally interacting with their infants from birth to three months old. The study found that, on average, fathers spent 37 seconds per day verbally relating to their infant.[3] Think about the impression the developing baby receives about Father God! If our early experience was like that, then we could grow into adulthood thinking that Father God does not have much time for us. We pray quickly and relate to God for short periods of time because, after all, God has only 37 seconds for us. He's too busy fighting famine, averting wars and alleviating poverty.

This may be an overreaction to the 37-second finding in the study, but it certainly drives home a point. Fathers need to spend much more time with their infants. Fathers provide a sense of security, protection and identity. Without father around much of these very significant aspects of life are, at the very least, weak in the child's developing personality.

Agnes' story

A young woman now, Agnes reports, "All my life I have had problems with my father. We had no relationship from the day I was born. There was no physical contact and no verbal interaction with him. He didn't even discipline me. I grew up thinking men were useless, helpless and wimps. I did not feel capable of communicating my needs to them. Actually, I saw men as needing someone to care for them, because they weren't capable of taking care of themselves. I was strongly motivated to take care of men. Yet, I feared getting involved and hated them at the same time."

We will return to Agnes in the section "Crying Requires Response."

Weeds and Roots

In this section we will consider each of the most important areas previously mentioned and point out what can happen in adult life when the infant is wounded at this age or not provided for as God intended.

Internal Existence

Babies who experience feeding problems such as allergies to

food, or digestive problems such as colic, experience a deterior-
ating self-image. They begin to incorporate an unhealthy self-
perception, which is then elemental to the formation of a poor
self-image. People to whom we have ministered over the years
who had colic or digestive problems as an infant, describe
themselves as insecure, and have a tendency not to feel good
about themselves.

Symbiotic Wounds

As discussed, symbiosis is the most impressionable relationship
in our lives. It sets the pattern for all future relationships
throughout life. When our needs at this time are not appropriately attended to by our mother, we continue throughout our
entire life to seek the satisfaction of these needs. However,
because these needs remain as *infant needs* they will go unmet.
No one will be able to meet them because they cannot go back in
time and take the mother's place. Yet, many people continue to
work at getting these needs met in their adult relationships. This
is why there are so many disappointments in relationships, so
many struggles, so many conflicts. It is not possible for anyone
to meet our unresolved infant needs. The only One who can is
Jesus Christ.

If a mother did not receive what she needed in the first
months of her own life, she will have difficulty meeting the
needs of her baby. Parents tend to wound their children at the
very ages they themselves were wounded. It is very difficult for
parents to give what has not been deposited in their lives: they
give what has been given to them (see Genesis 8:22; Galatians
6:7 – the law of sowing and reaping). What has been sown into a
life will provide like seed to be sown again into future lives.
Lifelong problems can result if babies are separated from their
mothers during this time of life, especially if the mother is gone
for several days. At this time babies do not perceive that they
exist separately from their mother. If this part of themselves goes
away for a long period of time, they perceive a major part of
themselves as not existing. If this separation is extended, it is
possible for them to begin to deteriorate physically.[4] In adulthood this problem manifests in an inability to understand their
existence or define who they are apart from others.

Another major problem occurs in the lives of people whose

mother was unresponsive to their needs, either because she consciously refused to provide them with nurturing or she was oblivious to their needs. Whether conscious or unconscious, the result was the same. They became wounded, and for the rest of their lives they work to set up symbiotic relationships with others in order to try to meet their infant needs. Are you in bondage to the wounds of your infancy? Only to the extent that you do not allow the Lord to reveal Himself in these areas of woundedness, heal you and set you free.

Other problems result if you were either neglected and under-protected, or overindulged and overprotected. Again, such a condition within the symbiosis results in a bondage motivating you throughout life to set up symbiotic relationships with others where you end up being neglected and abandoned, or over-protected and controlled (cf. Romans 6:16; 2 Peter 2:19).

The Word tells us that we are in bondage when we are enslaved to something or somebody. We will see this later in Martha's story which was introduced at the beginning of the chapter. Wounds inflicted on us in the symbiosis place us in bondage. We become enslaved. We are not free to develop and grow as God intended. We are unable to realize the fullness of what God has for our lives. Until we recognize this, accept it and stop denying our wounds we are destined to remain slaves to these abuses and deficiencies.

A third category of symbiotic wounding occurs when infants do not receive the proper parenting to become an independent person, apart from mom, capable of thinking, problem-solving and being responsible for their own behavior. This needs to occur with the resolution of symbiosis, which we will discuss in Chapter 4, "Terrific Twos."

In the symbiotic relationship, the mother is the responsible one. If mothers are dependent on their children for *their* value and worth, they will have difficulty giving up the caretaker role as their children grow and mature. They may not know how to encourage this maturity and independence. Thus, their children remain in bondage to immaturity. They are never really free. They become oppressed by an unhealthy dependent relation-ship with mother. Even when they leave home as adults, they remain in bondage, controlled by the very thing God originally provided to ensure their survival. This bondage destroys the fullness of what God intended for their lives. Due to problems during development, most people set up symbiotic relationships with others at various points in life. Over the years of ministry, we have discovered that people choose friends, marriage partners, occupations and numerous other choices based on unresolved symbiotic needs.

Keith's story

After eight years of marriage, Keith had yet to feel truly emotionally connected to his wife. He reported never having had the deep emotional closeness to his wife which he had always desired and expected to have. He knew the Lord had a great deal more for them within their marriage relationship. Keith reported not feeling any aversion to women. In fact, he got along better with women than men. He had a close relationship with his mother but he had no relationship with his father who died when he was only three days old.

We prayed and asked the Lord to reveal the root of his problem. Immediately, the Lord brought to Keith's memory the fact that he lost his father to a tragic accident only three days after his birth. As we asked the Lord to reveal what He wanted to show Keith about this time, he began to feel his mother's grief at the loss of her husband. He felt her fear as well. Then, as he was experiencing all the emotions from mom he became aware of an intense desire to take care of his mother. At that moment, three-day-old Keith became his mom's caretaker. He took on comforting her, protecting her and basically being to her what his father could no longer be. This role of being an emotional comforter and caretaker remained deeply entrenched and was not set aside when Keith was married. Therefore he was not free to connect emotionally to his wife because his mother already occupied that place.

The Lord revealed Himself to three-day-old Keith and showed that, in fact, He was his mother's Comforter, Protector and Caretaker. Keith released his mom to Jesus and felt assured that the Lord would be her husband (Isaiah 54:5). Keith felt release as the drive to care for his mother was removed by the Lord's presence and assurance. Finally, he prayed to break off all ungodly symbiotic bondages between him and his mother, and to be fully connected to his wife in the deep emotional areas once occupied by his mother.

Today, Keith reports that a major change has occurred in his feelings of closeness to his wife. He is more involved, interactive and responsive to her needs. His wife previously reported that she saw no problem in their relationship. This was because she knew him in no other way. Yet now, after the Lord set Keith free and healed him, she says he is much more involved at an emotional level. "I really enjoy my new husband!" she said.

We can all receive the healing we need for the wounds we suffered in the symbiosis. We can all be free of the bondages which imprison us in a continuous pattern of immaturity, failure, pain and suffering, and prevent us from experiencing the fullness of life's joy and the fulfillment of God's purposes for us.

Wounds from the Feeding Process

We have found that infants who did not make the connection between hunger pangs, crying and sucking, experience problems in their adult lives with thinking, problem solving and effectively dealing with the issues of life. Many of them were wounded in the feeding process. The most prevalent and major wound is inflicted by the use of scheduled feeding methods. This type of regime causes people to learn that solving problems is beyond their control and relegated to the control of others. It promotes pessimism, passivity and a fatalistic attitude to life's problems. God has built a unique "feeding schedule" into each child's life, to sustain his or her individual development, growth and maturity. Mom needs to learn this schedule. Babies should not be controlled by an imposed time frame designed for mom's convenience, which ignores their unique developmental needs. For example, if babies are placed on a four-hour feeding schedule, but are hungry in three hours, by design they experience a great deal of pain and thus cry for an hour before they are fed. In this setup, they learn that their needs and feelings are not important and incorporate the belief that they do not matter to anyone. They also learn that it takes too much energy to solve problems.

If this happened to you, you may have grown up feeling

controlled by others. As a result you will tend to be passive, ignore your feelings and avoid dealing with problems. You avoid problems because you feel there is just no possible way to do anything effective to solve them. Scheduled feeding cripples people in the area of appropriate feeling, thinking and doing, causing them difficulty in being effective and responsible later in life.

Feeding can also cause another type of problem in a child's development. If babies are on a three-hour feeding schedule, but do not become hungry for four hours, they never really experience the pain of hunger. They are not provided with the opportunity to make the connection between hunger, crying and sucking to solve problems. When they become adults, such people may find themselves unable to identify feelings, and, thus, unable to discern accurately how to respond to life's issues and problems. They may ignore problems to such an extent that they get hurt and so do their loved ones. They lack a fundamental skill for adult thinking and problem solving, which can be extremely tormenting as well as dangerous. Every infant is entitled to the freedom to discover his or her own feelings, thinking and doing without being oppressed by the external controls of a caretaker. The best feeding method is demand feeding, which allows babies to get in touch with their internal needs and learn to be effective in getting their needs met. This provides an excellent foundation for effective thinking and problem solving.

Damage as a Result of Control
Too much control at this age sets foundations for all future stages of development, causing young children to begin to relinquish control of their own internal impulses and processes to mother and to all authority figures hereafter. We have witnessed the implications of this in our ministry. Having learned to give up internal impulse control to an external source at this young age, these individuals will always require someone else to monitor and correct their behavior and will have difficulty developing "self-discipline." This is because their mother failed to allow them to develop their own control.

It must be remembered that what we sow, we reap (Galatians 6:7). If your mother imposed controls on you at a time when you needed to establish your own built-in ways of dealing with the world, you will have learnt how to be self-indulgent and controlling of others. This will cause you difficulty in learning the basic foundational Christian principles of fully giving your life to Jesus, crucifying self and giving to others. If parents and authority figures respected your needs at this crucial time of your life, you will have grown up learning to respect authority and being aware of the needs of others. We believe such fruit is what all parents want for their children.

Crying Requires Response

Let's return to Agnes now:

Agnes asked the Lord to reveal where her problem first took root in her life. The Lord revealed to Agnes a time when she was about four or five months old. Agnes reported, "I'm just laying there crying. I'm not hungry. I need some attention, to be picked up and held. I'm crying. There's a man standing over me. He seems afraid to pick me up." At that moment the Lord revealed to Agnes that the man standing over her was her father. Agnes continued, "All of a sudden, my father leaves. He just walks away, leaving me there crying. I feel fear and hatred of men taking root."

There is a general belief that there is no harm in allowing babies to cry for long periods of time in the first six months of life, perhaps allowing them to cry themselves to sleep. Some people also believe that babies are controlling their parents by crying. As we see in Agnes' case, infants have a different "belief." It is important to bear two considerations in mind: first, crying is the way babies communicate; second, how those caring for them respond to their crying affirms or undermines their existence. Thus, when babies are appropriately responded to, they are affirmed in their existence and encouraged to communicate their feelings.

Rage

We have ministered to many adults who have struggled with rage all their lives. Rage is a much more intense feeling than anger. It is uncontrollable and explodes from a person. One minute the person appears calm, the next minute he or she is overcome by violent emotion, often in response to frustrations or conflicts in life. Where the appropriate response might be anger or frustration, these people explode with rage. As we pray with people who suffer from this problem and explore the leading of the Holy Spirit, we are always directed to focus back on the early months of their life. Rage is a feeling incorporated by the infant within the first three months of life. It happens like this.

When babies have a need they cry to communicate the need. When no one responds, they will escalate the crying to signal the increased intensity of the feeling behind the need. When they are still not responded to, they begin to scream even more loudly to let someone know that if they are not cared for soon, they may not survive. The issue now becomes one of survival. It is a threat to their very existence. Hence, the fear of not surviving intensifies into desperation and an all out release of the urgency of the situation is now communicated. When babies cry, they are communicating a need. They are not trying to control their parents. Crying is a God-given mechanism to signal their needs. At this age, the fulfillment of needs affirms a person's existence and encourages him/her to survive. If no one responds, it threatens that very existence and survival. In order to find healing for the root of this problem, people need to return in their memory in the Lord's presence to the moment of time when the outbreak of rage occurred. The Lord Jesus reveals Himself to the crying infant and responds, Himself, to his or her need. The Lord always reveals Himself to the screaming infant as the Father who cares and the One who will provide what he or she needs in this moment of time.

Let's return to infant Agnes whose father ignored her crying.

Agnes again saw the picture of herself in her crib crying to be held. When she asked the Lord to reveal Himself she experienced Him pick her up, wrap His arms around her and hold her close. He spoke gently to her in comforting tones. His peace quieted her anxious heart. She could finally let go and relax: she was cared for.

Months later Agnes sent a testimony.

> "Gone is the fear and hatred of men. Gone is the desire to look for helpless, useless men to take care of. The Lord has shown me how to communicate with men. How to affirm men and communicate with them. How to communicate my needs without fear. How to affirm and encourage men to be what God wants them to be. Now, when I see a needy man, I pray for him. I see men totally different now. I am capable of relationship with men without feeling fear, hatred or a motivation to care for them because of their helplessness. Most exciting is my relationship to Father God. I never realized how distant I was from the Father until after my healing time of prayer. Now I feel much closer to Him than ever before. I am really feeling truly connected to Him now."

This is what it's all about. Allow the Lord to take care of the wounds in life that have pulled you further and further away from Him.

God's Intervention

Unless the Lord intervenes, bringing new life and His healing touch into these areas of woundedness, these same wounds will be repeated in future generations. The major premise of this book is that all of us have been wounded in childhood. Yet, if we allow Him to, the Lord will heal and set us free from the bondages of these wounds which hold us back from becoming all He intended us to be.

Let's now return to Martha' story:

> During ministry, Martha began to recognize that immediately at birth she felt strong expectations for performance. She knew her parents wanted a girl and got her. At birth and within the symbiosis she experienced major pressure to live up to her mother's expectations of what she believed her daughter should be like. From the beginning Martha felt a strong demand to be "the perfect baby girl." Then, the Lord revealed something to

Martha. She saw that there was an oppressive heaviness around her neck and shoulders crushing the life out of her. A yoke of slavery had been placed around her neck. This yoke was all the expectations to be the perfect daughter which had been heaped onto her by her mother. But that wasn't all. This yoke of slavery was perpetuated by fear, anxiety and a deep sense of shame at even the thought of failure.

As we continued to pray Martha shared what she was experiencing:

"I actually experienced Father God announcing my birth with great joy to everyone around. The Lord took me from my mother's womb and held me in His arms, close to His chest. There is such a look of love and overwhelming pride on His face for me, His daughter Martha. The only possible posture I can take at this moment is to just *be* ... I don't have to perform for His love, I'm just born, I can't. Yet, He is bursting with joy in the simple fact that I am brought forth into this world. What love I feel!! What freedom!! I didn't do a single solitary thing to deserve this love. The yoke of slavery I've carried around my neck for thirty-four years is shattered!! It has fallen away!! Along with the yoke went the fear, anxiety and the shame of failure."

Five years later, Martha reports in her testimony to God's faithfulness:

"In one word, FREEDOM! Freedom to try, freedom to fail, freedom to receive love from others without questioning it. Freedom to like myself. Freedom to say 'no' without feeling rejection. The pivotal point is the major change I have experienced in my thought life. God likes me! Just the way I am. He really likes me!!! This thought has lifted the perpetual darkness that crept into my life whenever I fell short of perfection. There is Light, now! I want to live life and somehow give out hope to others."

Even as this book is being written, Martha and her family are ministering to the destitute people in Bosnia-Herzegovina. She is having the opportunity she desired with all her heart to share with others what was deposited into her life by Father God and to minister hope to the hopeless. Thanks be to our wonderful Lord!!

Martha is just one of many, whom the Lord has touched and set free. Agnes and Keith can also be added to this list. We have consistently witnessed the Lord take broken, wounded lives and restore them to vibrant health. How faithful is the Lord to reveal Himself in every painful situation of our wounded past. He touches these times of pain and brings restoration and new life. There is nothing the Lord cannot touch and heal. He never refuses to heal the wounds that cause the pain and the many tears of our young lives. In fact, He assures us of just the opposite:

> *"Record my lament;*
> *list my tears on your scroll –*
> *are they not in your record?"* (Psalm 56:8)

> *"Then those who feared the* LORD *talked with each other, and the* LORD *listened and heard. A scroll of remembrance was written in his presence concerning those who feared the* LORD *and honored his name."* (Malachi 3:16)

> *"This is what the* LORD, *the God of your father David, says: I have heard your prayer and seen your tears; I will heal you."*
> (2 Kings 20:5)

Receive your healing from the Lord.

Truth: Facing the Pain

Consider the adult problems identified in this chapter. Do you recognize any of these problems in your life? Review Table 1 on page 174 and ask the Lord to show you if any of these apply to your life. Truth is the only way to freedom.

Revelation: Revisiting the Scene

What happened in our infancy is a mystery to us. Cognitive recall is not developed in the early months of life, yet the experiences of this time leave an indelible impression in our being that affects us even into adult life. We need the Holy Spirit to reveal what took root in our lives in these early months. The Lord promises in His Word:

> *"He reveals deep and hidden things;*
> *he knows what lies in darkness,*
> *and light dwells with him."* (Daniel 2:22)

> *"For there is nothing hidden that will not be disclosed, and nothing concealed that will not be known or brought out into the open."* (Luke 8:17)

> *"Ask and it will be given to you ... "* (Matthew 7:7)

Redemption: Healing and Deliverance

Redemption rescues us from loss: the loss of trust, the loss of the ability to solve problems effectively, the loss of self-esteem and the ability to communicate with confidence. The Father longs to heal us and provide the care we needed at this time of life. Our ability to trust, even trust God, is affected by what happened to us in this time. So it is easy to see why this stage is so important to us and our relationship to the Father. Our eternal Father always hears us when we cry.

> *"O people of Zion, who live in Jerusalem, you will weep no more. How gracious he will be when you cry for help! As soon as he hears, he will answer you."* (Isaiah 30:19)

Restoration: The Planting of the Lord

The process of restoration begins to take effect as Jesus reveals the Father to us. As we relive this phase of life with Jesus, He supernaturally imparts into our lives what the Father always wanted us to have. The old hurtful images and lies of the past give way to the new life-giving experience in the presence of the Lord, making us whole again.

Re-parenting: Father God, "Father" Us

Healing and deliverance frees us to begin to grow up. Restoration begins when the Lord uproots the weeds of destruction and plants the seeds of newness of life. Another hindrance to maturity is removed when we realize we have the power to walk free. Our relationship with the Father is vital after receiving healing of the wounds which occurred at this time of our development. Draw near to Him and come to know Him as He really is. Trust and faith develop through intimacy. As the Father "fathers" us, our infant needs are satisfied, our anxious hearts are quieted and the peace that passes understanding secures our life in Him.

Steps to Healing and Restoration

1. Identify the adult problems that apply to you (see Table 1 on page 174).

2. Ask the Holy Spirit to reveal the "root cause" of each problem. The root is whatever happened to you from birth to six months old that caused a wounding in your life and allowed the problem to take root. This revelation may be in the form of a memory, picture, impression, thought, awareness, or some other way of "knowing" (Luke 8:17).

3. Ask Jesus to reveal His Presence there with you. The presence of the Lord changes things (Hebrews 13:8; Psalm 31:14–16).

4. Tell Jesus what you are feeling and thinking in this revealed time, place, experience. Listen to His response (Psalm 91:14–16).

5. Ask Jesus to reveal what the Father intended for this time of your life. Jesus comes to show us the Father. He comes to care for your developmental needs, to heal you, to redeem all that was lost to you and to restore you to be all He created you to be (Jeremiah 29:11; Matthew 15:13).

6. Forgive your parents and all those who wounded you. Break any generational curses, if necessary (Matthew 6:14; Galatians 3:13; see also Appendix A, Generational Curses).

7. Take authority, in Jesus' name, over any demonic oppression or influences in your life that the Lord has revealed. Command them to leave in the authority of Jesus' name (Luke 10:19).

8. Break agreement with the lie planted in your heart and ask the Lord to uproot it. Embrace the truth that has the power to set you free, the Word of God. Proclaim the promises in God's Word that are His answers to your need (John 8:31–32; Matthew 15:13).

9. Receive Father God as your eternal Father and receive your inheritance of life in Christ Jesus (1 John 1:2).

10. Seek the Father each day to "father" you and ask the Holy Spirit to teach you how to walk in your "newness of life" (Hebrews 12:10).

Notes

1. Jacqui and Aaron Schiff, "Passivity," *Transactional Anaysis Journal* I, 1 (1971), 71–78.

2. Sandra Blakeslee, "Studies Show Talking with Infants Shapes Basis of Ability to Think," *New York Times* (17 April 1997), D 21; Sharon Begley, "How to Build a Baby's Brain," *Newsweek Special Issue* (Spring/Summer 1997), 28–32; Renee Baillargeon, "How Do Infants Learn About the Physical World?" *Current Directions in Psychological Science* (October 1994), 1331–40; Kathleen McAuliffe, "Making of a Mind," *Omni* (October 1985), 62–66, 74; Jacqui Schiff *et al.*, *Cathexis Reader* (New York: Harper and Rowe, 1975); Paul Chance, "Your Child's Self-Esteem," *Parents Magazine Enterprises* (January 1982).

3. F. Rebelsky and C. Hanks, "Father's Verbal Interactions with Infants in the First Three Months of Life," *Child Development* (1971), pp. 42, 63–68; Paul Roberts, "Father's Time," *Psychology Today* (May/June 1996), 48–55, 81.

4. Rene Spitz, "Hospitalization, Genesis of Psychiatric Conditions in Early Childhood," *Psychoanalytic Study of the Child* 1 (1945), 53–74; W. Goldfarb, "Psychological Privation in Infancy and Subsequent Adjustment," *American Journal of Orthopsychiatry* 15 (1945), 247–255; S. Provence and R. Lipton, *Children in Institutions* (New York: International Universities Press, 1962); Barry M. Lester, "There's More to Crying than Meets the Ear," *Childhood Newsletter*, Vol. 2, No. 2 (1983).

Chapter 3

Exploration

Six to Eighteen Months

"NO!!!" The shock of his mother's shout jolted Peter back from yet another futile attempt at exploring the world around him. He was confused, frustrated and "itching" to relieve the energy inside. Fifteen-month-old Peter experienced many such encounters with his parents. They were professionals, very successful and very much in control of their lives. They were highly respected by all who knew them. Yet, without realizing it, the pervasive pressure of their control was slowly and systematically crushing Peter's curiosity and desire to explore, tragically undermining the healthy development of his motivation, initiative, mobility and creativity.

The exploratory stage of development from six to eighteen months is a dynamic period of life, rich with wonder and intrinsic desire to experience and explore the world. Its primary goals are developing self-initiative, self-motivation, concept learning and mobility. The most important requirements for healthy development now are permission and protection in exploration. Self-initiative and self-motivation need to be encouraged without performance expectations, punishment or excessive restriction. Loss of parental nurturing, long periods of confinement and oppressive control are wounding as are performance expectations, punishment and lack of protection in exploration.

Adult Problems

Later in his life Peter came for ministry and counsel.

> Peter's jaw flexed as he shared the struggle he was having dealing with the authority figures in his life. Frustration and anger were feelings all too familiar to him. Throughout his life people in authority were either controlling him or criticizing him for *not* having any initiative or motivation. He felt driven to please others. Self-awareness and the Lord's direction for his life were muddled by the onslaught of the expectations and demands of others. It was true, Peter needed to get in touch with his initiative and self-motivation. He, in fact, was not only controlled by others but allowed the control. It was frustrating and oppressive, yet, paradoxically what he found to be most familiar to him. He was either being told what to do and when to do it or being criticized, and reprimanded for not taking initiative. Finally living in this "double bind" had taken its toll – the stress was unbearable.

Peter was an oppressed, demotivated, man-pleaser in bondage to the expectations and control of others. There are many such "Peters" in this world with similar stories. We will return to Peter's story later in the chapter.

What happened to you during this time in your development? The results are manifested in your life today. Do you lack initiative and motivation? Do you find it difficult to hear the voice of God and sense His direction in your life? Do you find it difficult to know what you are feeling? Is your behavior motivated by the fear of rejection or abandonment? Have you learned how to please others to the exclusion of your own needs for a balanced healthy life? Do you see a pattern in your life where people take advantage of you? Do you frequently feel overwhelmed or smothered by circumstances or the people closest to you? Do you struggle with passivity, over adaptation, anxiety or immobilization? The answers to many of these questions concerning the "roots" of such adult life manifestations can be found in understanding the developmental process between six and eighteen months of age.

Developmental Process

The world suddenly comes into vibrant focus and we are drawn out from our self-absorption to explore the wonders all around us. It is a time to experience and develop initiative, motivation, mobility, creativity, and an understanding of spatial and conceptual relationships. The problems and frustrations we encounter as we explore the world all help in the process of learning what we can and cannot do.

At this stage of development we are working through symbiosis (see p. 57) and beginning to do things on our own. In order to succeed we need to be encouraged. It is essential that we learn that exploring and developing will not result in abandonment, punishment or loss of nurturing. Unconditional love is required at this stage to maximize healthy development.

Before we go any further, ask yourself a question. Think about this past year. How many people with whom you have been involved, were highly motivated, full of initiative and very creative? What percentage of people would you say have these attributes? Maybe three per cent, five per cent or, if you were blessed, ten per cent? Why are there so few people who are highly motivated, full of initiative and creative? Let's explore the reasons.

Motivation, Initiative, Mobility and Creativity

We will only become self-motivated and creative adults, who are able to take initiative, if we are allowed to explore at this important phase of our lives. These characteristics need to be established, encouraged and rewarded. Getting in touch with our motivation and initiative helps us get in touch with ourselves.

We consistently find self-motivation, self-initiative and creativity snuffed out of people's lives. What happened? Due to a lack of understanding, parents, in their zeal to discipline, inadvertently destroy motivation, initiative and creativity. Inappropriate parenting can have a devastating effect on budding individuality.

It is important to be allowed, even encouraged, to use our own natural motivation rather than having to respond to the expectations and motivations of others around us. It is at this stage that these vital attributes begin, are encouraged and flourish, or are discouraged and wither away. Getting in touch with our motivation and initiative helps us get in touch with ourselves. Through exploration we discover what we can and cannot do.

Touching Machine

Personal experience is the best way to discover the world. While primary needs for nurture remain important, through exploration we begin to conceptualize the world around us. We learn the meaning of important concepts like near/far, over/under, hard/soft, hot/cold, big/little, crash/splash. We want to know what is under, behind, on top of, inside of every object we encounter. Curiosity about everything prompts mobility. We become "little explorers."

During these months of life we are best described as a "touching machine." We live to touch and we touch to live. This burst of energy and activity creates new challenges for parents. By giving us permission to explore they are stimulating our learning; by providing us with protection they are preventing the occurrence of wounding experiences which might cause us to shut down inside.

Scientific Confirmation

Scientific research in recent years has underscored how critically important this phase of child development is. At this stage the nervous system and muscle coordination are developing at their most rapid rate, with neural connections being formed at an explosive rate. Research reported in *Time* Magazine on 2 March 1997 states:

> "'What wires a child's brain,' say neuroscientists, 'is repeated experience. Each time a baby tries to touch a tantalizing object, or gazes intently at a face or listens to a lullaby, tiny bursts of electricity shoot through the brain, knitting neurons into circuits as well defined as those etched in silicon chips.'"[1]

These connections must be exercised by stimulation in order to be permanently established. The more the child is allowed to explore, touch and manipulate objects, the more neural connections are formed and the more enriched the nervous system becomes. The research of William Greenough of the University of Illinois confirms this: "A lot of organization (in the brain) takes place using information gleaned from when the child moves about in the world. If you restrict activity, you inhibit the formation of synaptic connections in the cerebellum."[2] If neural connections are not stimulated and exercised through exploration, touch and manipulation, they deteriorate, atrophy or waste away, and the nervous system becomes starved. The resulting deprivation is significant enough to cause problems later in life with reading, writing, thinking, conceptualizing and nearly all forms of learning.[3] "Deprived of a stimulating environment the child's brain suffers." Researchers at Baylor College of Medicine, for example, have found that the brains of children who don't play much or are rarely touched are 20–30 per cent smaller than normal for their age.[4] In contrast, babies who are given permission to explore within the freedom of a protected environment thrive.

Foundations for Adult Problem Solving/ Spatial Relationships

This is a critical time for the formation of spatial and conceptual relationships which are foundational in the development of all future thinking, learning and problem solving.[5]

In learning to understand spatial relationship we become aware of how objects are set up in space. How is a chair positioned in relationship to the floor and the table? How is the sofa positioned in relationship to the wall? How much space is there between the wooden bars on the railing of the stairs? In order to assess these relationships we must crawl or walk over to the object and explore its relationship to other things. So we push and squeeze our little bodies between the couch and the wall or stick our heads between the stair railing bars and get stuck. In this way we gain a "personal" understanding of spatial relationships. These early discoveries are vital if we are to think and solve problems effectively later in life. If we are restricted in how much we are allowed to explore by controlling, dominating, or overprotective parents, our spatial relationship skills do not develop sufficiently, which may result in difficulties with learning and problem solving later in life.

Conceptual Relationships

As well as an understanding of spatial relationships, conceptual relationships are also being developed at this stage. This is the ability to think about objects or places when they are no longer in our immediate surroundings. It is the ability to imagine. If we try to think about a place without having been there, we are unable to create an accurate image in our minds. If we have not explored something, seen it or had the opportunity to experience it, we will be unable to conceptualize it. Conceptualization, essentially, is the ability to create an image of something in our mind and it is an important tool in thinking effectively and functioning adequately in life.

Restricted mobility during this stage or the unavailability of objects to manipulate and explore can seriously affect our ability to function in this area. Being confined for long periods of time to "baby jail," commonly known as a playpen, or "bungey bondage" hanging from a suspended rubber-banded swing in a door frame, seriously restricts mobility and hinders exploration, causing conceptual and spatial relationship deficiencies.

Exploring the Existence of Things

Up to this stage, "out of sight" was "out of mind," the person or the object no longer existed when out of view. Now we learn that people can leave a room and still exist, and that things can be put away and still exist. Play involves putting things in places and taking them out again. We are working at developing fantasies and images regarding objects and the constancy of objects. This is the time when people play "peek-a-boo" with us and enjoy watching us laugh and get excited when they suddenly reappear.[6]

Jack's story
We ministered to a young man, Jack, who had feared abandonment all his life. The Lord revealed to him – and later it was

confirmed by his parents – that prior to seven months old and for a period of several months, he was frequently left with his grandparents on weekends while his parents went away. When the parents returned to retrieve Jack from his grandparents, they would find him reluctant to come to them. Jack appeared not to recognize his mom and dad. This occurred because Jack had not yet developed the cognition for "constancy of objects." His parents were, in a sense, unfamiliar to him because he did not remember them. Basically, Jack experienced abandonment, as all children of this age will if left by parents for extended periods of time.* In healing prayer, Jack experienced the presence of the Lord with him, caring for him when his parents left, healing the break in the bonding, releasing him from the fear of abandonment.

Mess is Best

We need freedom to be who God made us to be. We need to develop in the ways God has set within us. Now is the time for mess. It is important to be able to be messy without feeling parental rejection or repulsion. This stage may also be referred to as the "baptismal" stage of development.

At this age we enjoy spilling everything. It is exciting to watch all the wonderful things milk, juice, soup, etc., do when they splash. Smashing and squashing produce exciting new discoveries. If given the opportunity, we make a great deal of mess. The dried-on food decorating our face and hair adds to the messy look. This is developmentally normal, occurring around eight to ten months and continuing for several months. Unconditional love and attention is needed now, more than ever.

How mom reacts to us makes an indelible impression on our thoughts, feelings and behavior since the symbiosis between the mother and child is at its strongest.[7] If she reacts positively our self-image is enhanced, but if she reacts negatively it is diminished.

* *Note*: The symbiotic bond between the mother and child becomes stronger month by month reaching its strongest at eight months and then gradually diminishing in the months that follow. Separation from the mother in these first months is problematic for the child and in the seventh to eighth month it can be traumatic.

Testing Separation

At fifteen to twenty months, exploration really picks up. We are working through the symbiosis, when we depended on mom for everything, and finding out about separation. We are discovering what we can and cannot do. More than ever, we need to experience encouragement, freedom and support as we explore.[8] This is not the time for increased punishment, discipline or undue restriction in mobility. Important now is appropriate protection in exploration, avoiding the extremes of overprotection (that is, smothering and restriction) or a lack of protection (that is neglect and unresponsiveness). Either extreme adversely affects the quality of our exploration and ultimately undermines the development of maximum brain function.

Mom, I Want to Feed Myself!!!

Some time around ten to twelve months old, we need to be allowed and encouraged to feed ourselves. Feeding is another significant activity which encourages self-motivation and self-initiative through exploration.

Some children may be prevented from doing this because it makes too much of a mess or because they don't get enough food in their mouths. Rather than discouraging the child's desire it is more appropriate for child and parent each to have a spoon – which will hopefully ensure that at least some of the food will be eaten.

Let's consider, now, what can go wrong at this age and what impact this may have on healthy adult functioning.

Weeds and Roots

Let's return to Peter's story.

> When Peter was a child he was very active and curious. He would get into anything he could. The Lord revealed the extreme intensity with which Peter's mother and father would stop him from exploring. He once again experienced the long forgotten shock of his mother's piercing scream riveting him to the spot, cutting short his attempts at exploration.

What Happened to My Motivation?

If mobility is restricted, if permission to explore is replaced with constant discipline and punishment, we won't discover our capabilities and won't grow in self-motivation. Self-initiative and spatial and conceptual relationships will also suffer. If every effort to explore our world is stopped by "NO!!!" without any "YES" to redirect our energy, the energy diffuses in us and can cause us to be agitated, hyperactive and unable to focus.

In my experience as a psychologist in schools for fifteen years, I found that some learning disabilities are functional, related to inappropriate parenting, rather than organic in nature. As a result of inappropriate, ineffective parenting at this stage children develop difficulties with focusing, attending and learning later in life.

"Stop this Mess!"

There is a danger that, during this "messy" stage, you may have received the impression from mom that something was wrong with you. That you were somehow not right for her. You may have received these messages if you had a "super clean" mom who always cleaned you up immediately whenever there was the slightest mess. Such behavior instills a sense of rejection of who and what you are. Impressed upon your developing awareness and image of yourself is the nagging perception and belief that you are *not right*. You are left with the impression that something is wrong with you and you are not accepted for who you are or who you are becoming.

Does this sound familiar to you, now in your life?

Linda's story

Linda experienced rejection from her mother at this "messy" time of her life. She grew up with the obsessive belief that no one accepted who she was, especially authority figures. She had the self-perception that she was somehow dirty or unclean. She believed that no one could ever really love or appreciate her for *who* she was. She had received strong messages that she could not be who God had naturally made her to be, and felt that she needed to be something other than who she was to gain love and acceptance. God calls this "man pleasing."[9] Psychologists call this abandoning one's own identity.

When she asked the Holy Spirit to reveal the root cause of this she saw a picture of herself as a baby. Every time Linda was the least bit "messy," her mom looked at her in disgust, mumbled something and wiped her face or body until she felt it burn from the rubbing. She asked the Lord to reveal Himself in that time and show her what the Father wanted for her then. The Lord stepped in between Linda and her mom. He took the cloth from her mom and told her He would take care of Linda. Linda re-experienced this time with the Lord. Although she was "messy" He smiled at her and looked at her with great love. He even encouraged her to be messy. He loved and delighted in her in the midst of her messiness. Linda felt the knot in her stomach relax. She was set free by the Lord. His acceptance of her even in her mess was just what she needed to break free from the bondage of rejection. She was free to accept herself for who the Lord made her to be. No longer expecting rejection, she could begin to learn how to receive acceptance from herself and others.

Parents don't always consider the long-term effects of what they say and do on their children. They are then surprised when the fruit of what they have planted in their children's lives begins to manifest itself in later life. Children base their impressions, feelings and beliefs about themselves on their perceptions of how they are treated by those caring for them and what is said to them.

Don't Touch!?!?

Consider this real-life situation. I am fifteen months old and you are my parent. You take me into a crystal and china store. You have now created a problem for yourself and me if you expect me not to touch anything. Remember, I am a "touching machine." You now tempt my natural desire to touch and explore. I will be after everything in the store. To prevent me from breaking something, what must you do? You will need to tell me "NO!" continually to stop me from touching, frustrating my innate desire to explore. If you do not want me to touch, either hold me while we are in the store or, better still, don't take me in the store at all. But please, don't put me down on the floor and expect me not to touch. This is unrealistic and will only result in frustration for both of us. God does not tempt us, and neither should adults tempt their fifteen-month-old children.

Exactly What Part of "No" Don't You Understand?

Consider another real-life situation. Again I am fifteen months old and I go to touch something. You tell me "NO!" I go to touch something else and again you tell me "NO!" If there are numerous "blocks" like this throughout my day, what will happen to the energy in me that has not been given proper focused release? It remains inside me as undifferentiated and diffuse energy, which will manifest itself in my behavior as agitation. I will begin releasing it in unfocused, non goal-directed ways. Does this sound familiar? It might be that my behavior and inability to focus my energy lead to hyperactivity, which could then lead to a diagnosis of "Attention Deficit Disorder," also known as ADD.

Foundations of Fear

Some parents misunderstand this stage and, as a result, they discipline, restrain and correct their child too often. They do this for a variety of reasons, but one of the main reasons is fear. Either parents fear that other people will think they are raising an undisciplined, uncontrolled child (fear of man), or they fear their child will get hurt (fear of harm), or that the child might destroy something (fear of loss). Fear, then, becomes the motivation behind parental correction. A child who is restrained from exploring, initiating and self-motivating out of fear, will learn to connect these activities with fear. When carried into later life, fear is triggered in situations requiring these qualities, which will hold the individual back from functioning effectively and responsibly.

Does this strike a familiar cord with you? This is an issue we often encounter when ministering to people who have been subject to too much control during the exploratory stage of development.

Self-feeding: Mom Has the Food

As mentioned earlier, self-feeding is an activity which needs to be encouraged. If you were not allowed to explore self-feeding, you will have been discouraged from developing self-initiative and self-motivation and encouraged to be dependent. This may have resulted in you incorporating the distorted perception into your thinking that dependency on parents or authority figures is an attribute which should be developed. This then becomes a bondage in life and leads to the kind of situation where 35-year-old children are still living at home expecting their parents to "feed them." Excessive control at this stage in a child's development can be devastating to budding initiative and motivation.

I Want to Do It Myself

If, when you were exploring the world and learning to perform such tasks as stacking blocks or putting pegs in holes, etc., other people were constantly intruding and demonstrating the correct way to do it, you may have become demotivated. As a result you may still have the feeling that you can't do things well, that you are not capable, and that others can do things better than you. If there was too much intrusion in your activities, your autonomy, initiative and spontaneous motivation will probably have become diminished. Babies need autonomy to experience and manipulate objects within their environment.

Roots of Man Pleasing

Some people were encouraged by their parents to act "cute." If your parents did this, you may have learnt to perform for people and thus have become a man-pleaser (something God expressly forbids in Galatians 1:10). By being required to act "cute" or perform for others, you were placed at risk. Your own initiative and spontaneous motivation were infringed upon; you learnt to over adapt to others; you learnt to respond more to the demands of others than to your own internal processes. As an adult, you function out of the motivation of others rather than out of your own motivation and self-initiative which is left undeveloped or underdeveloped (as we see in Peter's story). Such people feel that their life is not their own – and it isn't. They have difficulty identifying their feelings and cannot seem to distinguish between their wants and their needs. They report having difficulty identifying what they need and asking for it. These people are always pulled along in life by the demands and expectations of others, rather than being prompted by motivation from within and the leading of the Holy Spirit. Without a developed internal awareness, it is hard to hear the voice of God. When our focus is external, we are vulnerable to being controlled by others.

What is Punishment Really Doing Now?

During this stage of a child's development it is very important that performance expectations are kept to a minimum. A heavy amount of discipline and punishment is also inappropriate. At six to eighteen months, it is more appropriate for a child to be guided and redirected than to be heavily disciplined and punished for age appropriate behavior. Structured consistent discipline needs to begin when the child reaches the age of two. Punishment any earlier than this is a direct attack on the development of initiative, motivation, creativity and mobility.

If you were punished regularly at this age, you will have become demotivated, lacking in initiative and either passive or hyperactive. You will also have become passive and prone to over adapting to the demands and needs of others.

Parents appear to be the ones who benefit most from punishment at this stage. For the child it only results in deactivating an otherwise active, curious human being.

Toilet Training Too Early

Between the ages of six and eighteen months children are not yet ready, developmentally, to begin toilet training.[10] All parent-initiated expectations should remain at a minimum to protect children from having to over adapt to the wants and needs of others. The more we are required to over adapt during this exploration stage, the more likely we are to develop a man-pleasing orientation to life, learning to discount our own needs and wants and operate out of the needs and wants of others. This can cause a loss of sensitivity to our internal life and make it difficult to hear the voice of God as we mature.

The most destructive impact of toilet training too early, however, is on the child's developing ability to learn self-control and impulse control. We have discovered that adults whose parents toilet trained them too early, give up the self-initiative and motivation necessary to establish their own self-control. They essentially abandon self-control while over adapting to the control of others.

If you struggle with such an orientation to life, you may struggle with an endless and frustrating cycle of sin and condemnation. Self-control/self-discipline, an important fruit of the Holy Spirit, will be totally missing from your life. However, do not despair: it is possible to develop this fruit of the Spirit in your life. Allow the Lord to reveal the wounds you suffered at this stage of life. He will uproot the destruction and redeem what has been stolen.

God's Intervention

Peter's healing ...

During prayer and ministry, the Lord revealed Himself to Peter and stood between him and his mother. He experienced the Lord comforting his mother, reassuring her that Peter would not grow up to be undisciplined if she allowed him to explore now. He instructed her that Peter needed the freedom to explore and discover without excessive correction and punishment to be healthy and well developed. Then Jesus came to Peter and removed the invisible force of control and fear binding him. He was free. He felt the release and life stirring within him. The fire of initiative and motivation was burning again. He knew the Lord was encouraging him to move out, to be motivated once again to explore. Peter felt a huge oppressive cloud lift from his life, he had never known life without it. He felt energy return to his body. He felt fear flee as the Lord walked with him through several adventures in exploration. The Lord had reawakened Peter's initiative and motivation. He was free. Free to experience the fullness of who he was created to be and what God originally intended for his life.

As we matured from a child to an adult, Father God wanted each of us to be creative and motivated with a high degree of initiative.

Truth: Facing the Pain

Do you find, in your life, that others are often explaining the consequences of your behavior to you? If you are honest with yourself, do you expect others to modify your behavior rather than taking responsibility for it yourself? If you answered yes to either of these questions, then it is a sure sign that your exploratory stage of development was unduly restricted and controlled. Developmentally inappropriate demands and expectations for performance were probably imposed on you. It is possible to be trained to behave in certain ways through "classical conditioning," even before cognitive "cause and effect" thinking has developed. This will be discussed in greater detail in the next chapter. If you were classically conditioned at this stage in your development, you never really developed your own self-initiated skills to use in modifying your behavior. You gave up internal self-control of your behavior to adapt to external control. The external control now comes from authority figures who provide the primary source of motivation for the way you operate in life.

Revelation: Revisiting the Scene

Stop for a moment and ask the Holy Spirit to take you back to this time in your development and reveal anything that may have happened to wound you. Jesus wants to reveal the Father to you and to parent you in the way He knew you needed for your healthy development. He will heal you, protect you from harm, set you free, uproot the destruction and supernaturally impart exactly what you needed for life and health at that time.

Redemption: Healing and Deliverance

The Father desires to set you free. He wants to heal your wounds. The Lord will minister to you back at the time when you were six to eighteen months old. Father God knows what happened in your life to diminish who He made you to be. You may not be in touch with your inner self at all; you may even feel dead inside, without any sense of your own needs or feelings. In order to be able to hear the voice of God and be led by the Spirit it is essential to be connected to your internal life, your heart. The Lord will uproot the destructive forces of control and fear and restore supernaturally your desire to explore with His protection. He will supernaturally impart what you needed to develop in your internal life, as He intended.

Restoration: The Planting of the Lord

The Father wants to restore what was lost – your initiative, motivation and creativity.

Most of all, He wants to breathe resurrection life into your "inner" self, your "heart life" that you may hear His voice.

Reparenting: Father God "Father" Us

The Father longs for you to be the person He created you to be. Freedom is only the beginning. He will be there to encourage and protect you in your renewed desire to develop your initiative, motivation, creativity, your internal life. He will be there to speak to you in your "heart" and lead you by His Spirit.

Steps to Healing and Restoration

1. Identify the adult problems that apply to you (see Table 1 on page 174).
2. Ask the Holy Spirit to reveal the "root cause" of each problem. The root is whatever happened to you at six to eighteen months old that caused a wounding in your life and allowed the problem to take root. This revelation may be in the form of a memory, picture, impression, thought, awareness, or some other way of "knowing" (Luke 8:17).
3. Ask Jesus to reveal His Presence there with you. The presence of the Lord changes things (Hebrews 13:8; Psalm 31:14–16).
4. Tell Jesus what you are feeling and thinking in this revealed time, place, experience. Listen to His response (Psalm 91:14–16).

5. Ask Jesus to reveal what the Father intended for this time of your life. Jesus comes to show us the Father. He comes to care for your developmental needs, to heal you, to redeem all that was lost to you and to restore you to be all He created you to be (Jeremiah 29:11; Matthew 15:13).

6. Forgive your parents and all those who wounded you. Break any generational curses, if necessary (Matthew 6:14; Galatians 3:13; see also Appendix A, Generational Curses).

7. Take authority, in Jesus' name, over any demonic oppression or influences in your life that the Lord has revealed. Command them to leave in the authority of Jesus' name (Luke 10:19).

8. Break agreement with the lie planted in your heart and ask the Lord to uproot it. Embrace the truth that has the power to set you free, the Word of God. Proclaim the promises in God's Word that are His answers to your need (John 8:31–32; Matthew 15:13).

9. Receive Father God as your eternal Father and receive your inheritance of life in Christ Jesus (1 John 1:2).

10. Seek the Father each day to "father" you and ask the Holy Spirit to teach you how to walk in your "newness of life" (Hebrews 12:10).

Notes

1. J. Madeleine Nash, "Fertile Minds," *Time* magazine (2 March 1997), p. 54.
2. L. Joseph Stone and Joseph Church, *Childhood and Adolescence* (New York: Random House, 1984), pp. 212–214.
3. Nash, "Fertile Minds," p. 51.
4. Ibid.
5. Stone and Church, *Childhood and Adolescence*.
6. Sharon Begley, "Your Child's Brain," *Newsweek* (19 February 1996), pp. 55–62.
7. Stone and Church, *Childhood and Adolescence*, p. 215.
8. J.H. Kennell and M.H. Klaus (eds.), *Birth, Interaction and Attachment* (Skillman, NJ: Johnson and Johnson), pp. 35–43.
9. E. Fenichel, *Learning through Supervision and Mentorship to Support the Development of Infant, Toddler and Their Families*, Zero-Three (1991), Annual Editions: Human Development (Guilford, Connecticut: Dushkin Publishing, 1996–97).
10. Stone and Church, *Childhood and Adolescence*, pp. 285–287.

Chapter 4

Free to Be Me

Two Years of Age

"Michael!!! Come here right now!!!" Michael stood firm ... his toes gripped the carpet, rooted in opposition. Every command from his mother sparked all the two-year-old anger, resistance and defiance little Michael could muster. His mother, confronted with this challenge, perceived it as a threat to her supremacy in the home. Determined to maintain her "iron grip" she escalated her anger to subdue him. These episodes only served to strengthen Michael in his resolve to fight the control. Michael had already learned to be very stubborn and rebellious because of all the control and "mother domination" he had lived with since birth. Again the battle was on!!! Mom v. Michael, who would win?!?

Two. What a terrific, turbulent time in our life! Time to break symbiosis with mom and become a separate person. Time to begin exercising our cognitive recall, also known as memory, and cause and effect thinking. Time to think and solve problems and become responsible for our own behavior. All these are important tasks now in our development. It is time to get free of self-centeredness and establish a social contract – that is, to find out how to live in society and learn to cooperate and share with others. Struggles with control, anger and opposition displace the blissful days of exploration.

Navigating these turbulent waters is difficult. Many get caught in the endless whirlpools of "self" and lose their way. It takes understanding and godly wisdom to hold the course steady and make it through this stage successfully. This time of our young lives is extremely significant on our journey to maturity. Wounds at this age cause major stumbling blocks for many of us. How many of us have yet to resolve these issues, even now, in our adult lives? Many are plagued with unresolved "two-year-old stuff" even in the later years of life. Some people never get victory in these areas, no matter how long they live.

Adult Problems

Being inconsiderate of others, lacking self-discipline, being oppositional, negative, competitive, controlling and self-centered are the most obvious adult manifestations of wounds which were inflicted upon the child during this stage of life. Many adults still suffer from the two-year-old syndrome, "I want it my way!" They are angry, negative, oppositional. They are always confronting life's issues and problems with a pervasive drive to compete with and control others. These people frequently struggle to be free of what they perceive as oppressive demands on their lives. They control others to get what they want. In the extreme, they are self-centered, abusive, narcissistic and demanding. They resist taking responsibility for their own feeling, thinking and doing and for the consequences of their behavior. They are involved in relationships where they can either control or be controlled by the other. In either relationship, they justify expressing their ever-present feelings of anger.

We believe most of us have some of these issues going on in our lives. It is time to face the truth and deal with them. It is time to learn to take personal responsibility instead of blaming others. It's time to take action. Go after these issues in your life: allow the Lord to reveal the roots and heal the wounds. When people are set free of "two-year-old stuff," the change is dramatic and life changing.

Michael's story continues ...

Michael was an angry, abusive, controlling husband. He came for ministry when his wife left him. He was shocked that she had abandoned him so abruptly. "After all these years, why did she just up and leave now?" Michael complained. He had been married for twenty years. He had no concept of the "we" aspect in the marriage relationship and no understanding of other people's feelings. All was done in his home the way he wanted it. He was not in the slightest bit aware just how self-centered and self-serving he was. No one ever confronted his selfishness because they feared his angry retaliation. Michael was really not a very nice man. The worst part of it was, he did not even realize how obnoxious he was to others. In his blindness, he could not see that he had destroyed his marriage.

So, how can we get "stuck" in two-year-old behavior?

Developmental Process

"NNNOOOO!!!" is the "battle cry" that resounds in the wake of little ones turned two as they dash away from mom. Overnight, it seems, they are transformed from sweet baby to tiny tyrant, becoming clearly negative, oppositional, even rebellious. God has given the two-year-old a one-word gift. It is the same word He gives every two-year-old in every language all over the world. The word is "NO!!!" – and they use it to reply to almost everything. Some people refer to this time as the "terrible twos," which is a decidedly negative perspective. We prefer to view this time as the "terrific twos." [1]

Much is happening now. It is a dynamic stage of development. It is the birth of our independence and the surging of our individuality as our unique personality begins to take shape. Many changes are occurring in our world and in our body. There are social rules and behavioral demands to deal with. At two years of age we are able to *begin* to discern right from wrong and so we can begin to learn responsibility for our behavior. These new challenges, along with internal physiological changes, cause us a great deal of discomfort, resulting in anger. The most dramatic opposition is with mom. As the need for the symbiosis, required for survival earlier in life, begins to break down, we begin to think independently and tackle small problems on our own. For example, we don't need mom to get all of our food – we know exactly where to go to get cookies! Parents, especially mom, can support their children by encouraging the budding independence while continuing to love, care for and nurture them – this is their main task now. Toddlers need to learn that they can think and become separate, and yet still receive nurturing and care. Basically the issue is, "Can I still get taken care of if I think for myself?"

Having lived their whole life within the symbiosis, challenging it is obviously a focus of concern, even fear. It is important for two-year-olds to learn that making decisions results in positive consequences in life.

Anger and the Social Contract

At fifteen months old, we spill milk to watch it splash and learn about all the wonderful things it does when it splashes. Little white drops run down mom's leg, slowly run down the wall and hit the floor. Wow, it's exciting! Now, at two years old, we spill the milk and watch mom's face with a defiant expression and learn about all the exciting things she does with her anger. This really creates excitement! We are angry, but don't know what to do with it; we don't know how to handle it. We need to learn. So, the best person to learn from is mom, to whom we are closely connected through the symbiosis.[2]

Anger is the primary mechanism used to break out of the dependency relationship with mom. Being responsible for our own feelings, learning to think independently and behaving appropriately are the ways we resolve the symbiosis.

If we are to become a fully functioning person able to manage our own feeling, thinking and doing effectively, we need mom's help. How mom handles her anger during these times of obvious challenge, provides instruction on how we are to deal with and express anger. When mom appropriately expresses her anger, we experience the consequences for our inappropriate behavior. We learn appropriate expression of anger and, with mom's direction, how to take responsibility for our behavior. This is our first encounter with a "social contract." A "social contract" means we agree to temper our own self-serving behaviors in order to get along with others, and still get our needs met. Through it we learn that other people have feelings and thoughts about what we do, which we must take into consideration. We can't just do or say whatever we want in complete disregard for other people. We learn to be aware of other people and learn that others are impacted by what we do.

The social contract provides us with the framework within which to operate in life, enabling us to cooperate and live in harmony with others. We also discover that we are no longer the "center of the universe," and this is something else that makes us angry. The world does not revolve around us and will not cater to our feelings, needs and wants alone. We must learn that the world is not defined by our feelings. We must also learn that we cannot control parents and the world with our anger, temper tantrums or rebellion. Anger and rebellion must be confronted.

Another revelation for us, regarding the social contract, is that there are things we must do, whether we want to or not, whether we feel like it or not. You may be shocked to discover some of these same issues surfacing, even now, in your adult life. God will provide the very situation designed to make such dross surface. "Two-year-old stuff" is alive and well, even in the church, even among Christians. I'm sure you have heard the "two-year-old" banter with a "religious twist" whenever there is an unpleasant job to do: "Oh, that's not my anointing;" "I don't feel led to do that;" "God hasn't given me that gift;" "I'm not called to that." No one is ever "led" to clean toilets or "anointed" to wash dishes or "called" to diaper changing in the nursery. They are not listed among the gifts of the Spirit. They are meant to be the "stuff" of character building which leads to dying to self in order to qualify us for the high calling.

Toilet Training, Cooperation, Impulse Control, Processing

WHAT?!? Yes, as improbable as it may seem, these activities are related. Toilet training is a foundational event at this stage of development. Toilet training is an external demand placed on an internal impulse. It is one of the major ways in which issues related to feeling, thinking and doing get worked out concretely. In addition, because toilet training requires the child's will-ingness and cooperation, it is an important way in which issues surrounding competition, control and cooperation are worked through. Successful toilet training incorporates effective prob-lem solving, self-control, impulse control and the willingness to cooperate into the child's developing personality characteristics. All these attributes are highly significant in establishing the social contract. Without them, the individual is poorly equipped to meet the challenges of future developmental issues and will continue struggling with two-year-old issues well into adult life. Later on in this chapter, we will discuss, in detail, what happens when a child has been wounded in the toilet training process.

Discipline

Discipline, appropriately applied, is crucial at this stage of development. It is important for parents to establish basic expectations and daily schedules to which the child must conform. We need confrontation to test our anger and other people's anger, and to learn limits and consequences for inappropriate behavior. We need to learn to make decisions, which, when carried out, result in appropriate and acceptable behavior.

Since many people have been wounded by corporal punishment, it would be in order here to have a brief discussion on disciplinary methods. What are the best methods to use to accomplish the desired results in a child at this stage? Many parents use corporal punishment, by spanking, hitting or, in some way, inflicting physical pain. This, as the belief goes, teaches the child that the consequence for misbehavior is getting hurt. The Christian community generally believe they have been specifically directed by God to spank their children, with reference always being made to scriptures referring to "rod" in the book of Proverbs.

There have been numerous studies conducted on the effectiveness of corporal punishment.[3] Basically, the findings of these studies reveal that, in fact, this method is a most ineffective form of discipline. In many cases it is counterproductive in teaching the child how to be a considerate, loving, responsible adult. Because this is not a parenting book, we do not intend to give an in-depth discussion of disciplinary methods, but we will present what the Lord has revealed to us over our years of ministry. Briefly, spanking a child does not make him/her think or make appropriate and acceptable decisions about future behavior, which is what all of us want from our children. The "rod" in Proverbs does not refer to a literal "beating stick," as many

Christians believe. The NIV Study Bible note for Proverbs 13:24 states: "Discipline is rooted in love. Rod is probably a figure of speech for discipline of any kind."

Remember, two-year-olders must be taught to think, solve problems and make decisions about behaving appropriately. The most effective discipline is that which promotes and models these behaviors.

Through angry encounters with mom and appropriate discipline, we come to realize that we are separate from mom and that our feelings are different from hers. We are now becoming responsible for our own feeling, thinking and doing. Parental discipline helps to establish the boundaries between self and others, thereby finally resolving the symbiosis. Testing those boundaries helps us to draw the line and establish what is and what is not under our control.

As we receive what we need, at this age, for healthy growth and development, we are prepared to meet the next stages of life. We have learned to think, solve problems and take responsibility for our behavior. We have established a "social contract," recognized we are separate from mom, and are beginning to learn about self-control and self-discipline.

Think back to your childhood: were you fully equipped to meet the challenges of your next stage of development? Let's now consider what has happened to cause so many people to struggle with two-year-old issues well into their adult lives.

Weeds and Roots

Let's return to Michael's story as the Lord reveals the roots of his pain.

Michael never cared about the impact he had on the lives of others ... until now. His wife's leaving was the motivation he needed to begin asking God why he had such a problem with his wife and where it all started in his life. Michael had been sitting in the seminar listening to the teaching about the two-year-old issues. He reported, "When you started talking about adult 'two-year-olders,' controlling mothers and social contracts, I could see myself in everything you said. I am still two years old! I have never committed to anything like a social contract and my mother wrote the book on control, she is a master at it!" To make matters worse, Michael's father was a rage-aholic who intimidated everyone with his outbursts. Everyone, except Michael's mother. Michael reflected, "Mom was the only one who kept dad in his place. That was her survival and my protection from him." The Lord revealed to Michael that even as early as two years old, he began making decisions about how he was going to survive in this world and that someone would have to pay the price for all the control he was being oppressed by. It was at this moment that the Lord revealed to Michael that he had been controlling, dominating and oppressing others all his life in retaliation for what he had suffered under his mother's domination and control. He learned well how to survive. The Lord revealed to him that his extremely destructive behavior toward his wife was the main way he was finally getting back at his mother. The person paying the price for his mother's control was Michael's wife. Michael was struck with guilt, grief and agony at this realization. He broke and a torrent of pain flooded out. As I held him in my arms, his sobs intensified and caught his breath ... The little child finally could release the grief and pour out the pain buried for so long.

Separating and Thinking

The birth of independence in separating from mom and learning to think on our own is a very real challenge to survival at this age. We are confronted with a paradox, "If I think and solve problems, will mom still take care of me? Will I be abandoned and left alone?" Fear of not surviving remains the basic issue. If, as a two-year-old, you were convinced that separation into independence and thinking for yourself threatened your mom and might result in her withdrawing care and threatening your survival, you may have decided to avoid thinking at all costs. As a result you may have lapsed into passivity. This happens in situations with insecure or fearful mothers who are so controlling that they perceive the child's budding independence as a threat to their authority. Perhaps mom was always there pulling you back, doing everything for you, smothering you with constant direction, threats and control, until you could hardly breathe, until the cry of your heart in frustration was, "Mom, I need to do it myself!!!"

Another, opposite but equally destructive, scenario is a mother who is so neglectful that becoming independent results in physical harm for the child. Rather than suffering under mom's wrath and anger, as in the example above, which is an obvious threat, now physical neglect threatens the child's survival. If this has been your experience, you work at remaining dependent on others so that others will solve problems for you. If you were controlled by mom, you have learned to get what you need by using control. "Not thinking" becomes a control mechanism, a protective device, used to deal with the potential dangers in life and to force others to solve your problems.

Anger and the "Social Contract"

Many people have difficulty dealing with anger because they did not learn how to express anger appropriately at this stage in their development. A two-year-older is skilled at getting mom and dad angry. You yourself felt angry and needed to learn how to deal with it. When you made mom angry and she expressed her anger by hitting you, she taught you a lesson. You learned very well that anger is expressed by hitting or hurting in some way, but you needed to wait until you were bigger than the other person.

Another problem may have occurred during this time if your anger, temper tantrums and rebellion intimidated your parents and they did not confront you. This resulted in you getting what you wanted, in you learning to control your parents and the world by using anger, rebellion and temper tantrums. Now, as an adult, you are bound by these same tactics in life.

Or, perhaps you were overpowered by the anger of your parents. They became very angry with you when you did your two-year-old rebellious routine, becoming more angry and ominous than your little being could handle. They frightened and intimidated you. As a result you grew up feeling intimidated by authority figures or, as in Michael's case, you learned to intimidate others with your anger to get what you want. Either way, the result is an unhealthy, even destructive, lifestyle that cripples you and prevents you from being able to live in harmony with others as God intends.

There are many "two-year-olders" in grown-up bodies walking around this world. They control through domination, intimidation and manipulation to get what they need and want. They may have learned something about a "social contract" when they were a child but have not yet agreed to it or signed it. They are still carrying the wounds they experienced as a two-year-old. These people will pass on this heritage to their descendants.

Toilet Training Wounds

When wounded during toilet training, individuals may struggle not only with issues of shame, but also with problems of self-control, impulse control and cooperation. If toilet training was too harsh or abusive, it adversely affects a child's willingness to cooperate, to think, to solve problems and to incorporate self-control. Instead, they become rebellious and resistant to authority. A "try and make me" attitude toward others, especially those in authority, can begin to form. The "social contract," which the child had begun to incorporate, will also be negatively affected. Usually it will become distorted and unhealthy, leading to the kind of person who is unwilling to cooperate readily with others or to submit to those in authority whom God puts in their life. The major problem becomes rebellion against God and an unwillingness to submit to His Lordship.

Toilet training too early can also have a negative impact on this stage of development.

Michael's story continues . . .

One of the significant memories the Lord gave Michael was the story he heard his mother tell in which she proudly proclaimed her skills at having toilet trained Michael by the time he was fifteen months old. How she started when he was twelve months old, and even though it took three months, she always boasted of this accomplishment.

As a result of Michael's mother's insistence on toilet training him too early, he never successfully made it through the two-year-old stage of development and never established a "social contract." Since, as in his case, early toilet training can only be accomplished by the use of classical conditioning methods – the type of conditioning experimented with by Ivan Pavlov and his famous "salivating dogs" – the desired behavior is achieved but the child is deprived of the opportunity to confront and accomplish the expectations when developmentally ready. In this way he or she is deprived of the opportunity to develop effective tools for problem solving.

In the case of toilet training, bowel control is a form of self-control and is one of the building blocks for developing self-discipline as an adult. If children are classically conditioned to perform this activity before ready, they are not given the opportunity to deal with the important issues of control and competition/cooperation. They are never really confronted with the opportunity to make a decision, in the strict sense of the word, to cooperate and commit to control their bowels because they have already been preconditioned by external controls. As mentioned in the previous chapter, being controlled by developmentally inappropriate external demands causes children to relinquish self-control of internal impulses and processes to the control of another person. Basically, children give up the ability to control internal impulses and processes to their parents, thus learning to abandon an internal disciplinary approach to life and embrace an external disciplinary focus and relinquishing the major foundation upon which self-discipline and self-control are built. Such children are often quickly labeled "problem" children and always seem to need parental discipline, correction and punishment. Parents have to monitor and watch them closely or they get into trouble. Is it any wonder they are problem children? They gave up their budding ability to incorporate self-discipline to dominating, controlling parents. Now, as adults, they may find themselves struggling with self-control and self-discipline. They may do and say things that provoke others to confront and correct them. Many adult Christians find themselves bound by the same sins which they repeat over and over again. They know they should not do certain things, but find it impossible to take control over these patterns of behavior. They keep doing them until someone confronts them and pressures them to change. Obviously, there are other reasons why people continue in the same sins or perform the same inappropriate, hurtful behaviors. Yet, it can often be traced back to having relinquished internal control to an external source.

Many adults – perhaps you are one of them – are held in bondage by this pattern of repeating the same sin over and over again. This lifestyle is most apparent in those who have grown up with controlling parents.

The reader is referred to the Appendix B at the end of the book: "Control: Brings Life or Brings Death."

Discipline Now

Lack of discipline or expectations, inappropriate discipline, harsh discipline enforced with extreme pressure or without having taught the consequences of behavior, results in people entering their adult years with many competition/control issues. They have the potential to become a negative, oppositional, rebellious adult who finds it extremely difficult to submit to authority, even to the authority of a living God. They become an uncooperative self-indulgent person who fears not getting what they need or want in life, so they intimidate, dominate or manipulate to accomplish their goals. Do you know anyone like this?

The Lord desires to set us free from these self-destructive bondages. We need to allow Him to show us the roots of these two-year-old wounds in our lives. He wants to touch these areas, heal our hearts and cleanse our minds. God is able.

"For Christ's love controls us ... " (2 Corinthians 5:14, NKJV)

"And God is able to make all grace abound to you, so that in all things at all times, having all that you need, you will abound in every good work." (2 Corinthians 9:8)

"To him who is able to keep you from falling and to present you before his glorious presence without fault and with great joy – to the only God, our Savior be glory, majesty, power and authority, through Jesus Christ, our Lord, before all ages, now and forevermore! Amen." (Jude 24–25)

God's Intervention

Again, the only way this cycle will ever be broken is to recognize it, take responsibility for the wounds in our lives, and let the Lord touch these two-year-old issues and heal them. When we become free, we can then pass this on as an inheritance to future generations.

Michael's story continues . . .

As we sat there, I prayed and asked the Lord to reveal Himself to Michael. A series of incidents when he was two to three years old replayed through his memory, incidents where he and his mother were locked in battles over who was going to get their way, Mom or Michael. In each situation where the control was oppressive, the Lord revealed Himself and protected Michael from the attack of the spirit of control. In situations where Michael was the one rebelling and controlling, the Lord again intervened to confront Michael and parent him, providing the correction and setting the boundaries he needed for security. In each memory, Michael experienced himself giving up control to the Lord and submitting to the Lord's corrective discipline. The Lord brought him through situation after situation for over an hour and revealed Himself in each memory, setting him more and more free of layers of "stuff." When no more memories came, Michael prayed to break the power of the spirit of control in his life, in the generations and over his wife. He repented and asked Father God to "father" him and guide him in situations where he would tend automatically to move into control. Another major result of this prayer time was that Michael committed to sign and live by a "social contract," symbolically, of course.

Over the past several years, it has not been easy for Michael. Yet, he is committed to work out what the Lord worked into his heart. Michael's wife has since returned. He is dramatically different in his behavior toward her and others. He still slips back into control now and then but, as soon as he recognizes it, he immediately deals with it and takes personal responsibility for his behavior. Another radical change is that Michael is now sensitive toward others and very much aware of the impact he has on them. He is no longer the prideful, self-seeking controller he used to be. He has moved on to pursue greater maturity.

There are many of us who have been wounded as Michael was. For some of us the wounding is more extreme, for others it is less extreme. No matter how deep your past wounds are, the Lord will walk through those experiences with you again and reveal the Father's intention for that time in your life. In His presence you will find the healing and the freedom you long for. The lies and bondages have no more power. The Truth Himself sets you free.

Truth: Facing the Pain

Although it is often viewed as positive, at the very least control is a counterfeit power. It relies on human strength or "the arm of flesh," as the Bible calls it. At its very worst, control is a spirit which influences words and actions and challenges the Lordship of Christ. In truth, when exercised over people, it is very destructive. Control hinders independence, thinking and problem solving and encourages inordinate dependence on authority. It breeds competition and conflict. A person wounded by control can grow up to be controlling, rebellious, or passive and submissive to a fault.

Revelation: Revisiting the Scene

Sometimes denial and familiarity can block us from seeing the truth. We need the Holy Spirit to break through, search our hearts and shine His light of revelation. Ask Him to show you the "roots" of any destruction in this time of your life. You need not face it alone, Jesus will be there to walk through that time again with you, just ask Him to reveal His presence.

Redemption: Healing and Deliverance

If we received what we needed at this stage of our development, we will be independent, able to think, to solve problems and to take personal responsibility for our behavior. But, if not, we need healing and freedom from the bondages that arrested our development. Control is a counterfeit of godly discipline. The Lord will uproot the destructive effects of oppressive or negligent parenting and restore the healthy limits and boundaries we need for security and healthy self-discipline in our lives. The Lord always redeems our life – our whole life.

Restoration: The Planting of the Lord

The Lord wants to restore you and provide what you needed for healthy development at this stage. He will again establish the boundaries you need for security and supernaturally impart into your life the foundation necessary for self-discipline. Under His lordship He promises you will find rest for your soul.

Reparenting: Father God, "Father" Us

Learning to submit to the Lordship of Jesus is a progressive pursuit, but without a healthy resolution of our "two-year-old stuff," it is impossible. Once healed and restored, the daily discipline of seeking the Lord, listening to Him and obeying Him will strengthen self-discipline and healthy submission to the proper authority God has placed over us for our good.

Steps to Healing and Restoration

1. Identify the adult problems or manifestations that apply to you. (See Table 1 on page 174.)
2. Ask the Holy Spirit to reveal the "root cause" of each problem, i.e. whatever happened to you as a two year old that caused a wounding in your life and allowed the problem to take root. The Holy Spirit may reveal this to you in the form of a memory, picture, impression, thought, awareness, or some other way of "knowing" (Luke 8:17).
3. Ask Jesus to reveal His presence there with you. The presence of the Lord changes everything (Hebrews 13:8; Psalm 31:14–16).
4. Tell Jesus what you are feeling and thinking in this time, place or experience. Listen to His response (Psalm 91:14–16).
5. Ask Jesus to reveal what the Father intended for this time of your life. Jesus comes to show us the Father. He comes to care for your developmental needs, to heal you, to redeem all that was lost to you and to restore you to be all He created you to be (Jeremiah 29:11; Matthew 15:13).

6. Forgive your parents and all those who wounded you. Break any generational curses if necessary (Matthew 6:14; Galatians 3:13; see also Appendix A, Generational Curses).

7. Take authority in Jesus' name over any demonic oppression or influences in your life that the Lord has revealed. Command them to leave in Jesus' name (Luke 10:19).

8. Break agreement with the lie planted in your heart and ask the Father to uproot it. Embrace the truth that has the power to set you free – the Word of God. Proclaim the promises in God's Word that are His answers to your need (John 8:31–32; Matthew 15:13).

9. Receive Father God as your eternal Father and receive your inheritance of life through Christ Jesus (1 John 1:2).

10. Seek the Father each day and ask Him to "father" you. Ask the Holy Spirit to teach you how to walk in your "newness of life" (Hebrews 12:10).

Notes

1. Bernice Weissbourd, "The Myth of the Terrible Twos: Rethinking Toddlers' Bad Rap (As They Grow: 2 Years)," *Parents Magazine* (October 1995), 70 n. 10, 77(2).
2. Nancy Samalin, "How to Love Your Child, Even When You're Angry," *Family Circle* (April 1996), 24 n. 5(2).
3. James and Mary Kenny, "Punishment Won't Make Your Kids Good," *U.S. Catholic* (July 1996), 26 v. 61, n. 7(5); Nick Gallo, "Why Spanking Takes the Spunk Out of Kids," *Child* (March 1996), 103, 146–147; "Public Spanking: Is It an Answer to Teen Crime?" *Current Events* (11 March 1996), 95, n. 21, 3(1); Ellen Wlody, "To Spank or Not to Spank?" *American Baby* (November 1995), 57, n. 11, 56(5); "Dr. Spock's Guide to Effective Discipline," *Parenting* (June/July 1995), 9 n. 5, 58(6); Nancy Samalin, "What's Wrong With Spanking?" *Parents' Magazine* (May 1995), 70 n. 5, 35(2); William Sears and Martha Sears, "8 Reasons Spanking Doesn't Work ... and 5 Kinds of Techniques That Do," *Redbook* (March 1995) 184 n. 5, 156; "Sparing the Rod to Save the Child" (Corporal Punishment in the United Kingdom) (editorial), *New Statesman and Society* (24 June 1994), 7 n. 308, 5(1); Hans-Joachim Heil, "Ein missverstandener Begriff: 'Zuchtigung' – was soll denn das?" *Der Auftrag*, Nr 61 (Dezember 1996), 58.

Chapter 5

Identity

Three to Five Years of Age

> Tom was just five years old, when his father returned from the war a broken man. During his father's absence, Tom's mother was lonely and very frightened about the future. She found her only joy was in raising her children, especially Tom who was her favorite. As her favorite, Tom was given special attention, sometimes in ways that confused him. A knot tightened in his stomach whenever she pulled him close to her. At times, when his mother was especially frightened and lonely, she would have Tom sleep beside her for comfort. Tom felt quite uncomfortable during these times.

Between the ages of three and five children learn to identify social roles and conceptualize what the world is about. What is seen is done; what is heard is repeated. It is time to incorporate identity, to discover what it means to be male or female. The family, social setting and culture all play an important role in shaping the development of young children of this age. Mother and Father are particularly significant role models.[1]

Adult Problems

Identity is knowing the truth of who we are, knowing who we were created to be. Adult problems affecting identity can have a devastating affect on our ability to recognize and fulfill our destiny. If we don't know who we are, how can we be who God intended us to be in this world and fulfill our purpose? In considering the importance of this stage of development, it is critical to recognize the adult problems that can take root during this time. Some of the most common struggles include: sex-role confusion, over adaptation, fears and phobias, fantasies without action, social ineptitude, rituals/compulsive behaviors, self-righteous/legalistic behaviors, distorted perceptions.

Tom's story continues . . .

Tom is a likable guy. He is well thought of by everyone in town, outside his home. Yet, deep inside, Tom was tormented by an oppressive sense of shame. He had struggled all his life with sexual identity problems, and was addicted to sexually explicit movies and porn on the Internet. Sexual relations with his wife had taken on more perverted patterns as the addiction tightened its grip. Tom and his wife had sought counseling with some results. Yet, the main issues of deep shame, sexual addiction, sexual perversion and a lack of emotional closeness had not been touched.

Tom is not alone. Sex-role confusion is more common than you might think. Many people struggle with insecurity in their identity as a man or a woman. The "blurring" of our sex-role differences in the present-day culture does not help the situation either. Sex-role confusion does not mean a person is homosexual but, rather, they are not completely comfortable and secure in knowing how to *be* and behave in appropriate ways for their sexual identity. Homosexuality is a much more severe identity crisis, related to many other influences that will be discussed in a later chapter. Do you feel compelled by others to say and do what you perceive they expect of you? Would you describe yourself as socially inept or an introvert, conversationally? Are you comfortable with the fact that God created you a male or female or do you struggle with your identity? Do you experience problems in the area of sex? Have you been tormented by fear for as long as you can remember? If you answered "yes" to any of the above questions, it's likely that the roots of such issues can be traced back to the time when you were three to five years old.

To get a better understanding of the roots of these problems, lets revisit the tender ages of three to five, and walk through our development again.

Developmental Process

Three Years Old

We discovered in the previous chapter that at two years old a social contract is established. Now a great deal of information gathering is necessary in order to put this contract to work. At three years old what we see, we do, and what we hear, we say. If it's OK for mom and dad, it's OK for me. It's likely we will say and do things learned from adults at the most inappropriate times, much to the chagrin of parents. Even so, parents love this age. They enjoy the welcome relief from the previous year's time of testing and opposition. Three-year-olders are very helpful, doing things for their parents, even without being asked. They are loveable, helpful and considerate.

Our insatiable drive for information motivates parents to consult the encyclopedia to answer the consistent and ever-present, "Why?" God gives all three-year-olds a one word gift, "Why?" Parents must work hard, at times, not to use the two-word response, "BE QUIET!" which can emerge out of frustration after the numerous whys. Do parents ever run out of answers? YES!!!

We are very perceptive now. Nothing seems to escape our awareness. We are collecting information about the world, and it's important we receive accurate information without being ridiculed, teased or made fun of. We are learning what people will and will not respond to. As much as we need to learn socially appropriate behavior, we also need to learn conversational etiquette. When it's OK to talk and when we must be polite and remain silent. What it is appropriate to say and what it is not. We experience our feelings and those of others around us and we must learn to integrate these feelings with what's happening in our environment. Parents need to spend some time helping us label feelings: "This is happy," "This is sad," "This is angry," etc. In this way we begin to understand the responses we and others have to the events happening around us. At this age we develop strong connections between feeling, thinking and doing. We test thoughts and perceptions in order to develop a foundational understanding of what it means to function socially, as a human being.

Four Years Old

By the time we are four years old, being well behaved becomes a major concern. We desire to be a good child for our parents. We've been collecting information for a whole year. The more we learn about the world, the more we begin to wonder if we will be good enough to make it in this world.

Fear Happens!!!

Have you ever noticed how, at four years old, children seem to get into fear? They begin to have nightmares, and talk about scary events and ghosts. They want you to read them stories of Jesus delivering people of demons. This is the age of the "night light" because it's dark and scary. As mentioned above, being well behaved is important for a four-year-old. Often, four-year-olds feel like they will not be good enough to make it in the world, and so, they discover a mechanism to make themselves behave: they scare themselves. For example, if people are overwhelmed with fear, they report being *frozen* with fear, not able to move. If you don't move you can't behave badly. This is the extreme case but you get the idea. Fear then becomes the self-imposed control mechanism to accomplish the goal of good behavior.

We need consistent, structured discipline at this age. The more we must control our own behavior without parental involvement, the more fear we will generate to accomplish this. The issue becomes one of parenting. The more structured and consistent the parents are in their discipline, the less the fear. We need to know that parents will be there to help us be the good child we desire to be. Yet, if parents are inconsistent in their discipline or do not provide enough parental structure for our needs, then greater will be the fear. At this time in our lives, we become susceptible to a spirit of fear taking hold and controlling us for the rest of our life. This might not make much sense to an adult but it makes perfect sense to a four-year-old.

If parents provided us with consistency and structure and if they did not reinforce the fear by using it against us as a disciplinary tool, then we were well prepared to meet the five-year-old issues with confidence and strength.

Five Years Old

By the time we are five years old we have established confidence in what is right and wrong. We know what is supposed to be done but will have trouble doing it. We will need to practice the "doing" which is what the six- to twelve-year-old stage of development is all about.

Self-righteous

This is a very self-righteous age. We see everything black and white, right and wrong. If you want to see what legalism looks like in its purest form, observe five-year-olds. There is little grace in a child of this age. Parents will need to be perfect in all their ways or the five-year-old will be there to remind them when they are not.

We become strongly acculturated at this age. We now incorporate many of the family standards, values and morays, as well as receiving a great deal of information about the roles males and females play in the family, the culture and the world. How do males and females fit into the family structure? How do males relate to other males and females? How do females relate to other females and males? We receive much training in these roles by observing and interacting with mother and father. Father becomes the major role model for sons and mother the major role model for daughters. Both parents give important information about what role we are to occupy as an adult in the family structure and society. Because social right and wrong is a major focus now, any time we observe anyone transcending what is socially acceptable, it will frighten us and threaten our developing sense of righteousness. When father drives faster than is allowed, with exuberance we will inform him of his sin.

I can remember a time when Todd, our son, was five years old and I took him to the market. A new shipment of grapes had just arrived and was out on the counter for sale. I decided to taste a grape to see if they were sweet before I bought some. I put one in my mouth and began to chew it. Shocked by what I had done, Todd shouted, at the top of his voice, "Daddy, Daddy, spit that out!" Startled, I spat out the chewed grape. I thought there was something terribly wrong with the grape. I said, "What, son!?" With tears in his eyes Todd said, "You're going to go to jail. You stole a grape." Legally, I had stolen a grape. The right thing would have been to allow Todd to see me ask permission to taste a grape before I did so. I could have avoided the embarrassment I felt as the people around me looked with disapproval at the thief in their midst. But, more importantly, I could have spared my son the shock he experienced when his sense of righteousness was affronted.

Many children become wounded in their sense of righteousness at this age, because significant adults in their lives do things that are inconsistent with their learning about what is right and appropriate, behaviorally and socially.

A Time to Pray

Because we have no trouble believing in God now, it is a good time to learn how to pray. I believe God really enjoys answering the prayers of five-year-olders. They can be formidable prayer warriors, who seem to get their prayers answered with very little delay on God's part. They have no trouble believing God. They know that if He said it He will do it. Their faith can, at times, far surpass the faith of many adults.

A father told me this story about a prayer time he had with his five-year-old. The father came home from work with a terrible cold. His nose was all stuffed up and he could hardly breathe through it. He sat down, on the couch, to rest. His son, seeing his father in great discomfort, walked over and asked if he could pray for him. The father, knowing five-year-olders get their prayers answered, said, "Yes, son, please pray for me." The son placed one hand on his father's nose and, with the other hand raised toward heaven, he spoke in the best prayer warrior voice he could generate, "Heal it ... or take it, Lord!" The father quickly responded, "Hold on ... I like my nose!"

The father's warning to me was, "Be careful *how* you teach your five-year-old to pray."

Sex-Role Identity Secure

By the end of these three years, we have a good understanding of our identity. We have incorporated the "shoulds" and "should-nots" from home and the society in which we live.[2] Armed with socially appropriate behavior, a secure identity and parent-instilled problem-solving structures, we are well equipped to experience and actively be involved in the next stage of child-hood, six to twelve years, and *active* it is.

Let's now look at some of the wounds which can occur at this age.

Weeds and Roots

Are You Ever Silent?

At three years old, we enjoy exercising our newfound verbal abilities. We talk a lot, ask a lot of questions and are very sensitive to our parents' needs.

Adults who feel socially inept or uncomfortable and fear asking questions, especially of authority figures, will often find the root cause back at three years old. Such feelings often arise when children feel pressurized to stop talking by parents who are frustrated with constant conversation and questions. Self-esteem is negatively affected and they begin to feel something is wrong with them. This sense of shame can then form the foundation for the belief that they are not significant, have nothing import-ant to say and have no right to assert themselves verbally. Living with such a bondage may create a pattern in life whereby they frequently make assumptions about what people mean, expect or want from them, without being totally sure. They con-sequently find themselves making errors of judgment, resulting in mistakes which cause problems for themselves and others.

People who feel teased or ridiculed during this time of information gathering, may find themselves having problems being serious about and focusing on learning new things, and may feel insecure in their perceptions of reality. Also, they may experience a great deal of skepticism when given new informa-tion because they don't trust the person who has provided it.

Fear is Incorporated

We have met many adults who have experienced a pervasive sense of fear nearly all their lives. These people had incorporated a spirit of fear at the time when they were most susceptible to it, when they were four years old.

Susan's story

Susan's request for prayer was motivated by a bondage to fear. This fear was robbing her of her joy and freedom in life. During prayer, the Lord revealed to Susan a time when she was four years old and she was riding her little three-wheel bike on the upstairs back porch of her home. Her younger brother began crawling swiftly toward the stairs which led down to the ground floor. Susan raced over with her bike to try and put herself between her brother and the stairs before he toppled down them. She just made it in time but in the process she managed to run over his little hand, and he began screaming. Susan was standing with her legs straddling either side of the bike at the edge of the top step. In fear, anger and frustration, her mother came running over and without asking what had happened she hit Susan for hurting her brother. When Susan was hit, she lost her balance and tumbled head over heels, bike and all, down the stairs. Susan landed on the ground floor, her arm was broken. She remembers screaming in fear and pain, and her mother running down the stairs crying out, "Oh Susan, I'm sorry ... Oh, Susan I'm so sorry!" By this time the intense fear evoked by the situation had created an opening for a spirit of fear in her life. Susan incorporated this fear and it remained as a pervasive controlling force up until the present time.

As we sat praying, we asked the Lord to reveal Himself in that memory. Susan experienced the Lord come to her, pick her up and console and comfort her. At that moment she felt an amazing peace come over her and experienced a dramatic release as all fear vanished from her mind. After a few moments, Susan prayed to forgive her mom and she took authority over the spirit of fear. She renounced this fear and proclaimed 2 Timothy 1:7: *"For God did not give us a spirit of fear ... "*. Susan was free. After twenty-three years of being controlled by fear, she was free!

There are many people like Susan who, at four years of age, incorporated a spirit of fear into their being. If fear is a problem in your life, it could be the result of a traumatic event you suffered at this age.

In some cases the problem is compounded by adults actually using the fear as a means of disciplining the child.

Frank's story

Frank was staying with his aunt and uncle for several weeks. One day Frank's aunt saw him hiding behind the bushes watching the men pick up the trash. Frank was obviously afraid of these men and his aunt recognized this. Later, when Frank was into some mischief, giving his aunt a hard time, she shouted at him, "If you don't behave, I will call those garbage men to take you away!" That was all Frank needed. He stopped his misbehaving. But, every night for twenty years thereafter, Frank had horrible, frightening nightmares of running in panic from men who were coming in garbage trucks to take him away. This is a big price to pay for a quick-fix disciplinary technique. Frank received ministry and was set free of the fear.

Fear will stop misbehavior but the price in terms of the enduring negative repercussions is too high. Was your four-year-old fear used against you because parents knew no other way to discipline your behavior? Any abuse, whether emotional, physical, or sexual, is deeply wounding during this stage of development. The heightened sensitivity to sexual identity and fear makes us more vulnerable to bondages and wounds taking root and the effects can be devastating throughout childhood and into adult life.

Whatever happened to you then, the Lord will easily and swiftly set you free now. *He is no respecter of persons* (Acts 10:34). What He did for Susan, Frank and many others, He will do for you.

Self-righteousness, a Bondage

Do you find yourself compelled and driven to "defend the faith"? To take a stand for righteousness, to identify with a cause or to correct those who are in error? The key words here are "compelled and driven." All healthy adults need to stand for their faith, to be righteous in their dealings with others, and to be accurate and truthful in word and deed. Yet, adults who were wounded in their sense of righteousness when they were five years old may find themselves in their adult lives with a driving, compelling need to correct people whom they perceive as unrighteous.

Edward's story

Edward would get furious when someone said or did something that was unacceptable or incorrect socially. He became even angrier if a religious leader said or did something he perceived as unrighteous by God's standards. Edward operated in life by the law. His self-righteous attitude got him into trouble many times, especially with his pastor. Many times he was told he was too fanatical and that he had a religious spirit, to which he reacted with "holy anger."

Edward had a very difficult time extending grace to others when he believed they were wrong. He was unable to walk away from what he perceived as obvious unrighteousness.

During prayer, the Lord revealed to Edward that when he was five years old, the time when children are most sensitive to issues of righteousness, he consistently witnessed his father committing obvious, unrighteous and inappropriate acts. He witnessed his father hitting his mother, stealing from stores, lying to people when Edward knew the real truth. He clearly remembered his father correcting him and punishing him for the very things he witnessed his father doing. Edward was wounded in his sense of righteousness. He made a decision at five years old that he would correct anyone who he perceived was acting unrighteously. After ministry, prayer and the Lord's intervention in many of Edward's five-year-old memories with his father, he was systematically set free. He renounced the decision he made to be the defender of righteousness and gave the responsibility back to Jesus, where it belongs. He asked the Lord to give him a revelation of His grace and mercy as he already knew about godly discipline and fear.

As the Lord brings to mind three-, four-and five-year-old childhood memories, His purpose is to revisit them with you and heal you of wounds you may have received. The Lord will set you free of the issues in adult life which are bondages and obstacles to growth and maturity in Him. Don't allow five-year-old self-righteousness, four-year-old fear or three-year-old shame and inadequacy to hold you back from allowing the Lord to touch these areas in your life. It is a free gift from God to you.

Sex-Role Confusion

Let's now look at the significant roots the Lord revealed to Tom. During the two hours we were together, Tom offered the following background information:

> Tom was the oldest of three children and the only boy. Tom's father was away at war during his first few years of life. The closeness that had developed between Tom and his mother became even more uncomfortable when Tom's father came home from the war. Tom's father, depressive, withdrawn and struggling with drug addiction, was incapable of attending to his wife's emotional needs. Tom, at five years old, began to feel quite embarrassed by his mother's attentions. He remembered nights when his father was not home and his mother would ask him to sit close to her on the couch. By the time he was six years old, this was causing him to feel enormous shame. He remembers the question was always in his mind, "Why do I feel so badly? Mom needs me." He remembers praying and asking God to bring his father home so he could go to bed, not wanting to abandon his mother.

As we began to pray, the Lord revealed significant roots to Tom's adult problems.

Since Tom's father was unavailable to meet his wife's emotional needs for companionship and support, as a husband normally does, she subconsciously turned to Tom for the emotional support she lacked. Tom became a surrogate husband for his mother. As well as receiving healthy nurture from his mother, Tom was being required to take her adult emotional needs on board. This mixture was a potent, destructive concoction which resulted in throwing Tom into emotional and sex-role confusion. Occurring as the situation did at the age when sex-role identity was a significant developmental issue, he became susceptible to sex-role confusion which created a perversion in Tom's attitudes about sex and sexual activity. This emotional confusion was the root of the intense shame Tom was experiencing (there was nothing of a sexual nature in his mother's interaction with him).

Such a situation in families can be considered "emotional incest." Tom's mother certainly did not intend this to occur in her relationship with her son, nevertheless when a mother's emotional needs for intimacy with her husband remain unmet, they can become mixed up with her normal emotional interactions with her children.

Tom also recognized that he had made a conscious decision to care for his mother and always be there for her, no matter what the cost. This decision was the root cause of why Tom and his wife had never been emotionally close to each other, which in turn was creating the same situation for Tom's wife that his mother had experienced with her husband. Tom's wife was turning to their oldest son for the satisfaction of her emotional needs in the same way that Tom's mom had turned to him. The problem was being passed on from father to son. Tom was shocked to recognize how such perversion and destruction could be handed from one generation to the next. (For more on this, see Appendix A.)

Tom is just one of many people we have met who have suffered with this problem, which appears more prevalent in some cultures than others. The attack on identity through this wounding is ruthless. Furthermore, we have found that such problems are not male-specific. Women experience similar distortion and perversion in their relationships with their mothers. When there is no son in the family or the son does not respond to his mother's emotional needs, the mother may take a daughter as a "surrogate spouse." If this occurs when she is between three and five years old, the sex-role confusion may have the added component of animosity or hatred toward men and a susceptibility toward homosexual abuses from women. Even though there is no overt physical sexual abuse the emotional sexual abuse is deeply wounding to sexual identity. When this unhealthy connection happens between a father and daughter, she grows up to disrespect men, often manipulating men through seductive behavior to validate her belief that they are weak and easily controlled. The fact that children forced into this role experience power over the parent for whom they are emotionally caring brings a love/hate dynamic into the relationship. On the one hand they hate being able to control the parent, but on the other hand they like the special favor and power they are able to exert. When a daughter is put into this position by her father, a sense of competition will be created between mother and daughter, which later displaces to women in general.

In all these cases, there will be problems in marriage relationships. When we are bonded wrongly to a parent, then our spouse is immediately displaced from his/her rightful position beside us. The perverted connection needs to be broken and our wounds need to be healed.

Tonia's story

Tonia is a stunning young woman. Her beauty and charm would have been lovely, had they not been distorted. Tonia was compulsively seductive. Her self-hatred and shame had brought her to the brink of suicide more than once. But this time she was finally ready to face the pain in her life. When she asked the Holy Spirit to reveal the "root" of her compulsion a clear memory came into focus. Tonia was her father's favorite, often displacing her mother in his affections and attention. When she was about five years old, her father demanded that she eat her porridge. She refused and stopped talking to her father for several hours. Finally, unable to bear her rejection of him, her father came and knelt in front of her, weeping and begging her to speak to him. She knew from that point on she was in control of her father. She hated his weakness but at the same time loved the power she had.

Now, as an adult, she played out the same scenario with men in authority. Only now she used seduction to manipulate them and had brought many men down in sexual sin, proving her belief. She said she targeted men who were full of pride, pretending to be strong when really they were weak.

Tonia could not bear the pain of her shame and guilt any more. She repented and asked the Lord to reveal His presence to her in that early time. He came to release her from the overwhelming "neediness" of her father and set her free to be a little girl. Jesus took her place and cared for her father. Jesus then broke the ungodly connection between her and her father. The Lord released her from the generational stronghold of a man-hating spirit and Tonia asked Jesus to restore to her a healthy view of men. She is learning to be the lovely woman God made her to be.

Tonia's perverted bonding with her father distorted her iden-tity as a woman. Because of her broken identity, she was vulnerable to the influence of the enemy. He was destroying her as well as the men she seduced. Jesus understands our pain and bondage. He is always ready to forgive us, heal us, set us free, and restore us.

Father God's Intervention

Tom's story continues ...

The time of prayer with Tom was emotional and dynamic. We asked the Lord to show Tom what had been significant in his childhood. Within moments the Lord revealed a time when Tom was laying in his bed with his mother laying next to him kissing him goodnight. He felt extreme shame, fear and revulsion. The Lord revealed that this particular incident occurred at a time when his mom's emotional needs were at an extremely high level. This was also the moment Tom made the decision always to take care of his mom. The connection was made and the torment began which Tom had lived with all his life.

We asked the Lord to reveal Himself in this memory. Tom reported, "Jesus is walking into my room. He's motioning to my mom to get off my bed and to come to Him. My mom is going to Jesus. He's taking mom in His arms and she's crying. Jesus is taking care of mom Himself. Jesus speaks to mom as He holds her. Then Jesus turns to me and tells me that He will care for mom. That it is not my responsibility. I feel the shame and fear go. I'm free!"

Tom then prayed to break all unhealthy emotional, sexual and symbiotic connections between him and his mother. Every tie, connection and attachment in his spirit, mind, will and emotions. Tom broke the power of perversion, confusion and shame in his life. He forgave his mom and asked the Lord to forgive her for what she did. He asked the Lord to forgive him for taking on responsibility for his mom when it really belonged to Jesus. Tom renounced the decision always to take care of his mom and always to remain emotionally tied to her so she could get her needs met. He prayed to finally leave his mom, break the bondage with her and family, to cleave to his wife and to work at becoming one flesh with her (Genesis 2:24). He then prayed to receive his wife by his side in her rightful place as wife, friend and lover. Tom was finally free to be the husband he wanted to be.

Your identity is critical to your future. If you don't know who you are, how can you lay hold of your rightful inheritance? If you don't know who you are created to be, how can you fulfill your purpose and destiny? The Father wants to heal you and restore what was lost. He wants to set you free.

Truth: Facing the Pain

The pain in our lives can only continue to hurt us if it remains hidden. When we bring it into the light and seek the Lord for healing, He will set us free. Let Jesus show you what He wants to deal with in your life from the ages of three to five years old. These formative years are critical to your personal identity and your cultural identity.

Revelation: Revisiting the Scene

The Holy Spirit knows the root of your pain. Allow Him to bring to your attention anything that happened in your life at this time that still hinders you today. He may give you a picture, a memory, an impression, an awareness, or some other way of "knowing." There is no need to fear. What the Lord reveals, He heals. The Holy Spirit knows just what we need to see in order to be set free.

Jen's story

Jen had been oppressed by fear for as long as she could remember. She was afraid to go out at night. She was afraid to be alone at night. The fear grew worse as the years passed. When she came for ministry we asked the Holy Spirit to reveal the root of her fear. She saw herself in a dark place when she was about four years old, and she heard a struggle and her mother crying, but she could not see clearly what was happening. She felt the fear come over her. We prayed and asked Jesus to reveal Himself in the picture. Jen could not see Him and began to panic. Then the Lord said, "Tell Jen to take a deep breath and tell you what she smells. When she took a deep breath she said, "I smell clean sheets!" Jesus told her, "I am here holding you close to My shoulder. This is not for you to see." Suddenly the realization came, "I smell Jesus!" Jen blurted and immediately the fear lifted. Jen commanded the fear to leave in Jesus' name and it did, never to return.

Redemption: Healing and Deliverance

In this time of development we may be wounded more by our perceptions of reality than by what actually happened. However, the wounds are just as real and need to be healed. Parents often do not know how to provide what we need for healthy development and we are left with unmet needs. Only Jesus can meet those needs now. Ask Him to reveal His presence in those times of need and fill up your empty places inside.

Restoration: The Planting of the Lord

The Father wants to redeem what was lost at this time in your life. He will supernaturally impart into your being the truth of your identity as a free child of the living God. He will answer all your "whys." He will even answer the "hard questions" harbored in your heart. Only Father God can quiet our anxious hearts – He alone gives the peace that passes understanding. He will invite you to embrace your true identity as a man or woman, according to His perfect plan for your life. His perfect love will cast out all fear and give you love, power and a strong mind.

Reparenting: Father, "Father" Me

Each day the Father waits for you to seek Him again, to hear from His heart, to receive all that He wants to teach you about

His ways. He wants to teach you, train you, correct you, nurture you – for your good, that you might share in His holiness.

Steps to Healing and Restoration

1. Identify the adult problems or manifestations that apply to you. (See Table 1 on page 174.)

2. Ask the Holy Spirit to reveal the "root cause" of each problem, i.e. whatever happened to you between the ages of three and five that caused a wounding in your life and allowed the problem to take root. The Holy Spirit may reveal this to you in the form of a memory, picture, impression, thought, awareness, or some other way of "knowing" (Luke 8:17).

3. Ask Jesus to reveal His presence there with you. The presence of the Lord changes everything (Hebrews 13:8; Psalm 31:14–16).

4. Tell Jesus what you are feeling and thinking in this time, place or experience. Listen to His response (Psalm 91:14–16).

5. Ask Jesus to reveal what the Father intended for this time of your life. Jesus comes to show us the Father. He comes to care for your developmental needs, to heal you, to redeem all that was lost to you and to restore you to be all He created you to be (Jeremiah 29:11; Matthew 15:13).

6. Forgive your parents and all those who wounded you. Break any generational curses if necessary (Matthew 6:14; Galatians 3:13; see also Appendix A, Generational Curses).

7. Take authority in Jesus' name over any demonic oppression or influences in your life that the Lord has revealed. Command them to leave in Jesus' name (Luke 10:19).

8. Break agreement with the lie planted in your heart and ask the Father to uproot it. Embrace the truth that has the power to set you free – the Word of God. Proclaim the promises in God's Word that are His answers to your need (John 8:31–32; Matthew 15:13).

9. Receive Father God as your eternal Father and receive your inheritance of life through Christ Jesus (1 John 1:2).

10. Seek the Father each day and ask Him to "father" you. Ask the Holy Spirit to teach you how to walk in your "newness of life" (Hebrews 12:10).

Notes

1. L. Joseph Stone and Joseph Church, *Childhood and Adolescence* (New York: Random House, 1984), pp. 333–416.
2. Ibid.

Chapter 6

Gifts and Callings

Six to Twelve Years of Age

> Markus had just come home from school; he was in the kitchen when the doorbell rang. His mother answered the door. It was a police officer bringing the tragic news that Markus' father had just been killed in an auto accident. His mother collapsed in shock, disbelief and grief. Markus, stunned himself, ran to his mom. They held on to each other as the reality slowly sank in.

What a tragedy for a nine-year-old child to be confronted with during this very formative time of his life.

This is the stage of life when children from the ages of six to twelve are concentrating on developing the skills necessary to survive in the world independently. This is the time when they are learning how to be effective and are developing the confidence that, "I can do it." They are developing a code of values and a strong moral foundation, and will work on being skillful in all areas, primarily learning how to learn. Doing is emphasized with feelings being a low priority. Healthy competition and skill-testing are paramount now.[1]

Adult Problems

> *Markus' story continues ...*
> Markus grew to manhood, married and had three lovely daughters. Although he was blessed with a lovely family, something was terribly wrong. Markus was tormented by the fact that his

relationship with his daughters, who were ten, thirteen and fifteen years old, was very unhealthy and destructive. He reported that his relationship with all three daughters always started out wonderfully and remained this way until each of them turned nine years old. At this time, his relationship with them dramatically changed. Overnight, it became destructive. He found himself being short tempered, extremely angry, and emotionally and verbally abusive with each one. He constantly reacted to them with the belief that they did not take what he said seriously. He felt as though they did not respect him, his ideas or his feelings. Basically, his relationship with his daughters was in shambles.

Are you inflexible, impatient and passively aggressive with people, especially those of the opposite sex? Do you rarely express your feelings openly when you're upset but your behavior signals just how angry you really are? Do you have difficulty prioritizing tasks? Do you procrastinate, having problems starting projects in a timely manner? Or do you have problems ending projects, having multiple projects hanging out there in various stages of completion? Are you in bondage to some form of addiction? Answering yes to any of the above questions will alert you to focus on this time of your life, six to twelve years old, to discover the roots of these problems.

Developmental Process

Competition and "The Grass is Greener"
A new era begins with the advent of school. We now spend long periods of time away from home learning about the world outside the family. We are developing, testing and fine-tuning skills in many areas. This is the age of healthy competition. Our life is centered on activity, with major emphasis on doing not feeling. We do things and get into activities because it seems like "a good idea at the time," and don't really consider the consequences of our behavior. Thus, we find the end result of what we sometimes do is less than appreciated by the adults in our life.

"Hey, John! I bet I can throw a rock closer to that window than you can without breaking it!"

"No you can't!"

Now, the competition is on. Rock throwing accuracy is put to the test. We each take turns throwing rocks closer and closer to the window. When all of a sudden, to our chagrin, I miss the mark and the window shatters. Dad comes running out, very upset, angry and quite vocal in his disapproval of our skill-sharpening activity.

"Gee, Dad, why are you so upset? I didn't mean to break the window. We were trying real hard not to break it. What can I say? I missed! I'm a bad shot! All I need is a little more practice!"

It seemed like a good idea at the time. We didn't consider the consequences of our behavior. Parents can use situations like these to instruct us in appropriate behavior and teach us about the consequences of what we do. Such mishaps do not necessarily indicate that we are a destructive or a delinquent child requiring punishment, but rather that we need parental guidance, instruction and discipline.

It is not only our physical activities that are put to the test: the values, ideals and beliefs of our parents are compared and contrasted with those of our friends' parents. Other adults besides our own parents begin to influence our values and ideals. In this way, we begin learning about the environment outside the family and begin to identify with society at large. This is necessary so that we can incorporate information about how we fit into society.

When comparisons with other families lead us to conclude that the grass is greener on the other side, we may find that the best solution to this revelation is to run away from home, as a story from my own childhood illustrates:

The day I reported to my father that I was going to run away from home was memorable. What my father did cured me, on the spot, from any future threats to run away. I had reported to dad that I was running away. I was going to live at my friend's house because I didn't like the rules at home.

Dad said, "OK." That was it!

I was excited! I ran to my room, packed my bags and turned to leave. There in the doorway, with hands on hips, was my dad.

With an inquisitive voice he queried, "Where are you going with those?", pointing at my bags.

"These are my clothes! I'm running away! I need my clothes!"

He quickly responded, "Drop 'em!" So, I did.

As I stood there in nine-year-old defiance, the competition was on. His next statement shocked me. I tried not to show my surprise.

Dad sternly commanded, "Take off your clothes, all of them!"

Somewhat deflated but not wanting to show it, I said, "Excuse me?"

Dad repeated loudly, "Take off your clothes!"

More deflated now, I asked, "Why, Dad?"

Then came the statement I will never forget for as long as I live.

Staring deep into my eyes, Dad said, "You came into this world naked, you will go out of this house naked!"

That did it. It was at that moment that I repented and asked Dad for permission to stay home and not run away. Dad congratulated me on my excellent decision and then said, "Come down to dinner when you're ready, son."

That worked for me. I never again threatened to run away. I may have thought about it but I chose to avoid challenging my dad with that again.

Exclusion of the Opposite Sex

Generally, this is the time when social activity and identification is oriented towards the same sex: boys stay with boys and girls stay with girls. This ensures the discovery and fine-tuning of our sex-role identification. However, some interaction with the opposite sex is also important. This will provide the information we need in order to be able to relate effectively to the opposite sex in adulthood. Both boys and girls also need involvement with adults of the same sex. In this way we learn appropriate ways of doing things in socio-cultural situations.[2]

Important during this time is that parents continue to provide parental structure, deal with conflicts that arise, encourage the excitement of learning, and set reasonable standards and expectations.

This is an age when we argue and hassle quite a bit. Such behavior is now being used to prove that we are a separate person, an individual. It is a way to test ideas, values and the validity of what we are learning. Mom suffers more from this hassling than dad. This is to ensure the earlier stage of mother/child symbiosis remains broken. If it hasn't been broken, as in many cases, these hassles are a further push for the symbiotic break finally to occur. We need to prove to both mom and ourselves that we are a separate person from her – that we are an individual with our own ideas and ways of doing things.

It is important that parents work with their child around this issue of hassling. They need to affirm their child's separateness and teach him/her how to be separate without having to hassle to prove it. Children need to learn that it's OK to think, have their own ideas and develop their own ways of doing things. They need to know they can do this and still be cared for and loved by their parents. Hassles and conflicts, then, are normal and necessary. They allow us to define ourselves. Even Father God allows us to argue with Him (Isaiah 43:26). But children do need to learn during times of hassles and arguments how to account for and respect other people's ideas and beliefs. These encounters also encourage them to establish their own reasons for their beliefs and for the things they do, which provides a strong foundation for adult beliefs, values and ideals.

Let's Do Something Else!!!

There are so many things to do, so much we want to do, that we move from one activity to another. It may appear to parents that we are unable to stay with any one task or activity for any extended period of time, but it is very important now that we are allowed to change activities, after a reasonable amount of time, without being made to feel like a quitter. Or, being made to feel irresponsible. This is the age to learn about a wide range of activities. In this way we learn how to prioritize tasks, how to begin projects and how to finish them. Such encounters also provide us with the opportunity to assess our skills and talents.

Rather than make their children feel like a quitter and trying to intimidate them into staying with one activity, parents can more appropriately provide them with guidance and direction in starting and stopping activities or tasks.

This is a very industrious stage in life. Foundational decisions are being made about our life-plan, vocation and profession. This is the time for dreams and visions which accompany the "When I grow up ..." statement burning in our heart. The methods, skills, values and morals we learn and incorporate now provide the material needed to advance into our teen years with excitement, confidence and security. Let's consider some of the more obvious wounds that can occur during these formative years which result in adult problems.

Weeds and Roots

Let's pick up Markus' story where we left it at the beginning of this chapter.

Markus' story continues ...

During the time of ministry Markus shared, "I never saw mom so full of pain, fear and sadness. I knew she was not only sad and lonely but also worried about having enough money to live. I thought, I'm now the man of the house. I need to find out how I can make money for mom and the family. The majority of my waking hours were occupied with such thoughts. One day mom sat me down and said, "Markus, you are not to worry about money for this family. You are not responsible for taking care of me, financially." How do moms know what sons are thinking? I never said anything about this to her. Mom always seemed to know what was going on with me. It was almost as if she could read my mind. I remember, not too long after mom told me not to worry about finances, that she made a request of me. One evening, just before bedtime, she asked me to sleep next to her in her bed because she was feeling so lonely, sad and afraid.

I slept in mom's bed that night. I remember feeling very uncomfortable, shameful and angry but I never spoke a word to mom about my feelings. I didn't want to hurt or upset her any

> more than she already was. From that night on I slept with mom
> until I was twelve years old, when I moved back to my own room.
> The whole time I suppressed my feelings of discomfort, shame
> and anger. I can remember thinking that this was the way I could
> care for my mom.

Markus was nine years old when his father was killed and he
began sleeping in his mother's bed beside her. This stage of
development is characterized by a tendency to repress feelings,
which is exactly what Markus did. He was unwilling to express
his feelings of shame and anger to his mother and so he just
covered them up. Yet, this caused a deep wound of resentment
in him toward his mother and he became more argumentative
than usual for a child of his age. Passive-aggressive behavior and
continuous hassling became characteristic of his relationship
with his mom. He could not remember one day where he did not
have an argument with her. Subconsciously he was fighting
against the sleeping arrangement which he found uncomfortable and was trying to make his statement, more than ever
before, that he was separate from her.

As stated earlier in the chapter, hassles and arguments are used
by children at this age to define their individuality, to prove they
are separate, especially from mom. Markus could never resolve
his feelings of torment about sleeping with his mom. She wanted
him close every night and he complied. Thus, Markus became
stuck in passive-aggressive, hassling and argumentative behavior
patterns. He was never able to resolve these feelings during the
developmental stage, when they should have been resolved.
Such patterns of behavior continued throughout Markus' life. In
fact, these very patterns were characteristic of the relationship
he now had with his daughters. He was beginning to discover
the roots of this destructive relationship.

Wounds Affect School Performance

The first three years of this developmental stage are crucial for
healthy adjustment to formal education provided by public and
private school systems. Circumstances can occur during this
time that can severely inhibit academic success.

Daniel's story

Daniel was now twenty-two years old. When he was seven years old he had developed an extreme learning disability. He had become dyslexic and was unable to read or comprehend the written word. There were no signs of this problem prior to seven years of age. For fifteen years he had struggled with this problem, which was never remediated. Daniel was also tormented by the fear of going crazy, pervasive feelings of shame, uncleanness and confused sexual identity. He was led by the Holy Spirit to attend the Human Development Seminar, believing God wanted to heal him and set him free. Thus, he came with high expectations. During the time of ministry with Daniel, the Lord revealed the sexual abuse he suffered in his family, which he had denied and repressed for years. At about the age of seven, Daniel suffered regular and excessive sexual abuse by his older brother, which went on for several years. At the time the abuse began, Daniel's ability to function in school was dramatically affected. Overnight, he became unable to read and comprehend. He became overwhelmed with shame and feelings of uncleanness, and was tormented by a belief that he would become mentally insane. This fear of insanity is characteristic of people who have been abused by a family member (incest), as was true in the case of Tamar, David's half-sister who became desolate after Amnon sexually abused her (2 Samuel 13:20). This same potential for desolation exists in all people who are sexually abused by a family member. The one place where children should find safety and protection in this world is in their family. If a child is unable to find safety and protection there, then where else can they possibly find it? Abuse within the family is extremely devastating for children and causes major destruction in their developing young lives.

As we prayed the Lord revealed Himself to Daniel in a powerfully intense way. He experienced the Lord entering a memory of one of the times when his brother began to abuse him. Jesus suddenly burst into the scene in a blinding light of glory. Spirits of sexual abuse, destruction, perversion and uncleanness exposed in the light of the Lord's presence scattered in every direction, fleeing in terror. Daniel with eyes closed watched the vision unfold. He reported, "The Lord is dealing with the situation. He's protecting me. He's coming between my brother and me. He's confronting my brother. I feel like the Lord is bringing safety, security and protection into the situation and into my life. Jesus is talking to my brother. I feel like he's commanding every bit of perversion out and away from him." Daniel began praying, taking authority over everything that had tormented him and tried to destroy him these past fifteen years. He knew something happened.

Late that night, Daniel opened a Bible and to his amazement he began to read with miraculous fluency. Not only that, he was able to understand everything he read. This was a miracle. He exploded with tears of joy, praising the Lord at the top of his voice. He was so excited that he ran throughout the place he was staying, waking people up to show them how he could now read and understand. God had taken away his dyslexia and restored him to wholeness. When the Lord heals, He does a complete work. Daniel, once unable to read and comprehend his native English, has now mastered the Chinese language and is fulfilling his call, ministering in China. All the praise goes to the Lord.

Sharing Daniel's story is not in any way meant to suggest that all learning problems have a root of woundedness that can be traced back to an early stage of development. But Daniel's story and the stories of other individuals recounted in this book clearly show that many people are seriously affected by wounds which occurred at critical points in their development.[3] We believe the Lord wants each of us to be free of the wounds and abuses suffered during childhood, in order to fulfill the destiny He has for us.

Injustice: "It's just not fair!"

During this age-group the most prevalent area of wounding is in the area of injustice. Many people between the ages of six and twelve years old have been unjustly, even severely punished for behavior that was age appropriate and not meant to cause anyone any harm. They had simply not considered the consequences of their actions.

As we explained earlier, children at this age do things because it seems like a good idea at the time – like the stone-throwing contest earlier in this chapter. Parents need to teach their children the consequences of their behavior and need to carry out proper discipline. However, severe punishment for age appropriate behavior can and usually does result in wounds which will manifest later in life. One of the most troubling age appropriate behaviors parents are required to deal with at this age is hassling, arguing and fighting. Because these behaviors are being used by children to define their individuality and to prove they are a separate person from mom, dad, sister and brother, if handled inappropriately by parents they can cause problems later in life.

Rolf's story

Pastor Rolf shared that he lacked true compassion for people. This manifested in hidden feelings of happiness and arrogant sarcasm which arose from deep inside him when other leaders in opposition to his beliefs would have problems in their lives or ministries. Rather than have compassion and pray for them he would secretly experience satisfaction about their difficulties. He was aware this attitude was sinful and destructive and he wanted it out of his life.

As we prayed the Lord brought Rolf back to the time when he was six to twelve years old. Rolf began to share, "I am three years younger than my brother. We shared the same room during this age and I remember my brother fighting and hassling with me. My brother was much stronger and always had the advantage in a physical altercation. Our parents would always intervene in our fights and my brother would always get punished, sometimes severely, because, my parents said, he took advantage of my being so much younger. Even when I provoked the fight, my brother would get punished for it. I remember feeling happy when my brother was punished. Yet, to be honest, the punishment he received was too severe and definitely unjust for most of the situations."

The Lord revealed to Rolf how he had incorporated these feelings and attitudes when he was seven to nine years old and how he had carried them into his adult life, so that this way of reacting to the parental punishment suffered by his brother had become a bondage in his life.

As we continued to pray, Rolf remembered one fight for which his brother had received a particularly severe punishment from his parents. The Lord revealed himself in this memory and justly handled the situation between Rolf and his brother. Rolf then took authority over the inappropriate feelings and attitudes that had been strongholds in his life. The Lord also revealed a generational root to the joy and arrogant sarcasm he felt over other people's misfortunes. Rolf's mother and father had modeled this for him and his brother. When people they knew suffered misfortune, they showed no compassion or mercy, but in fact always appeared joyful about it. Rolf prayed and dealt with this stronghold in the generations. He shares that the joy he now feels is not due to people's misfortune but due to the compassion he now feels. He also shares, "The Lord has definitely taken away the arrogant sarcasm and in its place has deposited grace and compassion for others."

Are You a Quitter?

Other problems which result from wounding at this age are procrastination and the tendency to have multiple projects in various stages of completion. These problems may have arisen if your parents didn't understand that this stage of your life is meant as a time for surveying skills and abilities. If out of concern that you would never be able to commit yourself to anything, they forced you to remain at one task or activity, you may now experience difficulties in starting a project and carrying it through to completion, or stopping a project and starting another one. As a result you may find yourself being one of the many people in this world who have trouble beginning projects. Instead, you work back from deadlines, waiting until the last possible moment to begin and then working furiously to complete the task. Or you may have no problem beginning projects – in fact, you easily begin them and have a number in progress – but you find difficulty in bringing them to completion.

The people whom we have ministered to with such problems, have found healing by focusing on the damage they have suffered as a result of parental pressure to stick to one activity during this time of their lives. It would be appropriate to add here that we are not proposing that children of this age should not be taught to persevere in some things. Yet always to evaluate the child's desire to begin something new as an inability to persevere is extreme and if handled inappropriately can cause the types of problems mentioned above.

Is God able to do the things we share in these chapters? Yes! He is not only able but He is definitely willing. Our responsibility is to admit we are in bondage and to desire to be free. It is God's responsibility to do it.

Addiction: The Essence of Destruction

The last problem to consider here is that of addiction. Our intention here is not in any way to refute the many long-standing and comprehensive studies on the causes of addition, nor to attempt to give our own all-inclusive theory. However, in our ministry to numerous people who were in bondage to some form of addiction, we have observed a functional-developmental component to the problem, which we hope, when added to the other research, will increase understanding about this very destructive problem.

As we have previously explained, the six- to twelve-year-old stage of development is a time of industry, of engaging in many activities in order to discover, develop and fine-tune the skills, talents and abilities children will carry into adulthood. These are skills which will ensure success in a profession, in the family, in the community and in society at large. However, in certain situations, a person will almost inevitably become susceptible to the bondage of addiction.

People may become prey to an addiction as a result of being made to feel inadequate, inferior and/or helpless in their abilities, skills and talents during this stage of development as a result of not being allowed or encouraged to develop their own ways of doing things. Instead, mom stepped in and did many of the things for them which they should have been learning to do on their own. It may have been wonderful. Mom may even have felt that she wanted to do these tasks for them because she loved them so much. Or maybe she was doing more for them than necessary because she was trying to compensate for the lack of a father in their life. Whatever the reasons, this was destructive to their developing sense of adequacy in life. They were made to remain dependent on their mother when they should have been learning to solve their own problems and learning ways of doing things for themselves. They were being trained to be dependent. They were not being trained to develop their own capabilities and adequacies to enable them to succeed in life as an adult. Adolescence, then, became an extremely stormy time for such people because they were having to cope with these deficiencies. As a result they experienced feelings of such inferiority and inadequacy that they needed something to depend on in order to make it in the world. Having not been taught to develop their own thinking and doing, they were not equipped to meet the challenges of adolescence with a foundation of self-developed skills and talents already in place. They began feeling inferior, inadequate, helpless and unable to think independently. They may not even have felt in the least bit confident in their ability to solve problems or deal with difficult situations. Of course they didn't admit to any of this. They were grown up now. They were too "with it" to admit to such weakness. Now, pride entered to influence and assist them in the end result which, we believe, is the ultimate goal of all addictions: to bring destruction.

One additional ingredient must be considered. Since feelings are repressed at this stage of development more than at any other, these six to twelve-year-olds may not be prepared for the resurgence of intense emotions at the onslaught of adolescence. They may have no way of dealing with these overwhelming feelings, especially if their parents have not provided an environment within which feelings can be expressed and dealt with, and so they have to find some other way of handling the problem. Having been trained in dependency up until now, they will continue in what they have learned. They will find something (or someone) outside of themselves on which to become dependent. They will turn to anything that can keep their feelings under control – anything they can depend on to help them through the stormy challenges they are now facing in their life. It is important to note that they will choose something (or someone) which will assist them in what they believe about themselves. Something that concurs with their view that they are inadequate, inferior and helpless to do anything effective on their own; that they are unable to think, solve problems and deal effectively with the difficult situations in life. If father, mother or family members in past generations have had problems with addictions, then they are quite likely to follow the same destructive pattern. Addictions provide a false sense of comfort. They mask feelings of inadequacy, inferiority and helplessness. They continue the life pattern of being dependent on something or someone outside of oneself. Ultimately, they bring to completion the deep-seated belief that a person's only way out is to destroy him or herself.

It is quite probable that some people who are reading this are themselves struggling with some form of addiction. Please hear God's heart. He is much bigger than any addiction you are struggling with. He is more powerful than any bondage. As we minister to those under the oppression of addiction, the Lord faithfully reveals Himself as the Supreme Authority. He destroys every bondage and every stronghold which addictions have over His people. He drives out the spiritual forces which accompany all addictions. He then moves to heal the multiple wounds inflicted by the cloak of dependency thrown over you. He puts to death inadequacy, inferiority and helplessness. In their place He builds up, encourages and edifies. This is His new beginning for you. Then, it is time for you to do your part. Specific behavior patterns are characteristic of all addictions and you will need to change them in order to work out what Jesus works in. You will need to commit to major changes in these old behaviors. Each day you will need to receive direction from the Lord in what, when and how to do things. Obviously, this requires you to draw close to Jesus. To depend upon Him for everything. But isn't that what we all need to do?

God's Intervention

Back to Markus:

> The Lord revealed to Markus the overwhelming effect the unspoken feelings he experienced at nine years old had had on his life since that time. How, because Markus was unable to speak to his mom about his feelings, he was now displacing these old feelings of resentment and anger on his daughters. The Lord also gave Markus the understanding that his relationship with his daughters became destructive when they turned nine years old.

This was the same age Markus was when the problem started for him with his mother. His daughters becoming nine years old was the catalyst that ignited all the nine-year-old feelings he carried for his mom. What a revelation this was for Markus!

The Lord then began to reveal Himself to Markus in a memory he had of being in his mother's bed. He reported, "The Lord is removing me from mom's bed. He's revealing to me that the care of mom's emotions and her life are His responsibility, not mine." Markus then released his mom to the Lord, renouncing all the shame, resentment and anger he had towards his mom and letting it go. The Lord healed the wounds in Markus and began to input into his life the appropriate fathering he needed so that he could care for his daughters in a healthy, loving way.

Markus knew the next step in this process was to deal with each daughter individually. He needed to share what the Lord had revealed to him and healed him of today. He made a commitment to ask his daughters to forgive him and to pray with each daughter and ask the Lord to heal them of every wound he had caused in their young lives.

The Lord Jesus has done all that is necessary for our healing: He endured the cross (Hebrews 12:2) and despised the shame; He took all our infirmities, sickness and disease (Isaiah 53:5). It is our responsibility to recognize areas of bondage in our lives; to desire freedom from them; to ask the Lord to set us free; to receive what the Lord deposits in each of these areas; to do what He instructs us to do. It is a simple procedure, yet so difficult for those of us who are plagued by the most ancient hindrance to God's work in our lives: *pride*. But this can also be torn down and trampled under our feet by humbling ourselves before the Lord.

Christian's story

Christian remembered clearly the day he rounded the corner on his way home from a friend's house, where he had spent the night, to see his house engulfed in flames. In a surreal nightmare of reality, the shock distanced him from the screaming sirens of fire engines rushing past him to the scene. He stood frozen in disbelief for what seemed like hours as neighbors ran past him. Finally he moved hesitantly toward the house, fearing the worst.

Christian vaguely recalls a neighbor coming to console him. Both his parents were killed in the fire. All he could think in that moment was, "What am I going to do?" He was only nine years old.

As an adult, Christian, now an expert consultant on Personal Safety for the Home and Workplace, needed to be healed and restored from the devastation of sudden abandonment that left him an orphan. In the healing experience the Lord spoke to Christian and told him that his chosen profession was also part of God's plan to redeem. Although he was not able to prevent his parents' death, he had been used by God to prevent the harm and death of others as he taught Personal Safety. The Lord had redeemed the tragedy of Christian's life and was working it out for good.

We have seen this many times over the years: police officers raised in family violence now working to protect; gifted entrepreneurs raised in poverty now financing opportunities for orphans and others bound in poverty; physicians who grew up with the devastation of sickness and disease in their families now bringing healing. Often God redeems in this way as well. Turning what the enemy meant for harm in our lives to great good.

Truth: Facing the Pain

The pain of injustice is not always easy to recognize in itself, but it becomes clear in our behavior. This wounding makes us vulnerable to offense whenever we encounter injustice. We can be so sensitized to injustice that we are too easily offended and can be predisposed to carrying the offenses of others. With this perspective, it is easy for us to fall into the false belief that we are to dash about on our white horses "righting all wrongs." It seems like a noble pursuit but in the end it only leads to exhaustion and at its worst can bind us up in offenses we have no power to resolve because they are not ours. It is time to face the truth:

> *"There is a way that seems right to a man,*
> *but in the end it leads to death."*   (Proverbs 14:12)

Revelation: Revisiting the Scene

Ask the Holy Spirit to reveal what happened in your life between six and twelve years of age. Injustice and other problems that take root at this time of life directly hinder your release in the gifts and callings of God. Sometimes even being able to recognize the gifts and callings in your life depends on what you experienced in this time of development. Jesus will never leave you. He will be there with you to walk through whatever you need to face. It's time to be free.

Redemption: Healing and Deliverance

The Lord wants to release you from the pain of injustice and insecurity regarding your abilities. He wants to listen to your thoughts and feelings and help you sort out the internal conflicts you struggle with. He will be your advocate and establish justice in those unjust situations you were wounded by. Most of all, He wants to restore your gifts and callings and encourage you to dream again.

> *"A bruised reed he will not break,*
> *and a smoldering wick he will not snuff out.*
> *In faithfulness he will bring forth justice;*
> *he will not falter or be discouraged*
> *till he establishes justice on earth."*   (Isaiah 42:3–4)

Restoration: The Planting of the Lord

You were born for a purpose and the Lord wants to restore your eternal destiny. Whatever has happened to destroy the dream in your heart, the Lord will plant it again and nurture it to maturity as you listen to Him, believe His Word and obey what He asks you to do. It is not too late! All things are possible in Him.

Reparenting: Father God,"Father" Me

Probably the greatest challenge for all of us at this stage of development was learning how to argue our point of view in a healthy, respectful way. It is impossible to learn how to do this without practice and correction. We need to get into the struggle with Father God and work through it with Him. He even invites us to do it: *"Review the past for me, let us argue the matter together ... "* (Isaiah 43:26).

God always wins, but He is willing to hear us out, and that is the "fathering" we most needed then, and the "fathering" we most need now.

Steps to Healing and Restoration

1. Identify the adult problems that apply to you (see Table 1 on page 174).

2. Ask the Holy Spirit to reveal the "root cause" of each problem. The root is whatever happened to you between six and twelve years of age that caused a wounding in your life and allowed the problem to take root. This revelation may be in the form of a memory, picture, impression, thought, awareness, or some other way of "knowing" (Luke 8:17).

3. Ask Jesus to reveal His Presence there with you. The presence of the Lord changes things (Hebrews 13:8; Psalm 31:14–16).

4. Tell Jesus what you are feeling and thinking in this revealed time, place, experience. Listen to His response (Psalm 91:14–16).

5. Ask Jesus to reveal what the Father intended for this time of your life. Jesus comes to show us the Father. He comes to care for your developmental needs, to heal you, to redeem all that was lost to you and to restore you to be all He created you to be (Jeremiah 29:11; Matthew 15:13).

6. Forgive your parents and all those who wounded you. Break any generational curses, if necessary (Matthew 6:14; Galatians 3:13; see also Appendix A, Generational Curses).

7. Take authority, in Jesus' name, over any demonic oppression or influences in your life that the Lord has revealed. Command them to leave in the authority of Jesus' name (Luke 10:19).

8. Break agreement with the lie planted in your heart and ask the Lord to uproot it. Embrace the truth that has the power to set you free, the Word of God. Proclaim the promises in God's Word that are His answers to your need (John 8:31–32; Matthew 15:13).

9. Receive Father God as your eternal Father and receive your inheritance of life in Christ Jesus (1 John 1:2).

10. Seek the Father each day to "father" you and ask the Holy Spirit to teach you how to walk in your "newness of life" (Hebrews 12:10).

Notes

1. L. Joseph Stone and Joseph Church, *Childhood and Adolescence* (New York: Random House, 1984), pp. 419–495.
2. Barrie Thorn, *Gender Play: Girls and Boys in School* (Rutgers University Press, 1993), pp. 27–47.
3. Sharon Begley, "How to Build a Baby's Brain," *Newsweek* (Spring/Summer 1997), 28–32.

Chapter 7

Independence vs. Dependence

The Early Teen Years

Since his teen years Graham had been overwhelmed by severe insecurities and panic, especially when speaking publicly or in a business context. He was literally paralyzed by fear and insecurity. He also struggled with symbiotic relationships, being far too dependent on others for his own sense of worth. He could not understand why he was experiencing these problems. What had happened in his teen years? What had changed?

Teens, instilled deep in our psyche are the lifelong impressions of the agony and ecstasy of those tumultuous years. Emotional reawakening and surging hormones herald the onset of adolescence when we shake off the long emotional dormancy of the latent years and begin to feel again. The focus now is on social skillfulness, with friends and relationships a high priority. Tasks, studies, etc., tend to fall like a brick to the bottom of our conscious awareness.

God in His wisdom built redemption into the developmental process during the teen years. Adolescence is the bridge between childhood and adult life, providing an opportunity for us to revisit all the earlier stages of development for a final resolution of issues.[1] It is a chance to correct and complete unfinished business from the earlier developmental stages. Since it is also the time when our sexual identity begins to mature, puberty adds an interesting twist to the adolescent process.

Adolescent resolution involves the integrating of earlier development with the relationship and life skills being developed in the teen years. If it is successful, the complete, mature person will function effectively as an individual and will have the capability to initiate and maintain healthy relationships. However, successful integration is rare. The wounds of our early life hinder our maturing process and there is a sense of "déjà vu" as we confront certain problems over and over again. We find ourselves going around the mountain only to find ourselves back in the same spot time after time, seemingly unable to get out of the "rut" and move on. The apostle Paul said it best,

> "I do not understand what I do. For what I want to do I do not do, but what I hate I do . . . For what I do is not the good I want to do; no, the evil I do not want to do – this I keep on doing . . . What a wretched man I am! Who will rescue me from this body of death? Thanks be to God – through Jesus Christ our Lord!"
>
> (Romans 7:15, 19, 24, 25)

What is happening?

Adult Problems

Trouble in early teen years shows up in our adult life in a variety of ways. Specific adult problems rooted in this stage of development are:

- difficulty with time structuring and task priority
- struggle with thinking and problem solving
- insecurity regarding limits
- symbiotic relationships
- inappropriate expression of anger
- eating disorders
- addictions.

Graham's story continues . . .
Graham's mother had died when he was ten years old and his father remarried when he was about thirteen years old. His

stepmother proved to be the antithesis of his own natural mother. All the good that she had woven into his life was systematically undone under the severe emotional abuse of his stepmother. She "railed" at him from dawn 'til dusk, nothing he did was good enough for her. Her tirades and curses terrorized Graham, leaving him with bouts of fear and insecurity to deal with, even into his adult life, that often undermined his personal and professional success.

To understand better how these problems get a foothold, it is important to consider what is needed for healthy development in the early teen years.

Developmental Process

Oral issues, time structuring, anger, rebellion, opposition and independence are all challenges teens face. If you have been around young teens you are probably aware of the "mouth" issues. "In the head out the mouth", as the old saying goes. The fine art of discretion has not yet been mastered. Generally speaking, girls are into the "snap, crackle and popping" of chewing gum and talking nonstop to relieve oral stress, while boys are exploring the range and variety of noises that the human mouth is capable of – you will often hear them coming long before you see them. Eating everything in sight is a favorite pastime for boys at this age. Of course, there are exceptions to every rule and both boys and girls can be indulging in these annoying habits. This oral agitation is one signal that early adolescence has arrived.

In our early teens we are not self-starters when it comes to anything vaguely related to task or work. Parental guidance in learning task priority and time structuring is essential now. Even the most diligent, task-oriented individuals hit a bit of a slump in this early transition. The good news is: it is normal. This is not to say we should be allowed to be irresponsible, but it helps to know it is normal. Parental intervention is needed to learn how to balance responsibilities with social relationships.

Also normal now are bouts of anger, rebellion and opposition as we struggle to separate and establish our independence.

Developmental Needs: Twelve–Thirteen Years Old

The earliest stages of development are now being recycled. Young teens often seem to regress in their maturity causing parents great consternation, but understanding "recycling" can help put things into perspective. Issues from babyhood are surfacing to be resolved. Young teens often exhibit behavior reminiscent of "baby days" – they love to eat, sleep, play and cry. They become nostalgic about the "good old days" of symbiosis, when mom did all the "work stuff." Young teens want mom to take care of them and do things for them again. In short, young teens try to reestablish symbiosis. The parents' task now is to resist dependency. Teens need to learn how to ask for what they need and learn that asking is the way to get taken care of. The scripture confirms this truth: *"Ask and it will be given to you . . . For everyone who asks receives"* (Matthew 7:7–8). Jesus said it!

In our young teen years we are very self-critical and insecure. We need affection and affirmation as well as correction. Painfully aware of our every flaw and failure, we need some honest encouragement and genuine praise to help us weather the intensity of self-criticism we inflict on ourselves.[2]

Time Structuring

Teens need to learn time structuring. We are not self-starters now: when it comes to tasks we need structure. It is important for us to learn to order time so that we are able to get everything done that we are responsible for. It is also imperative for us to have input to help us establish reasonable time frames for completing our studies, chores, etc. Teens need to experience this mutual respect and cooperation with parents in order to learn healthy submission to authority.

Sexuality

Puberty gives rise to a natural curiosity about sexuality. Teens need clear, accurate information from a healthy, godly perspective. Without this, we are vulnerable to searching out information on our own from various sources, not all of which will provide us with healthy options.

Boundaries and Limits

With the reawakening of feelings young teens now crave sensory stimulation. Structure and boundaries are needed for protection as they begin to explore again. Curiosity and the lure of sensory stimulation can lead to experimentation with substances such as drugs and alcohol. This can be a very destructive period if there is too much freedom. Young teens need as much supervision as they did when they were toddlers, with boundaries and limits being clearly defined. Boundaries and limits are not there to restrict young people, but to protect them. They have a false perception that they can handle their own lives and do not need to be treated "like a baby." In fact, they need to be protected and watched over in their ever-expanding exploration of the world.

Real Values

Teens at this stage begin to identify with "real values." They test family values to decide which they will incorporate and live their lives by. When they see adults living according to the values they profess, they are much more likely to accept and incorporate those values into their own life.

Developmental Needs: Fourteen Years Old

Anger, opposition and rebellion are the hallmarks of this age. The fight is on for separation and independence. Individuation is the goal. Testing authority and negativity are on the rise again. This is the "sequel" to the two-year-old phase, revisited in a bigger body! "NO" is the teens' war cry of independence! Often they oppose adults just to assert their separation from them. No matter what adults say some teens will be oppositional just to be different. On the other side there is a strong tendency to conform to peers to be accepted. Anger erupts and we are engulfed in negativity. The pressure is on – we must think and solve problems, and meet social demands and responsibilities, all while our hormones are raging. Often growth spurts cause us to feel awkward in our own bodies, so, needless to say, with all this going on we can sometimes be a bit "testy." In our early teen years we are masters of "reverse psychology:" we hassle parents to give into our demands but deep down we really don't want them to. Truth is, we want and respect strong parents, who model what they require of us, and are willing to be the "bad guys" and set unpopular limits when necessary.

Anger

Inappropriate expression of anger signals a need for parenting. Overstepping boundaries is a way of testing authority. Do you really mean what you say? Teens will attempt to shift responsibility at this age: it's the "make me do something" stage. At fourteen, we need to learn how to manage our anger appropriately. As scripture says, *"In your anger do not sin"* (Ephesians 4:26). Anger is an ever-present reality to us at this stage, which makes it a prime time to learn and incorporate the healthy management of anger.

Many Christians struggle with what to do with anger, most often because of misguided beliefs that are not scriptural. Anger is not sin. What we do with it can be, if we don't learn to manage it for good. God's anger is recorded several times in the Old Testament (e.g. Psalm 18:7ff.), and Jesus rearranged the furniture in the temple outer courts in righteous anger (John 2:12ff.). Neither the Father nor Jesus ever sinned, so it must be possible to be angry and not to sin. Anger is an emotion given by God that energizes us to action in order to deal with problems and correct wrongs.

The following practical steps are very helpful in beginning to learn anger management.

1. Years of built-up anger and resentment need to be released to the Lord. It can be overwhelming to process all that backlog, but it needs to be done. If there are any circumstances that need to be dealt with specifically, the Lord will reveal them and direct you through the process (Hebrews 12:15).

2. Recognize your anger. Acknowledge it when you feel it (Ephesians 4:26).

3. Anger has energy: externalize the energy of the anger. Verbally expelling it may be enough for small frustrations,

like being left alone to clean up after a church fellowship gathering. But greater anger may require more physical activity to release it. For such occasions cleaning the house, garage, tearing up overgrown gardens, or for the sports-minded, running, cycling, soccer, etc., can offer the needed release. This helps to focus the energy of the anger in a constructive way.

4. Go to the Lord and sort it out with Him first. He will help you get your heart right (Psalm 139:23–24).

5. Go to the one who has wronged you and work out the offense (Matthew 18:15–17).

6. Pursue resolution and reconciliation (2 Corinthians 5:18–19).

7. Pursue peace. Develop a practical strategy to avoid the same problem in the future (Psalm 34:14; 1 Peter 3:11).

Thinking

At this stage it is important to integrate thinking and problem solving more fully. Taking personal responsibility for our behavior, being held accountable and facing the natural consequences for our choices are all important for our character development. Breaking symbiosis with mom, once and for all, is essential in order to become a fully functioning, responsible individual.

Social Contract

If all has gone well, we emerge from this time with a clear social contract. The social contract, in essence, is, "There are things I must do in life, whether I want to or not, whether I feel like it or not. Other people have feelings about what I do, and I must consider others. The world does not revolve around me." Needless to say, there are many people in the world who have not gotten this insight yet.

Decisions About Life and Self

The experiences we have during this time of development result in an impression about ourselves that becomes part of our belief system. We may come to the conclusion that there is or there is not an order to my life; I can or I cannot think and solve my own problems; I am or I am not separate from my parents (especially mother). Ultimately, what we believe to be true about ourselves will affect our thinking and behavior. *"As* [a man] *thinks in his heart, so is he ... "* is a powerful truth (Proverbs 23:7, NKJV).

Weeds and Roots

The problems that take root at this time of our life have a direct impact into our adult years. The wounds of the first months of life will also come up for resolution during the early teen years, as the following story poignantly illustrates.

The story of a contentious son

A mother came for counseling regarding her thirteen-year-old son. He had always been resistant to her from the time he was a baby, but now the contentiousness was becoming increasingly more hostile. As we prayed and asked the Lord to show us the root of this problem, He took her back to the early months of the boy's life. The mother had been ambivalent about having another child, since her husband was often traveling away from home and she had to care for the children on her own most of the time. Her husband, however, had wanted another child and had promised her he would be home more to help care for the family. She had relented and had soon become pregnant. In the first months of her pregnancy, he had been more attentive and present to care for the family, but just before the son was to be born the father had fallen back into old habit patterns and she had felt betrayed and abandoned. Deep resentment for her husband and bitterness had grown in her heart. As the mother nursed her son in bitterness and resentment, he became deeply wounded. When he rejected the breast his mother was forced to bottle-feed him. As he grew more independent, he pulled away from his mother and grew increasingly resistant, even rejecting in his reactions to her. He would not allow her to be close to him. Over the years, the mother felt "a wall" between them.

In the prayer time the Lord revealed that her son had sensed the resentment she had felt for her husband, but had wrongly interpreted it as being against him and so, in defense, he had pulled away from her to survive. She was shocked, totally unaware of the impact her heart attitudes had had on her son. As she prayed and repented before the Lord, we asked the Lord to heal his wounds and restore them to right relationship.

A few hours later she called to tell us of the miraculous change in her son. The mother had gone to pick him up from soccer practice. During the drive home, he began to share how he had realized how mean he had been to her and asked his mom to forgive him. He didn't know why he had been like that. She was able to share with him what the Lord had revealed in the time of ministry and asked him to forgive her. They then prayed together for the Lord to heal and restore them and their relationship. As they hugged for the first time in years, she knew the Lord had done a miracle of restoration.

Pain and Addictions

With the onset of teen years comes the reawakening of feelings. For those who have had a relatively stable, healthy childhood, this is merely a new phase of their development as a person. But for others the reawakening of feelings brings the resurgence of deep pain and shame which has remained unresolved from the early years. Dealing with these feelings can be excruciating and bewildering particularly when added to the stresses they are already facing. The disabling pain and shame often drives young teens to drugs and alcohol to "medicate" the symptoms. The "root" of drug and alcohol addiction is pain. It is critical to get to the pain to be free, but this is not an easy task after years of repressed feelings. It is easy to move into denial and keep the pain buried, in order to avoid having to face it. The problem is exacerbated when the teen develops a tolerance level to the drug or alcohol and it takes increasingly larger amounts to get the relief they crave. With the help of the Holy Spirit and the focus on the pain, it is possible to get to the "root cause" and experience the healing necessary to quell the need for addiction.

Eating Disorders

In the United States of America about 7 million women and 1 million men are afflicted with an eating disorder. One in ten cases of anorexia nervosa leads to death from starvation, cardiac arrest or suicide according to the National Institute for Mental Health.[3] Girls traditionally have been more susceptible to eating disorders; however this is currently changing as boys are feeling similar pressures to be thin and muscular. "Ten to twenty-four percent of male adolescents report bingeing and one to two percent report engaging in vomiting or use of laxatives or diuretics."[4] Male athletes pushed to maintain low weight are especially susceptible to the development of eating disorders. "A study of eighty-four German university athletes (wrestlers and rowers) reported that 52 per cent engaged in binge eating and 11 per cent had a number of eating disorder symptoms."[5]

Eating disorders often surface in the teen years. The most common are anorexia nervosa, bulimia nervosa and compulsive eating. Clinical treatment often involves a team approach as the disorders touch on many areas of a person's life. These disorders have a complex root system involving addiction, generational curses, wounding in the feeding process, controlling environments, sexual abuse, and other trauma or emotional pain. Being healed of the wounds that started the problem and set free from the bondages associated with it, is only the beginning for the person with an eating disorder. The most effective course of action is a combination of prayer ministry and counseling providing practical information, support and accountability. Let's take a brief look at each one in turn.

Anorexia Nervosa

Anorexia nervosa is characterized by self-starvation and excessive weight loss. The individual experiences an intense fear of gaining weight, a feeling of being fat even though underweight, and a denial of the seriousness of the low body weight. Physical problems that are associated with this disorder include damage to the heart and other vital organs, low blood pressure, slow heartbeat, abdominal pain, loss of muscle mass, constipation and sensitivity to cold.[6, 7]

Bulimia Nervosa

Bulimia nervosa is characterized by a secretive cycle of binge eating followed by purging using vomiting, laxatives, diuretics or compulsive exercise in order to prevent weight gain. The person feels a lack of control over eating behaviors during binges and has a preoccupation with weight, body shape, and appearance. Complications associated with bulimia include damage to the heart, kidneys, reproductive system, intestinal track, esophagus, teeth and mouth.[8]

Compulsive Eating/Binge Eating

Binge eating disorder is a syndrome in which an individual eats large amounts of food in a short period of time and feels a lack of control over their eating during the binge. The person consumes food more rapidly than normal, eats until uncomfortably full, ingests large amounts although not physically hungry, and eats alone due to a sense of embarrassment. Feelings of distress and intense feelings of depression or guilt follow.

The sufferer may undertake sporadic fasts or repetitive diets, and therefore body weight may fluctuate from normal to obese. Physical complications associated with this disorder include diabetes, hypertension, circulatory problems, degenerative joint disease, hormonal imbalances and cardiovascular disease.[9]

Anika's story

Anika was alarmingly frail when we first met her. Gaunt and ashen she gazed at us through lifeless, hollowed eyes. There was an urgency in the Spirit to get to the "root cause" of this horrifying oppression in her life. She was bound in denial and deception and had no understanding of what was happening to her or why. Before we could even move into healing prayer we needed to take authority over the spiritual forces of deception and denial in Jesus' name (Luke 10:19) and command the "god of this world blinding her mind" to remove the blind so that she could see the truth (2 Corinthians 4:4). When we asked the Lord to reveal the root, He gave us a picture of Anika's mother nursing her as an infant. She was obsessive about her baby's weight and would not feed her very much. As a result of never being allowed to take in sufficient nourishment, Anika was always on the edge of hunger. Since her mom was pleased that Anika was tiny, Anika incorporated the association, "Mom is pleased when I am starving." The Lord also revealed that addiction was in the family and Anika had inherited that bondage as well. Anika asked the Lord to reveal Himself in her memory. He took Anika in His arms and gave her a bottle which she devoured and another besides, as He encouraged her to take in nourishment until she was satisfied. In that experience the Lord "uprooted" the lie that she must starve to please her mother. He exposed the deception that blinded her from seeing how her body really looked, and he restored a healthy appetite. Anika prayed to break the generational bondage of addiction and broke agreement with the spirit of death in Jesus' name, embracing the gift of life He gave her. He released her from the hold of the enemy and set her free to live. After this session, she continued in counseling, knowing she needed to learn how to work out her healing. She needed to learn how to eat in a healthy way and learn how to have a healthy perception of her body. Today she is a healthy young woman with a strong athletic build, as God created her to be.

Hannah's story

Hannah was a beautiful young woman but she was seriously overweight, which was the reason she came for ministry and counseling. She wanted to get her fluctuating weight under control. She would have extreme weight fluctuations from the obese condition she was currently in to near starvation after prolonged fasting. She felt trapped in this pendulum of destruction, never having been able to break the cycle. When we asked the Holy Spirit to reveal the "root cause" of this perplexing cycle, He revealed Hannah in the womb. Hannah saw herself as a tiny, tiny baby. When we asked the Lord what this meant He showed us Hannah's mom, who was only a young teen weeping and fearful. As we prayed, the Lord revealed that Hannah's mom had conceived Hannah out of wedlock and, fearing her father's wrath, was trying to hide the pregnancy. She was not eating, thinking this would keep her from gaining weight and being discovered. What she did not realize in her youth was that she was seriously jeopardizing her baby's health. By the time the pregnancy was discovered and she was taken to the doctor the baby was in crisis. The doctor rebuked the young woman and told her if she did not eat her baby would die. Not ever having intended to hurt the baby, Hannah's mom went into alarm and started overeating to compensate. Hannah survived but in her subconscious was indelibly imprinted a compulsive eating pattern that triggered in her adolescence and continued into her adult life. Fasting until she nearly starved, then compulsively overeating to the point of gorging until she was dangerously obese. Although she had been in counseling for years, she had not been able to break free from the compulsion. In the prayer time the Lord broke the curse and the destructive cycle, and she broke the power of the addictive spiritual forces driving her. The freedom from bondages and patterns imposed on her in the womb made it possible for her to incorporate the healthy eating habits she had been learning.

Individuals troubled by eating disorders need to be released from generational bondages and spiritual forces of addiction and compulsion (see Appendix A on page 179), and need healing prayer for wounds and wrong associations in the feeding process, and for freedom from control and oppression in family relationships. They are then able to begin to make healthy choices that are right for them. Counseling is most effective after a person is set free in the Spirit and has walked through a healing experience with the Lord when the problem took "root" in the person's life.

Hypocrisy

Teens, who are very sensitive in this time of development to inconsistencies in the lives of authority figures, can be deeply wounded by hypocrisy. Hypocrisy fuels the fires of rebellion and erodes respect for authority. Without healthy, godly role models they are set adrift and have a hard time identifying and incorporating values by which to live their lives. It is especially destructive when someone in Christian leadership they look up to and admire fails them. The sense of betrayal and mistrust can be overwhelming and difficult to come to terms with at this tender age, and its effects can carry over into adult life, causing people to become skeptical and cynical and making it hard for them to submit to rightful authority.

Insecurity

Insecurity is also rooted in this time of development. Insecurity regarding limits, ego boundaries and expectations all come as a result of insufficient parenting. One of the biggest mistakes that parents make now is to assume young teens are as mature on the inside as they appear on the outside and give them too much freedom without enough adult supervision. Insufficient limits and boundaries can leave young people vulnerable in a world of challenges and confrontations that they are not yet emotionally prepared to deal with. Too much freedom too soon can be very destructive, causing serious wounding and long-term negative repercussions into adult life. For young teens to feel secure, they must be given clear limits and boundaries. They need as much protection now as they did when they were toddlers: without it they get hurt.

Symbiosis and Dependency Reinforced

Equally harmful now is reinforcing dependency by allowing the symbiosis to be reestablished. If this happens, people remain helpless and dependent, and spend their whole life seeking out symbiotic relationships. Too often moms are not willing to allow their sons to grow up and keep them dependent by doing everything for them. Because most boys do not want to hurt mom, they stay dependent and get "stuck" in immaturity, which gives rise to all kinds of problems in adult life, especially in relationships. Individuals who have never broken symbiosis wander through life with their invisible umbilical cord, on a mission to seek out and connect up with people who will take care of them and satisfy their unmet needs. This is "mission impossible" unless they connect with Jesus. Only He can fill their emptiness and be the strength in their weakness.

Displaced Anger

Learning to manage anger in a healthy way is one of teens' most important needs at this stage. Displaced anger or inappropriate expression of anger leads to sin and often results in someone getting hurt. This usually happens because parents do not know how to deal appropriately with their own anger – another case of you cannot give what you do not have.

The sin of anger can have the following consequences:

1. it can hurt others physically or emotionally;
2. it can destroy property;
3. it can hurt ourselves.

Most of us would agree immediately that the first two are sin, but the third one is the sin we commit most often. We hurt ourselves by holding anger inside, instead of feeling it and learning to express it appropriately to bring needed change.

Internalizing anger is self-destructive in the following ways:

1. People may swallow their anger because they were not given permission to be angry in their family as they were growing up, or they saw too much violent anger and vowed never to be angry themselves. Usually, they end up "unloading" the anger inappropriately by displacing it onto someone. The resulting feelings of shame lead to a renewed vow not to be angry and, thus, the cycle starts again. This is very destructive to our relationships.

2. Denying and repressing anger leads to depression, hypertension, colitis, ulcers and a myriad of other stress disorders. In the extreme, unresolved resentment has been linked to rheumatoid arthritis.

3. Unrestrained, nurtured anger also results in serious physical disorders and is especially harmful to the cardiac system.

Sexuality

At this age teens are naturally curious about sex and need to be given accurate information. Lack of information or insufficient information compels them to seek out other sources. Often they consult their friends which can be "the blind leading the blind", so to speak, and we know how that ends up. Even worse, they may end up turning to pornographic material and media or other questionable resources to satisfy the need to know. This covert searching opens the door to perversion and can lead to addiction.

Father God's Intervention

Graham's story continues . . .

Graham hesitated – even the thought of facing that painful time again seemed unbearable. Yet, living in fear and torment was an even more painful option. As we prayed and asked the Lord to reveal the root of Graham's problems, he saw the situation in a new light. Not only was he being oppressed by his stepmother but his father was under her control as well. Graham had needed his father to protect him but his father was also under oppression. Then Jesus revealed the truth: Graham's stepmother was herself filled with fear and was being controlled through fear by an abusive evil spirit. As Graham watched, the Lord drove out the spiritual forces of abuse, fear and control and his stepmother was suddenly softened. The fiery darts of her verbal abuse were quenched and Jesus removed each one, breaking the power of the curses and speaking the blessing that He had wanted Graham to receive at that time.

The power of the fear and insecurities was broken and a deep peace quieted Graham's anxious heart. With this new perspective, Graham was able to forgive his stepmother and his father and walk free. Today Graham is a very successful business man, leading many to the Lord through his testimony of the practical, life-changing encounter with Christ that transformed his life.

Truth: Facing the Pain

Acknowledging the problems in your life is the first step to overcoming them. These problems are keeping you from being all that you can be, all that God intends for you to be. Take a look at Table 1 on page 174 and consider which adult manifestations in your life may signal a problem rooted in this stage of your development.

Revelation: Revisiting the Scene

These problems need to be "uprooted" by the Lord. Ask the Holy Spirit to reveal where the problem began. He wants to do this for us: *"You do not have, because you do not ask"* (James 4:2). As we seek His help He is faithful to reveal how the whole mess started. Denial often protects us from remembering painful events that we were not able to cope with at the time, but at the right time the Holy Spirit helps us to remember the significant experiences. Ask Jesus to walk through this time with you.

Redemption: Healing and Deliverance

As we remember these experiences with the Lord, He reveals the Father to us, caring for us and providing for our every need. When we have received healing, we often need new boundaries, which the Lord sets in place for us. As He reparents us, He "corners" us (cf. Psalm 139:5) to redirect us on the right path, sets boundaries and limits so that we will feel secure, and imparts into our lives an ability to trust and a willingness to submit to His Lordship.

Restoration: The Planting of the Lord

As past hurts and wounds are healed and lies uprooted, a planting of the Lord is put in their place. Our unmet needs are satisfied by the presence of the Lord, and a sense of peace and wholeness settles our anxious hearts. There is a tangible experience of healing and freedom as peace and confidence replace anxiety and insecurity.

Reparenting: Father, "Father" Me

Once we have been set free, we face the challenge of learning to walk in new ways according to God's Word. Scripture admonishes us, *"work out your salvation with fear and trembling ... "* (Philippians 2:12). What does that mean in concrete terms? It means learning to be taught by the Holy Spirit. It means learning to work out the healing and deliverance the Lord has given us in daily life. It means humbling ourselves before God to acknowledge we don't know how to live and learning to listen and obey as He teaches us how to live in freedom and wholeness according to His Word. In a very real way Father God wants to teach us as a father teaches his child. Just as Jesus learned special obedience through the things He suffered, so do we. Seeking Father God in the morning, opening our hearts to receive His instruction and committing ourselves to obey His directives, will result in a day of walking in righteousness in the way that pleases Him. Jesus is our model. He said: *"I do nothing of my own but speak just what the Father has taught me"* (John 8:28). Jesus always lived a life pleasing to the Father.

Along the way the Father may need to discipline us to break old destructive habits that were linked to our bondage and woundedness. He will begin to pry our fingers off these old habits and the "survival mechanisms" we took on to try and make it on our own, enabling us to walk in greater freedom in Him. This fruit of change is always the evidence of what the Lord has done to set us free. For some the change is instant and dramatic; for others it is a process yielding greater freedom over time. God restores us in the way He knows is best for each of us. We are unique and precious in His sight and Father God restores us individually, to His original intention.

Steps to Healing and Restoration

1. Identify the adult problems that apply to you (see Table 1 on page 174).

2. Ask the Holy Spirit to reveal the "root cause" of each problem. The root is whatever happened to you during your early teens that caused a wounding in your life and allowed the problem to take root. This revelation may be in the form of a memory, picture, impression, thought, awareness, or some other way of "knowing" (Luke 8:17).

3. Ask Jesus to reveal His Presence there with you. The presence of the Lord changes things (Hebrews 13:8; Psalm 31:14–16).

4. Tell Jesus what you are feeling and thinking in this revealed time, place, experience. Listen to His response (Psalm 91:14–16).

5. Ask Jesus to reveal what the Father intended for this time of your life. Jesus comes to show us the Father. He comes to care for your developmental needs, to heal you, to redeem all that was lost to you and to restore you to be all He created you to be (Jeremiah 29:11; Matthew 15:13).

6. Forgive your parents and all those who wounded you. Break any generational curses, if necessary (Matthew 6:14; Galatians 3:13; see also Appendix A, Generational Curses).

7. Take authority, in Jesus' name, over any demonic oppression or influences in your life that the Lord has revealed. Command them to leave in the authority of Jesus' name (Luke 10:19).

8. Break agreement with the lie planted in your heart and ask the Lord to uproot it. Embrace the truth that has the power to set you free, the Word of God. Proclaim the promises in God's Word that are His answers to your need (John 8:31–32; Matthew 15:13).

9. Receive Father God as your eternal Father and receive your inheritance of life in Christ Jesus (1 John 1:2).

10. Seek the Father each day to "father" you and ask the Holy Spirit to teach you how to walk in your "newness of life" (Hebrews 12:10).

Notes

1. Pamela Levin, *Becoming the Way We Are* (Deerfield Beach: Florida, Health Communications, Inc., 1988), p. 74.
2. David Elkind, *A Sympathetic Understanding of the Child*, 3rd edition (Needham Heights, Massachusetts: Allyn & Bacon, 1994), pp. 232, 235–236.
3. Cesar G. Soriano and Michelle Hatty, "Eat or Die," *USA Weekend* (20–22 February 1998).
4. Deirdra Price PhD, "About Eating Disorders, Facts and Figures," *Diet Free Solutions*, http://www.dietfreesolution.com/dfs/disorder.htm, p. 3.
4. Ibid., p. 4.
5. Ibid., p. 2.
6. "What Is an Eating Disorder?", *Eating Disorder Recovery Online*, http://www.edrecovery.com/information.html, p. 1.
7. Price, "About Eating Disorders, Facts and Figures," p. 2.
8. "What Is an Eating Disorder?", *Eating Disorder Recovery Online*, p. 1; Price, "About Eating Disorders, Facts and Figures," p. 2.
9. "What Is an Eating Disorder?", *Eating Disorder Recovery Online*, p. 2.

Chapter 8

Destiny Defined

Mid Teens to Young Adult Years

Emma's story
Emma curled up in her bed and wept bitterly, bewildered at how this same nightmare could be happening again. She had trusted this woman friend, a Christian, she thought. Why was this happening to her? She never seemed to see the signs that danger was near.

This final phase of our development in teen years is filled with challenge and the thrill of our growing independence. We tend to feel very "grown up" now and certain we can manage our life without any more help from our parents. Sex-role identification is being incorporated and integrated. Issues surrounding independence/dependence have been resolved, and, having established our separation, we are "psychologically" ready to leave home. We are equipped to take full responsibility for ourselves and our behavior. This is also the time when we are refining and integrating professional and life skills to prepare for independent living. The "light at the end of the tunnel" is clearly visible and "adolescent resolution" is imminent. If all has gone well, we are able to integrate into a unified whole the resolutions of our earlier development with the relationship skills, independence, professional and life skills of adolescence, thus becoming a fully functioning, healthy individual. Unfortunately, for most of us, all has not gone well.

Adult Problems

Problems from this stage of development center around identity issues, especially sex-role identity and male/female relationships. Insecurity and unhealthy dependency can give rise to symbiotic relationships instead of the desired separation, independence and development of personal responsibility. Sex-role confusion undermines confidence and security in knowing how to be and behave appropriately. The resurgence of wounds from our early development complicates matters as well. Tendencies toward legalism and battling real or imagined injustices can also put stress on relationships with others. These problems cause serious disabilities in being able to function as a mature adult in society and greatly hinder fulfilling our destiny in the Kingdom of God. Let's consider what should have happened during these years to prepare us for the plan God had for our lives.

Developmental Process

The storms of "negativity" have passed and we sail into relatively tranquil waters in this next stage of development. We are a bit calmer and find it easier to flow in cooperation with parents and family. We are taking more responsibility for our life and preparing for eventual separation from our family to become an independent, responsible individual in society.

Developmental Needs: Fifteen Years Old

Sex-role Identification
Sex-role identity becomes our focus. The inevitable "why" is back, as we revisit the three- to five-year-old stage to settle any unfinished business. This time our "why" is a social "why:" "Why can't I?" "Why won't you let me?" "Why don't you trust me?" etc., etc., etc.

Fear and righteousness are recurring themes as we reprocess "old stuff" once more. We have many questions regarding male/female relationships and have a desire to know about our parents' social history. In order to embrace confidently our identity as a man or woman and acknowledge that it is good to be who God made us to be, we need parental guidance and healthy role models. Daughters are attentive to fathers now and need "father" love to develop a healthy self-image as a woman. Fathers need to give daughters affirmation and protection to communicate how valuable they are. Through a healthy relationship with fathers, daughters learn to expect to be treated with love and respect, as the woman of God that she is. Sons are attentive to mothers and need to receive permission and encouragement to "grow up" and become independent. It is also important for mothers to affirm their sons in developing responsibility. This then gives the son the release from mother without fear of hurting her. It frees him to become the godly man he is destined to be.[1]

Developmental Needs: Sixteen to Thirty Years Old

Separation and Independence
Yes, sixteen to thirty. Current research indicates that due to the highly technological society in which we live, training for professions now takes much longer and can cause a young person to remain economically dependent for a longer period, even up to thirty years of age.

This was a great encouragement to a pastor at one of our seminars recently. He came up afterwards to tell us what a relief it was to know that his son was "normal." His son had left home three times to live on his own and for various reasons had ended up back home again. But since he was not yet thirty, he was still in the normal range of development. Now he was preparing to leave home again, hopefully for the last time. Hallelujah!

Separation and independence are important for us in these closing years of adolescence. We need to function independently and take personal responsibility for our life. Left-over issues from the six- to twelve-year-old period will surface again to be resolved, especially issues of injustice. It is a time when we look back and reflect on the successes and failures of the past, as well as looking forward and planning for the future. It is time to begin the transition and prepare to leave home. Parents need to support us by "letting go" and being available for consultation as needed. We need to take charge of our life and begin to move out into the world.[2] We need to be blessed by our parents and released back to our eternal Father God to serve Him with our life.

Decisions About Life and Self
What happens to us in these closing years of adolescence either enhances or diminishes our self-confidence as an adult. The major issues for us now are: It is good to be male/female; I can/can't handle responsibility.

Weeds and Roots

The wounds we suffer in our mid- to late-teens transition immediately into our adult life. Sex-role confusion, symbiotic relationships and an inordinate sensitivity to unrighteousness and injustice are the most common problems rooted in this time.

Sex-role Confusion
Sex-role confusion is fairly common in the wake of the feminist movement and the blurring of the differences between men and women in modern western culture. Simply defined, it is a lack of security in sexual identity, not knowing what it means to be a healthy man or woman. This can be slight or severe depending on what has happened in the earlier stages of a person's life. The absence of a father or mother can leave an individual without a role model for his or her sexual identity, or, much more seriously, sexual abuse or exploitation in the teen years can cause a confusion or revulsion of identity. In cases where there has been a history of sexual perversion in the family for generations, there is an even greater risk. A family history of sexual perversion creates a demonic stronghold that causes vulnerability to a broad spectrum of sexual perversions including homosexuality.

If you suffer from sex-role confusion, the important thing to realize is that these wounds can be healed and you can be restored to wholeness. The Father has made a way.

Emma's story continues . . .
Emma in her late forties had allowed a lady friend, who seemed like a lovely Christian, to move in to share her home. It was only

after she had been there for some months that the relationship began to change. Emma found herself more and more controlled by her housemate and, not wanting to cause friction, she submitted. It wasn't long before she felt like a prisoner in her own home. To make matters worse this lady was into strange "spiritual activities." Emma wanted her out but felt trapped.

Symbiotic Relationships

Insecurity leads to symbiotic relationships. If people are unable to manage their feelings or are incapable of thinking and solving problems on their own, they become vulnerable to symbiotic relationships, which are based on an unhealthy dependency on others. They then relinquish responsibility for these areas to someone else. In effect, they give others control of their life and expect them to manage all or parts of it for them. This often turns into a "double-edged sword," since, although they want to be taken care of, at the same time they resent the control. They can become passive aggressive, and vindictive. Most often this happens because people were "smothered" and controlled during key stages of their development and not allowed or encouraged to become responsible for their lives. Overprotective parents who shield their children from the invaluable learning experiences of natural consequences do them a great disservice. They leave their children with the impression, "I am not capable, I am not responsible, I am simply helpless" – and it is very scary to feel helpless in the world. Helplessness can pave the way for addiction. Even people who are quite intelligent and capable will sometimes become addicts to sabotage their success and maintain their belief that they are helpless and incapable.

Aaron's story

Aaron was out with his friends at a popular teen "hang out" one Friday night when one of the kids in the group got the brilliant idea it would be great fun to "bolt" (i.e. leave without paying for the food they had eaten), which is what they did. However, the next day the owner, who knew Aaron, called his home. I was sitting in their kitchen at the time the call came. Lara, his mother, was so embarrassed and upset she told the man she would come down right away and pay the bill. "Wait a minute," I said. "Whose responsibility is this?" After she calmed down she realized Aaron needed to go and pay the bill and apologize to the owner. It is an awful feeling to "get caught" doing something wrong, but facing the consequences of our behavior is what builds character. Needless to say, having to face the owner and ask forgiveness and pay the entire bill left a lasting impression on Aaron, which will ensure he will never do *that* again!!!

Dealing with the natural consequences of our actions is the "stuff" of character building and growing in responsibility. I also personally believe it is the "grace" of God in our lives to keep us on track.

Father God's Intervention

Emma's story continues ...

Emma was quite ill when she came for prayer. She thought she was going insane but in fact she was under an attack of witchcraft. When we prayed, the Lord revealed the truth. This woman was not a Christian and was in fact operating in the occult. As we came into agreement in the name of Jesus, the power of the witchcraft was broken, the heaviness and oppression lifted, and she was free. We asked the Lord to reveal the root of this destructive cycle in which Emma continuously found herself, trusting blindly and always getting hurt. The Lord gave Emma a picture of her mother constantly hovering over her controlling her every move even into her teen years. Her mom was so strong she just submitted, not feeling strong enough to take her mother on and fight for her freedom. She opted for peace at all costs. In the long run the cost was too high. In submitting to the control of her mother she came under the oppression of the spirit of control and, to make matters worse, she was also under the fear of man. The Lord revealed the picture of Emma all tied up and blindfolded. She wanted to be free and asked the Lord to come to her. He removed the blindfold and cut off the ropes binding her. It was time to leave her father's house and become independent. She broke the symbiotic tie with her mother and commanded the fear of man and the spirit of control out of her life. Finally she stood against the witchcraft commanding it out of her life in Jesus' name. She went home armed for battle to get the woman out, only to find that as she had committed herself to the Lord the "enemy had fled before her." The woman and all her belongings were gone without a trace. Now Emma, submitted to the Lord and under His protection, never makes a serious decision without asking her First Love, her Redeemer King, who watches over her life. She is safe in the secret place; her life is hidden in Christ and in God.

Truth: Facing the Pain

We all have problems, shortcomings, "hang ups" in our lives. It is no shame to have needs – but it would be a terrible shame to allow them to continue to hinder you from becoming all that God created you to be. Review Table 1 on page 174 to see if there are any of the adult manifestations which relate to this stage of development in your life. No matter what you are bound by, Jesus can set you free. What the Lord reveals, He heals.

Revelation: Revisiting the Scene

The Holy Spirit is the revealer of truth. Sometimes we don't see the cause of our problems clearly; we don't recognize the connections of certain early experiences with the trouble in our life today. We need the Holy Spirit to reveal the "root cause" and its connection to the challenge in our present life. Walk through the revelation with Jesus. In His presence everything is made right.

Redemption: Healing and Deliverance

Jesus comes to reveal the Father. He see the destruction planted in our life and He uproots it to prepare us for restoration and redemption.

The Father created you as a man or woman according to His perfect plan for your life. Security in your identity is critical to becoming all that the Father created you to be. Allow the Father to provide the support, protection, healing and restoration you need to be free.

The Father knew we needed to become independent and confident in our abilities to make it in life. He wants to give you the support and encouragement He knows you need. He wants to free you from the struggles of immaturity, the pain of addiction, the bondage of controlling symbiotic relationships. He wants to restore your gifts and callings, healthy life-giving relationships, eternal destiny, purpose and freedom so that you can continue to mature and become more and more like Jesus.

Restoration: The Planting of the Lord

The Father restores and supernaturally imparts into your life your true identity in Him. He wants to restore your healthy self-image. He wants you to see yourself as He sees you, and to be secure in your uniqueness. There are "Deborahs" and there are "Ruths;" there are "Davids" and there are "Peters:" all godly in their being, yet all unique and different from one another in their manly and womanly expression. Let the Lord restore your identity in Him.

The Father also wants to restore your gifts and callings, your destiny in His Kingdom that you were born to fulfill. It is time to dream again: it is time to dream the Father's dream for your life.

Reparenting: Father, "Father" Me

The Father waits to meet you every morning. He longs to nurture you, teach you, train you and bring you into maturity. Jesus is our role model. All that we have missed out on in our lives, we can learn from His life and from fellowship with Him. As we grow in godly maturity, the Father can release greater spiritual authority to us by His Spirit and together we can become the glorious Church, the radiant Bride of Christ, that we are meant to be: *"the planting of the LORD for the display of his splendor"* (Isaiah 61:3).

Steps to Healing and Restoration

1. Identify the adult problems that apply to you (see Table 1 on page 174).

2. Ask the Holy Spirit to reveal the "root cause" of each problem. The root is whatever happened to you during your late teens and early adulthood that caused a wounding in your life and allowed the problem to take root. This revelation may be in the form of a memory, picture, impression, thought, awareness, or some other way of "knowing" (Luke 8:17).

3. Ask Jesus to reveal His Presence there with you. The presence of the Lord changes things (Hebrews 13:8; Psalm 31:14–16).

4. Tell Jesus what you are feeling and thinking in this revealed time, place, experience. Listen to His response (Psalm 91:14–16).

5. Ask Jesus to reveal what the Father intended for this time of your life. Jesus comes to show us the Father. He comes to care for your developmental needs, to heal you, to redeem all that was lost to you and to restore you to be all He created you to be (Jeremiah 29:11; Matthew 15:13).

6. Forgive your parents and all those who wounded you. Break any generational curses, if necessary (Matthew 6:14; Galatians 3:13; see also Appendix A, Generational Curses).

7. Take authority, in Jesus' name, over any demonic oppression or influences in your life that the Lord has revealed. Command them to leave in the authority of Jesus' name (Luke 10:19).

8. Break agreement with the lie planted in your heart and ask the Lord to uproot it. Embrace the truth that has the power to set you free, the Word of God. Proclaim the promises in God's Word that are His answers to your need (John 8:31–32; Matthew 15:13).

9. Receive Father God as your eternal Father and receive your inheritance of life in Christ Jesus (1 John 1:2).

10. Seek the Father each day to "father" you and ask the Holy Spirit to teach you how to walk in your "newness of life" (Hebrews 12:10).

Notes

1. David Elkind, *A Sympathetic Understanding of the Child*, 3rd edition (Needham Heights, Massachusetts: Allyn & Bacon, 1994) pp. 242–246.
2. Ibid., pp. 246–251.

Table 1: Healthy Development

Stage of Life	Significant Issues	Developmental Task (needed for healthy development)	Adult Manifestation
In utero	Existence: To be/Not to be Acceptance/Rejection Belonging/Not belonging	Bonding/Connecting with mother Receive acceptance Receive birthright Embrace life Embrace intrinsic identity	Secure in existence and life Secure in belonging Secure in acceptance Secure in intrinsic identity Secure in Christ
Birth to 6 Months	Existence/Basic trust Self-concept foundation Problem solving foundation Foundation for communication	Healthy symbiosis with mother Unconditional love Define internal and external existence Integrate feeling, thinking, doing Incorporate communication skills	Trust in Father God Establish healthy relationships Secure in relationships Identify feelings/Healthy expression of feelings Aware of internal and external boundaries Trust in others
6 Months to 18 Months	Exploration: mobility Initiative, motivation, creativity Concept learning	Permission to explore Protection in exploration Explore self-motivation Learn spatial and conceptual relationships Explore self-initiative Unconditional positive affection	Self-motivated, self-initiated Healthy social interaction Accept own wants and needs Balance in caring for self and others Sensitive to the Holy Spirit Free in the Lord

Age			
2 Years	Anger, opposition, rebellion Independence, thinking Establish "Social Contract" Separation; control Cooperation v. competition	Initial breaking of symbiosis Establish separateness Incorporate "Social Contract" Learn limits and boundaries Accept discipline/Learn cooperation Develop cause and effect thinking	Considerate of others Think effectively: problem solver Submit to rightful authority Self-disciplined, cooperative Synergistic relationships* Submit to Lordship of Jesus Cooperate with the Holy Spirit
3 Years to 5 Years	Identity: How to fit in Sex-role identification Effect on relationships Information gathering Social and conversational skills	Identify with healthy role model Appropriate answers to "why" Information seeking encouraged Connections made between feeling and thinking Learn to define and label feelings Appropriate conversational and social behavior learned	Acceptance of identity Healthy sex-role identity Secure in social situations Strong connections with feeling, thinking, problem solving Social and conversational appropriateness Unshakable identity in Christ
6 Years to 12 Years	Argue, hassle, disagree Competition Skill learning	Establish separate identity Find own methods of doing things Life skills surveyed and developed Learn how to learn Task priority and completion Values and rules connected to reasons	Prioritize activities/Complete tasks Creative in problem solving Healthy development of social and emotional skills Strong sense of values and rules, applied with grace Confident in own methods of doing things Secure in challenges of life Knowing and fulfilling God's destiny in life

Table 1: Healthy Development (*cont.*)

Stage of Life	Significant Issues	Developmental Task (needed for healthy development)	Adult Manifestation
12 Years to 13 Years	Revisit in utero to 18-month-old issues Time structuring Task priority Relationship skills	Adjust, refine, finalize in utero to 18-month-old tasks Internalize appropriate time structure Learn to get needs met by asking Established order in life Explore social involvement	Incorporate and integrate: in utero to 18-month-old resolutions Appropriate time structure Healthy task priority Godly discernment God's order in life
14 Years	Revisit 2-year-old issues Test life values	Adjust, refine, finalize 2-year-old tasks Final breaking of symbiosis: separation Finalize "Social Contract" Final incorporation of values Learn to manage anger in healthy way	Incorporate and integrate: 2-year-old resolution Independence "Social Contract" Accept responsibility for self Anger is managed constructively Integrity in real life values
15 Years	Revisit 3–5-year-old issues Sex-role identification	Adjust, refine, finalize 3–5-year-old tasks Sex-role identity in relationships	Incorporate and integrate: 3–5-year-old resolution Security in identity Effective relationship skills Operate in grace and mercy of God

16 Years to 30 Years		
Revisit 6–12-year-old issues Integration Adolescent resolution	Adjust, refine, finalize 6–12-year-old tasks Establish professional/occupational skills, life skills Independent/Dependent struggle resolved	Incorporate and integrate: 6–12-year-old resolution Strive to improve in profession and occupation Train and mentor others Dynamic, continuous growth toward maturity Continue to mature in the Lord

** **Synergy**: (1) The working together of two (or more) to produce an effect greater than the sum of the individual effects; (2) The doctrine or belief that the Human Will cooperates with the Holy Spirit and with Divine Grace, especially in the act of conversion or regeneration (Collins English Dictionary).*

Table 2: Unhealthy Development

Stage of Life	Significant Issues	Developmental Wounding	Adult Manifestation
In utero	Acceptance/Rejection Existence: To be/Not to be Belonging/Not belonging	Needs ignored Existence discounted Treated with ambivalence or rejected Lack of or insufficient bonding Abandoned Abortion/Attempt or threat Curses	Existence issues Autistic "behaviors" Rejection issues Oppressed by death Anxiety disorders/Insecurity Panic attacks Insecure in Christ
Birth to 6 Months	Existence/Basic trust Self-concept formation Problem solving foundation Foundation for communication	Disturbances in symbiosis with mother Parent-imposed feeding schedules Parent-imposed expectations Inappropriate response to cry Reaction that increases discomfort Unresponsiveness Internal disturbance and pain	Lack trust in Father God Rage Discount problems Difficulties in relationships Lack ability to trust Problems with thinking and problem solving Discount feelings Poor self-concept Unable to communicate needs

6 Months to 18 Months	Exploration: mobility Initiative, motivation, creativity Concept learning	Unhealthy symbiosis/Learn dependency Lack of protection in exploration Restricted mobility Frequent punishment or discipline Performance expectations Premature toilet training	Lack motivation and initiative Lack impulse control Problems with control Lack self-control Feelings seen as problems and discounted until build up to eruption Relationships are symbiotic Man-pleasing/Overadaptive Lack freedom in the Lord Difficulty hearing God's voice
2 Years	Anger/Opposition Rebellion, independence Thinking, "Social Contract" Separation Control Cooperation vs. competition	No discipline or expectations Consequences of behavior not taught Expectations too high or enforced with extreme pressure Parents demand dependency Anger not confronted and dealt with Control issues not confronted Inappropriate modeling of anger by parent No clear boundaries/limits	Inconsiderate of others Lack self-discipline Oppositional, competitive, controlling Symbiotic in relationships Self-centered Difficulty thinking effectively and problem solving Anger that discounts others Oppose/Resist the Holy Spirit

Table 2: Unhealthy Development (*cont.*)

Stage of Life	Significant Issues	Developmental Wounding	Adult Manifestation
3 Years to 5 Years	Identity: How to fit in Sex-role identification Effect on relationships Information gathering Social and conversational skills	Lack of healthy role models Sexual abuse Inconsistent, unstructured parenting Parenting excludes child's thinking Fear reinforced or used against child Socially appropriate behavior not taught Sense of righteousness affronted	Overadaptive/self-righteous Self-righteous/legalistic Sex-role confusion Inept in social situations Poor connections between feeling, thinking, doing/problem solving Lack social and conversational skills Rejection of identity Fear used to motivate self Over adapt to others Oppressed by spirit of fear Tenuous identity in Christ
6 Years to 12 Years	Argue, hassle, disagree Competition Skill learning	Rules and values too rigid Rules or values lacking or inconsistent Unable to argue rules with reasons Made to stick to one task or activity Starting and stopping projects not taught Punishment harsh and unjust	Inflexible with rules and values Problems with task priority and task completion Addictive personality traits Passive/aggressive behavior Compelled to war against injustice Use feelings on others to control Use feelings on self to punish; guilt ridden Unaware of destiny in God Insecure in gifts and callings

Age			
12 Years to 13 Years	Revisit in utero to 18-month-old issues Time structuring Task priority Relationship skills	In utero to 18-month-old tasks unresolved Incapacitate self with feelings Time structure lacking Lack of/or insufficient boundaries Overprotected from natural consequences of behavior Hypocrisy	Struggle with in utero to 18-month-old issues Insecurity with self and life Symbiotic/unhealthy relationships Insecure with limits Problems staying on task Addictive personality structure Lack "godly discernment" No "godly order" in life
14 Years	Revisit 2-year-old issues Test life values	2-year-old tasks unresolved Discipline lacking Anger not confronted Limits and boundaries not enforced Dependency fostered Symbiosis reinforced Hypocrisy	Struggle with 2-year-old issues "Social Contract" weak or lacking Narcissistic; self-centered Control by domination, intimidation and/or manipulation Destructive competition Dependent on others Addictive personality structure Lack integrity in real life values Control new moves of God
15 Years	Revisit 3- to 5-year-old issues Sex-role identification	3- to 5-year-old tasks unresolved Sexual exploitation/abuse Unhealthy or unrighteous role models Consistent failure in relationships Reinforce inappropriate sex-role identification Hypocrisy	Struggle with 3- to 5-year-old issues Absence of real life values Insecure and/or confused sex-role identity Socially inept Addictive personality structure Bound by religious tradition Function legalistically

Table 2: Unhealthy Development (*cont.*)

Stage of Life	Significant Issues	Developmental Wounding	Adult Manifestation
16 Years to 30 Years	Revisit 6- to 12-year-old issues Integration Adolescent resolution	6- to 12-year-old tasks unresolved Independence discouraged Control/inhibit separation/ independence Skill learning not provided or encouraged Hypocrisy	Struggle with 6- to 12-year-old issues Struggle with immaturity Rigid and inflexible Passive-aggressive lifestyle Activities exclude opposite sex Addictive personality structure Lack God's vision for life

Appendix A

Generational Curses

Breaking the Inheritance of Destruction

It is time to awaken from our "sleep" of complacency. It is time to become alert to the reality that the fullness of our true inheritance has been stolen by the enemy. The Lord does not want us to be ignorant of Satan's schemes (2 Corinthians 2:11). One major strategy of the enemy is to take whole families captive through generational curses and bondages. Once the enemy gets into our family, he begins to build a stronghold over our minds and hearts. The word in the Greek language for "stronghold," as used for example in 2 Corinthians 10:4 (KJV), is *ochuros* and means "a hard place." It refers to a place on the battlefield that is an entrenchment or a fortress. As a verb it means "to fortify" or "make firm" and is used both literally and figuratively. Generational curses and bondages are strongholds of the enemy in our life that we inherit from our forefathers. Just as we inherit physical characteristics from our ancestors, so we also receive a spiritual inheritance of blessings and curses. For the blessings we can be truly thankful. The curses need to be broken.

It will be important to consider certain aspects of this biblical truth in order to grasp fully what generational curses and bondages are and, most importantly, how to break them in our lives and in the lives of our children. Scripture tells us:

> *"The LORD is longsuffering, and of great mercy, forgiving iniquity and transgression, and by no means clearing the guilty, visiting the iniquity of the fathers upon the children unto the third and fourth generation."* (Numbers 14:18, KJV)

It is clear from this scripture that iniquity in past generations opens a door to the enemy and gives him legal access into the family to oppress the children to the third and fourth generation. This opening into a person's life, that he or she may or may not be aware of, allows demonic oppression to operate covertly and cause havoc. Generational curses and bondages are the result of sin (Exodus 20:5), lack of knowledge (Hosea 4:6), or a family history of life without God (Ephesians 2:12). The curses and bondages are then passed on as an inheritance from generation to generation until they are broken by the power of the blood of Jesus.

Recognizing and acknowledging generational curses and bondages is the first step to freedom. Whenever problems have a generational "root," certain characteristics are discernible. A person in bondage to a particular sin or destructive patterns of behavior, emotions or thought feels powerless and "driven" by compulsions, even though he or she is desperate to be free and truly repents. They are often tormented by guilt and condemnation and feel trapped or enslaved by their vulnerability or oppression.

Another indicator is when a person is vulnerable to being victimized by the sin of others, as in the case of abuse, for example, and there is also evidence of the sin, curse or bondages in past generations. In such cases a person can look back and detect a similar pattern in their parents and other family members over the generations.

The destruction, devastation and death brought on by generational curses and bondages is staggering. Because the degree of destruction does not remain the same but rather increases exponentially from generation to generation, annihilation is the ultimate end. The third and fourth generations are being targeted for destruction by the enemy. Demonic manifestations may occur if the enemy is firmly entrenched over three or four generations and those in bondage can be under strong deception and spiritual blindness, unable to see the truth or receive correction until the curse and bondage is broken.

The "good news" is *"the curse causeless shall not come"* (Proverbs 26:2, KJV). The devil has no power without permission or a legal opening into our lives. If great grandma let him in, you can kick him out and shut the door.

"Christ redeemed us from the curse of the law by becoming a curse for us ..." (Galatians 3:13)

Jesus Himself said,

"I have given you authority to trample on snakes and scorpions and to overcome all the power of the enemy; nothing will harm you." (Luke 10:19)

Jesus went to the cross not only to save us from eternal separation from God but also to redeem our families from the curse of the law in this life on earth. Once we have received revelation, knowledge of our need, and humble ourselves before God, He will redeem us and our children and set us free from the curses and bondages inherited through our natural bloodline. In exchange we will receive an eternal inheritance of life and peace through Christ Jesus.

The prophet Daniel received revelation of the sins of his forefathers that hindered the Israelites from returning to the Promised Land. As he humbled himself and stood in the gap to ask the Lord to forgive the sins of his forefathers, the bondage was broken and Israel was set free (Daniel 9:1–6).

Today is the day of salvation. Today is the day to set ourselves and our children free. The Lord has made a way.

"Know therefore that the Lord your God is God; he is the faithful God, keeping his covenant of love to a thousand generations of those who love him and keep his commands." (Deuteronomy 7:9)

It is time to reclaim our lost inheritance in the Kingdom of God. Jesus still comes to set the captives free.

Summary
Simply stated, generational curses are a "breach" in the person's life, of which he or she may or may not be aware of. This opening, which may take the form of actual curses, sins or bondages, gives access for demonic oppression to operate under-cover and cause havoc in a person's life.

Causes

Iniquity and Sin

"The Lord is longsuffering and of great mercy, forgiving iniquity
and transgression, and by no means clearing the guilty, visiting
the iniquity of the fathers upon the children unto the third and
fourth generation." (Numbers 14:18, KJV)

Lack of Knowledge

"... my people are destroyed from lack of knowledge:
Because you have rejected knowledge,
  I will also reject you ...
because you have ignored the law of your God,
  I will also ignore your children." (Hosea 4:6)

Family History of Life without God

"Remember that at that time you were separate from Christ ...
foreigners to the covenants of the promise, without hope and
without God in the world." (Ephesians 2:12)

One thing is for sure, there has to be a cause if the person is a
Christian.

"... the curse causeless shall not come." (Proverbs 26:2, KJV)

Salvation

Most importantly, there is an answer. What the Lord reveals, He
heals.

"Christ redeemed us from the curse of the law, by becoming
a curse for us, for it is written: 'Cursed is everyone who is hung
on a tree.' He redeemed us in order that the blessing given to
Abraham might come to the Gentiles through Christ Jesus, so
that by faith we might receive the promise of the Spirit."

(Galatians 3:13–14)

Breaking Generational Curses and Bondages

- **Identify the generational sins, curses and bondages in your family.** Ask the Holy Spirit to reveal the hidden ones (Matthew 10:26; Luke 8:17; Luke 12:2). Ask the Lord to forgive the specific sins of the past generations revealed by the Holy Spirit. If you personally have committed the sin, repent and receive forgiveness (Daniel 9:1–6; 1 John 1:9).

- **Break all curses, bondages and demonic strongholds in the name and authority of Jesus Christ** (Luke 10:19; 2 Corinthians 10:4).

- **Receive freedom from the curse through Jesus Christ** (Galatians 3:13–14; 1 Peter 1:18–19).

- **Release your children from the curse and any effects of it.** Establish Father God's legacy for your family, namely "blessings for a thousand generations."

- **Proclaim the blessings of Deuteronomy 28:1–14 over yourself and your children** (Deuteronomy 7:9; Exodus 20:6; Leviticus 26:39–45; Deuteronomy 28:1–14).

Appendix B

Control: Brings Life or Brings Death

Over the past several years much has been written on the destructive nature of control. We have also been fighting the battle to reveal the devastating results that control brings into the lives of people, organizations and cultures. This Appendix contains some of our research, revelation and findings on control.

There are various forms of control:

- self-control which is a fruit of the Spirit;
- necessary, God-given control which is given to individuals, leaders and authority figures for the process of carrying out dominion, rightful authority and responsibility in areas under their charge. This type of control takes the form of leading, guiding and directing. It brings order, focus, clarity, safety and discipline. The results of this type of control are positive, bringing life, health, growth and freedom to individuals, relationships, organizations and cultures;
- quality control which assures that products produced are of high quality. The need for this type of control is obvious.

In addition, there is, of course, the type of control on which we will focus:

- control which is used by man to fulfill the goal of maintaining power and influence over individuals or people groups, where the intent is to pressure individuals, organizations or cultures to accomplish self-seeking, arbitrarily established sets of desired results. This form of control is rooted in fear. Since our God has not given us a spirit of fear, this form of control is motivated by Satan himself. It is manifested in domination, manipulation and intimidation, and its results are negative, bringing death, destruction and bondage to people, relationships, organizations and cultures.

The first three types of control listed are developmentally healthy. They result in healthy growth and maturity. They breed independently responsible people and ensure personal rights and freedom. The last form of control is developmentally destructive. It results in arrested growth and immaturity, and breeds dependency on the controlling agent, ensuring the obstruction of personal rights and placing others in bondage.

Amongst their other definitions of "control" most dictionaries include one similar to the following: "A personality or spirit believed to activate the utterances or performances of a spiritualist medium." In our view this definition cuts to the very heart of negative control. Control is so destructive because it is not a personality characteristic or trait, but is a spirit. This type of control manifests itself in three ways: *intimidation, domination, manipulation.*

There is nothing good about this form of control. It is motivated by fear, having been initially learned in the symbiosis and incorporated by the developing person for the purpose of survival. When the infant is controlled by caretakers from birth, control is learned as the only acceptable way to get needs met to survive. Fear is first incorporated by the newborn baby: fear of not having survival needs met unconditionally. Fear then becomes the motivation behind incorporating an approach to the world which requires control to get the needs for survival met. Once this spiritual force takes hold, it becomes the primary way in which an individual ensures his or her needs, wants, desires and goals in life are satisfied and fulfilled.

This control has the following results:

- it builds weakness in the one using it because it reinforces dependence on the use of external forces and factors to get things done;

- it builds weakness in the person being controlled, stunting the development of independent reasoning, growth, self-discipline and self-control, which is a fruit of the Spirit.
- it builds weakness within the relationship in which it is being exerted.[1]

Because fear is the motivation behind this spiritual force, fear replaces cooperation causing the people involved to become arbitrary, at odds with each other (adversarial), competitive and defensive.

In addition, where the spirit of control is in operation there usually exists a counter spiritual force: rebellion. Wherever you find control, you will eventually find rebellion. The reverse is also true. Wherever you find rebellion, the oppression of control is either in operation or once was in operation in the person's life.

We believe people control because they do not know any another way to get a job done or to ensure that their needs are met. Control is addictive. When it works once it remains as a behavior of choice to fulfill needs, wants and desires. All of us learn control from the way our parents handled us and our needs during infancy and childhood. This form of control is very often generational, handed down from generation to generation. It must be dealt with, not only in the person's life in the present, but in the past generations as well.

We are saddened by the many infants who are being raised under this form of control. In our ministry, we are confronted by its destructive results again and again.

In 2 Corinthians 5:14 (NASV) we find clearly stated, *"For the love of Christ controls us ... "* Here we see a biblical principle for relationships, which makes a clear link between love and control. When the love of others and their love of us "controls" our relationships, molding us and leading us, the result will be healthy, desirable benefits and outcomes. When the main ingredient of love is missing from the equation, then we must realize that control becomes an entity in and of itself. Control becomes the ultimate force which drives us and others to satisfy our needs, to fulfill our desires and to accomplish our goals.

We learn in 1 John 4:18 (NKJV) that when love exists, fear does not. In fact, perfect love casts out fear. Again, the foundation is fear. If fear is cast out because love exists, then there is no motivation for control and thus no need to control. We then come back to 2 Corinthians 5:14 and will choose to walk in the reality of 2 Timothy 1:7.

As we have already said, the foundation and motivation behind this form of control is fear. When a situation arises that causes fear and the individual does not deal with it in prayer, asking the Holy Spirit for direction and guidance, he or she risks getting into "self-designed" methods to find a solution. These "self-designed" methods replace Holy Spirit initiated action and thus can only be empowered and maintained by human effort. The energy for this human effort is sustained by control because the person has not submitted to the Holy Spirit, who now steps aside. Control is now free to take over as the motivating force behind the individual's feeling, thinking and doing. Control takes the place of the Holy Spirit in a person's life and becomes lord, with the destructive outcomes previously listed. This is truly a tool of the enemy which is designed to torment and destroy Christians and non-Christians alike.

We believe the Lord recognizes and understands how people get into this form of control. He does not condemn us for this but He does expect us to get out of it as soon as we recognize what has happened.

To understand more about this type of control, we encourage you to attend one of the many seminars we conduct on God's Plan for Human Development, in which we deal with the issue of control, its origins, motivation and outcomes and specifically minister into this destructive aspect of human interaction.

Note
1. Stephen R. Covey, *Seven Habits of an Effective Leader* (New York: Simon & Schuster, 1990), p. 39.

Bibliography

Armstrong, Thomas. *The Myth of the ADD Child*, Penguin Group Publishing.

Blankeslee, Sandra. "New Connections: When It's Time to Make Changes in Your Life, What Role Does Your Brain Play?" *American Health*, March 1990, pp. 74, 76, 78.

Dobbins, Richard D. *Venturing into a Child's World*, Akron, Ohio, Emerge Ministries, Inc., 1985.

Venturing Into a Teenager's World, Akron, Ohio, Emerge Ministries, Inc., 1987.

Elkind, David. *A Sympathetic Understanding of the Child*, 3rd edition, Needham Heights, Massachusetts, Allyn and Bacon/Paramount Publishing, 1994.

All Grown Up and No Place to Go, New York, Addison-Wesley Publishing Co., 1984.

Miseducation: Preschoolers at Risk, New York, Alfred A. Knopf Inc., 1987.

The Hurried Child, New York, Addison-Wesley Publishing Co., 1988.

Erikson, Erik H. *Childhood and Society*, New York, W.W. Norton & Co. Inc., 1963.

Gibbs, Nancy. "The EQ Factor: New Brain Research Suggests That Emotions Not IQ May Be the True Measure of Human Intelligence," *Time Magazine*, 2 October 1995, pp. 60–66, 68.

Ingelman-Sundberg, A. *A Child Is Born*, New York, Dell Publishing Co., 1979.

Levine, Pamela. *Cycles of Power*, Deerfield Beach, Florida Health Communications, 1988.

MacNutt, Frances and Judith. *Praying for Your Unborn Child*, Doubleday Publishing Co., 1988.

Schiff, Aaron Wolfe and Jackie Lee Schiff. "Passivity," *TAJ* 1:1.

Shephard, Sharon. "Television: The Prime Time Invader," *Christian Parenting Today*, September/October, 1989.

The DICTIONARY *of*
BUSINESS
BULLSHIT

The DICTIONARY *of*
BUSINESS
BULLSHIT
The World's Most
Comprehensive Collection

Kevin Duncan

LONDON   MADRID
NEW YORK   MEXICO CITY
BOGOTA   BUENOS AIRES
BARCELONA   MONTERREY

PUBLISHED BY
LID Publishing Ltd.
6-8 UNDERWOOD STREET
LONDON N1 7JQ (UNITED KINGDOM)
INFO@LIDPUBLISHING.COM
LIDPUBLISHING.COM

A member of:

BPR
Business Publishers Roundtable

www.businesspublishersroundtable.com

PRINTED IN GREAT BRITAIN BY T J INTERNATIONAL LTD.

ISBN: 978-1-907794-30-8

ARTWORK COVER AND PAGE DESIGN: E-DIGITAL DESIGN LTD

*Dedicated to Rosanna, Shaunagh and Sarah
—my RSS feed.*

Foreword

"*This dictionary easily ranks as one of the greatest single achievements of scholarship, and probably the greatest ever performed by one individual who laboured under anything like the disadvantages in a comparable length of time.*" (Walter Jackson Bate)

No, not *this* one in your hand, but rather the one compiled by the dyspeptic poet, essayist and all-round Enlightenment man, Dr Samuel Johnson.

That one was written primarily to settle the use and spelling of English at a time when more and more of the population needed to know the agreed definitions of meaning, usage and spelling. And it was at least partly funded by printers who had real need of knowing the correct way to spell, for example, the word dictionary and understanding what it meant.

Johnson went about his task by using "custom" as the equivalent of legal precedent to set the standard on all these dimensions.

"*The rules of stile, like those of law, arise from precedents often repeated, collect the testimonies of both sides, and endeavour to discover and promulgate the decrees of custom, who has so long possessed whether by right or by usurpation, the sovereignty of words,*" he explained.

This dictionary has a very different purpose: it collects our terribly loose custom in a catechism of cliché and an encomium of euphemism not merely to describe our dire contortions of the language and logic but *to condemn them and shame us from using them.*

Too often we simply glue words and ideas together and – pleased by the familiar ring of them – attach them to some more loosely related ones. George Orwell pointed out in *Politics and the English Language* that too much of our prose is like this:

"Prose consists less and less of words chosen for the sake of their meaning, and more and more of phrases tacked together like the sections of a prefabricated hen-house."

All of which might make you think this book sounds like a terrible old bore but like all of Kevin's writing it's actually incredible fun. I keep dipping into the copy I've got as a kind of anti-thesaurus (no, you can't use that phrase). It's sharp, tight and all too true.

So here's my proposal.

Buy one of these for a businessperson in your life and challenge them not to use any of the words and phrases in Duncan's Dictionary.

In fact, why don't you buy several? The more the... (Ed. is that allowed?)

Do it and we might start to speak more clearly in business, and in doing so, think more clearly.

Which would be an excellent thing all round.

Mark Earls, author of *Herd* and *I'll Have What She's Having*

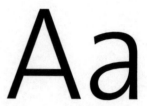

ABC, easy as: 1. A complete doddle; something you could do in kindergarten. 2. A task only suitable for total idiots, which probably says more about the person being asked to do the job than they would care to admit; piss-easy; pride before a fall, as in *"This is easy as ABC Derek"*, shortly before realizing that it is in truth quite complicated. (*see Art form, got it down to an; Cooking on gas; Falling off a log*)

ABC session: 1. Meeting in which all staff are graded in their absence. 2. Management immediately uses findings of said session to instigate a ruthless cull; superb opportunity to display flagrant nepotism and favouritism. (*see Axe, face the; Destaff; Headcount; LIFO; Phone list, go down the; Powwow*)

A-Z: 1. Fully comprehensive; covering absolutely everything. 2. We can't decide which bit to concentrate on, so we're asking you to do everything before we decide; not comprehensive at all, but claiming to be so for marketing purposes; starting at A, but petering out horribly after E and F. (*see Chapter and verse; Full Monty, the; Zee, we've covered everything from A to*)

Above and beyond: 1. More than was originally asked for. 2. Totally unnecessary over-delivery fuelled by rampant ambition and sucking up to the boss – guaranteed to annoy all colleagues; plaintive mantra of Terylene-wearing Sales Directors from Land's End to John o' Groats, as in *"Come on guys, we need to go above and beyond in this sales period!"* (*see Quarter, one, two, three, four; Team, take one for the*)

Above board: 1. Correct, proper or legal. 2. This is a bit dodgy but we need to create the semblance of being whiter than white otherwise we'll be fired; barely legal; just about okay; marginal. (*see Cook the books; Fiscal juggling*)

Absolutely: 1. Totally or completely. 2. Maybe, actually probably not; I've just added an authoritative-sounding adverb to reassure you, but I'm none the wiser frankly; not in the slightest; it's never going to happen. (*see At the end of the day; Basically; Frankly; Literally*)

Accelerator, take one's foot off the: 1. Lose energy and enthusiasm for a project or initiative. 2. Decide you can't be arsed because the whole thing's pointless; one of many automotive analogies that makes wishy-washy male executives feel particularly virile; suggestion of speed and power, but in reality slowing down; much-loved rallying cry for oppressed managers, as in *"Guys, we mustn't take our foot off the accelerator on this one."*

Access to information: 1. Ability to see what a department or company is up to. 2. You can't have access; "Restricted Access", otherwise known as none at all; a cover up; a sham; don't ever let this get out or else we're all doomed. *(see Need to know basis)*

Accountable, accountability: 1. We are truthful and reliable, and our numbers really do add up if you check them. 2. We will never be held accountable, because we have set up impenetrable and arcane structures so you can't get us; we have absolutely no accountability; we don't trade in this country at all – it's all based overseas, but we're not telling you where. *(see Buck stops here, the)*

Achieve learning outcomes: 1. Get something done based on sensible information. 2. Set woefully low standards and repeatedly fail to live up to them, despite plenty of warning signs. *(see Fall short)*

Achilles heel: 1. Back of the ankle (anatomical). 2. Fatal flaw suddenly exposed through fundamental incompetence, especially of those who lied on their CV. *(see CV)*

Acid test: 1. A rigorous test of authenticity, from the testing of gold with nitric acid. 2. Nasty moment when it becomes apparent that it's simply not going to work; time to retire hastily to the pub to lick wounds and have a re-think; conclusive proof that it's a shambles; irrefutable evidence of incompetence. *(see Blue touch paper, light the; Proof of concept)*

Across the board, right: 1. Everywhere. 2. Sweeping implementation that will give everyone an unexpected surprise; complete closure of company; meltdown; Armageddon; comprehensively wrong everywhere; not everywhere actually, just at head office in Aldershot. *(see Niche, carve out a, market _____; Pan-global, -European; Swingeing cuts)*

Act, getting our _____ together: 1. Being competent. 2. We are not competent and we're about to be found out. *(see Ducks in a row, get our)*

Action (vb.), actioned, actioning: 1. Taking action. 2. Taking no action at all; ignoring completely; delegating by email in order to avoid; idling; going to the pub; taking the day off; skiving; buying an extra jacket and hanging it over your chair so that people think you are in the office; blocking; obstructing; making niggardly changes to a draft so that it has to be done again. *(see Goal-oriented; -driven; Outcomes, negative, positive; Outputs)*

Action list: 1. A list of things to do. 2. A bird's nest of jumbled notes shoved into a drawer. *(see Snake's honeymoon)*

Activation: 1. Making something happen. 2. Pretending to make something happen, but not really doing much.

Activity, lack of, planned: 1. Planning or doing stuff. 2. Not planning or doing stuff; cleverly creating the appearance of activity when nothing much is really happening; calling a meeting to avoid having to do any proper work.

Acumen, commercial: 1. Smart business intelligence. 2. Judgment utterly warped by the filthy lucre; blind obsession with cash; money at all costs; an eye for a dollar; quality much prized in Finance Directors, who then spend all their time generating impenetrable spreadsheets that no one can fathom.

Adhocracy: 1. Management that reacts to urgent problems rather than planning to avoid them. 2. Company in which everything is done on the hoof as a matter of course; most companies. (*see Pants, fly by the seat of our; SNAFU*)

Administrivia: 1. Trivial administration. 2. Civil servant job description. (*see Bread and butter; Bureaucracy; Jobsworth; Panjandrum; Process; Target manager; Timesheets*)

Advisorial: 1. Relating to advice. 2. Fabricated Americanism alluding to taking advice; a euphemism for a direct order; word to the wise; side remark that is more weighty than what is being said in the main body of the meeting. (*see FAQs; Hints and tips; Practical advice; Shell-like, a word in your*)

Agenda, hidden: 1. Meeting plan, concealed. 2. Devious intention to hijack or derail intended topic of meeting; scheme to ignore topic altogether, or table a completely new one; murder plot, Ides of March style; plan for coup d'état, usually of Managing Director or Chief Executive. (*see Agenda, own the, set the*)

Agenda, own the, set the: 1. A list of items to be discussed. 2. A list of items you had no idea existed; swathes of material for which you have done no preparation at all; topics deliberately kept secret from you to retard your career progress. (*see Agenda, hidden*)

Aha moment: 1. Moment of realization or sudden understanding. 2. Fanciful notion that someone will see your amazing product or presentation and shout out loud *"Aha! Finally I get it! Thank you so much for enlightening me!"* (*see Enlighten me; FMF; Light bulb experience*)

Aims: 1. Intentions or purpose. 2. Hopelessly unachievable targets that will never be met; comprehensive fiction invented at the beginning of every financial year. (*see BHAG; Fiscal juggling; Objectives; Target, hit the _____, miss the point, miss the _____ left right and centre, moving*)

Air cover: 1. Protection from above to allow *"the troops"* to get on with their work. 2. Total absence of management, whose main role seems to be to go on holiday precisely when any important issue needs to be addressed. (*see Empower; Enablement; Forces of darkness, deploy the; Piggyback; Shit hits the fan, when the*)

Alarm bells, set the _____ ringing: 1. Trigger warning system because there is a fire. 2. Cause total panic amongst colleagues by doing something distinctly unnerving, such as wearing trainers with suits, reaching inside a room from the corridor when a meeting is in session and turning the light switch repeatedly on and off for five minutes, or insisting on being called Colin when your real name is Samantha. (*see AWOL, go; Ballistic, go; Box of frogs, mad as a; Bundle, one stick short of a; Gene pool, swimming in the shallow end of the; Mid-life crisis; Moon, barking at the, over the, through the; Picnic, one sandwich short of a; Plot, lose the; Pram, to throw one's toys out of the; Radar, off; Rails, gone off the*)

Albatross around our necks: 1. A burden. 2. Poorly-informed bastardization of Coleridge's *The Rime of the Ancient Mariner* metaphor, without any particular knowledge of the origin or context.

Align, aligned: 1. In line with. 2. Categorically not in line with; unaligned; nowhere near agreeing; not interested; in desperate need of a complete rebrief. (*see FIFO (2); Hymn sheet, singing from the same; Realignment*)

All over bar the shouting: 1. Finished, unless something truly unexpected happens at the very last minute. 2. This was dead in the water years ago; it always was a non-starter; misguided from the outset; doomed. (*see Fat lady, it's not over till the _____ sings; Horse, flogging a dead*)

All-singing, all-dancing: 1. The full works, with no expense spared, particularly with regard to presentation. 2. Much fanfare with precious little content. (*see Bells and whistles; Hype; Pull out all the stops; Push the boat out*)

All staff memo: 1. Announcement to the whole company. 2. Momentous announcement for three possible reasons: 1) Most of you are fired. 2) We've gone bust. 3) Just to let you know that you may spot in the papers tomorrow that the board have awarded themselves a massive pay rise when none of you have got one – this is because we have hit the targets we set for ourselves and you haven't.

Always on: 1. Paying attention at every moment of the day. 2. Intensely annoying to colleagues and family due to total inability to relax or generate any form of work-life balance. (*see Amber as red, treat every; Constantly striving; Expectations, exceeding; Mission statement; Sun, the _____ never sets at; Passion, passionate; 24/7/365; Work-life balance*)

Am I right, or am I right?: 1. I'm right. 2. I'm right and I'm in charge, so do what you're bloody well told or you'll be fired. (*see Dejob; Follow, do you*)

Ambassador, brand; team: 1. A person who represents the cause in an appropriate way. 2. C-list celebrity signed up at great expense who will probably disgrace the company when found face down in a pole dancer's lap after a night of drunken debauchery.

Amber as red, treat every: 1. Be on permanent alert, even if nothing is urgent or critical. 2. Panic every working moment; generate paranoia amongst all colleagues; fret unnecessarily; mainline on coffee and hard drugs to stumble through; lose wife and family due to permanent obsession with trivial work matters. (*see Always on; 24/7/365*)

Ambition, ambitious: 1. Intent on making progress. 2. Prepared to kill women, children and colleagues in order to secure promotion; ruthlessly selfish. (*see Driven*)

Ambulance chasing: 1. Following emergency services in the hope of picking up business (*insurance industry*). 2. Frantic and merciless pursuit of any business at any cost. (*see Bottom feeding; Scraping the barrel*)

Analysis, paralysis by, in the final: 1. Incapable of taking action due to being overwhelmed by too much data. 2. Too dim to understand basic numbers. (*see Brain dump; Crunch the numbers; Data dump*)

Anonymise: 1. Make anonymous. 2. Don't tell a soul I did this or I'll get the boot. (*see Team, take one for the*)

Another day another dollar: 1. I earned some money yesterday and I intend to do the same thing again today. 2. I am obsessed with making money and will do anything to get it, including parroting trite aphorisms like *"Another day another dollar"*.

APAC: 1. Shorthand for Asia Pacific region. 2. Job title offering the broad excuse to fly round the Far East hurling abuse at the locals and surreptitiously shagging diminutive hookers and/or ladyboys. (*see EMEA*)

Apples with apples, not comparing: 1. These two data sets cannot be compared. 2. I am totally baffled; my brain is too small to compare two slightly different things without melting down; I am dim and blinkered; unless it's blindingly obvious I simply won't get it; please don't show me any facts because I'll just apply the same bias I always have anyway. (*see Merger; Mix, the right, the wrong*)

Apple cart, don't upset the: 1. Don't make a fuss. 2. The Chairman is always right, even when he is wrong. (*see Natural order of things, don't upset the*)

Appraisal, one degree: 1. An authoritative one-dimensional view of a subordinate. 2. Utterly prejudiced view that flies in the face of all prevailing opinion; one-eyed bias. (*see Appraisal, 360 degree; Riot act, read the*)

Appraisal, 360 degree: 1. Appraisal in which everyone with whom you work is consulted, regardless of status. 2. Annoying, touchy-feely modern HR development in which the tea lady has a say about whether you get a pay rise or not; fertile opportunity for colleagues to shaft you completely, whilst hiding behind the veil of anonymity; erratic and inconsistent scoring system which seems to have no pattern from one review to another; confused even further by having a different appraiser every time; pointless, ill-informed chat with so-called line manager who doesn't give a shit. (*see Appraisal, one degree; Line manager; Performance review; Shafted down the river, yourself*)

Architecture, brand _____, business _____: 1. The component parts of a brand or business. 2. Classic wank word to suggest that the brand or business has solid foundations. (*see Foundations, lay the, firm, shaky; Overarching; Positioning*)

Armageddon plan: 1. Crisis management plan. 2. Daily occurrence; permanent panic mode; firefighting; tail chasing; chaos. (*see Doomsday scenario; Efficiency drive; Scenario, best-case, nightmare, worst-case; Scorched earth policy; SNAFU*)

Arse about face, you've got that: 1. The wrong way round. 2. Hopelessly inappropriate; so bad that it is effectively the opposite of what is needed to do the job; completely off brief; useless (*item or person*).

Arse covering: 1. Protecting one's position or job. 2. All-pervasive frame of mind in which the perpetrator can never admit that it was their fault; generating a massive email trail proving that everyone else is responsible, but not me; enormous dossier of evidence that verifies beyond a shred of doubt that the client is in the wrong, because I am perfect; sole activity of control freaks who don't care what they work on, so long as they are always right. (*see BCC; Call report; CC; Control freak; FYI*)

Arse in alligators, up to my: 1. In danger of being eaten by an aggressive crocodilian; very busy; in a spot of bother. 2. About to be fired, or carried away by a team of medics in white coats; not coping at all; stacking lie upon lie to get out of a metaphorical hole that is only getting bigger by the minute; seconds away from defenestrating a colleague, or oneself; seriously considering self-immolation. (*see Defenestrate, defenestration; Full-on; Postal, go*)

Arse, up your own: 1. Self-obsessed and usually spouting nonsense. 2. Utterly unbearable; insufferable; effectively impossible to work with, as in *"He was so far up his arse they could have shared a hat"*. (*see Loose cannon*)

Art form, got it down to an: 1. Mastered a successful formula that can be repeated again and again. 2. Taken a series of crass shortcuts to knock something up in as quick a time as possible so we can all go to the pub; skimmed it; mapped out a simplistic framework that will just about do; plagiarized someone else's method and passed it off as our own; stole intellectual copyright lock, stock and barrel, whilst claiming barefaced that it was all your work. (*see ABC, easy as; Cooking on gas; Falling off a log*)

ASAP: 1. As soon as possible. 2. Now; yesterday; actually any time you like, I'm just trying to make it sound as though everything is vitally urgent when it isn't really, which makes me feel important and gives me wood. (*see ETA; PDQ*)

Ask, big: 1. A substantial request, usually involving a lot of work or onerous responsibility. 2. Impossible task dressed up as a flattering and significant thing to do; a project that genuinely cannot be completed in time or for the budget; a pup; an instruction that will almost certainly lead to termination of employment. (*see Hospital pass; Opportunity; Poisoned chalice; Team, take one for the*)

Asking a duck to bark: 1. Requesting something impossible. 2. Deliberately requesting something impossible in order to humiliate a subordinate, preferably in public; blindly refusing to accept that something cannot be done. (*see Bark into the wind, up the wrong tree; Impossible, nothing is*)

Aspirational: 1. Something to aspire to. 2. Vain and insubstantial; deeply unfulfilling within seconds of purchase; fleeting dopamine high followed by profound and sustained depression; addictive and yet unsatisfying; jealous yearning for someone else's job or possessions; shallow characteristic displayed by thousands of talent show contestants; in total denial about skills and wanting something beyond one's capability. (*see Capability gap; Deeply shallow*)

Asset: 1. Anything valuable or useful. 2. Anything we can flog, frankly, and quite a lot of things that we can't; toadying descriptor of workforce often deployed by HR directors, as in *"Our greatest assets walk out of the office every night – our staff!"*; any cash we can get for nothing, usually filed under *"goodwill"* in the accounts so that shareholders can squeeze more money out of ignorant investors.

Assimilation: 1. Process of absorbing. 2. Process of ejecting, such as during mergers and takeovers when half the staff are sacked; of individuals, total failure to absorb any relevant information due to daydreaming, hangovers, or plain boredom. (*see Merger; Mix, the right, the wrong; Integrate, integral, integration*)

At a stroke: 1. In one go, sometimes of a pen. 2. In a horrible split second, as in *"Did you hear about Darren? He was dejobbed at a stroke"*. (*see Dejob; One fell swoop, in*)

A-team, this calls for the: 1. We urgently need our senior team on this. 2. The management has severely neglected this project and now it's a monumental cockup so they are going to position themselves as the only people who can get us out of a hole; B, C, or D-team – we don't actually have an A-team. (*see Cavalry over the hill; Dream team; Eleventh hour, at the*)

At, where I'm: 1. This is my point of view. 2. Nowhere – my brain is so small I just can't work it out; I've made cock-all progress on this since I last saw you because I am too (a) busy, (b) lazy and (c) retarded to have a view. (*see Coming from, where I'm*)

At the end of the day: 1. When a day is finishing, somewhere between 11pm and 12pm. 2. Totally pointless beginning or ending to a sentence that adds nothing to its meaning whatsoever. (*see Absolutely; Basically; End of play; Frankly; Literally; Net net; Put to bed*)

At this moment in time: Now. (*see At this point in time; End of play*)

At this point in time: Now. (*see At this moment in time; End of play*)

Attention-getting: 1. Someone who gets attention, usually Sally on reception with the large Charlies. (*see Attention-seeking*)

Attention-seeking: 1. Someone who seeks attention, usually Sally on reception with the large Charlies. (*see Attention-getting*)

Aunt Sally: 1. Something set up as a target for disagreement. 2. Egregiously sub-standard proposal or piece of work that has no hope of doing the job, but is lobbed into the presentation anyway to make it look as though more work has been done than truly has; item included on the agenda for the sole purpose of rejecting it and humiliating your main rival for promotion. (*see Agenda, hidden; Know it when I see it, I don't know what I want but I'll _____; Sacred Cow; Straw Man*)

Authenticity: 1. Relating to anything that is authentic. 2. Totally false, such as *"This product was lovingly forged in the crucible of time"*; quality constantly demanded of staff in over-earnest companies. (*see Passion, passionate; Provenance; Rebrand*)

Autocorrect: 1. Feature that corrects spelling on computers and mobile devices. 2. Frequently annoying function that makes you say something you don't want to; source of occasional massive faux pas such as *"I can't come out tonight, I'm cleaning my Mum's vagina"*, shortly followed by *"China, I meant china!!"* (*regular examples of this phenomenon at damyouautocorrect.com*)

Autonomy: 1. Ability to do something on your own, and without interference; complete executive authority. 2. No freedom in which to move whatsoever; constantly being monitored. (*see Control freak; Micromanaging*)

Autopilot: 1. Machine that can control a plane. 2. Zombie-like state prevalent first thing in the morning after the office party or a Bank Holiday; near total absence of brain activity, often witnessed on the second day of an *"off-site"* awayday after overshooting in the hotel bar the previous night. (*see Awayday; Office party; Off-site*)

Awayday: 1. A day away, usually from the office. 2. Large-scale excuse for the board or an entire department to wear ill-advised *"mufti"* clothes, play golf badly and eat unfeasible quantities of boiled sweets and biscuits; embarrassing escapade to an eye-wateringly expensive country retreat, accompanied by a programme of excruciating team-bonding exercises, facilitated by a ruddy-cheeked woman called Amanda. (*see Autopilot; Bad idea, there's no such thing as a; Bonding, team; Brainstorm; Executive retreat; Flip chart; Off-site; Workshop*)

AWOL, go: 1. Absent Without Leave (*military*). 2. Nowhere to be seen, as in *"Where the f**k is Dave?"*; throw a sickie; not turn up; do a runner; leg it; quit the scene at once, sometimes permanently. (*see Ballistic, go; Pear-shaped, it's all gone; Plot, lose the; Postal, go; Pram, to throw one's toys out of the; Radar, off; Rails, gone off the; Tits up, it's all gone*)

Axe, face the: 1. Be a candidate for dismissal. 2. Be summarily dismissed, despite a sham of a *"consultation period"*. (*see ABC session; Can, carry the; Consultation period; Decruit; Dejob; Downsize; Phone list, go down the*)

Bb

Back burner, we'll have to put that on the: 1. Make that low priority from now on. 2. We announced this project in a blaze of glory but it has now become apparent that it's doomed, so ignore it – but if anyone asks, don't tell them we cocked it up. *(see Front burner, let's bring that onto the)*

Back end architecture: 1. The design bit at the end of the project or product. 2. Desperate scrambling around at the last minute to rectify all the bugs in the project or product that were never anticipated due to lack of foresight or blatant incompetence. *(see Front end)*

Background noise: 1. Irrelevant static that should be ignored. 2. Vital signals that would have warned us that the whole project would be a disaster if only we hadn't been so intent on doing it anyway because the boss insisted on it, despite all sensible advice to the contrary. *(see Static; White noise)*

Backlash: 1. Nasty reaction to an action. 2. Vicious witch-hunt to find someone else to blame. *(see Blame culture; Witch-hunt)*

Backroom: 1. The room at the back where no one ever goes. 2. The place where all the truly valuable work is done, despite the claims of the self-appointed glory boys from the sales department. *(see Frontline; Jazz hands)*

Back-to-back: 1. A segue between one thing and another, with no gap in between them. 2. A relentless mad scramble caused by chronic lack of organization and institutional incompetence. *(see Cocks on the block; Stacked, completely; Under siege; Wall-to-wall)*

Back to basics: 1. A return to first principles, also often referred to as the drawing board, or square one. 2. We massively over-elaborated this due to a mixture of hubris, over-confidence and sheer arrogance – simple would have been far better. *(see Drawing board, back to the)*

Backs to the wall: 1. A desperate rearguard action. 2. We could well be fired for this, mainly due to amateurish misjudgment and over-confidence. (*see Cocks on the block*)

Back stabbing: 1. Apportioning blame to someone when they are not present to defend themselves, or even deny that they were responsible. 2. Merciless accusation of a colleague in order to save your own skin. (*see Blitz; Front stabbing; Rowing in the same boat, direction*)

Bacon, bring home the: 1. Get the job done. 2. Take all the credit for a successful sale or presentation when in fact other people did all the work.

Backwards, bend over: 1. Do everything possible to help. 2. Drop all the important stuff and leave everyone else in the lurch just to brown-nose the boss. (*see Brown-nosing*)

Bad apple: 1. Rotten piece of fruit. 2. Poisonous member of staff with dreadful attitude. (*see Draining the swamp*)

Bad idea, there's no such thing as a: 1. Say what you like – all thoughts are welcome, no matter how poor they sound. 2. We are incapable of distinguishing between a good and bad idea; most ideas are rubbish and these are no exception; we don't care how much crap we generate in this session so long as it looks as though we are working when in fact we are just eating biscuits. (*see Awayday; Brainstorm; Conceptual thinking; Idea, big; Lateral thinking; Off-site*)

Baked in: 1. An intrinsic part of the whole, as in a thoroughly cooked pie or loaf of bread. 2. Tragically inane metaphor drawn from the culinary world, much loved of *"digital natives"* (qv.) as in *"We must ensure that social media is fully baked in to the brand's DNA"*. (*see Digital native; DNA*)

Balanced scorecard: 1. A wider set of measurements of business performance than simply finances, invented by Harvard Business School professor Robert Kaplan in 1992. 2. Semi-useless ragbag of vague characteristics only loosely relevant to the business, most commonly used as a smokescreen to disguise inept performance; godsend for poor managers, giving the impression of a pseudo-science and thereby adding legitimacy to shocking failures in competence. (*see Snake oil salesman; Vin ordinaire*)

Ball, take one's eye off the: 1. Fail to concentrate sufficiently. 2. Fail to concentrate sufficiently, for a split second or several years, resulting in dismissal; daydream; cockup. (*see Decruit; Drop a ricket*)

Ballbreaker: 1. Tough female executive. 2. Tough female executive who revels in the ritual humiliation of male colleagues just for the sport of it; woman with "issues"; resentful divorcee; aggressive lesbian on a mission; miserable harridan without an inch of compassion. (*see Control freak; Gynocracy; Nutcracker; Rottweiler*)

Ballistic, go: 1. Adopt an approach relating to the flight of projectiles; become enraged or frenziedly violent. 2. Hurl objects around the office, sometimes including members of staff; go AWOL; have a paddy; embark on childish tantrum; have a fit; become incandescent with rage. (*see AWOL, go; Defenestrate, defenestration; Mid-life crisis; Moon, barking at the, over the, through the; Nuclear, go; Plot, lose the; Postal, go; Pram, to throw one's toys out of the; Radar, off; Rails, gone off the*)

Ball juggling: 1. Handling several issues or projects at the same time. 2. Failing to cope on all fronts; attempting to create the impression of all-round competence but failing miserably; standing up in the middle of an open plan office and shouting *"I've got 15 balls up in the air on this project and two of them are mine!"*; surreptitiously fiddling with one's testicles in a tiresome board meeting. (*see Balls in the air, on the block, to the wall; Plate spinning; Python, wrestling with a*)

Balloon has gone up, the: 1. The action has started. 2. Quick, leave the building immediately and don't ever go back – we've been rumbled; sudden and fatal discovery of financial mismanagement. (*see Fiscal juggling*)

Ballpark figure: 1. An estimated number. 2. Comprehensive fiction; nowhere near the true amount; out to the tune of millions; flagrant lie; random guesswork. (*see Cover all the bases; Zone, in the*)

Balls in the air, on the block, to the wall. 1. Genitals not entirely where they should normally be. 2. Reputation in near-tatters; chances of ever working again diminishing by the second; sweating profusely on the outcome of a tribunal after a misdemeanour with Jemma from the typing pool. (*see Ball juggling; Cocks on the block; Plate spinning; Python, wrestling with a; Under siege*)

Banana, stabbing a seal with a: 1. Using a tropical crescent-shaped fruit to terminate the life of an aquatic mammal of the phocidae or otaridae families. 2. Hopelessly equipped for the job; using entirely the wrong tool to get something done; repeatedly using the same technique again and again hoping in vain for a different result; too dim to change tactics. (*see Bark into the wind, up the wrong tree; Grasping at fog; Nailing a jelly to the wall, trying to*)

Banana skin, political. 1. Issue with the power to trip someone up. 2. Terminal booby trap that leads to dismissal, either via the window or after a slow, painful death. (*see Consultation period; Defenestrate; defenestration*)

Bandwagon, jumping on the, negative _____, positive _____: 1. A wagon carrying a band in a parade. 2. Blindly following what everyone else is doing for no particular reason, for better or worse; joining in a craze without thought; triumphantly shouting *"I am an individual!"* whilst joining a million other people doing the same thing; failing to have an original thought, ever. (*see Outcomes, positive, negative*)

Bandwagoneering: 1. There is no correct definition for this word, because it doesn't exist. 2. Exploiting a trend in order to make stack loads of cash out of it; agreeing with lots of other hip people in the vain hope that you will look hip too. (*see Mid-life crisis*)

Bandwidth, he doesn't have the: 1. Not intelligent. 2. He's thick as a brick; dead from the neck up; relentlessly useless at work; no help at all, in fact, a downright hindrance; 100% incompetent. (*see Intelligent, if you were any less _____, I'd have to water you once a day; Mental furniture; Obvious, firm grasp of the; Psychic RAM; Shilling, not the full; WOMBAT*)

Bang the drum: 1. Hit a percussion instrument. 2. Make a disproportionate racket about something in a futile attempt to rally support or gain interest. (*see Tub thumping*)

Bar chart: 1. Histogram showing data or sales performance. 2. Work of fiction designed to mislead potential customers or shareholders; cunning deployment of distorted axes to create the impression of success; baffling array of similarly-coloured towers depicting nothing intelligible whatsoever; one of 127 similar charts in a tedious research debrief with no discernable conclusion. (*see Histogram*)

Bark into the wind, up the wrong tree: 1. Attempting something that is never going to work. 2. Too unintelligent to rumble that the current approach will consistently fail. (*see Asking a duck to bark; Banana, stabbing a seal with a; Dialogue, continuous consumer, meaningful; Herring, chasing a different*)

Barnstorm: 1. To tour rural districts putting on shows (*chiefly USA*). 2. Take a meeting by storm, for better or worse; be brilliant and win; be utterly useless and fail miserably in public; throw a wobbly and lose it completely in front of the entire board; experience a burst of Tourette's in front of a senior visiting customer.

Barriers: 1. Things in the way. 2. Thoroughly legitimate reasons why prospective customers refuse to buy your sub-standard products, as in so-called *"barriers to purchase"*; obstructive colleagues who block your every proposal.

Baseline: 1. An agreed point from which other points can be measured or compared. 2. Ever-shifting criteria only called upon to trumpet imaginary success; infuriating chimera that never quite arrives nor truly exists. (*see Ballpark figure; Fiscal juggling; Hopper, pour into the; Horizon, above the, change the, below the, small ripple on the; Re-baselining; Touch base*)

Basically: 1. In a fundamental or elementary manner. 2. This word has marginal meaning and rarely adds anything no matter where it is used. (*see Absolutely; At the end of the day; Frankly; Literally*)

Basket case: 1. Merciless US slang term for a person with all limbs amputated. 2. Total buffoon; complete no-hoper; an idiot in search of a village. (*see Box of frogs, mad as a; Mid-life crisis; Picnic, one sandwich short of a; Postal, go*)

Bath, take a: 1. Conduct ablutions in a body-sized, water-bearing vessel. 2. Lose the lot; nose dive spectacularly; crash violently in full view of all colleagues; experience absolute humiliation in all-company meeting. (*see Catch a cold; Gung ho*)

Battleground: 1. Place where a battle is fought. 2. Pathetic deployment of the military metaphor to something truly bland, such as toilet cleaner market; heroic but pointless attempt to make dreary subject matter seem more appealing, as in *"We're going to take the curtain ring market by storm guys!"* (*see Flagpole, run it up the _____ and see who salutes; Jungle out there, it's a*)

Bazooka after a fly, we're not going to send a: 1. We won't devote disproportionately large resources to this. 2. It's a piss-pot little project so we'll let it wither on the vine; outrageous budget request, as in *"Brian, the board has decided that the £1 million sign-off for the jasmine and sesame seed line extension will sadly not be forthcoming."* (*see Drop a ricket; Feet, to dive in with both; Nut, sledgehammer to crack a; Platform, eat one's own*)

BCC: 1. Blind carbon copy. 2. My intention is to humiliate you convincingly in public by letting everyone see your crass rantings in full; tangible equivalent of a vindictive outburst along the lines of *"Don't f**k with me you little shit, I have the proof!"* (*see Arse covering; Blame culture; CC; Email; FYI; Voice mail*)

Beaconicity, predictors of: 1. Factors that will indicate what will stand out. 2. Truly shocking piece of government rubbish, inventing *"beaconicity"*, the capacity to shine or stand out; originating from the correct word for a signal fire or light on a hill, and horribly migrated to any areas acquiring *"beacon status"*, and thus qualifying for special funding; the addition of the suffix -icity and a predictive element make this a car crash of gargantuan proportions.

Be-all-and-end-all: 1. Ultimate; final; crucial. 2. Nothing of the sort; quintessentially unimportant, but dressed up to sound as though it is; irrelevant; incidental; of no real interest; inconsequential.

Beanbags: 1. Large soft cushions. 2. Large soft cushions much loved by reclining semi-stoned hippies; similar brightly-coloured *"furniture"* totally unsuited to the office environment; popular, in-vogue items to scatter around so-called *"soft areas"*; near-flattened blob of material still bearing the unmistakable imprint of the rear end of Sylvia from HR, who has a *"big personality"*. (*see Blue sky thinking; Brainstorm; Breakout groups; Soft area*)

Bean counter: 1. Accountant or Finance Director. 2. Intensely irritating man in a bad suit who is never seen without a spreadsheet; incapable of any basic social skills; champion of the hilarious Donald Duck tie; also inclined to wear hooped red socks with unpolished brown shoes; likely resident of Ruislip or Rickmansworth; humourless numbers person with borderline halitosis and a disconcerting leer – to be avoided at all costs at the Christmas party.

Beans, spill the: 1. Drop a number of leguminous plants of the genus phaseolus on the floor. 2. Let slip something highly inappropriate in a crucial meeting; get pissed and reveal vital trade secrets to a competitor; blurt out confidential information at a trade conference or interview. (*see Chinese whispers; Drop a ricket; Loop, out of the, keep in the*)

Beavers, defending it like: 1. Tenaciously backing a cause. 2. Completely inaccurate analogy attempting to specify anthropomorphic qualities which the beaver does not in fact possess; starting a sentence without knowing how to finish it and randomly grabbing at a member of the animal kingdom to finish the job. (*see Seals, left them clapping like; Wildebeest in a row, has the lion got his*)

Bear with me: 1. Give me a moment. 2. I desperately need to stall for time; I have no executive authority to deal with this problem, despite claiming I did.

Bee's knees, it's the: 1. It's brilliant. 2. It's the same as the leg joints of a hymenopterous insect of the superfamily apoidea, which is really saying something; curious piece of vernacular with no discernible purpose. (*see Dog's bollocks; Mustard, cut the, that's _____ that is*)

Begs the question: 1. Why? 2. Why oh why?

Behavioural economics: 1. Pseudoscience suggesting that pure economic theory is a poor indicator of human behaviour. 2. Spectacular smoke and mirrors job much loved by advertising agencies; random series of anecdotes about the vagaries of human decision-making; not a discipline at all, having resisted a clear definition in the entire academic canon that describes it. (*see FAQs; Grasping at fog; Hints and tips; Smoke and mirrors job*)

Bells and whistles: 1. Lots of fancy stuff. 2. Pointless superfluous fanfare surrounding something actually quite ordinary; scores of additional features on a piece of technology that nobody uses but which make the designer look clever and get him promoted. (*see All-singing, all-dancing; Hype; Pull out all the stops; Push the boat out*)

Bench, has this got: 1. Does this team have strength in depth, as verified by the quality of the players on the substitute's bench? 2. Truly dire phrase pilfered, once again, from the verbal swamp that is American sport; is this idea any good, or is it pure bollocks? (*see Legs, it's got; Real estate, how much _____ does this have; Success, what does _____ look like?*)

Benchmarking, category, industry: 1. Making a mark as a reference point for surveying. 2. Incessant paranoid comparison between the performance of your business and that of a competitor; incapacity to have one iota of original thought; relentless plundering of copycat ideas from a more inventive rival. (*KPIs; Markers, put some _____ down; Metrics; Milestones*)

Best practice: 1. How something should be done, ie. properly. 2. Standard that companies and individuals consistently fail to reach; shoddy fudging; skimming; quality never achieved, but regularly hyped up; something that is practiced but never enacted; abstract concept often discussed without any reference to how it can actually be done.

BHAG: 1. Big Hairy Audacious Goal, invented by Jim Collins in 2001 in his book *Good To Great*. 2. Tediously macho *"vision"* mapped out by unintelligent business leader, usually just after reading said book or failing to complete an

MBA; vacuous collection of bland and predominantly meaningless adjectives supposedly intended to *"direct"* the staff; random verbal guff entirely interchangeable with that on the boardroom wall of a main rival. (*see Aims; Aspirational; Greatest Imaginable Challenge; Impossible, nothing is; MBA; Objectives; Unthinkable, think the*)

Bias for action: 1. Tendency to get things done rather than just talk about them, first proposed by business writers Peters and Waterman in their 1982 book *In Search of Excellence*. 2. Loud but hollow mantra frequently peddled by vacuous macho managers, as in *"We need a bias for action on this one guys!"*, when in truth they have no intention of lifting a finger to help, ever.

Big boys, playing with the: 1. Competing against the biggest and best there is. 2. Scrabbling around with the same old has-beens; frantically playing catch-up; vainly trying to move out of the second or third division.

Big fish: 1. Large marine animal; significant player or prize. 2. Tired aquatic scale reference, usually involving being a big fish in a small pond, or a small fish in a big pond; rarely mentioned as a big fish in a big pond for some unknown reason.

Big cheese: 1. Large chunk of dairy produce, such as Gorgonzola. 2. The boss; the person at the top; supposedly famous visiting dignitary. (*see Fromage, grand; Head honcho; Head office, I'm from _____ and I'm here to help; Player, big*)

Big enchilada: 1. Large tortilla fried in hot fat, filled with meat and covered in chilli sauce. 2. The boss, or if not, then a big presence in the office. (*see Big cheese*)

Big match temperament: 1. Disposition suitable for important occasions. 2. Disposition utterly unsuitable for important occasions; prone to childish outbursts. (*see Pram, to throw one's toys out of the*)

Big picture: 1. A large painting. 2. Apparent ability to see beyond the trivia, when the trivia is actually more interesting; strategic wibble that excuses someone from having to do any work, on the grounds that they are *"strategizing"*. (*see Blue-sky thinking; Brainstorm; Helicopter view; Holistic; Strategy, strategize*)

BlackBerry prayer: 1. Leaning forward, as if praying, to check emails surreptitiously in meetings. 2. Incapable of paying attention to those present due to absolute addiction to one's own mobile device; total ennui with regard to present company; belief that one's own affairs are intrinsically more interesting than anyone else's; odd belief that one's own activities elsewhere must somehow be more interesting than what is happening in front of you, despite repeated evidence to the contrary. (*see Death by PowerPoint; Meetings; Moi presentation*)

Black arts: 1. Black magic used for evil purposes. 2. Obscure chicanery used by shady executives to achieve their nefarious ends. (*see Cook the books; Fiscal juggling*)

Black hole, disappeared into a: 1. Astronomical phenomenon so dense that that its escape velocity exceeds the speed of light. 2. Catastrophic loss of income or flaw in system; near-total loss of customer base overnight; instant sacking, never to be seen again; immediate imprisonment for fraud. (*see Blood bath, on the walls; Game is up, the; Leaky bucket*)

Black swan: 1. Large and dark aquatic bird; random event that cannot be predicted, as explained by Nassim Nicholas Taleb in his 2007 book of the same name (*all swans were assumed to be white until overseas travel revealed the existence of black ones*). 2. Disastrous development that no one saw coming, and that destroys everything; total crash; meltdown; catastrophe; career-threatening cockup. (*see Bounce out of the norm; Crystal ball; Event; Futureproof; Game plan; Head office, I'm from _____ and I'm here to help; Navel gazing; Risk management*)

Blame culture: 1. Work place in which people have to prove that they are genuinely doing something constructive, or face the consequences. 2. Vicious atmosphere in which finger pointing and character assassination are the norm – it's dog eat dog, and anything goes so long as it's definitely not your fault. (*see BCC; Backlash; Back stabbing; Fear; Front stabbing; Hospital pass; In the same boat; Witch-hunt*)

Blank canvas: 1. A clean sheet; starting from scratch. 2. Highly dangerous non-brief allowing a completely free rein, often leading to disastrous consequences; permission to run riot and go completely off-piste, much loved of creative and design folk; irresponsible grey area allowing people to do exactly what they want, which usually means going to the pub.

Bleeding edge: 1. Blood dripping from the corner of a sharp object such as a knife. 2. Hideous bastard son of the phrase *"leading edge"*, impossibly suggesting something even more advanced than the most advanced thing. (*see Cutting edge; Leading edge; Next-generation; Pioneering*)

Blitz: 1. Violent and sustained attack. 2. Violent and sustained attack on a colleague after years of persecution. (*see Back stabbing; Front stabbing*)

Blood bath, on the walls: 1. Massive fight, leaving significant evidence. 2. Total carnage in the office; wholesale sacking of an entire department; full-scale walkout of majority of the board to form a rival breakaway; dramatic eviction of Finance Director in hand cuffs following appalling exposé of malfeasance. (*see Armageddon plan; Black hole, disappeared into a; Fiscal juggling*)

Blow it: 1. Fail to take an opportunity. 2. Crash and burn at the vital moment, such as breaking wind loudly at interview; allow inner monologue to surface during a crucial client meeting, as in *"Oh for f*@k's sake Brian, just get on with it!"*

Blue-chip: 1. A company whose stock is considered reliable for dividend income and capital value, named after the gambling chip with the highest value. 2. Lazy catch-all descriptor to suggest anything of high quality, particularly by companies claiming that all their customers are *"blue-chip"*, or by job candidates portraying a supposedly "blue-chip" CV; not high quality at all – in fact, distinctly average; just as likely to go bust tomorrow as an iffy start up. (*see CV*)

Blue in the face, talk until you're: 1. Talk for a long time. 2. Say nothing of consequence for a whole day. (*see Awayday; Brainstorm*)

Blue sky, to: 1. To think theoretically without any regard to future application of the result. 2. Shocking verb-cum-noun-cum-adjective much loved of Americans, roughly denoting to think broadly and vaguely; useless hot air session in which many attendees talk drivel for a sustained period, congratulate themselves on a *"highly constructive session"*, and then sod off to the golf course to wear dreadful trousers. (*see Blue-sky thinking*)

Blue-sky thinking: 1. Purely theoretical thinking. 2. Waffle; static; hot air; piffle; inconsequential rubbish; stuff that will never happen in a million years. (*see Beanbags; Big picture; Blue sky, to; Blue yonder; Brainstorm; Static; White noise*)

Blue touch paper, light the: 1. Set something running, then stand back and watch the consequences. 2. Cause complete chaos; do something thoughtless without due regard for the consequences; set in train a cataclysmic chain reaction; fail to spot the link between several related things. (*see Acid test; Dropping grenades in fishponds; Proof of concept*)

Blue yonder: 1. A long way over there in the distance. 2. Metaphorical place where all the pointless blue-sky thinking ideas go, never to return or be enacted. (*see Blue-sky thinking; Head of the valley syndrome; Horizon, above the, change the, below the, small ripple on the*)

Bob's your uncle: 1. Robert is your father's brother. 2. Hey presto!; there you have it; trite throwaway phrase much loved by self-appointed office wags who are never as funny as they think they are; daft nonsensical aphorism frequently trumpeted by the annoying maintenance man when completing a perfectly simple task such as fixing a shelf.

BOGOFF: 1. Buy one get one for free. 2. This tat is so low quality we're giving it away.

BOHICA: 1. Bend over here it comes again. 2. Look out, you're about to get shafted for the umpteenth time; scatological rallying call for procurement executives about to screw their suppliers for the fourth year in a row. (*see Compliance; Cost effective; Drop our trousers; Sprat to catch a mackerel*)

Boil the ocean, you can't: 1. It's impossible to make the sea turn from liquid to vapour. 2. This task simply can't be done.

Bollocks, talking: 1. Testicles that can speak. 2. Sustained burst of total rubbish blurted out in answer to an unexpected interview question; patchwork of platitude and cliché designed to confuse; mission statement contents; any acceptance speech; 100% of proclamations made by politicians or sportsmen. (*see Bullshit; Obfuscation*)

Bombs, box of: 1. Container of explosives. 2. Lethal, career-threatening material lurking ominously in in-box, whether physical or electronic; accident waiting to happen; project that will detonate the moment it is touched; important meeting with trouble written all over it; annual review at which a severe dressing down will undoubtedly be administered. (*see Ask, big; Catching a falling knife; Curved ball; Dyke, finger in the; Hospital pass; Minefield, complete, tiptoeing through a; Poisoned chalice*)

Bombshell: 1. Unexpected news; attractive blonde woman. 2. Combination of the two, as in discovering that the attractive blonde woman is up the duff, and the child is yours; marching orders. (*see Bullet, get the; Marching orders, get your*)

Bonding, team: 1. Joining together, not always using adhesive. 2. Dreaded verb referring to the abhorrent process of *"getting to know your colleagues better"*, probably originated by well-meaning and touchy-feely HR people intending to improve morale; butt of thousands of awayday jokes referring to disastrous *"team-bonding"* exercises, typically building a pontoon over a river with limited materials, or having the courage to fall backwards into the team's arms from a great height. (*see Awayday; Partners; Share and air; Show and tell; Strategic alliance; Touchy-feely*)

Bones, put flesh on the: 1. Provide detail to explain the broad concept. 2. Add extraneous layers of blether when the gist is already evident; massively pad out with dross; confuse the issue with irrelevant material; obfuscate; waffle; drone on purely to hear one's own voice; showboat; bore for England, or any nation that will listen.

Boomerang effect: 1. A person or thing that comes back. 2. Awful unintended repercussion; unexpected reaction to something you originally thought was of no great consequence; trainee you badly mistreated returning to company some years later as Chief Executive, with inevitable effect; tit for tat retaliation to office prank leading to dismissal.

Boss: 1. Person in charge. 2. Incompetent prat.

Bottleneck: 1. The top of a bottle where the flow of liquid is most squeezed. 2. Chaotic log jam of projects and workload that can cripple a company in a matter of days; complete deadlock when no one will work with you because of your appalling office habits; paralysis caused by one power-crazed maniac insisting on signing off every bit of paper in the company. (*see Control freak*)

Bottom feeding: 1. Eating material on the floor of a river, sea or fish tank. 2. Hoovering up any crap that has settled on the bottom; dealing solely in the dross; working with or for the cheapest and worst possible exponents in the market; actively pursuing low-rent customers, and to hell with the consequences. (*see Ambulance chasing; Scraping the barrel*)

Bottom line: 1. The figure at the bottom when all the others have been added and subtracted. 2. Maze of chicanery and falsehoods, bearing no resemblance to the true state of the business; work of supreme fiction. (*see Fiscal juggling; Topline*)

Bounce ideas off: 1. Discuss a concept with a colleague. 2. Random word dump after jumping a colleague unexpectedly in the corridor just outside the toilets; sustained monologue trying to impose one's own view; blunt refusal to accept any idea deviating from one's own preconceived bias; bawl out subordinate for no particular reason other than being in a bad mood. (*see Brain dump; Brainstorm; Word dump*)

Bounce out of the norm: 1. Deviate from what is normal. 2. Veer horribly off-piste; discover utterly unexpected sales figure (*almost always negative*); random occurrence that really should have been anticipated. (*see Black swan*)

Box, think outside the, try and put a _____ round that one: 1. Nine-dot matrix game usually called the Gottschaldt figurine, which challenges the solver to join all nine dots with four lines without removing the pen from the paper – it can only be solved by taking the lines outside the perceived square, hence the phrase. 2. Hackneyed piece of nonsense used as a euphemism for having a perfectly average thought; plaintive plea for originality that is almost never answered; all-round conspiracy designed to convince one and all that everyone is rather intelligent. (*see Blue-sky thinking*)

Box of frogs, mad as a: 1. Mad. 2. Utterly ga-ga; loopy; not well, by any stretch of the imagination; incomprehensible; likely exponent of bullshit. (*see Basket case; Gene pool, swimming in the shallow end of the _____; Mid-life crisis; Moon, barking at the, over the, through the; Postal, go; Picnic, one sandwich short of a*)

Braggadocious behaviour: 1. Vainglorious, empty boasting, after a character in Spenser's *Faerie Queene*. 2. Vainglorious, empty boasting, all day every day at work; tedious windbag very keen on him or herself; convinced of one's own self-importance; principle characteristics of Chairman. (*see Chairman; Large, giving it*)

Brain dump: 1. Outpouring of thoughts. 2. Outpouring of thoughts on a colleague without any warning; random musings of a muddled fool; ill-prepared ragbag of half-baked clichés; so-called briefing. (*see Analysis, paralysis by, in the final; Bounce ideas off; Breeze, shooting the; Data dump; Waffle; Word dump*)

Brainstorm: 1. Ideas session. 2. Curious gathering of hapless individuals who have never had a decent idea in their lives, in the vain hope that suddenly they will; badly cast group who neither know nor like each other; international coming together of global network staff who claim they are *"one big family"* when in fact they have never met before; tedious powwow in which Geoff from production puts a downer on everything with the immortal phrase *"That'll never work will it?"* (*see Aha moment; Awayday; Bad idea, there's no such thing as a; Beanbags; Big picture; Blue-sky thinking; Flip chart; Lateral thinking; Light bulb experience; NPD; Off-site; Outcomes, negative, positive; Outputs; Think-tank; Workshop*)

Brain surgery, it's not: 1. It's not like cutting someone's head open and performing an intricate operation. 2. Actually it is – politics and backstabbing make this an impossible task. (*see Open-heart surgery, it's not; Rocket science, it's not*)

Brand onion; pillars, pyramid, values: 1. Diagram designed to clarify what a brand stands for. 2. Horribly contrived bastard son of a management consultancy chart, densely populated with meaningless catch-all adjectives such as *"passion"*, *"innovative"* and *"leading edge"*; unintelligible child's drawing resembling a car crash of imagery and words, vaguely reminiscent of Stonehenge, the Egyptian pyramids or an unspecified vegetable. (*see Brand strategist; Foundations, lay the; Guardian, brand ; Guidelines, brand, corporate; Innovation, innovative, innovatively; Passion, passionate; Positioning; Promise, brand, broken:*)

Brand strategist: 1. Person in charge of the direction a product or service is taking. 2. Purveyor of endless diagrams; generator of impenetrable jargon; conjurer. (*see Architecture, brand _____, business _____; Brand onion, pillars, pyramid, values: Marketing; Marketing guru; Needs and wants; Overarching; Positioning; Rebrand; Smoke and mirrors job; Time-poor, time-rich; User experience*)

Bread and butter: 1. Standard, workaday stuff; ordinary 2. Drudgery; slave labour; tedious, relentless administration. (*see Administrivia; Target manager*)

Break the ice: 1. Smash up frozen water. 2. Frantically attempt to butter up a frosty customer; smile weakly and ask a question about the family, where they live or the weather; try to establish basic eye-contact despite the other person having disconcerting designer glasses that create an impenetrable, inscrutable impression.

Break the mould: 1. Take a mould and break it, for reasons unknown; try to do something different. 2. Hackneyed catch-all phrase meaning *"For God's sake, we've seen all this stuff before Derek. Can't you do something original for once?"*; oft-used expression in creative industries, as in *"Come on guys, we need to break the mould here!"*, although why anyone would want to break a mould when they have spent so long designing it remains unclear. (*see Game-changing; Groundbreaking*)

Breakout groups: 1. Small sub-sets of a larger group, not necessarily broken. 2. Supposedly trendy term for awayday attendees when asked to sod off from the main room and have a decent idea for once; all the smokers at said event standing on the balcony puffing furiously under the guise of thinking; similar gathering at coffee refill station, where Brenda and Stephanie from Accounts can be found scoffing custard creams and moaning about the management. (*see Awayday; Bean bags; Come on people; Off-site; Soft area*)

Breath of fresh air: A person or idea that brings something entirely new to the matter in hand. 2. Thoroughly dangerous new recruit, often senior, who wants to change everything on their first day; terminal bore who keeps repeating *"That's not how we did it at my old place"*; genuinely inspiring new person with loads of good ideas who only lasts a few months before being fired. (*see Bull in a china shop; Broom, new; Compatible, not*)

Breathes through his arse: 1. Physical impossibility, alluding to an ability to talk consistently without appearing to breathe. 2. This bastard never comes up for air; talks non-stop; only interested in the sound of one's own voice. (*see Bark into the wind; Dialogue; Fire hydrant, trying to drink from a*)

Breeze, shooting the: 1. Firing shots into thin air. 2. Wibbling for no apparent reason; boring a colleague senseless; boring an entire audience senseless. (*see Blue-sky thinking; Brain dump; Word dump*)

Bridge too far, it may be a: 1. This may be more than we can handle. 2. This is definitely more than we can handle so we may as well admit defeat now. (*see Capabilities*)

Broad brush: 1. Wide painting utensil for covering a wide area. 2. Total fudge; failure to come to point; obfuscation; vagueness; sweeping attempt to avoid coming to the point. (*see Gloss over; Keep it dark; Strategy*)

Broad canvas: 1. A big surface area on which to paint. 2. Massive subject area about which a person knows very little, or naff all; diffuse area of over-claim, as in *"Of course Nigel these proposals can be applied across a very broad canvas"*, without actually specifying what, when or where; favourite hazy domain of politicians and Chief Executives where no one can be held accountable.

Broad church: 1. Religious building with a wide aisle; diverse gang of people, or broad-minded attitude. 2. Suggestion that work force is drawn from a wide spectrum, as in *"Of course we have a very broad church here Martin"*. (*see Diversity; Multicultural*)

Broom, new: 1. Freshly-purchased household cleaning instrument. 2. New boss, who knows nothing, and never will. (*see Breath of fresh air; Bull in a china shop*)

Brownie points: 1. Notional mark to one's credit based on the mistaken idea that the Brownie Guides earn points for good deeds. 2. Seldom-quantified suggestion that a number of good achievements at work all add up to something helpful, such as promotion or a pay rise; odious sucking up to the boss in a pathetic attempt to curry favour. (*see Brown-nosing*)

Brown-nosing: 1. Scatological reference to placing one's nose where the sun doesn't shine. 2. Obsequious behaviour towards anyone in a more senior position; toadying approach; automatic agreement with whatever the boss says; blind acceptance of what management decrees. (*see Backwards, bend over; Brownie points; Ego; First past the post; Hedge our bets; Team, take one for the; Where the sun don't shine, stick it*)

Buck, pass the: 1. In poker, a marker that reminds a player they are the next dealer. 2. Outrageous abdication of responsibility; total failure to live up to job description; automatic raising of hands as if to say *"Nothing to do with me!"*, almost always preceded by complaint that said individual is *"not being given enough respect or responsibility"*. (*see Empower; Hospital pass; Micromanaging; Pass the baton; PDQ; Riot act, read the; Wash our hands of it*)

Buck stops here, the: 1. I/we am/are fully responsible for everything, and am/are prepared to take the consequences. 2. I/we truly love everything that power brings – the money, the status, the women on tap – but try to hold us to task for anything untoward and we'll deny everything. (*see Accountable; Delegate, delegation*)

Bucks, bang for your: 1. Number of satisfying explosions, or possibly orgasms, for an amount paid. 2. Value for money; nothing whatsoever to do with value for money – more a case of desperately trying to receive more for less; vain cry of under-resourced manager, as in *"I need more bangs for my buck, Fiona!"* (*see Dial up*)

Bugs, iron out the: 1. To remove beetles from an article of clothing with a hot pressing implement. 2. To eliminate critical flaws in a product or service; start from scratch; return to the drawing board. (*see Crafting, it needs a bit of; Drawing board, back to the; Optimal; Sub-optimal*)

Building bridges: 1. Constructing ways over water or valley. 2. Try to make amends after a total breakdown in relations; bring flowers to colleague after throwing up on them at the office party; offer olive branch to new boss who beat you to the promotion; buy chocolate biscuits for receptionist following highly inappropriate physical approach the day before. (*see Burning bridges*)

Building the plane as we fly it: 1. Literally, aeronautical construction on the wing, if it were possible. 2. Overly-macho notion that we are so clever we can rectify any unforeseen problem as it arises, without preparing first; hubris; misplaced confidence, usually followed by a loud crash; phrase much loved of self-styled Internet entrepreneurs. (*see Digital native; Fly by the seat of one's pants; SOP*)

Built to last: 1. Classic management book written by Jim Collins and Jerry Porras in 1994, explaining how companies can generate long-term success. 2. Peculiar exhortation of short-term managers who have no intention of staying in the job for more than 18 months; sham expression designed to fool colleagues into believing that you give a dam, as in *"We need this built to last guys!"* (*see Good to great*)

Bull in a china shop: 1. Someone causing a lot of trouble in a delicate environment. 2. Loose cannon; horribly off-brief colleague; all Chairmen who haven't read their briefing notes and who think they can wing it; every politician that ever existed. (*see Breath of fresh air; Broom, new; catalyst; Dropping grenades in fish ponds; Flight path; Gung ho; Loose cannon*)

Bullet, bite the: 1. Face up to; be stoical. 2. Run for the hills; leave the building; resign; shift the blame onto someone else. (*see Blame culture; Bombshell; Hospital pass*)

Bullet, get the: 1. Experience execution. 2. Be fired. (*see Decruit; Defenestration; Marching orders, get your*)

Bullet, magic, silver: 1. Single cure, answer or solution. 2. Deflective verbal ruse of squirming bosses and politicians, as in *"There is no silver bullet here guys!"*; weak excuse; unwanted component if playing Russian roulette.

Bullet points: 1. A series of points on a chart. 2. PowerPoint's undying lethal gift to the world of business; list of objectives on a brief, whose true number is infinite; number of things required by customer yesterday; competition to see how many items can be placed on a chart before they are illegible, or the audience shoots the presenter. (*see Bullet, magic, silver; Death by PowerPoint*)

Bullshit: 1. The excreta of a large male bovine. 2. Technically endless supply of waffle and nonsense uttered in business meetings; cunning wordsmithery that is neither on the side of the false nor the truth; verbal expedience; the entire contents of this book. (*see Bollocks, talking; Doughnut rather than the hole, it* would be wise to concentrate on the; Obfuscation; Off the top of my head; Static; Talking out loud; Waffle; White noise; Word dump)

Bun fight: 1. Violent disagreement in a bakery (*causes various*). 2. Dust up; brawl; mild difference of opinion leading to outright fisticuffs; suit-ripping incident at sales conference; abuse (*or vegetables*) thrown at awards ceremony; principle activity at office party. (*see Consensus*)

Bundle, one stick short of a: 1. A lightweight collection of fire wood. 2. Not the full shilling, not quite the ticket; slow; dim. (*see Box of frogs, mad as a; Gene pool, swimming in the shallow end of the; Mid-life crisis; Picnic, one sandwich short of a; Shilling, not the full*)

Bureaucracy: 1. System of administration. 2. Pointless rules and processes that take all the fun out of business; pen-pushing twaddle; form filling. (*see Administrivia; Jobsworth; Panjandrum; Process; Target manager*)

Burn the candle at both ends, the midnight oil: 1. Stay awake too long; get very little sleep. 2. Be worked like a dog by one's boss; have a job with perfectly ordinary working hours but then spend inordinate amounts of time in bars and nightclubs; sleep under one's desk.

Burning bridges: 1. Set light to bridge and thus prevent the chance of going back. 2. Tell the boss in no uncertain terms to f*@k off; deliver similar message to important customer; shag secretary; shag boss's wife; shag both; ruin one's life in an ill-advised instant. (*see Building bridges*)

Burning platform: 1. Rostrum or dais in flames; impossible position that will inevitably end in disaster. 2. A firm favourite of sales people who have boxed themselves into an awkward corner; death wish; shades of self-immolation; suggestion of so-called platform as physical manifestation of ethereal concept such as customer base. (*see Foot, shoot oneself in the; Hoist by one's own petard; Kamikaze; Object, defeating the; Own goal, spectacular; Platform, online, sales, user; Platform, eat one's own; Platform, exceed the*)

Bus, who's driving the: 1. *"Is this double-decker operated by a robot?"* 2. *"Who the f*@k's in charge here?!"*; euphemism for weak, or totally absent, senior direction; strategy-free zone; complete lack of leadership. (*see Rowing in the same boat, direction; Train, who's driving the*)

Buy-in: 1. State of purchasing something and consuming it at home. 2. Agreement or approval from a colleague, as in *"We'll need Geoff's buy-in on this one."*; poisoned blessing which doesn't mean approval at all, simply permission to go ahead and humiliate yourself. (*see Green light; Greenlit; Issues , I have _____ with that; Problem, I don't have a _____ with that; Redlit; Run it past; Unhappy, I'm not _____ with*)

Buzz: 1. Annoying sound made by insect. 2. Annoying sound made by public relations executives called Emma when waxing lyrical about the coverage they will achieve for a client; static; hot air; gossip; wibble; abject failure of said campaign to generate any publicity at all; sound of Chief Executive's intercom when calling the PR agency into his office to be fired for failing to *"generate buzz"*. (*see Hype*)

By the board: 1. Next to a piece of board, just there. 2. Absolutely nowhere at all; certainly not there; redundant; dead; passed over.

B2B: 1. Business to business. 2. Squeamish mnemonic denoting subject matter between two businesses; childish shorthand; wince-making collision of verbal and numerical components. (*see B2C; One-to-one*)

B2C: 1. Business to consumer. 2. Something straight out of kindergarten class; random abuttal of letters and a number; lazy shorthand to suggest that the writer is "in the know" when it comes to industry lingo. (*see B2B*)

Cc

Calibrate: 1. Determine the accuracy of a measurement. 2. Fabricate a totally false scale in order to make sales or profits look impressive, when in fact they are disastrous. *(see Cook the books; Fiscal juggling)*

Call report: 1. Record of conversation between a company representative and a client or customer. 2. Pack of lies noted down as an afterthought to protect oneself from gross incompetence and failure to complete a simple instruction; additional pack of lies that uses the spurious authority of type to note things that were never agreed at all; pure fiction. *(see Arse covering; Contact report)*

Call to action: 1. Request to do something. 2. Desperate plea for a colleague or customer to acknowledge that your hopeless job or product is even worth a second of their time.

Campaign: 1. Sustained programme of events to achieve an objective. 2. Overly-macho expression plundered from the military to lend undeserved credence to a random selection of lacklustre ideas.

Can, carry the, left holding the: 1. Take the blame, right now or at some later time. 2. Get it comprehensively in the slats when it was absolutely nothing to do with you. *(see Above and beyond; Team, take one for the)*

Can, we need to _____ it: 1. We need to stop doing something. 2. This is utter crap – cease work on it immediately.

Can do attitude: 1. A constructive, positive approach. 2. Pointless blind optimism flying in the face of all sensible known information, deployed to impress a boss or colleague of the opposite sex. *(see Doable; Easy tiger; Failure is not an option; Impossible, nothing is)*

Cane it: 1. Beat something too hard or go too fast. 2. Completely overshoot despite all previous experience, usually in reference to alcohol or drugs.

Capabilities: 1. Range of skills. 2. Enormous selection of lies perpetrated on one's CV. (*see Bridge too far, it may be a; CV; Competencies, core*)

Capability gap: 1. Difference between what can and can't be done. 2. Sudden revelation that a colleague is incapable of doing the job in hand, despite their claims at interview. (*see Aspirational; CV; Potential*)

Carbuncle, unwanted: 1. A nasty boil. 2. Undesirable colleague who really should have a bath.

Card, red: 1. Severe or final warning; outright dismissal. 2. Removal from job, or meeting room; humiliating public dress down; red card offence that strangely results in no disciplinary procedure or dismissal, but is merely described as such by relieved macho colleagues; awestruck reflections of other members of team in the pub after a disgraceful scene at work, as in *"Gary should have had a red card for that"*.

Carrot, big, _____ and stick: 1. Incentive to do something; blend of reward and sanction. 2. Blend of slave-driving and pitifully small *"bonus"* much loved by macho organizations trying to suggest they have a passable approach to staff welfare; small carrot; no carrot at all; a derisory £25 shopping voucher apparently as reward for 12 months of hard labour; bowl of gruel. (*see Incentive, staff; Incentivize*)

Cash flow: 1. Flow of cash through the company accounts. 2. Complete absence of flow of cash through the company accounts. (*see Cook the books; Fiscal juggling*)

Casting: 1. Choice of personnel for a task, or to work on a particular account or customer. 2. Huge error of judgment in choosing the wrong person for the job; erroneous selection of bearded, skateboarding digital native for serious piece of corporate business; futile attempt to match the right people to the right business, as in *"We really need to get the casting right on this one guys!"* (*see Digital native; Dress to impress; Fish up a tree, he looks like a; Food chain, a long way down the, higher up the; Mix, the right, the wrong*)

Catalyst: 1. Person or substance that causes change. 2. Reckless newcomer, usually a Sales Director or Managing Director, who changes everything and wrecks it in the process; annoying self-appointed *"Minister for Fun"* who pisses everyone off so badly that they all leave. (*see Bull in a china shop; Broom, new; Loose cannon; Minister for fun*)

Catch a cold: 1. Contract viral infection of the upper respiratory tract; lose on an investment. 2. Lose everything after a gung ho bet; blow everything on the nags; under estimate the amount of preparation required for a crucial meeting. (*see Bath, take a; Gung ho*)

Catch-22: 1. Paradoxical set of rules that always lead nowhere, or to disaster, coined in the book of the same name by Joseph Heller in 1961. 2. Deadlock state of affairs; personal dilemma involving only nasty options such as dismissal, embarrassment, demotion, humiliation in front of the whole company, or wife. (*see Square the circle*)

Catching a falling knife: 1. Foolishly attempting to grab a sharp kitchen implement when it slips off the work surface. 2. Idiotic attempt to intervene that will only lead to pain or severe injury; stupidly claiming to be able to save the day in order to impress, only to discover the true horror of the problem. (*see Bombs, box of; Hospital pass; Poisoned chalice*)

Category of one: 1. Area of business with no other competition. 2. Mathematically inane suggestion that the company or brand is invincible; abject failure to spot that an as yet unknown rival will steal all your customers by Christmas; tub-thumping claim to uniqueness, almost always false.

Cavalry over the hill: 1. It's time to put proper resource on this for once. 2. It's all hands to the pump and those senior people who have horribly neglected the task will be the first to claim hero status for apparently bailing everyone else out when in fact they should have paid proper attention to it in the first place. (*see A-team, this calls for; Eleventh hour, at the; Lead from the front*)

CC: 1. Carbon copy. 2. Sustained campaign to smear a colleague for incompetence; relentless email trail proving that you are in the right and it's everyone else's fault; career-spanning, arse-covering exercise, much loved of administrators the world over. (*see Arse covering; BCC; Email; FYI; Voice mail*)

Centre of excellence: 1. Place where stuff is done well. 2. All-too-rare outpost of an organization where they really do know what they are doing; somewhere, but not in your organization; in the Head Office of your main rival, but not in yours.

-centred, -centric: 1. Having a centre; anchored in the middle. 2. Nasty, roughly interchangeable, suffix pairing; frequently added mindlessly to any word the author can get their hands on; examples include customer-centric, goal-centred and media-centric, when in fact the correct usage is to be found in words such as concentric, eccentric and heliocentric. (*see -driven; -focused, people-, goal-; -oriented*)

Chairman: 1. Person, annoyingly usually male, who looks after, or sits in, a chair. 2. Mysterious shadowy figure at the top of many companies; so-called eminence grise; unnecessary overhead; inveterate meddler in other peoples' work; person whose role is almost entirely unknown; walking embodiment of the phrase *"out of touch"*; consistently unaware of what the company is actually doing; elderly irritant who should in all probability be put out to grass; prone to making long, rambling speeches about nothing in particular; windbag. (*see Braggadocious behaviour; Gloss over; Heavy hitter; Player, big*)

Chairman's wife: 1. Woman married to your boss. 2. Extremely attractive woman married to your boss, with whom eye contact must be avoided at all costs; extremely unattractive woman married to your boss, with whom eye contact must be engaged at all costs; knackered old harridan who has the Chairman under her thumb and as such runs the company in a surrogate fashion; woman with irrational objections to simple things, such as the colour blue, as in *"The 3,000 outlet refit has been shelved at the last minute because the Chairman's wife doesn't like blue"*. (*see Charisma bypass; Movers and shakers; Prejudice*)

Challenger brand: 1. Any brand that isn't number one but would like to be. 2. Clapped out selection of has-beens and also-rans in any market; semi-macho lingo designed to improve morale in mediocre companies, as in *"Good news guys, we're not bottom of the market – we're challengers!"* (*see Market-leading; Mediocracy; Thought leadership; World class*)

Challenges: 1. Things to do, some of them quite tricky. 2. Things to do, all of them very tricky; impossible selection of tasks set out thoughtlessly by boss; so-called *"opportunities"* that are actually booby-trapped. (*see Ask, big; Opportunity; Poisoned chalice; SWOT analysis*)

Champion (vb.): 1. To be an ambassador for; to support; to promote something. 2. To take the credit when everyone else has done all the work; to agree to back a proposal and then vote against it in a crucial meeting, to the amazement of all colleagues; to vacillate and prevaricate; to lie outright in order to avoid a conflict with one's team members.

Change drivers: 1. To give control of the steering wheel to someone else. 2. Factors that might affect whether things change or not; factors that probably won't affect anything at all; bleating set of mission or *"value"* statements that all staff will ignore as a matter of urgency; hypothetical blether that probably has no bearing on anything; axiomatic twaddle hastily woven together in order to secure a publishing contract. (*see Drivers, key; Values; Vision, visioning*)

Chapter and verse: 1. Exact authority for something. 2. Tautological battle cry usually decreed by desperate managers wanting to know why something has failed miserably, as in *"I want chapter and verse on this one guys!"*; catch-all receptacle for anything supposedly comprehensive, but in truth shallow and hastily cobbled together. (*see A-Z; Full Monty, the; No-quibble guarantee; Zee, we've covered everything from A to*)

Charisma bypass: 1. Total absence of character. 2. Sales Director; Finance Director; Geoff in Production; Alan in IT; any of various insufferably dull people one has to endure at work. (*see Chairman's wife*)

Chasing eyeballs: 1. Pursuing vital visual organs, for reasons unknown. 2. Unspeakably bad phrase for encouraging people to watch something on a screen, usually the television or their computer.

Cherry pick: 1. Pluck red round fruit of the rosaceous genus Prunus. 2. Take all the interesting work for yourself; demonstrate disgraceful favouritism by only selecting your drinking buddies for a project, or the well-stacked Julia from procurement for slightly different reasons; ask Julia for a *"one-to-one" after work to "discuss some issues"*. (*see One-to-one*)

Chinese walls: 1. Structures that hold up ceilings in China. 2. Metaphorical barriers between teams or departments, purported to retain client confidentiality; free-for-all of information exchange for maximum benefit; hotbed of gossip; industrial espionage; flagrant cross-fertilization of market knowledge to increase bonus levels.

Chinese whispers: 1. Chain of message passing that results in a distortion of the original message. 2. Thoroughly illegal passing on of information, all of it 100% accurate and highly damaging; ill-advised momentary lapse of discretion at office party usually leading to dismissal. (*see Beans, spill the; Loop, out of the, keep in the*)

Choiceful: 1. Full of choice. 2. Offering no choice at all, as in *"Guys, can we make this offering more choiceful?"* (*see Insightful; Meaningful*)

Chop, for the: 1. About to be fired. 2. About to be physically removed from the building. (*see Decruit; Defenestrate, defenestration*)

Christmas party: 1. Festive celebration. 2. Carnage; unwanted collision between management and staff; only moment when Phil from IT is brave enough to tell the Managing Director what he always thought of him; bacchanalian orgy in which an appalling volume of bodily fluids is exchanged; vomit-fest best avoided, every year. (*see Office party*)

Chuggers: 1. Elision of *"charity"* and *"muggers"*; charity representatives in the street who press unsuspecting pedestrians to sign up to the cause. 2. Feral gangs of students with clipboards and relentlessly cheerful smiles; gap year mercenaries intent on securing a sale to bolster their Peruvian cycling trip fund. (*see Cold calling; Experiential marketing; Hot lead*)

Churn and burn: 1. Process fast and move on; attend to, then ignore or discard. 2. Cynical exploitation of customer base; obsession with winning new customers, only to ignore existing ones; similar attitude to staff, utilizing a hire and fire policy. (*see In for the long haul; Leaky bucket*)

Circular file: 1. Wastepaper basket. 2. Last resting place of sanctimonious all-staff memos; unsavoury mélange of old banana skins, nail clippings and desk detritus; health hazard; fire hazard; surreptitious dumping ground for illicit porn; occasional vomit bucket. (*see Christmas party; FIFO; LIFO*)

Clapham omnibus, man on the: 1. Male of the species, found aboard a London bus in the SW4 postcode. 2. Derogatory descriptor for an *"average"* customer, whatever that may be; Joe Bloggs; John Doe; John Smith; supposed pig-ignorant mug who will buy our sub-standard product regardless of all evidence to the contrary. (*see Consumer-focused; Focus group*)

Clarity: 1. Clearness, of expression or water. 2. Total absence of clarity; opacity; obscurity; scrabbling around trying to find out the truth. (*see Focus; Obfuscation*)

Clear-cut: 1. Evident. 2. Vague as hell; trumped-up; biased; loaded to suit one's needs.

Clicks and mortar: 1. Related to online assets and retail estate. 2. Awful bastard son of *"bricks and mortar"*, in which the genuine components of a building have been twisted to suit online needs; the total value of our online assets is nothing, as is the value of our shops; inability to distinguish between the value of either. (*see Concretize; Foundations, lay the; Offline, let's take this*)

Close but no cigar: 1. Not bad, but you don't win a prize. 2. Utter second-rate rubbish; woefully inadequate; failing even to reach a very low standard; shoddy; crap.

Closer look, stand back and take a: 1. Curiously contradictory phrase suggesting that a broader view may allow greater understanding of the detail. 2. Supreme example of management bollocks, in which distant managers envy the detail shown by micro managers, and vice versa. (*see Big picture, Deep dive; Helicopter view; Loose-tight properties; Micromanaging; Marathon not a sprint, it's a; No stone unturned; Overview; Witch-hunt; Wood, can't see the _____ for the trees*)

Closure: 1. To declare the end of an issue; 2. Peculiar matrimonial Americanism originally referring to a person who is finally able to stop bleating about their ex and boring everyone rigid, including their therapist; business equivalent in which a member of staff simply will not stop referring to a long-gone disastrous project or obsolete working practice that went out with the ark. (*see Jobsworth*)

Clout: 1. To cuff stiffly, usually on the head; degree to which an executive can pack a metaphorical punch. 2. Dick-swinging bravado; testosterone-fuelled show of strength evident in any all-male boardroom; peacock-strutting display of power, often with no back-up whatsoever. (*see Cojones; Dick-swinging*)

Coalface: 1. The exposed seam of coal in a mine. 2. Patronizing management term for the environment in which the people who do all the work have to operate; bear pit; shit hole; dump; pressurized customer interface; the sharp end; appalling frontline job that no one should have to endure; sales region in Wales. (*see Frontline; Ground, on the*)

Coals, hauled over the: 1. Given a severe dressing down. 2. Humiliated in public in front of everyone who needs to know.

Coals, send _____ to Newcastle: 1. Something supplied where it is already plentiful. 2. Pointless duplication; misguided decision; adding resource where none is needed; attempt to fix something that isn't broken.

Coals, walk on hot: 1. Tread dangerously. 2. Embark on a perilous sequence of blunders, such as losing a major customer, insulting the Chairman and sleeping with the receptionist, often all in the same day. (*see Hand rails, hold the; Last chance saloon, drinking at the; Postal, go; Riding the razor blade; Saddle, cycling with no*)

Cocks on the block: 1. In an extremely uncomfortable position. 2. With genitals metaphorically on the chopping block, knife poised. (*see Backs to the wall; Back-to-back; Hand rails, hold the; Last chance saloon, drinking at the; Over a barrel; Postal, go; Riding the razor blade; Saddle, cycling with no*)

Cockup: 1. Something done badly. 2. Poor show; disaster; lousy job. (*see Pig's ear*)

Coffee, wake up and smell the: 1. Face up to reality. 2. Emerge from haze of self-delusion; stop pretending to have skills you don't possess; cease and desist from Nero-like delusions of power; resign and let someone properly qualified handle it. (*see Nero syndrome*)

Cohesive: 1. Sticking together. 2. All over the place; not joined together at all; random and unrelated, as in *"a cohesive package of measures"*.

Cojones: 1. Spanish word for testicles. 2. Sheer front; balls; guts; chutzpah; audacity. (*see Clout; Dick-swinging*)

Cold calling: 1. Soliciting people you have never met for business. 2. Relentlessly hard sell business approach; systematically telephoning hapless potential customers; doorstepping; chugging (*charity mugging*), usually in busy streets. (*see Chuggers; Doorstepped; Doorstopped; Hot lead*)

Collaboration: 1. Working together. 2. Totally shafting a colleague or sister company by pretending to work together whilst undermining their efforts and/or taking all the credit for anything good, and denying responsibility for anything bad. (*see Turf wars*)

Collars and cuffs, I bet the _____ don't match: 1. All is not what it seems. 2. Sleazy, sexist remark referring to a woman's hair colour being unlikely to match that of her pubic region; linguistic genre much used by greasy Terylene-clad salesmen who have never had a decent shag in their life; regular refuge of ugly, lecherous men often working the security night shift. (*see Kimono, open the; Matching luggage; Playtex strategy*)

Collateral: 1. Security pledged for a loan repayment; situated or running side by side, literally co-lateral. 2. Perfectly good word hi-jacked by Americans to denote a suite of stuff or materials (*no genuine dictionary contains this definition*); arsenal, and probably deployed by an arse; faux suggestion of a vast phalanx of resources when there are none; mock toolkit that is in fact empty. (*see Cross-collateralization; Tools, management, unique*)

Collect your P45: 1. Visit the finance department and pick up your last evidence of employment. 2. Take marching orders; move on; leave in disgrace; precursor to setting fire to the boss' desk and marching triumphantly to the pub.

Come a cropper: 1. Hurt oneself, or fail badly at something. 2. Cock it up completely; crash and burn; sustain severe injury (*often self-inflicted*) and report to hospital forthwith. (*see AWOL, go; Ballistic, go; Crash and burn; Fly in the face of; Postal, go; Radar, off; Rails, gone off the*)

Come on people: 1. Please back me up. 2. Plaintive request in the face of widespread derision, as in *"Come on people, all join hands in the team bonding game!"*; happy-clappy exhortation much loved of hippy HR managers. (*see Bean bags; Breakout groups; Off-site; Soft area*)

Come up to scratch: 1. Reach the required level. 2. Exasperated exhortation to reach the required level, for once in your life; desperate plea from boss to ineffective and feckless subordinate; set low standards for oneself and consistently fail to meet them; underachieve.

Comfort zone, out of one's: 1. Beyond the level or nature of work in which one feels comfortable and competent. 2. A tiny fraction of what a person is asked to do;

unpleasant sinking feeling that you haven't a clue what you are doing; blatantly ill-equipped; in a canoe without a paddle. (*see Micromanaging*)

Coming from, where I'm: 1. Direction of travel based on where I was before. 2. Directionally-challenged remark confusing opinion with physical position; this is my view and I wish to prevail over yours; I'm your boss so shut up and get on with it. (*see At, where I'm; SUMO*)

Coming or going, he doesn't know if he's: 1. He is confused, or dithering. 2. He's a blithering idiot; incompetent; indecisive; conflicted; self-styled *"entrepreneur"* who makes a lot of U-turns and then claims they were intentional *"pivots"*. (*see Evolving to meet customer demand; Pivot; Tweak; U-Turn*)

Commit, committed, commitment: 1. Pledge or align oneself to a particular cause. 2. Run a mile from any such agreement; use macho vocabulary to imply *"commitment"* whilst intending nothing of the sort; hang colleague out to dry by suggesting backing and then pulling it in a crucial meeting; quality perpetually demanded by macho Sales Directors but rarely delivered; principle that flies straight out of the window in the face of a job offer with a bigger salary.

Commoditized: 1. Turned into a commodity. 2. Horrible addition to the seemingly endless production line of Americanisms in which a perfectly good noun has once again been turned into a verb; paranoid (*or possibly quite true*) feeling that one's product is bog standard, despite brash marketing claims to be *"premium"*. (*see Concretize; Democratize; Diarize; -ize; Monetize; Premium; Socialize*)

Communication, lack of, plan, skills: 1. Convey something to someone else. 2. Total breakdown in understanding; complete failure to have a meeting of minds; static; hot air; piffle; conveying the opposite of what was intended. (*see Non-verbal; Static; White noise*)

Compatible, not: 1. Unable to exist together harmoniously. 2. Totally incompatible; at loggerheads; likely to come to blows; daggers drawn; full of hate for each other; extremely likely to take a swing after a few drinks (*see Breath of fresh air; Office party*)

Competencies, core: 1. Things a company or person can do properly. 2. Utterly bizarre extension of the word *"competence"*, in itself perfectly capable of conveying precisely the same meaning; stuff that any fool or organization worth its salt should be doing; basics; lowest common denominator activities to even warrant being in business in the first place; bog standard stuff. (*see Bridge too far; Capabilities; Core; CV; Knitting, stick to the*)

Competitive advantage, edge: 1. Something compelling that makes us better than our competitors. 2. Sinking feeling based on the dawning realization that we are clearly no better than our competitors; on further examination, alarming discovery that we are actually much worse than our competitors; trumped up piece of corporate puffery to claim competitive advantage where there patently is none. (*see Leverage*)

Competitive review: 1. Analysis of what your competitors are doing. 2. Paranoid sweep of what all the others are doing; flagrant theft of ideas from all competitors in the absence of having any decent ones of one's own; pointless collection of tedious data that will never lead to action. (*see Data dump*)

Competitiveness: 1. Desire to compete; winning drive. 2. Determination to win at all costs, regardless of the effect on others; ruthless streak; thoughtless quality; macho tendency to stomp all over colleagues, women, children, puppies and anything else that gets in one's way. (*see Ambition; Drive*)

Compliance: 1. Act of complying; acquiescence. 2. Shadowy department that insists that everyone *"follows the rules"*; total capitulation; giving in; getting shafted comprehensively; dropping one's trousers; losing out completely on price to the extent that one will make a whopping loss. (*see BOHICA; Drop our trousers; Jobsworth; Panjandrum*)

Conceptual thinking: 1. Thinking concerned with concepts. 2. Ludicrously abstract; so-called *"ideas"* that are impossible to implement; hot air; waffle; the entire output of an awayday; intellectually lazy bollocks with no practical application whatsoever. (*see Awayday; Bad idea, there's no such thing as a; Lateral thinking; Off-site*)

Concretize: 1. To turn into concrete; make solid. 2. Thoroughly annoying noun-turned-verb suggesting the solidification of an idea; pseudo construction industry term suggesting strength, usually where the idea is intrinsically flimsy; vain attempt to make a weak thought into a better one; yet another attempt to make a non-physical entity appear physical. (*see Clicks and mortar; Commoditized; Democratize; Diarize; Foundations, lay the; Granular, let's get; Monetize; Premium; Socialize*)

Conductor's baton, wave the: 1. To direct effectively; issue instructions. 2. Tenuous attempt to imbue the world of business with some of the subtleties of the world of music; futile suggestion that mundane business operations can somehow be compared with lyricism or melody; vainglorious claim by deluded boss to be *"conducting an orchestra"* when in reality he or she is in charge of a ragbag of greasy executives in a warehouse in Redcar. (*see Orchestra Model; Pull out all the stops*)

Conference call: 1. Phone conversation with more than two people. 2. Total waste of time in which several people in a badly decorated room address their remarks to a box in the middle of the table, loudly; superb opportunity to hit the mute button and spend an hour looking at porn; excuse to do nothing in bursts of 15 minutes, interspersed with an occasional comment such as *"I completely concur with David on this – we've had exactly the same experience here in the UK"*; technique designed to assert authority over executives in a different time zone without the faff of having to get on a plane and visit them in person. (*see Head office, I'm from _____ and I'm here to help*)

Connect with our audience: 1. Have a customer pay attention or react in some way to one's marketing. 2. Catch-all wibble to suggest some sort of emotional connection with customers; concept that becomes more and more improbable the less interesting a sector is, as in *"Come on guys, we really need to connect with our audience over these panty pads!"* (*see Consumer-focused; Customer experience*)

Connectivity: 1. State of connecting. 2. Ubiquitous term describing things that join together, particularly in technology companies; obsession with joining everything together. (*see Joined-up thinking; Seamless; Segue*)

Consensus: 1. Widespread agreement. 2. Widespread disagreement; anarchy; what the boss says. (*see Bun fight*)

Consigliere: 1. Adviser or counsellor to the boss. 2. Rather unnerving lifting of mafia term to refer to what should be quite innocent advisory board duties; hints of the mob and nefarious dealings. (*see Consultant; Non-exec*)

Constantly striving: 1. Trying all the time. 2. Being very trying all the time; dreary over-claim suggesting that the company thinks about its customers incessantly. (*see Always on; Continual improvement; Expectations, exceeding; Passion, passionate; Sun, the _____ never sets at; 24/7/365; Work-life balance*)

Consultant: 1. A specialist who gives expert advice. 2. Charlatan who charges a fortune for simply chatting; silver-haired eminence grise who cruises their former industry dispensing pearls of apparent wisdom; person with no executive responsibility or accountability at all; shadowy septuagenarian who really should have hung up his boots years ago; annoying occasional presence at advisory board meetings who refuses to write anything down lest it destroy the conversation flow, and then fails to remember to do any of the items discussed. (*see Consigliere; Non-exec*)

Consultation period: 1. Time span in which discussions can be had. 2. Time in which no discussions are had at all; silent spell when all those due to be axed are kept in the dark and ignored; frustrating month for management in which all the people they have decided to fire are annoyingly still in the building. (*see Axe, face the; Banana skin, political; Can, carry the; Decruit; Downsize*)

Consumer-focused: 1. Concentrating on what customers want. 2. Ignoring what people want whilst claiming rapt attention; incapable of having an original idea before asking a group of housewives in Bromley. (*see -centred, -centric; Clapham omnibus, man on the; Connect with our audience; Constantly striving; Customer experience; Focus group*)

Contact report. 1. Record of meeting between two parties. 2. Fantastic work of fabrication that bears no relation at all to what was discussed; heavily-biased representation of the issues at hand; close cousin of Tolstoy's *War and Peace* outlining in minute detail a near-verbatim account of immensely tedious meeting. (*see Arse covering; Call report*)

Context, the power of: 1. Significant influence of circumstances on subject matter. 2. Brilliant deception in which style overcomes substance; spectacular charade disguising utter lack of content; any presentation by an advertising agency.

Contiguous niches: 1. Series of small pockets that join together. 2. Forlorn effort to suggest that a few patches of hopeful activity can somehow be viewed as a universal success; deliberate use of an on obscure adjective in order to imply competence. (*see Coterminous; Long tail, the; Niche, carve out a, market _____*)

Continuous improvement: 1. Getting better all the time. 2. Consistent underachievement; relentless programme of HR initiatives designed to buck up an ineffectual workforce; work in progress. (*see Always on; Constantly striving; CPD; Expectations, exceeding; 24/7/365; Sun, the _____ never sets at*)

Control freak: 1. Executive who cannot delegate. 2. Executive who cannot delegate due to (a) a fear that everyone else will discover how mundane their work is or (b) an unstinting belief that they are the only person capable of doing something. (*see Arse covering; Autonomy; Ballbreaker; Bottleneck; Comfort zone; Micromanaging; Nutcracker; Rottweiler*)

Cooking on gas: 1. Performing really well. 2. Giving the impression of outstanding forward motion, but only because the job is piss-easy to do. (*see ABC, easy as; Art form, got it down to an; Falling off a log*)

Cook the books: 1. Move money around to make things look better. 2. Lie comprehensively about projected income to justify bonuses for the directors or impress ignorant shareholders. (*see Above board; Black arts; Calibrate; Crunch the numbers; Fiscal juggling; Massage the numbers; Numbers, the*)

Core: 1. The innermost part of something; the bit in the middle. 2. Lazy catch-all for anything routinely done; dull, workaday; perfectly serviceable as a noun but sorely abused as an adjective, as in *"Guys, let's stick to our core beliefs here"*. (*see Competencies; Knitting, stick to the; Non-core; Principle, core*)

Corporate governance: 1. Correct and proper running of a company. 2. Flabby and pompous phrase that somehow tries to raise the status of running a company to that of running a nation.

Cost-effective: 1. Good value. 2. We screw our suppliers so hard that we make a massive profit and they can barely eat. (*see BOHICA*)

Coterminous: 1. Having a common boundary. 2. Colliding nastily. (*see Contiguous niches; Niche, carve out a, market _____*)

Cover all the bases: 1. Be prepared for any eventuality. 2. Another in the seemingly never-ending supply of American sport phrases; fail to make a decision. (*see Ballpark figure; Zone, in the*)

CPD: 1. Continuous Professional Development. 2. Erratic, occasional bursts of staff motivation; naked favouritism shown to a favoured few. (*see Continuous improvement; Fast track*)

Crack it: 1. Break the code. 2. Rather over dramatic way of saying that you have worked out how to do something, or completed even the simplest of tasks.

Crafting, it needs a bit of: 1. Further work is required on this. 2. This is sub-standard rubbish and needs to be done again. (*see Bugs, iron out the; Drawing board, back to the; Optimal; Sub-optimal; Tools, management, unique; Woodwork, spanners in the, spanners jumping out of the*)

Crash and burn: 1. Sustain impact, then burst into flames. 2. Fail spectacularly; fly high, then fall to earth; pride before a fall, followed by fall; public display of incompetence, preceded by hubristic claims of technical expertise. (*see Come a cropper; High risk; Maxed out; Needle, moving the; Needle, pushing the; Nightmare, utter; Plate spinning; Pushing the envelope; Wheels coming off; Wind, sailing close to the*)

Credo: 1. Belief or principle. 2. Self-aggrandizing word, much loved by advertising agencies, to explain what they stand for; how we do it round here.

Crisis: 1. Crucial development or unhelpful period. 2. Permanent state of affairs in many companies; meltdown; systemic inability to cope.

Criteria, key: 1. Some important points. 2. One criterion after another in a seemingly never-ending list; not *"key"* at all; cobbled together ragbag of disparate thoughts masquerading as a brief. (*see Key; Word dump*)

Critical path: 1. Timing plan. 2. Perfectly ordinary sequence of events that should occur in order to make something happen effectively; not critical at all, in fact, quite humdrum and workaday; almost nothing to do with a path in the normal sense of the word.

Cross-collateralization: 1. Blending of various materials. 2. Woeful verbal car crash combining incorrect use of the word collateral, the classic American suffix –ize extended into an -ation, and a cross-prefix thrown in for good measure. (*see Collateral, -ize*)

Crunch the numbers: 1. Do some calculations. 2. Make a big deal out of doing some calculations; use a calculator; flounder around, having barely any capability at maths; design a ridiculously large spreadsheet to disguise the fact that the numbers are either unhelpful or unintelligible. (*see Analysis, paralysis by, in the final; Brain dump; Cook the books; Data dump; Fiscal juggling; Massage the numbers; Numbers, the*)

Crystal ball (vb.): 1. Predict the future. 2. Risible attempt to work out what will happen next, with absolutely no chance of getting it right; plaintive call to action all-too-familiar to economists and weathermen everywhere, as in *"We need to crystal ball this guys!"* (*see Black swan; Futureproof; Navel gazing; Strategy, strategize*)

CSR: 1. Corporate social responsibility; a policy explaining how a company conducts its business in an ethical and appropriate manner. 2. Fawning set of half-truths and broken promises that comes nowhere near explaining the full operational horror of what the company does; all-encompassing manifesto explaining whiter-than-white approach to everything from employee benefits to working conditions; joyous geographical trip around the globe showing delirious, exotic workers in conditions of sheer bliss; improbably equal set of photographs representing every race, colour and creed, all smiling by the company logo. (*see Exit interview; Transparency*)

Culture, company: 1. The atmosphere in a company. 2. Curious, ethereal attempt to describe what companies are like; strange belief that what people are like may have a bearing on whether they can do the job. (*see Grasping at fog; Vision, visioning; Values*)

Culture, Curved ball: 1. A ball that swerves in mid air. 2. Another baseball reference courtesy of the USA, referring to something that's quite tricky to deal with; nasty booby trap. (*see Ask, big; Bombs, box of; Catching a falling knife; Hospital pass; Poisoned chalice*)

Custodian: 1. Somebody looking after the welfare of something or someone. 2. Somebody totally ignoring the welfare of something or someone; just passing through; deriving maximum personal benefit and then sodding off; itinerant job hopper; self-appointed *"brand guardian"* who ruins it completely before being ceremonially fired. (*see Guardian, brand*)

Customer experience, -centric, -facing, -focused, journey, satisfaction, value: 1. Talking to customers, looking after them and making them happy. 2. Hotchpotch of drivel designed to convince customers that anyone gives a damn about them; not facing the customer at all, in fact probably looking the other way; self-deluding fabrication of so-called *"customer journey"* to suggest proper service; consistently low ratings for satisfaction and value. (*see Connect with our audience; Expectations, exceeding, failing to achieve, living up to, managing, meeting; Seamless*)

Cut our losses: 1. Quit whilst behind. 2. Compound our losses; go bust; fail; file for bankruptcy.

Cut through, cut-through: 1. Sever something. 2. Odious verb-cum-noun prevalent in the communications industry; strange allusion to media messages somehow being physically tangible, as in *"We need to cut through the clutter here guys"*; even worse, *"We need to generate cut-through"*, thus turning an active verb into a spurious noun.

Cutting edge: 1. The sharp edge of something like a knife. 2. Macho, semi-military descriptor to suggest that something is particularly advanced or ingenious, when it probably isn't; noun morphed into an adjective, as in *"This is truly cutting-edge technology, Malcolm"*, when referring to something perfectly straightforward such as a bicycle or paper clip. (*see Bleeding edge; Leading edge; Next-generation; Pioneering*)

CV: 1. Curriculum Vitae (Latin). 2. A total pack of lies and fabrication bearing no relation to the true (in)competence of the candidate. (*see Achilles heel; Blue-chip; Capabilities; Capability gap; Drop a ricket; FNG*)

Dd

Damage, collateral: 1. Unintentional damage caused to civilians and property by military action. 2. Disastrous chain reaction following an appalling blunder – easily capable of bringing an entire brand or company down if the person is stupid or clever enough, as in Leeson or Ratner.

Data dump: 1. Download of large amount of information. 2. Large scale vomiting of factoids or statistics without due heed for the intended audience, or indeed any useful outcome – much loved by researchers with only average intelligence. (*see Analysis, paralysis by, in the final; Brain dump; Competitive review; Crunch the numbers*)

Dead cat bounce: 1. Temporary recovery in prices after a substantial fall, but not a true recovery. 2. Futile attempt to suggest there is still potential in a project or product when the wheels fell off ages ago; desperately clinging on to any tiny glimpse of good news whilst simultaneously flying in the face of all rational information. (*see Entering a new plateau; Flatline; Negative growth, profit; SNAFU*)

Dead wood: 1. Arboreal matter that is no longer growing. 2. Any long-term colleague you genuinely dislike and would like to see fired, or an entire department meeting the same criteria.

Death by PowerPoint: 1. Extremely long and boring presentation. 2. Interminable drivel given credence by near-universal software package; default setting for all bad presenters who, on being asked to write a presentation, rush to their work station and immediately open a PowerPoint file called *"Presentation to X"*, without any thought about the line of argument; deck of impenetrable charts offered up by fawning management consultancy to justify exorbitant fee; receptacle for juvenile clip art; vehicle for thunderously boring research debrief; all-day briefing nightmare; cure for insomnia; showboater's paradise; colossal time wasting mechanism. (*see BlackBerry prayer; Bullet points; Full Monty, the; Kitchen sink; Meetings; Moi presentation*)

Decision maker, decision-making process: 1. An individual or system whose purpose is to decide what to do. 2. A dithering individual or neutered committee whose sole purpose is in fact to avoid decisive action. (*see Deconflicted*)

Deconflicted: 1. Free of conflict. 2. Emerging from a dark period of indecision and self-loathing. (*see Decision maker*)

Decruit: 1. Relieve of employment. 2. Fire; sack; physically eject from the building without warning; defenestrate spontaneously (*advertising industry only*). (*see Axe, face the; Defenestrate, defenestration; Delayering; Dejob; Downsize; Human resources; Phone list, go down the*)

Dedication: 1. Complete and wholehearted devotion. 2. Pathetic adherence to the corporate creed, and the working of inhumane hours, in the vain hope of a pay rise or viable pension.

Deep dive: 1. Close and detailed look. 2. Frantic plunge into the issues to see what exactly has gone so horribly wrong, usually following a holiday or sustained period of reckless neglect of a project. (*see Closer look, stand back and take a; Drains up, have the; Drill down; No stone unturned; Root-and-branch review; Witch-hunt*)

Deeply shallow: 1. Of nearly no substance. 2. Inspired oxymoron defining someone's complete lack of backbone or integrity, as in *"One thing one can say about Barry is that he is deeply shallow"*. (*see Aspirational*)

Defenestrate, defenestration: 1. The act of throwing someone out of a window. 2. Dismissal from a company by the same technique, sometimes followed by a range of office furniture and a pot plant; swift eviction method much loved by advertising agencies. (*see Alligators, up to my arse in; Ballistic, go; Bullet, get the; Chop, for the; Exit strategy; FIFO (2); Marching orders, get your; Mid-life crisis; Moon, barking at the, over the, through the; Postal, go; Radar, off; Rails, gone off the; Show the door*)

Dejob: 1. Remove from current job. 2. Construct a farrago of lies to suggest why one's current role is no longer valid, thereby justifying firing, redundancy or a move to the Faroe Islands, or Staines-on-Thames. (*see At a stroke; Axe, face the; Decruit; One fell swoop, in; Phone list, go down the*)

Delayering: 1. Taking away layers. 2. Firing everyone except the management. (*see Decruit; Dejob; Destaff*)

Delegate, delegation: 1. Pass on a job to a subordinate. 2. Get rid of entire workload to subordinates; do nothing; idle. (*see Buck stops here, the; Deploy energies, resources*)

Delighting customers: 1. Making customers happy. 2. Annoying customers over a sustained period through persistent pestering. (*see Customer journey; Desired consumer response; Expectations, exceeding; Loyalty beyond reason, customer, staff, team*)

Deliver: 1. Cause to arrive. 2. Often, completely fail to arrive, as in fail to deliver.

Deliverables: 1. Things that should be delivered. 2. Condemning rap sheet of items that palpably failed to happen; wish list; wishful thinking; not a cat in hell's chance of occurring; much-abused default position for lazy managers wishing to appear practical, as in *"What are the deliverables on this guys?"*

Delivery of outputs: 1. Things that should be delivered. 2. Even longer-winded and more pointless phrase for stuff that hasn't been done. (*see Inputs; Outputs*)

Democratize, democratizing the idea: 1. Make the people's property. 2. *"Down with the kids"* verb invented by self-styled *"hip populists"* in social media, having established that all companies and capitalists are bad; *"democratizing the idea"* returns power to the people, apparently. (*see Commoditize; Digital native; -ize; Monetize; Productize*)

Demographic: 1. Relating to demography. 2. Hybrid noun referring to a demographic segment, as in *"Hey guys let's not forget which demographic we are targeting here"*. (*see Target*)

Deploy energies, resources: 1. Decide how to spend time or effort. 2. Put feet up and get everyone else to do the work. (*see Delegate, delegation*)

Derive synergies: 1. Create benefit(s) from working well together. 2. Squeeze extra profit out of already strained workforce by combining two departments and sacking half the people. (*see Synergy*)

Desired consumer response: 1. How a customer will ideally respond. 2. Vacuous wish list of reactions that will never come to pass. (*see Customer journey; Delight customers; Expectations, exceeding*)

Destigmatize: 1. Remove stigma from. 2. Try to resuscitate project or colleague when all hope of survival is long gone; attempt to improve image but actually make it worse. (*see Turd, polishing a*)

Destaff: 1. Reduce number of employees. 2. Fire as many people as possible, as fast as possible. (*see ABC session; Defenestrate, defenestration; Decruit; Dejob; Delayering; Marching orders, get your; Phone list, go down the*)

Details, god is in the: 1. Phrase coined by Mies van der Rohe to suggest that the importance of detail cannot be overstated. 2. Mindless, glib parroting of same phrase by smug managers when horribly out of their depth; desperate attempt to plaster over the cracks of vacuous waffle outburst with a semblance of practicality; massive hospital pass masquerading as a compliment. (*see Buck, the _____ stops here; Hospital pass*)

Development: 1. Unfinished work; new event. 2. Work that will never be finished because it is, and always will be, *"in development"*; nasty turn of events that will ruin everything. (*See Black swan; WIP*)

Devil and the deep blue sea, between the: 1. On the horns of an uncomfortable dilemma. 2. Clichéd excuse of all lazy sales executives; suggestion of conflict where none exists; weary bleating of executive who has never seen (a) the devil or (b) the deep blue sea, having never left Solihull.

Devil's avocado: 1. Fruit owned, or indeed possessed by, Lucifer. 2. Variation on devil's advocate; deliberate taking of the opposite view; attempt to diffuse uncomfortable conflict in meeting, as in *"I'm just trying to play devil's avocado for a minute here guys"*.

Dial up. 1. Telephone a number. 2. Irritating modern expression for increasing the strength of something; much used in the world of media, as in *"We need to dial up this TV plan guys"*; randomly used regardless of resources, budget or any reference to investment likelihood. (*see Bucks, bang for your*)

Dialogue (vb.): 1. To talk with. 2. Redundant noun-cum-verb, as in *"I'm going to dialogue with Nigel on this one tomorrow"*. (*see Triangulate*)

Dialogue, continuous consumer, meaningful: 1. Conversation with customer or colleague, intended to have some meaning. 2. Intersecting monologues; no conversation at all; shouting into the void. (*see Bark into the wind, up the wrong tree; Human wind tunnel*)

Diarize: 1. To put in a diary. 2. Lamentable *"action oriented"* verb created by Americans. (*see Commoditize; Democratize, -ize; Herding cats; Locked into; Monetize*)

Dick-swinging: 1. Moving genitals from side to side. 2. Overbearingly macho, despite possessing rather small genitals; priapic posturing; peacock strutting; boasting. (*see Clout; Nero syndrome*)

Difference, make a: 1. Make a difference. 2. Pretend to make a difference without influencing anything at all; talk about *"making a difference"* without actually making a difference.

Digital native: 1. Person, usually young, fully-versed in all matters relating to the Internet and modern technology, having grown up with it. 2. Potentially pejorative, borderline racist term for a hairy bloke called Dean who skateboards dramatically into the office, and then sits in the corner with his headphones on all day furiously tapping on a keyboard; any person who knows more about the Interweb than you do. (*see Democratize; Drive traffic; Free-roaming experience; iGod; Monetize; On-rails experience; Productize; User experience*)

DILLIGAF: 1. Do I look like I give a f**k? 2. Profane rhetorical question disguised as acronym and designed to humiliate the listener absolutely. (*see Enlighten me; FOFO; Follow me, do you; Lips, read my; Respect, with*)

Dinosaur: 1. Prehistoric animal. 2. Ancient or old-before-time member of staff who keeps referring to "the good old days", or beginning sentences with *"Of course in my day..."* (*see Jobsworth; Halcyon days; Rose-tinted*)

Direction, lack of; strategic: 1. Intended line of travel; vector; course. 2. Abstract and diffuse notion designed to suggest that everyone knows what they are doing, when they probably don't. (*see Aims; Grasping at fog; Objectives; Strategize*)

Disaster, total: 1. Mishap. 2. Meltdown; absolute failure; catastrophic collapse in capability. (*see Armageddon plan; Scorched earth policy*)

Disconnect: 1. To unplug an electric appliance. 2. Utter failure to connect; complete void in communication or understanding, as in *"Do we have a disconnect here, Colin?"*

Disinvestment: 1. Removal of funds. 2. Annual removal of funds at exactly the same moment after the traditional three-month budget bidding round; February 15th, after only six weeks of financial support; pulling the plug. (*see Dog, this is a*)

Disseminate: 1. To distribute or scatter about. 2. To vaguely announce; fail to announce at all.

Diversity: 1. Mixture of X and Y; varied mix. 2. Inability to hire anyone different to oneself; flagrant nepotism; refusal to accept findings of psychometric testing that suggests a broader blend in the team would be beneficial. (*see Broad church; Multicultural*)

DNA: 1. Deoxyribonucleic acid, the main constituent of chromosomes responsible for transmission of hereditary characteristics. 2. Intensely annoying shorthand to describe *"the character of a brand"*, as in *"The brand's DNA is crucial here guys"*. (*see Baked in; Brand strategist; Mission critical*)

Doable: 1. It can be done. 2. Sometimes offered in a genuine way, as in *"Yes Steve, that's definitely doable"*; more commonly used when it can technically be done but it's neither advisable nor likely to be any good, as in *"It's doable Jane, but it'll be crap"*. (*see Can do attitude*)

Dog, this is a: 1. Death knell for a product or brand after analysis using the Boston Consulting Group matrix deems it so. 2. It's rubbish, kill it now. (*see Disinvestment; Duck, lame*)

Dogs bark but the caravans move on, the: 1. Nothing really changes. 2. Amusing imagery of strays howling at a passing vehicle, as though it will make a difference; metaphor for the futility of much office work, as with *"The flies change but the shit stays the same"*.

Dog's bollocks: 1. Canine testicles. 2. Brilliant; superb; enviable, as in *"Can you lick yours then?"* (*see Bee's knees, it's the; Mustard, cut the, that's _____ that is*)

Done deal: 1. A deal that has been done. 2. Pipe dream; pie in the sky; categorically not in the bag; classic over-claim of Terylene-suited sales managers when returning from a meeting without a signed contract. (*see Door, knocking on an open; In the bag; Paving the way; Pipeline, in the; Seals, left them clapping like; Slam dunk*)

Doomsday scenario: 1. Moment of reckoning. 2. Ultra-bleak possibility of everything going horribly wrong; crisis planning; strong likelihood of total nightmare; time to leave the office rapidly, or resign. (*see Armageddon plan: Scenario, best-case, nightmare, worst-case*)

Door, knocking on the; pushing at an open: 1. Attempting something that will certainly receive a positive response. 2. Pride before a fall; unwarranted hubris of the over-confident salesperson; not in the bag at all; only a distant possibility. (*see Done deal*)

Doorstepped: 1. Caught at one's front door or unexpectedly in the street without prior warning. 2. Unnervingly intercepted by Bernadette from accounts when you least expect it; confronted at one's desk by her ample midriff, disconcertingly at face level. (*see Cold-calling; Doorstopped; Heavyweight*)

Doorstopped: 1. Wedged a door open. 2. Comprehensively blocked by Bernadette from accounts outside the gents in a tight space; prevented from escaping an unwanted conversation about a spreadsheet; total eclipse of the corridor. (*see Cold-calling; Doorstepped*)

Dosser: 1. Lazy person; idler. 2. 99% of any workforce, including the post room, maintenance, IT helpdesk, accounts, "human" resources, security staff, Managing Director and your boss.

Dotted line: 1. Line broken into a series of dashes. 2. Seemingly innocuous device found on organizational charts that wreaks utter havoc by leaving all concerned totally confused about who reports to whom; source of hundreds of office brawls. (*see Hierarchy; Matrix; Non-hierarchical; Organogram; Pecking order; Pull rank; Snake's honeymoon*)

Double-loop learning: 1. Management process coined by Harvard professor Chris Argyris in the 1970s in which executives continually question the policies within which their decision-making power is constrained. 2. Anarchy in which no one does what they are told; overwhelming feeling that the law is an ass, and that you are absolutely right; cocky, self-righteous attitude of new graduate who believes they know everything, and that the world owes them a living; privately-educated toff with similar beliefs.

Double whammy: 1. Negative impact, occurring twice. 2. Sucker punch; knockout blow; straight in the slats immediately after receiving a hit to the slats; one on each testicle; minimal chance of recovery; down and out for good; the end. (*see Sucker punch*)

Doughnut rather than the hole, it would be wise to concentrate on the: 1. Look at the relevant bit of the problem. 2. Slightly surreal, semi-culinary analogy to allude to the irrelevant part of an issue; stop talking about the stuff that doesn't matter and get to the point; this person is way off brief. (*see Waffle*)

Downside: 1. Disadvantage; the con to the pro; the bit where things go wrong. 2. Overwhelming reason why something should certainly not be done; pitfall; certainty of failure; long list of cons that heavily outweigh any suggested pro. (*see Upside*)

Downsize: 1. Reduce the size of, usually workforce. 2. Weasel word to disguise anything from mild reduction to total annihilation; dastardly retention of the word *"size"* in the body of the new word allows macho managers to imply that scale remains part of the action, whereas in fact it doesn't. (*see Decruit; Lay off; Negative growth, profit; Quantitative easing*)

Draconian: 1. Harsh, severe (*after the strict rules of Draco, Greek lawmaker*). 2. All-encompassing; total and utter; everyone out; last one out turn the lights off; complete company or departmental meltdown; factory closure or punitive outsourcing decision (*see Across the board, right; Armageddon plan; Scorched earth policy; Swingeing cuts*)

Draining the swamp: 1. Turning boggy area into dry land. 2. Purging company or department of horribly poisonous member of staff; weeding out constant moaners; working out weasels who smile obsequiously to members of management whilst slagging them off in private; purge; cleanse. (*see Bad apple*)

Drains up, have the: 1. Examine sewage system. 2. Find out what's really going on in a company; discover nasty truth of working reality; pay attention for the first time; annual review with unpleasant consequences. (*see Deep dive; Drains up, have the; Drill down; Flush out; Forensic, send it down to the boys in; Lift up a rock; No stone unturned; Root-and-branch review; Warts and all; Witch-hunt*)

Drawing board, back to the: 1. Return to the original design or blueprint. 2. Begin again, having got nowhere; complete rethink; start from scratch; write off millions of investment money having made the wrong choice; plaintive cry of New Product Development managers from Penzance to Preston, as in *"Right guys, it's back to the drawing board!"* (*see Back to basics; Bugs, iron out the; Crafting, it needs a bit of; Evolving to meet customer demand; Optimal; Rebrand; Redesign; Sub-optimal*)

Dream team: 1. Assembly of the best possible people for the job. 2. Random ragbag of semi-qualified personnel; anyone who isn't on holiday or off sick; whoever is left after we fired everyone; two trainees and an overstretched director; the tea lady and the bloke on security; two people who know nothing whatsoever about the subject matter but are quite good at finding things on the Web; interns being paid nothing; B, C or any other lower grade team. (*see A-team, this calls for the*)

Dress to impress: 1. Put on clothes that will create a favourable impression. 2. Choose completely the wrong suit for a crucial meeting, such as pinstripe to meet a whizzy entrepreneur or a purple one with an eerie sheen for an investment bank; ill-advised selection of *"office jester"* tie for annual pay review. (*see Casting; Minister for fun*)

Drill down: 1. Drill down. 2. Find out what's really happening; discover the awful reality; usually, the first time that the Chief Executive has realized the true nature of the business they are running; moment of reckoning; dawning of real understanding; find out that the business is fundamentally flawed, or dangerously teetering on the edge of bankruptcy. (*see Drains up, have the; Granular; Needs and wants; No stone unturned; Root-and-branch review*)

Drive: 1. Golf shot; to operate a car (vb.); ambition. 2. Naked ambition; preparedness to tread on any colleague to win or be promoted; machismo; greed; selfishness;

self-centred motivation at any price; undesirable quality in a colleague, but much-prized by macho Sales Directors, as in *"Yes, Martin's figures are good but has he got the drive to be regional manager?" (see Ambition; Competitiveness; Driven)*

Drive a coach and horses through: 1. Find many flaws in an argument. 2. Totally dismantle; humiliate a rival in an important meeting; tear to shreds, piece by piece; reduce subordinate to tears; savagely deploy superior intellect to undermine less bright colleague or customer; publicly execute.

Drive it home: 1. Transport unspecified object to its dwelling, probably in a car. 2. Repeat a point again and again, even though everyone else in the room knows precisely what you are saying; drone on; preach; incessantly say the same thing over and over after realizing that you only have one point and have run out of material. *(see Waffle; Word dump)*

Driven. 1. Taken somewhere, perhaps by a chauffeur or friend. 2. Possessed of *"drive"* (qv.); overtly ambitious, but only on behalf of oneself; adjective describing a total arsehole whom everyone universally despises; narcissistic; loathsome; riddled with self-perception problems; determined to own a Porsche by the age of 30; prone to celebrate sales achievements by spending thousands on champagne and cocktails; inclined to show off and humiliate as many other people as possible, including wife, children and parents; twat-like. *(see Ambition; Competitiveness; Drive; Hungry, are they _____ enough?)*

-driven: 1. Suffix denoting something that has been pushed in a certain direction, such as change-driven or market-driven. 2. Egregiously bad bastardization of almost any word that requires macho turbo charging (qv.); devious method for changing any verb into an adjective, as in needs-driven, consumer-driven, web-driven and so on, ad infinitum; possible technique for retrieving some humour from a bad situation, as in idiot-driven, boss-driven, tosser-driven, etc. *(see -centred, -centric; -focused, people-, goal-; –oriented; Results-driven; Turbo charge)*

Drive traffic: 1. Encourage quantity of customers to use or do something. 2. Pointless pseudo-automotive phrase usually associated with websites, as in *"We need to drive traffic to our site guys!"*; curious suggestion that we are somehow driving everyone else's cars, whilst presumably driving our own; odd implication that the collective effect of customers' buying decisions is akin to the flow of vehicles on a road; staple phrase of hairy computer coders throughout Shoreditch. *(see Digital native)*

Drivers, key: 1. People operating vehicles, presumably in possession of an ignition key; important influences that make things happen. 2. Hideous catch-all phrase to describe anything and everything to do with how a market works; random hotchpotch of stuff to do with the matter in hand; lazy, default phrase for Marketing Director or advertising executive referring to things that may or may not make a difference; not drivers at all, and certainly not "key"; passive constituent parts that have no bearing on anything at all. (see Change drivers; Key criteria; KPIs)

Drop a ricket; 1. Make a mistake. 2. Lose it completely; fail to live up to boss' expectations; fail to display any of the basic qualities claimed at interview. (*see Ball, take one's eye off the; Bazooka after a fly, we're not going to send a; Beans, spill the; CV; Drop the ball; Platform, eat one's own*)

Drop our trousers: 1. Take our pants off (USA). 2. Reduce price significantly; make a whopping loss; offer a loss leader in the hope of more profitable work to come; get comprehensively shafted. (*see BOHICA; Compliance; Flexible; Pants down, caught with our; Sprat to catch a mackerel*)

Drop the ball: 1. Relinquish control at a crucial moment. 2. Fail miserably; blow it; demand greater responsibility and then fail to deliver; be found in the pub when supposed to be in a crucial meeting; not turn up; struggle to cope with a delegated task. (*see Ball, take one's eye off the; Drop a ricket; Hospital pass; Pass the baton*)

Dropping grenades in fishponds: 1. Detonating hand-held incendiary devices in small aquatic environments; generating a dramatic outcome via use of excessive firepower. 2. Causing absolute chaos; destroying everything one touches; being a total liability; wreaking havoc in a department or company; slashing and burning; changing all the rules on first day in job; acting before taking advice; executing decrees without considering the possible consequences; being a thoughtless prat. (*see Blue touch paper, light the; Bull in a china shop; Gung ho*)

Duck, lame: 1. Aquatic bird that has trouble walking. 2. Project that will never get off the ground; no-hoper; doomed case; non-starter; sudden realization that the company's star project or product is deficient; exasperated cry of Chief Executive on discovering that Project Dominatrix is a comprehensive failure and has soaked up millions in investment money. (*see Dog, this is a; SNAFU*)

Ducking and diving: 1. Deploying a range of evasion techniques. 2. Bobbing and weaving; hiding in the toilets so as not to bump into boss; refusing to answer the phone to suppliers needing to be paid; avoiding client interaction of any kind in case one is found wanting; nipping off to the pub rather than facing the music; throwing a sickie; wandering around the park trying to work out how not to be fired on returning to the office.

Ducks in a row, get our: 1. Take some aquatic birds (that we own) and arrange them neatly; make sure we know what we are doing. 2. Rush around in a blind panic trying to create some vague semblance of order; generate an illusion of organization where there is none; bluff; lie; pretend we know what we're doing when we patently don't; frantically draft an impressive looking chart that suggests structure, rigour and process. (*see Act together, getting our _____: Hymn sheet, singing from the same; Realignment; Wavelength, on the same, not on the same; Wildebeest in a row, has the lion got his*)

Dumbing down: 1. Making simpler. 2. Making simpler because we don't understand it; making simpler because our customers don't understand it; making simpler because no one understands it; make simplistic because everyone is too dim to get it when it's actually very simple; drawing a childish diagram because the words are just too much, frankly.

Dyke, finger in the: 1. Small intervention holding back what could be a massive flood. 2. Digit ill-advisedly inserted into lesbian; sticking plaster approach to business; problem about to explode; hopelessly ill-equipped solution to a problem; bomb waiting to go off. (*see Bombs, box of*)

Dynamic: 1. Concerned with energy. 2. Lacking in any form of dynamism whatsoever; listless; of a product or person, inert; the opposite of what is claimed on a CV, as in *"Dynamic personality"*; Bernard from accounts, who likes to push the boat out with a half of bitter on pay day.

Ee

Ear to the ground: 1. Well informed. 2. Phenomenally nosey.

Earn-out period: 1. Time during which the price of a company sold will eventually be paid. 2. Shorter-than-expected passage of time during which the person who sold the company walks out in disgust at the antics of the new owners, and simultaneously loses more than half of what they agreed to sell it for.

Ease the throttle back: 1. Reduce speed. 2. Skive; neglect; take the piss; ignore; skim; cut corners in the hope of getting away with it.

Eastern front, this is like the _____ when the bullets didn't turn up: 1. Archaic military reference to Napoleonic or World War in which troops did not have the right equipment. 2. Any occasion on which the team is woefully under-equipped. (*see Paper cup, here's a _____, there's a tidal wave coming; Pathologist's interest; Titanic, rearranging the deckchairs on the*)

Easy answers, there are no: 1. This is actually quite difficult. 2. I haven't got a clue what I'm talking about, but I don't want anyone to rumble it so I am using a broad platitude as a distraction. (*see Quick fix; Magic ingredient, there is no*)

Easy tiger: 1. Calm down. 2. *"I know we encourage blind enthusiasm round here but now you're getting on my nerves, so shut up!"* (*see Can do attitude*)

EBITDA: 1. Earnings Before Interest, Taxes, Depreciation and Amortization. 2. Any fabricated figure that makes it looks as though profits are healthy, regardless of a range of skeletons in cupboards. (*see Fiscal juggling; Skeletons in the cupboard*)

Educating consumers: 1. Letting customers know what we offer. 2. Patronizing the people who buy our products, because we are much more intelligent than they are.

EDLP: 1. Everyday Low Pricing. 2. Cheap tat.

Ego: 1. The self of an individual. 2. Massively over-inflated opinion of oneself, most commonly fuelled by status, power, money, perceived gonad size or the sycophancy of subordinates. (*see Brown-nosing*)

Effectiveness: 1. Degree to which something has an effect. 2. *"Professional"* word much loved by creative industries desperately trying to prove that they are indeed professional; broad term that usually yields no quantification; pseudo-rigorous hint at return on investment when in all probability there is none. (*see ROI*)

Efficiency drive: 1. Concerted effort to be more efficient. 2. Massive purge of everything; decimation of anything within reach; sacking of entire workforce; disposal of all factories and real estate; cancelling of all contracts; screwing every supplier; pawning of desk lamps; selling of grandmother and office cat. (*see Armageddon plan; Efficiencies, finding; Scorched earth policy*)

Efficiencies, finding: 1. Discovering ways to run a business more efficiently. 2. Deviously seeking out more ways to cut costs to the bone; freezing all pay rises; refusing to sign expense forms; allowing dilapidation of offices; failing to replace broken sign over entrance to office; downgrading all international travel to economy class; insisting salesmen sleep in their cars rather than check in to a hotel; cancelling office party; giving oneself a pay rise and no one else. (*see Efficiency drive*)

80/20 rule: 1. The Pareto principle, named after the 19th-century professor who spotted that the majority of activity in most markets was accounted for by a minority of operators. 2. Faux mathematical platitude that frequently bears no relation to the matter in hand at all; brilliant catch-all for innumerate sales people wishing to add a dash of quantification to a meeting, as in *"Of course, this is the old 80-20 rule isn't it guys?"*, when it's actually nothing of the sort. (*see Peter principle, the*)

Elasticity: 1. Stretchiness; flex. 2. Scope to wriggle out of almost anything; superb cover word for reneging on everything that was agreed last week; massive downgrading of forecast or target; weasel word to escape from any awkward situation, as in *"Well naturally there's a certain amount of elasticity in those figures, Brian."* (*see Flexible, flexibility*)

Elephant in the room: 1. Big issue that is being ignored. 2. The main point of almost every meeting that is never discussed, such as catastrophic sales figures, or the fact that the Chief Executive is paid millions for doing sod all whilst everyone else works like a slave for a pittance. (*see Emperor's new clothes; Fat man in the canoe; White elephant*)

Eleventh hour, at the: 1. We have barely any time left. 2. I am pathologically incapable of doing anything until the very last minute. (*see A-team, this calls for the; Cavalry over the hill; Essay crisis*)

Email. 1. Electronic communication. 2. Fantastic medium with which to delegate and abdicate all responsibility. (*see BCC; CC; Voice mail*)

Embedding: 1. To fix firmly in a surrounding solid mass. 2. Verb borrowed from the construction industry in a vain attempt to give solidity to ephemeral ideas such as culture and creativity, as in *"We really need to embed these values guys!"*

EMEA: 1. Shorthand for Europe, Middle East and Africa. 2. Job title offering the broad excuse to fly round Europe and the Middle East hurling abuse at the locals and surreptitiously shagging well-stacked hookers, or drinking illicit booze in gambling dens. (*see APAC*)

Emotional intelligence: 1. Awareness of one's own emotions and those of others. 2. Curiously fluffy phrase much-loved of HR personnel from Land's End to John o' Groats; touchy-feely; technically incompetent but 'really good with people'; vague excuse for being nice and useless at the same time, as in *"I know Jane has her weaknesses but she has high emotional intelligence."* (*see Empathy; Minister for fun; Touchy-feely*)

Empathy, empathetic: 1. The power of understanding someone else's feelings. 2. Strange connective quality, usually offered by Barbara from Human Resources; endless ability to have cups of tea and chat; adjective describing the broad phenomenon that is encapsulated by the phrase *"Let's sit down and talk about it"*; annoying ability to see everyone else's point of view; total inability to have a point of view; vicarious living of office life entirely through the actions of others; lack of originality and character; sympathetic but not really cut out for any particular job function. (*see Emotional intelligence; Minister for fun*)

Emperor's new clothes: 1. Short story by Hans Christian Andersen featuring a suit whose material is invisible to those unfit for their positions. 2. Hubris of many senior executives; inability to realize one is metaphorically naked in front of colleagues and clients; titanic self-delusion; failure to spot the blindingly obvious; flat refusal to confront the truth; delusional stupidity of the highest order. (*see Elephant in the room*)

Empire building: 1. Increasing power and land ownership on a large scale. 2. Nakedly trying to be in charge of as many people, and as much budget, as possible; obsessed with numbers, as in size of workforce who report to you; power crazy; prone to exaggeration at interview or on CV, as in *"I have 10,000 direct reports"*. (*see Dick-swinging; Nero syndrome*)

Empower: 1. Give someone the power or authority to do something. 2. Do nothing of the sort; suggest autonomy whilst constantly peering over someone's shoulder; offer power and simultaneously take it away; undermine; erode; flatter to deceive; deceive outright; over-claim; overstep one's brief; pass the buck. (*see Air cover; Buck, pass the; Enablement; Hospital pass; Micromanaging; Riot act, read the*)

Enablement: 1. Provision of the adequate means, opportunity or authority to do something. 2. Nothing of the sort; fail to back up or protect properly; permission to hang oneself; hoisting by petard, not usually one's own; opportunity to be ritually humiliated under the guise of new responsibility; poisoned chalice. (*see Air cover; Empower; Hoist with one's own petard; Poisoned chalice*)

End of play: 1. When a theatrical production has finished; after everyone has left the office. 2. At the very last minute; not today, tomorrow in fact; never; at some unspecified point in the future, maybe; broad cover-up for hoping that the requester will forget what they have asked for, as in *"I'll get that over to you by the end of play, Steve"*. (*see At the end of the day; At this moment in time; At this point in time; Put to bed*)

End-to-end: 1. From one end to the other. 2. Possessing significant gaps; patchy; hastily cobbled together; apparently comprehensive, but not really, as in an *"end-to-end user experience"*. (*see Seamless*)

End user: 1. Someone who uses something. 2. Pointless modifier to a perfectly good word; no different from a *"beginning user"*; a user, full stop. (*see End-end user*)

End-end user: 1. User at the very end of the process. 2. Even more pointless modifier to a perfectly good word; no different from a *"beginning user"* either; a user, full stop; additionally annoying trumped-up adjective to suggest that the user at the end is strangely not at the end at all, but some kind of false one, thereby requiring another end, called an end-end. (*see End user*)

Enduring: 1. Lasting a long time. 2. Short-lived; ephemeral; fly by night; fair-weather; flaky; self-serving and fame-seeking, as in *"What's our enduring legacy here guys?"*

Enemy, sleeping with the: 1. Procreating, or possibly just dormant with, an adversary. 2. Utterly unscrupulous; happy to do business with anyone just to gain a sale or promotion; amoral; immoral; illegal; uncaring; doing anything for a legover. (*see Collars and cuffs; Get into bed with; Kimono, open the; Matching luggage; Scratch my back and I'll scratch yours*)

Energies: 1. Sum total of vigour or vitality. 2. Woeful Americanism that turns a perfectly good word, energy, into an unnecessary plural; peculiar office-based life force that bears no relation to one's home-based vim level; weirdly fluctuating indicator of output that vacillates between full throttle and can't be arsed, depending on a range of factors including hangovers, looming pay day, impending appraisal or resignation, day of week, time of day or distraction by large-breasted new receptionist. (*see Geography, geographies*)

Engage, engaged, engagement: 1. To involve. 2. Straightforward verb now transmogrified into a grotesque bastard son of its original form; *"customer engagement"* has nothing to do with an impending marriage, but simply refers to their paying attention; *"engaging the staff and stakeholders"* simply means getting them to agree to something as opposed to rejecting it outright. (*see Stakeholder*)

Engender: 1. Bring about or give rise to. 2. Weasel word for bring about or give rise to, as in *"We really need to engender customer loyalty guys"*; start; begin; get on with; persuade; do something; get going; pull one's finger out. (*see Pull your finger out*)

Enhance, enhancement: 1. To intensify or increase in quality 2. Annoying verb or descriptor to suggest that something is somehow better or more *"premium"* than it probably is; redundant modifier, as in *"enhanced outcomes"* and *"product enhancements"*; direct substitute for improve or improvement. (*see Premium*)

Enlighten me: 1. Increase my understanding. 2. Hugely patronizing imperative that aims to assert the intellectual superiority of the asker; shades of the enlightenment, or some higher power or deity; roughly translates as *"I am a lot cleverer than you but if you really must say something I suppose I'll have to indulge you, you dimwit"*. (*see Aha moment; Follow, do you; FMF; Lips, read my; Respect, with; Teach your grandmother to suck eggs, don't, would never, would you; Word dump*)

Ensuing: 1. Following. 2. Slightly more pompous and smug than simply following, as in *"The ensuing carnage wasn't pretty"* when describing a nasty round of blood-letting, or the rather dreadful *"What implications will be ensuing from this?"*

Entering a new plateau: 1. Flatlining again. 2. Stasis; nothing happening; business as usual; stagnant; lifeless; moribund business performance; near terminal. (*see Dead cat bounce; Flatline; Negative growth; SNAFU*)

Entrepreneur, entrepreneurial: 1. A businessperson who takes risks, from the French *entreprendre*, to undertake. 2. Tremendously over-used term to describe anyone who runs a small business, or who has made a staggering number of cockups before getting it right, if at all; smug and self-deluding personal introduction at networking meetings, as in *"Pleased to meet you, I'm an entrepreneur!"*; ubiquitous descriptor for any perfectly ordinary person running a business from home. (*see Coming or going, he doesn't know if he's; Marketing guru; Multitasking; Pivot*)

Environment, business, challenging: 1. External conditions or surroundings. 2. Vastly over-used word to describe the context in which business is being conducted; suggestion that the business is operating on a far greater scale than is truly the case; desperate attempt to imply that the company trades beyond Rochdale, or the panty pad market, as in *"This is a really challenging environment"*; approximate translation: things are difficult at the moment. (*see Battleground; Jungle out there, it's a; Out there*)

Equity, brand: 1. What a brand might be worth. 2. Finger in the air guesstimate of value in order to inflate the worth of a company's intangible assets, having sold all tangible assets; comprehensive guesswork; shareholder ruse to fleece buyer for higher price; fabrication.

Essay crisis: 1. Cramming too much work into too little time. 2. Continuing utterly flawed student cramming behaviour into (so-called) professional work life, working through the night fuelled only by a range of semi-legal substances. (*see Cavalry over the hill; Eleventh hour, at the; ETA; Maxed out; Pushing the envelope; Needle, pushing the*)

ETA: 1. Estimated time of arrival. 2. Whenever; when I get round to it; possibly never. (*see ASAP; Eleventh hour, at the; Essay crisis; PDQ*)

Ether, float into, lost in the: 1. Hypothetical medium formerly believed to fill all space and support the propagation of electromagnetic waves. 2. I have no f**king idea where it's gone; it was there seconds ago, honestly; disappeared without trace; total deletion of email inbox, generating initial panic, followed by all-embracing elation and a sweet feeling of release. (*see Smoke and mirrors job*)

Event: 1. A thing happening. 2. Word usually surrounded by dramatic (*and usually untrue*) hyperbole, such as launch, one-off, or once-in-a-lifetime; nothing much happening at all; trumped-up non-event hyped to within an inch of its life by over-excited public relations agency; pure fabrication, as in most news stories; almost the entire editorial *"content"* of most news programmes. (*see Black swan*)

Evidence-based: 1. Based on evidence. 2. Deeply suspicious qualifier immediately suggesting that the proposal may actually be based on no evidence at all; instant alarm bell hinting at no basis whatsoever; evidence-free; without any justification; baseless; poorly informed; plain wrong; trumped-up; done on the fly; on a whim; in all probability, total bollocks.

Evolving to meet customer demand: 1. Changing, based on what customers have requested. 2. Radically departing from original intentions; overhauling; changing completely; ignoring customers and doing what we want to do, because the Chief Executive says so. (*see Coming or going, he doesn't know if he's; Drawing board, back to the; Pivot; Reverse gear; Tweak; U-turn*)

Exceptional: 1. Not ordinary; the exception. 2. Not extraordinary at all; total crap; euphemism for totally unexpected, as in *"I was gobsmacked by Dave's exceptional performance"*.

Executive: 1. Person or group responsible for the administration of a project. 2. Overpaid boss; underpaid underling; catch-all word for anyone unfortunate enough to work in an office; in its collective form, a toothless committee of time wasters intent on doing sod all other than eating biscuits on company time.

Executive retreat: 1. Time out of the office for management to contemplate long-term strategy. 2. Costly excuse to play golf, visit a posh hotel and demonstrate appalling taste in casual clothing; ill-advised chino and polo shirt wearing *"opportunity"*; astonishingly high consumption of complementary mints, chocolate rolls and evil-looking lime cordial. (*see Awayday; Brainstorm; Off-site; Workshop*)

Exit interview: 1. Chat when leaving a company. 2. Pathetically earnest set of questions levelled at someone who has just been made redundant for no particular reason; annoying and pointless gathering of opinion to which no one will play a blind bit of notice; complete waste of time for all concerned; charade. (*see CSR*)

Exit strategy: 1. Plan to get out. 2. Plan to get out very fast indeed; rapid extrication from tricky situation; absolute removal from market when it becomes apparent your product or service has been found sadly wanting; scheme to leave building, painfully or otherwise. (*see Defenestrate, defenestration*)

Expect more: 1. Exhortation or statement based on level of expectation. 2. Odd incitement from company to prospective customer suggesting that they *"expect more"*, as though they expected anything in the first place; disappointment-tinged phrase familiar to anyone who has experienced an unsatisfactory appraisal, as in *"I'm afraid to say, Andrew, we expected more from you"*. (*see Expectations, exceeding, failing to achieve, living up to, managing, meeting*)

Expectations, exceeding, failing to achieve, living up to, managing, meeting: 1. Doing more, less or about as much as necessary for someone to think you are doing okay. 2. Debatable notion that customers give a shit about what a company does; diffuse set of things that consumers apparently *"expect"* from a company; notional *"benchmark"* much loved of HR, as in *"I'm afraid to say, Nigel, you failed to live up to expectations"*, when none have ever truly been articulated; thoroughly biased basket of attributes made up by your boss when he wants to fire you; even more biased set of attributes conjured up by Sales Director who wants to give a bonus to his favourite protégé for *"exceeding expectations"*. (*see Always on; Constantly striving; Customer journey; Expect more; Go off half cock; Sun, the _____ never sets at; 24/7/365; Valued customer; Work-life balance*)

Experiential curve: 1. Learning through experience, intended to be on a metaphorical rising curve. 2. Regular repetition of exactly the same mistake, again and again, by a company or individual incapable of learning anything at all; harsh lesson; kick in the slats one may or may not forget, depending on brain power. (*see Learnings; Learning curve, steep, vertical*)

Experiential marketing: 1. Branch of marketing that gives potential customers a chance to experience the product for free in the hope that they become true customers. 2. Frantic mass giveaway of product in desperate hope that some interest is generated; brutal and random assault of unsuspecting commuters at busy railway termini offering them free yoghurt, toothpaste or pile ointment when on the way to work; marauding gangs of scantily-clad, stick-thin blondes called Stacey let loose in shopping centres wearing promotional t-shirts. (*see Chuggers*)

Eyes and ears: 1. Visual and aural body parts. 2. Crucial components in the arsenal of industrial espionage; phrase much loved by secretive executives, as in *"I want you to be my eyes and ears on this one Brian"*; unnecessarily clandestine phraseology usually deployed by member of a Research and Development team who mistakenly believes (a) that they are living in a Robert Ludlum novel or (b) that anyone gives a shit about their new product.

Ff

Face the music: 1. Take the consequences. 2. Hope to get away with something dreadful but fail utterly. *(see Can, carry the; Team, take one for the)*

Face time: 1. Speak to someone in person. 2. Try to work out the time by staring at someone; use conventional time-honoured communication technique when all crap modern alternatives have failed completely. *(see Face-to-face; Heads up; Interface; One-to-one)*

Face-to-face: 1. Two people facing each other, possibly speaking, possibly not. 2. Nauseating phrase depicting two people meeting and emphasizing, possibly inaccurately, that they are facing each other; failure to acknowledge that many people do not face each other when meeting, and sometimes deliberately so, as in embarrassing meetings. *(see B2B; Face time; Heads up; Interface; One-to-one)*

Facilitate, facilitation: 1. Make easier, assist the progress of. 2. Dominate proceedings in an all-day workshop, refuse to let anyone else speak their mind and steamroller your view through regardless.

Facts, cold hard: 1. The untainted truth. 2. What's left after all the bullshit has been stripped away; most commonly exposed as nothing of substance at all.

Fag packet, back of a: 1. A quick summary or overview. 2. A hopelessly inadequate case – badly thought through or not thought through at all.

Failure is not an option: 1. We must win at all costs. 2. If we lose I'll get fired, so I'm using a macho metaphor to put the pressure on everyone else. *(see Can do attitude; Face the music; Go the extra mile; Land, we need to _____ this one; Unfair advantage; Unthinkable, think the)*

Fall on your sword: 1. Take the blame. 2. Take the blame for everyone else's incompetence. *(see Spear, fall on one's; Team, take one for the)*

Falling off a log: 1. Really simple. 2. Apparently easy, but probably horribly booby-trapped. (*see ABC, easy as; Art form, got it down to an; Cooking on gas; Halcyon days*)

Fallout, coping with the: 1. Handling the consequences (*of something bad, such as a nuclear explosion*). 2. Sweeping up the chaos after something has gone spectacularly wrong. (*see Team, take one for the*)

Fall short: 1. Fail completely. 2. Fail, but re-express the abject failure in relation to some spurious or non-existent target that everybody has long since forgotten. (*see Achieve learning outcomes*)

FAQs: 1. Frequently asked questions. 2. Fatuous checklist of trivia thinly disguised as patronizing advice for customers; kindergarten series of basic common sense. (*see Advisorial; Behavioural economics; Hints and tips; Practical advice*)

Fast track: 1. Vector of travel that gets you there quicker than another comparable one. 2. Claimed shortcut to promotion, pay rise and fame that has a strange habit of never arriving; El Dorado, Shangri-La or promised land. (*see CPD*)

Fat lady, it's not over until the _____ sings: 1. It's not necessarily a failure until we reach the very end. 2. It's a total failure – we just haven't got the humility to admit it even though we are now flogging a dead horse. (*see All over bar the shouting; Horse, flogging a dead; Setback; Win or lose, we're in with a chance*)

Fat man in the canoe: 1. Obvious and out of place element. 2. Palpably inappropriate for the circumstances; ill-equipped; not remotely in control of one's situation or equipment. (*see Elephant in the room; Push the boat out; Rock the boat, don't; Rowing in the same boat, direction*)

F-Bomb, drop an: 1. To use the word f**k in a business meeting or encounter. 2. Profane outbursts spanning the two extremes of (a) persistent swearing as the norm, as in *"This f**king product will never see the f**king light of day in a million f**king years"*, or (b) a totally unexpected ejaculation from someone who is normally polite, as in a one-hour presentation extolling the virtues of a premium brand followed by *"Oh for f**k's sake Brian, that'll never bloody work you f**king idiot!"*; both approaches usually result in a failure to secure the business or disciplinary action for the perpetrator.

Fear: 1. Feeling of distress or apprehension. 2. Permanent state of affairs at work; horrible feeling that something, somewhere is going horribly wrong. (*see Blame culture; SNAFU*)

Feedback: 1. Amplifier distortion much loved by Jimi Hendrix; comment from boss or customer. 2. Unwanted comment; litany of complaint; long list of moans and misgivings; chapter and verse on your personal deficiencies providing the company with every possible reason not to give you a pay rise; debrief from boss after a disastrous client meeting; ominous preface to a conversation you know you don't want to have, as in *"May I give you some feedback Kevin?"* (*see Bombs, box of; Pushback: Quality feedback*)

Feet, to dive in with both: 1. Rush into a situation rashly and clumsily; illegal football challenge liable to break an opponent's leg. 2. Thunder into a meeting without any prior briefing; accuse boss of malfeasance, having no evidence to prove it at all; blame colleague for an outcome before said outcome is even known; fly off the handle for no apparent reason; hurl punch at office party after one cocktail too many; hammer fist on meeting room table to emphasis a point, as in *"Over my dead body will we have moist toilet paper in the gents!"* (*see Bazooka after a fly, we're not going to send a; Bull in a china shop; Nut, sledgehammer to crack a; Platform, eat one's own*)

Fence mending: 1. Fixing a divider between two pieces of land. 2. Eating significant quantities of humble pie; apologizing profusely after jumping to conclusions and getting it all wrong; buy flowers for receptionist after inappropriate fumble in the lift. (*see Feet, to dive in with both*)

Ferret on amphetamines: 1. Feisty mammal made even feistier by stimulant drugs. 2. Irritating, over-zealous colleague; relentlessly enthusiastic member of staff whose energy levels expose the feckless nature of the rest of the workforce; goody-two-shoes universally loathed by all but slave-driving boss; Rottweiler puppy. (*see Rottweiler*)

FIFO (1): 1. First In First Out, usually with reference to material in an in-tray or email inbox. 2. Ignored; left unattended; long forgotten; deleted; archived; passed over; junked; binned; trashed; delegated; filed. (*see Circular file; FIFO (2); LIFO*)

FIFO (2): 1. Fit In or F**k Off. 2. Frank observation about one's current status by new boss; no-holds-barred assessment of immediate employment prospects, not necessarily to one's advantage; not to be confused with FIFO's alternative meaning, although if you are the first into the boss' office, you may well be the first out – of the company. (*see Align, aligned; Defenestrate, defenestration; FIFO (1); Hymn sheet, singing from the same; Realignment*)

Fire hydrant, trying to drink from a: 1. Attempting to imbibe from a highly forceful source. 2. Attempting a genuinely impossible task; unable to cope; drowning; failing spectacularly; going down in flames, in full view of all colleagues. (*see Breathes through his arse; Human wind tunnel*)

Firing on all six, on all cylinders: 1. Fully operational; running smoothly; optimum performance. 2. Feeling rather self-satisfied after a supposedly *"stellar"* performance in an important meeting; smug; pride before a fall, as in *"We were awesome guys!"* – only to find the day after that you did not win the contract. (*see Great guns, going; Rubber hits the road, when the*)

First mover advantage: 1. Gains arising from being first in a market. 2. Management consultant's wank phrase asserting a colossal collapse in logic – that being first is always an advantage; subsequently discredited by hundreds of shrewder companies who have deliberately allowed rasher competitors to thunder into a market, make a stack of mistakes and thus unwittingly equip all other entrants with the wherewithal to do better; macho concept based entirely on the obsession of business with speed. (*see First past the post; Pacesetter; Pre-emptive strike; Retaliation, get your _____ in first*)

First past the post: 1. Winner, originally in horse racing. 2. Whoever got there first, regardless of merit; first person in the meeting room gets all the biscuits; first one into the office gets to impress the boss. (*see Brown-nosing; First mover advantage; Pre-emptive strike; Retaliation, get your _____ in first*)

Fiscal juggling: 1. Moving money from one part of the financial year to another. 2. Incessant gerrymandering of spreadsheets to confuse anyone and everyone; legerdemain, literally lightness of hand; adding costs to reduce profit; removing costs to increase profit; changing financial years; shifting from quarters to tertials or vice versa; deliberately generating multi-sheet spreadsheets with hidden layers in order to obfuscate; pursuing opacity at all costs; using arcane financial language to disguise the working reality; all in all, a huge battery of techniques to prevent anyone understanding the monetary truth. (*see Above board; Aims; Balloon has gone up, the; Baseline; BHAG; Black arts; Bottom line; Calibrate; Cook the books; Crunch the numbers; Markers, put some _____ down; Massage the numbers; Numbers, the; Obfuscate; Quantitative easing; Quarter; Re-baselining; Tertial*)

Fish up a tree, he looks like a: 1. Not comfortable; out of context. 2. Horribly exposed; hugely miscast; patently in the wrong job; out on a limb; in for a fall, probably today; drowning or possibly asphyxiating. (*see Casting*)

Fish where the ducks are: 1. Suggestion that the chances of catching a fish may be increased by the proximity of ducks. 2. Errant nonsense that fails to rumble that ducks are vegetarian and have no bearing on the presence of fish; car crash metaphor grabbed from the natural world at short notice; floundering grab for even the most crass analogy to add colour to a drab objective.

Flag up: 1. Mention; point out. 2. Alert; draw frantic attention to; state quite clearly that there will be shocking consequences of this decision; protest; object in the strongest possible terms; state one's case firmly but be overruled by boss who doesn't give a damn; fail to prevail with view; be blamed subsequently for not mentioning there was a problem. (*see Team, take one for the*)

Flagpole, run it up the _____ and see who salutes: 1. Raise a flag and establish whether anyone nearby is in the military, or is behaving as though they are; try something out and see if anyone reacts. 2. Another in a long line of military metaphors subverted for the cause of business; somewhat quaint suggestion that companies are akin to armies; vainglorious belief by Chief Executive that he is somehow a field general of some kind; mini-burst of pomp and circumstance, likening the launch of a new flavour of crisps to a new government policy. (*see Battleground; Launch; Watch the boards light up*)

Flagship: 1. Ship flying a flag; most important item. 2. Best example of product or store as it really should be, when in fact all the others are crap or not up to scratch; isolated case; only asset that has received any support or investment for years; exception to the rule; worryingly exposed element carrying the full weight of the business on its shoulders, as in *"OMG guys, our flagship store is flagging!"*

Flak, take the, dish out the: 1. Give out or take anti-aircraft fire, from the German acronym Fl(ieger)a(bwehr)k(anone), literally: aircraft defence gun. 2. Hurl abuse or receive it; unseemly office ruck; corridor disagreement that can be heard at the other end of the department; final snapping of uneasy entente (not so) cordiale; blazing row with no holds barred; fist fight; bitchslapfest in the reception café, inappropriately occurring in front of visiting clients. (*see Soft area*)

Flatline: 1. To die or be so near death that vital sign monitoring equipment registers nothing. 2. Lifeless; beyond hope; bereft of any vitality; dead in the water; truly not happening, despite being on the status report for months. (*see Dead cat bounce; Entering a new plateau; Negative growth, profit: WIP*)

Flexible, flexibility: 1. Malleable, accommodating. 2. Prepared to do anything to win the business; having no principles or ethics at all; of any target, double what you can realistically achieve with current resources or time; inflexible; a direct order that cannot be challenged, as in *"I need you to be flexible on this one Tony"*. (*see BOHICA; Drop our trousers; Elasticity; Stretch target*)

Flip chart: 1. Large sheet of paper on a stand for taking notes at meeting. 2. Seemingly inoffensive and inanimate object that can cause utter havoc for years to come; receptacle of some of the worst ideas in business history, ever; childish doodle pad allowing Barry from production to show everyone that he can draw; cartoonist's paradise; home to semi-offensive caricature of bald and chubby Chief Executive hidden on chart three, only revealed when Barry's group make their presentation. (*see Awayday; Bad idea, there's no such as a; Brainstorming; Off-site*)

Flight path: 1. Direction or vector taken by aircraft. 2. Unshakable course determined by over-zealous Managing Director on a mission; line of travel best avoided unless imminent trampling underfoot is the desired endgame; beeline taken by Marjorie from the legal department upon discovering a deal has been signed without her presence; resulting contrail leaving singed carpet and hingeless doors in its wake. (*see Bull in a china shop; Hell in a handcart, we're all going to*)

Flip side: 1. Another aspect of a person or thing. 2. Shocking, two-faced quality; total opposite of normal character; Jekyll to a person's Hyde; werewolf-like ability to transform in seconds from a perfectly nice colleague into a many-headed monster; Medusa in disguise; schizoid quality only revealed when under extreme pressure or sleep deprived from social overshooting. (*see Office party*)

Flounder: 1. European flatfish; to struggle. 2. Panic; flap; lose one's marbles; sweat profusely; do a runner; hide in the stationery cupboard until it's all over; throw a sickie; flee; jump; *"nip to the toilet"* and never return, having legged it through the window; not cope.

Flush out: 1. To rouse wild game; expose. 2. Reveal the unpalatable truth; uncover shocking evidence of malpractice; root out someone to blame for unholy mess on your watch; find scapegoat; take evidence to Chief Executive, only to find that she authorized it. (*see Drains up, have the; Lift up a rock; No stone unturned; Witch-hunt*)

Fly by the seat of one's pants: 1. Operate an aircraft by instinct rather than knowledge or experience, presumably sitting down. 2. Make it up as one goes along; bluff; bluster; busk it; improvise; career into a meeting breathless, clutching a set of charts you have never even looked at; take briefing in cab on way to pitch; have no proper grasp of the issues but start talking regardless; standard operating procedure in advertising and public relations. (*see Building the plane as we fly it; SOP; SNAFU; Woods, not out of the _____ yet*)

Fly in the face of: 1. To act in defiance of. 2. Ignore entirely; fly solo; go out on a limb despite all best advice from wiser colleagues; embark on glory trip; fly blind; gamble dangerously; disregard warning signs; crash and burn due to crass ignorance. (*see Come a cropper; Flying unstable*)

Flying unstable: 1. Pushing aeronautical tolerances to the limit in order to break speed records. 2. Reckless behaviour by any normal standards; lethal; hazardous to colleagues; stressed, prone to inappropriate decisions and actions; on the edge; about to blow; likely to crash at any moment; disconcertingly unreliable; utterly unpredictable; teetering crazily on the brink. (*see Come a cropper; Fly by the seat of one's pants; Fly in the face of; Pushing the envelope; Wind, sailing close to the*)

FMF: 1. F**k Me Factor. 2. Supposed magic ingredient that impresses someone so much they shout *"Fuck me!"* out loud; debatable idea that being shafted is somehow a good thing; unrealistic expectation that anything business related could invoke so much joy. (*see Aha moment; Wow factor*)

FNG: 1. F**king New Guy. 2. New person who knows nothing because they haven't been briefed or trained properly; new person who can't do the job because they lied on their CV. (*see CV*)

Focus: 1. To see more clearly. 2. Comprehensively over-used and abused word that used to be the sole preserve of opticians; effort to concentrate, a facet seemingly beyond many employees; opinion; point of view; also used as verb to exhort colleagues to wake up and pay attention; main staple of idiotic big picture/small picture discussions, as in *"There's a focus here we can see beyond, Steven"*, and *"We need to stand back and take a closer look"*. (*see Clarity; Closer look, stand back and take a*)

Focus group: 1. Group of people, usually around eight of them, gathered to chat about a product or service in the name of market research. 2. Eclectic mix of individuals who may or may not have any interest in the subject matter; random selection of misfits picked up in the Arndale Centre; people with nothing to do, enticed by the promise of free wine and crisps; unreliable collection of charlatans who have no intention of buying the product ever, despite claims to the contrary; friends and family of the recruiter using pseudonyms to make up the numbers; euphemism for one of the most unreliable research techniques ever invented. (*see Clapham omnibus, man on the; Consumer-focused; Rebrand*)

-focused, people-, goal-: 1. Concerned with people, goals, etc. 2. Hideous, mutated suffix universally applied to any word that comes to mind, as in people/goal/target/market/consumer; pointless modifier that hints at comprehensive lack of focus in the normal course of events, or at least prior to *"focus"* being mentioned; as redundant as "going forward"; worst of all, frequently misspelled as *"focussed"*. (*See –centred, -centric; –driven; Going forward; Grounded; -oriented*)

FOFO: 1. F**k Off and Find Out. 2. Stop asking stupid questions; exasperated cry of frustrated boss when faced with gormless subordinate; don't ask me; use your initiative for once; show some gumption. (*see DILLIGAF; RTFM*)

Fog, grasping at: 1. Trying to understand something that defies understanding. 2. Desperately floundering around in a futile attempt to rescue a lost cause, or comprehend a concept that exceeds one's brain capacity. (*see Jelly, nailing a _____ to the wall*)

Follow, do you: 1. Do you understand what I am saying? 2. Do you get it, you f**king idiot?; if you were any less intelligent I would have to water you; is this simple enough for you?; patronizing question to assert intellectual authority, especially when uncertain of subject matter. (*see Am I right or am I right?; DILLIGAF; Enlighten me; Intelligent, if you were any less _____, I'd have to water you; Lips, read my; Respect, with; Teach your grandmother to suck eggs, don't, would never, would you*)

Food chain, a long way down the, higher up the: 1. Hierarchy of which species eats, or is eaten by, another. 2. Unfortunate power pyramid topped by an apex predator, usually a chisel-jawed American called Doug or Todd; bad brief for the minnows at the bottom, liable to be corralled into a bait ball and swallowed whole for breakfast; failure to meet with appropriately senior level person in client company. (*see Casting*)

Foot, shoot oneself in the: 1. Inflict damage on oneself. 2. Score spectacular own goal; problem entirely of one's own making; personally generated cockup; no one else to blame but oneself; self-immolation; hoisted by own petard; chewing your own ear off. (*see Burning platform; Hoist with one's own petard; Kamikaze; Mountain to climb; Object, defeating the; Own goal, spectacular; Platform, eat one's own; Shafted down the river, yourself*)

Forces of darkness, deploy the: 1. Use every trick in the book to achieve your goal. 2. Enlist everybody and everything to win; rope in Chief Executive to ram the point home; sign up celebrity to endorse dubious brand or product; use dark arts and subterfuge, espionage and general skullduggery; cheat. (*see Air cover; Unfair advantage; Voodoo, corporate*)

Forensic, send it down to the boys in: 1. Have something properly analyzed in minute detail. 2. Crawl all over; send in the pathologists; scrutinize painfully; look for a scapegoat; find hidden reasons where none may exist; have the floorboards up; search high and low for a culprit; conduct post-mortem on failed pitch and conclude you *"came a close second"*; discover sod all after a huge amount of wasted time and energy. (*see Drains up, have the; Drill down; Flush out; Lift up a rock; No stone unturned: Pathologist's interest; Pulse, check the, finger on the*)

Forward-looking: 1. Looking forward. 2. Paying attention, no more, no less; futile adjective stressing some sort of forward orientation, as though backward-looking is a serious alternative; often backward-looking, particularly in relation to competitive reviews and tedious historical data; not looking at anything at all, just staring blankly into space or out of the window; daydreaming; navel gazing. (*see Going forward; Navel gazing*)

Forth Road Bridge, like painting the: 1. Never-ending process or project. 2. Outdated analogy based on the old adage that by the time the painters of the famous bridge finish the job, it needs doing again – longer-lasting paint has since been invented; dreary default phrase for anything taking a long time, usually uttered by the person doing the least work; world-weary bleating of middle manager in boozer whilst drinking half a pint of real ale, as in *"Cor, dear me, it's typical isn't it, Project Hatstand has turned out to be like painting the Forth Road Bridge!"* (*see Jobsworth*)

Foundations, lay the, firm, shaky: 1. Structural underpinnings, solid or not. 2. Another piece of blether half-borrowed from the construction industry in a vain attempt to imply structure and solidity where there almost certainly is none; part of a suite of materials including concrete, bricks, and mortar that lend spurious reassurance to otherwise completely nebulous concepts; suggestion of architectural rigour; likening of diffuse brand-related nonsense to physical structures such as pyramids; close ally of *"overarching"*. (*see Architecture, brand _____, business _____; Clicks and mortar; Concretize; Over-arching; Penthouse, furnishing the*)

Framework, operating, overarching: 1. Parameters within which work is conducted. 2. Annoying chart with arbitrary boxes and clusters of words dumped inside them; incomprehensible flow diagram signifying nothing; semblance of system that fools client into believing there is a sequence to things; spider diagram where everything is inextricably linked to everything else; vacuous word much-loved of pedestrian politicians, as in *"This is the overarching operating framework we will be concretizing going forward"*. (*see Foundations, lay the; Snake's honeymoon*)

Frankly: 1. In all candour. 2. Not frank at all; I'm lying to you. (*see Absolutely, At the end of the day; Basically; Literally*)

Free lunch: 1. Midday meal, gratis. 2. Bonus with no strings attached; pleasant break from work; congratulatory repast; blowout gourmet interlude; phenomenal piss-up, with a tiny finger buffet; liquid lunch; sprint to the boozer at lunchtime with no prospect of ever returning to the office; evil-looking cling-filmed sandwiches, with side tray of nuts, olives and twiglets, sitting on plastic trays in a meeting room. (*see Free ride, there's no such thing as a*)

Free ride, there's no such thing as a: 1. Everything has a price. 2. Tedious platitude often trotted out by world-weary traveling sales managers; cynical world view spouted by hangdog bar stool preachers who have made little progress in life; resentful side swipe at anyone who has indeed experienced a free ride, thus disproving the statement altogether. (*see Free lunch*)

Free-roaming experience: 1. One where the user decides where to go next; something that happens when wandering about untethered. 2. Gibberish jargon from the world of so-called digital devices, where everything is *"experiential"* or linked to the *"user experience"*; shades of organic claim, as in *"free range eggs"*; visions of feral gangs of digital natives roaming the country *"having an experience"*, possibly induced by mind-bending drugs. (*see Digital native; On-rails experience; User experience*)

Fromage, grand: 1. Big cheese (French version); very senior person. 2. Heavyweight visiting dignitary; chairperson; client with ability to hire and fire; pompous and overweight man in pinstripe suit; windbag; perennial bore. (*see Big cheese; Head honcho; Heavy hitter; Human wind tunnel; Player, big*)

Front burner, let's bring that onto the: 1. Make this a priority now. 2. We've flagrantly ignored this for far too long and now it's even worse, so remedial action is required immediately. (*see Back burner, we'll have to put that on the*)

Front end: 1. The bit at the beginning of a project. 2. The start of the project where no one gives a toss because the deadline is so far away. (*See Back end architecture*)

Frontline: 1. First line of attack, or defence; line of military or sporting deployment. 2. Coalface; sharp end; metaphorical place where hapless executives do the work and take all the pressure; woefully under-resourced "thin blue line"; first port of call for customer complaint and, in many cases, downright abuse. (*see Backroom; Coalface; Ground, on the*)

Front of mind: 1. Being thought about right now. 2. Irritating advertising and media phrase to suggest a consumer is thinking about your product every second of the day; curious division of the brain into front and back; inference that back of mind is somehow undesirable; blind faith that front of mind is the best place to be, when any presence of mind would be a start. (*See Frontofmindness*)

Frontofmindness: 1. State of being *"front of mind"*. 2. Hideously mutated noun-cum-adjective suggesting a state of actively thinking about something; four syllable car crash much loved by designers and self-styled *"brand strategists"*. (*see Brand strategist; Front of mind; Here-and-now-ness; Worklessness*)

Front stabbing: 1. Blaming someone to their face. 2. Deliberately blaming someone in front of the boss to avoid personal criticism, regardless of the truth of the matter. (*see Back stabbing; Blitz; Rowing in the same boat, direction*)

FUBAR: 1. F**ked Up Beyond All Recognition. 2. Truly unrecognizable from the original; utterly destroyed; annihilated; blown to smithereens. (*see FUBB: SNAFU*)

FUBB: 1. F**ked Up Beyond Belief. 2. Horrible mutated version; conceptually ruined; twisted poor relation of what was intended; massive own goal; spectacular cockup when doing it well would have been easier. (*see FUBAR; SNAFU*)

FUF: 1. F**k Up Factor. 2. Likelihood of going spectacularly wrong, always high.

Full Monty, the: 1. Everything; the lot; the whole shooting match. 2. Make it look as if we've covered everything by putting on a great show. (*see A-Z, Chapter and verse; Death by PowerPoint; Jazz hands; Kitchen sink*)

Full-on: 1. Busy; on all the time. 2. Stacked; swamped; overloaded; not coping; overworked; doing the work of three people. (*see Arse in alligators, up to my; Stacked, completely*)

FYI: 1. For your information. 2. Just so you know; to remind you I'm doing this, not you; to prove I've done this, so you can't point the finger later; to cover my arse. (*see Arse covering; BCC; CC*)

FULLAB: 1. Fat, ugly, looks like a boy. 2. Appalling, sexist, chauvinistic, non-politically correct acronym to describe woman not blessed in the looks department; last bastion of sweaty fat salesmen in Beckenham who desperately want sex but can't get any; after work pub *"badinage"* run amok after two small Martinis. (*see Collars and cuffs, I bet the _____ don't match; Kimono, open the; Matching luggage*)

Future-facing: 1. In the future; from now on. 2. Abstract concept strangely pointing to a time yet to come, as though past-facing is helpful to anyone other than a historian. (*see Futureproof; Going forward*)

Futureproof: 1. Protecting against future developments. 2. Self-deluding notion that forthcoming events can be predicted accurately; soothsaying; crystal ball gazing; navel gazing; pure guesswork; placing finger in the air and whistling Dixie. (*see Black swan; Crystal ball; Navel gazing*)

Gg

Game-changing: 1. New, revolutionary. 2. Extraordinarily perverse piece of logic that suggests that if you can't win the game you are playing, you should move on to another game entirely; quite how this helps anyone in business is a total mystery. *(see Break the mould; Groundbreaking)*

Game plan: 1. What you have decided to do. 2. Rambling document full of half-truths and guesses; so-called *"five-year plan"* that flies in the face of all modern business development such as pace of technological advance and a series of worldwide financial crashes; supreme work of fiction whose contents never come to pass. *(see Black swan; Strategy)*

Game is up, the: 1. We've been rumbled. 2. And we've been fired. *(see Black hole, disappeared into a; Blood bath, on the walls)*

Gangbusters, it's going: 1. Things are going very well. 2. We're all on a caffeine-fuelled rollercoaster that we can't get off, usually headed by a narcissistic Chief Executive desperate for a knighthood. *(see Mega; Meta; Monster, it's a; Net net)*

Gap analysis: 1. Identifying where the gaps are, usually in a market. 2. Desperately flailing around with a flipchart and an overly simplistic diagram trying to convince all present that you've spotted something that no one else has; last refuge of crap facilitators the world over.

Gene pool, swimming in the shallow end of the: 1. Not intelligent. 2. Wry notion that the gene pool is akin to a real life swimming pool, with a shallow and deep end. *(see Box of frogs, mad as a; Bundle, one stick short of a; Mid-life crisis; Picnic, one sandwich short of a; Postal, go)*

Geography, geographies: 1. The study of the natural features of the earth. 2. Any region in which Americans do business and attempt world domination, as in *"As you know Todd, we operate in a number of geographies"*; pointless plural of the word geography. *(see Energies)*

Get ink. 1. Persuade a journalist to write something (preferably favourable) about your product or service. 2. Get a hack so paralytic that they write a good review, or slip them cash to achieve the same end.

Get into bed with: 1. Sleep together, often sexually. 2. Embark on a sleazy and incestuous business relationship for mutual benefit or status. (*see Collars and cuffs, I bet the _____ don't match; Enemy, sleeping with the; Kimono, open the; Matching luggage; Scratch my back and I'll scratch yours; Playtex strategy*)

GIGO: 1. Garbage In Garbage Out. 2. If the original data are rubbish, then any subsequent conclusion drawn from analyzing them will be too. Much loved of computer programmers, often heard exclaiming mournfully *"This is GIGO – all we're doing here is polishing a turd!"* (*see RIRO; SISO; Putting lipstick on a pig; Turd, polishing a*)

Global, globalization, globally: 1. All over the world. 2. Croydon borders; a bit further than most hard-pressed executives have been: somewhere really scary where the food is different and they talk funny. (*see Sun, the _____ never sets at*)

Glocal: 1. Attempting to reflect worldly and local characteristics at the same time. 2. Wince-inducing elision of *"global"* and *"local"*; abject failure to comprehend that world domination is a rather different thing than a homespun approach; classic desire to have cake and eat it; impossible brief, as in *"target teenagers but don't alienate pensioners"*; consummate twaddle.

Gloss over: 1. Add shiny coat of paint; skim fast to avoid detail. 2. Avoid the point at all costs; circumnavigate; duck; dive; dodge; evade; flim; flam; embark on extended analogy to detract from main theme; have no working knowledge of any main theme; filibuster. (*see Broad brush; Chairman; Keep it dark; Mum, keep; Strategy*)

Goal-oriented, -driven: 1. Someone who concentrates on, or is motivated by, what they are trying to achieve. 2. Self-evident piece of nonsense that adds nothing to a person's understanding of the job in hand, ever; close contender for the worst piece of business bullshit ever, coming a close second to *"Going forward"*; complete waste of a rainforest every time it is written down; energy sapping and depressing when spoken; absolute drivel. (*see Action; Aims; -driven; Going forward; Objectives; -oriented*)

Goal posts, move the: 1. Move football target to a different place. 2. Change objective entirely; ask for one thing then expect another; fail to brief accurately; have no idea what is wanted in the first place; mislead; dupe. (*see Wild-goose chase*)

Gobbledegook: 1. Pretentious or unintelligible jargon, such as used by officials; bullshit. 2. Nonsense; piffle; static; hot air; tripe; codswallop.

Going forward: 1. The opposite of backwards. 2. Truly a king amongst kings; the undisputed champion of utter bullshit, with the possible exception of *"proactive"*; entirely pointless modifier somehow designed to suggest a forward-looking demeanour, when any fool knows that a backward one would be detrimental for everybody, except possibly historians who should indeed adopt a backward-looking approach; selfish waste of time perpetrated by anyone using these two utterly redundant words – those subjected to them could probably increase their life expectancy by removing themselves from the room immediately whenever they are spoken, thus saving years of meeting time. (*see -focused; Forward-looking; Future-facing; Futureproof; Goal-oriented; Here-and-now-ness; Momentum; Proactive*)

Golden goose, bite the hand of the, milking the: 1. Take advantage, or ruin, a decent opportunity. 2. Bizarre bestial car crash with extremely confusing anatomical reference points; a goose is made of gold, apparently; it has at least one hand; it has breasts that can be milked; all very confusing.

Golden handcuffs, handshake, hello, goodbye: 1. Money handed over to stay or go. 2. Strange two-faced expression with variations; cash provided to stay at a company (presumably good, but not necessarily if you have sold your soul to Mammon); cash provided to go away (possibly bad if you liked the job, or good if you couldn't stand it); money on arrival (great); money on departure (even better).

Gold-plated: 1. Covered with a layer of gold. 2. Suggestion of quality but without going all the way; a level down from pure gold; runner up; highish quality, but not the very highest; pretty good but not the best. (*see Premium*)

Good to great: 1. Classic management book by Jim Collins in 2001, selling over 1 million copies and adorning the bookshelves of most CEOs. 2. Rallying cry of Terylene-suited sales managers across the country, as in *"We have to move this from good to great guys!"*; diffuse and arbitrary reference point for the quality of any project, none of which anybody truly understands. (*see Built to last; Great, good is the enemy of*)

Go off half cock: 1. Embark on a task when not fully prepared. 2. Damp squib; half-baked effort; wet firework; non-dramatic fizzle rather than spectacular launch; crash and burn; suffer significant humiliation in presentation when proposal is found to be seriously wanting; return to office with tail between legs; fall well below expectations (*see Expectations, exceeding, failing to achieve, living up to, managing, meeting; Launch*)

Goose it up: 1. Liven it up a bit; put finger up someone's bottom. 2. Once again anthropomorphic observations prove irresistible to all and sundry; unusual inference that geese are somehow full of energy and pep.

Go round the houses: 1. Circumnavigate a number of dwellings. 2. Comprehensively fail to take the direct route; faff about unnecessarily; sod around when doing some work would be the easier option; procrastinate; prevaricate; search for, and always find, displacement activity; do absolutely anything other than the task in hand; stare out of the window; daydream; navel gaze; pick fluff from navel. (*see Navel gazing; Research*)

Go the extra mile: 1. Travel one mile further than necessary to reach required destination, presumably overshooting it in the process. 2. Pathetic distance-related cri de coeur from management determined to pump one last bit of sweat out of already beleaguered workforce; fantastically eclectic mantra hinting at sport, warfare, marches to conquer the pole, etc. in the vain hope of attaching some sort of macho endurance theme to the otherwise workaday nature of business; annoying yet somewhat hilarious *"If you do this you'll be as revered as Captain Scott"* implication; comprehensive failure to spot that anyone genuinely going the extra mile will not have arrived at the intended destination, but in fact somewhere entirely different. (*see Failure is not an option; Go the whole hog; Push the boat out*)

Go the whole hog: 1. Meaning obscure: to go all the way, or perhaps eat an entire pig. 2. Do it all, for better or worse, depending on the context; finish the job comprehensively (good); shag Darren from Accounts after office party (bad). (*see Go the extra mile; Office party; Pull out all the stops; Push the boat out*)

Granular, let's get: 1. Let's study grains intensely; let's get into detail. 2. Rather vexing idea that looking at sand intently is an interesting thing to do; probably sourced from geology or mining world; yet another attempt by business to appear more credible when dealing with elusive, ethereal or conceptual material. (*see Concretize; Deep dive; Drains up, have the; Drill down; Unbundling*)

Grasp the nettle: 1. Take a firm hold of a plant in the full knowledge that it will sting you; tackle an unpleasant problem. 2. Strangely foolhardy piece of advice; go ahead, hurt yourself; dive right in, regardless of the consequences; self-harm. (*see Kamikaze*)

Grasping at fog: 1. Attempting an impossible task. 2. Brilliant undoable metaphor for grappling with an intangible item. (*see Banana, stabbing a seal with a; Behavioural economics; Nailing a jelly to the wall, trying to*)

Gravitas: 1. Heaviness; weight; import. 2. Nebulous idea that certain people have more weight than others, irrespective of their physical mass; implication that this has some bearing on the outcome of important decisions, as in *"I think Nigel has the sort of gravitas that we need for this business."*

Great, good is the enemy of: 1. Settling for good may prevent the achievement of greatness. 2. Trite mantra trotted out in all creative industries, with the sole intention of suggesting the highest possible standards, whether they exist or not; platitudinous deflection technique to gain more time when no idea has been generated at all, be it good, great or piss-poor; suggestion of quality through apparent *"company philosophy"* where none may exist. (*see Good to great*)

Great guns, going: 1. Going well. 2. Feeling rather macho; pretending that selling bathroom fittings is akin to being Billy the Kid; gunslinger; packing a punch. (*see Dick-swinging; Firing on all six, on all cylinders*)

Greatest imaginable challenge: 1. The most ambitious thing you can do. 2. Testosterone-fuelled ambition finely crafted by chisel-jawed Chief Executive and self-styled *"brand strategists"*, hired at great expense; over ambitious target that will never be achieved. (*see BHAG; Dick-swinging; Impossible, nothing is; Unthinkable, think the*)

Green light: 1. Signal to go. 2. Annoyingly flip, semi-automotive, word pairing to indicate approval, as in *"That's a green light on Project Pilchard, Barry"*; worse, deployment as an active verb, as in *"I'm prepared to green light Project Centipede now, Monica"*. (*see Buy-in; Greenlit; Issues , I have _____ with that; Problem, I don't have a _____ with that; Redlit; Unhappy, I'm not _____ with*)

Greenlit: 1. Past tense of giving something a green light. 2. Horrible application of past tense of the word *"light"* added to a colour to generate a mutant child; further mutation into a verb, as in *"I've greenlit Project Cummerbund, Steve"*; still disastrous as an adjective, as in *"This is a greenlit project, as you well know, Richard"*. (*see Buy-in; Greenlit; Issues , I have _____ with that; Problem, I don't have a _____ with that; Redlit; Unhappy, I'm not _____ with*)

Ground, on the; 1. Not in the air, or underground. 2. Doing the work rather than just talking about it; much loved phrase of those who haven't a clue what is really going on, as in *"We need to talk to the troops on the ground, Gemma"*; further overuse of the military metaphor. (*see Coalface; Frontline*)

Groundbreaking: 1. Destroying terra firma; genuinely new or pioneering. 2. Macho imagery of rock breaking, chain gangs, construction, pick axe-wielding, drilling and digging to imbue lightweight project with semblance of authority; not remotely heavy duty; flimsy, but with a hard sounding adjective attached for ballast. (*see Break the mould; Game-changing*)

Grounded, people-, theory-, strategy-: 1. People, theory or strategy at ground level; level-headed; anchored in. 2. People, theory or strategy; meaningless modifier. (*see -focused*)

Grow a pair: 1. Miraculously develop testicles; get a backbone. 2. Applicable to either male or female; toughen up, as in *"For God's sake Colin, grow a pair"*. (*see Man up*)

Grown-ups: 1. Mature people. 2. Immature people who happen to run the company; anyone paid more than you; anyone credible, unlike most of the hapless jokers at our disposal; court jesters, but in more expensive suits.

Growth trajectory, personal, explosive: 1. Direction of travel, individual or otherwise. 2. Pseudo-scientific term to suggest physics and quantification of personal or company direction; introduction of some pyrotechnics to imply quantum progress. (*see Launch; Learning curve, steep, vertical*)

Grunt work: 1. The workaday, practical stuff. 2. Activity comprehensively avoided by all board members.

Guardian, brand: 1. Person or company in charge of a brand's direction or reputation. 2. Self-appointed overseer of *"brand health"*; prone to outbursts of rules and regulations surrounding brand trivia such as size of logo or minute pantone shade difference; *"brand guru"*, apparently possessing an alchemist's touch when it comes to simple decisions such as how to phrase a voiceover; author of impenetrable diagrams purporting to explain what the brand stands for. (*see Brand onion, pillars, pyramid, values; Brand strategist; Custodian; Monitoring*)

Guidelines, brand, corporate: 1. Guidance manual that explains how a brand or corporation should be portrayed. 2. Chapter and verse on every arcane detail that makes the Bible look like a short read; mindless, seemingly infinite portrayals of logos, typefaces, colour swatches and letterhead examples; tedious examples of *"how we do it round here"*, as though anyone cares; trite diagrams covering every possible eventuality; gravy train for design agencies and self-appointed *"brand strategists"*. (*see Brand onion, pillars, pyramid, values; Brand strategist; Guardian, brand; Tramlines*)

Gung ho: 1. Extremely enthusiastic, sometimes to excess; keen to participate in military combat; pidgin English from mandarin Chinese kung (work) and ho (together). 2. Completely over the top; unsubtle; careening into meetings without due care and attention; blunderbuss; liability; liable to cause intense damage to proposals, plans and, on occasion, property. (*see Bath, take a; Bull in a china shop; Catch a cold; Dropping grenades in fish ponds; Pull out all the stops; Ton of bricks, subtle as a*)

Gut feel: 1. Instinct about what to do, not necessarily rational. 2. Whim; madcap notion; unexplainable desire; pure guess; strange belief that decisions should be based on the state of one's intestines; visceral decision. (*Must, this is a; Pants, fly by the seat of our; Pull rank*)

Gynocracy: 1. Company run by, or consisting entirely of, women. 2. Extremely scary place for men; male no-go zone; sorority; sisterhood; lesbian enclave. (*see Ballbreaker; Mediocracy; Nutcracker*)

Halcyon days: 1. Happy and carefree days symbolized by the fabulous winter solstice bird from the Greek myth. 2. Piss-easy phase, probably somewhere in the eighties, when doing business was as easy as making one phone call and then going smartly to the pub. *(see Falling off a log; Marriage made in heaven; Rose-tinted)*

Halo effect: 1. Reflected glory from someone else's efforts. 2. Disastrous feedback loop in which everything gets progressively worse following an ill-advised decision.

Hand over fist: 1. A hand over a fist (self-evident this, no dictionary required). 2. We are losing money at an alarming rate and can't do a damn thing about it.

Handrails, hold the: 1. Brace yourself – things are about to get rough. 2. Everything's shot to bits as usual and we have no sensible coping strategies; we're understaffed and overstretched due to years of mismanagement and a succession of executives siphoning off funds for their personal benefit. *(see Coals, walk on hot; Ride, bumpy, along for the, roughshod over; Riding the razor blade)*

Hands-off: 1. Happy to delegate and let trusted staff get on with it. 2. Conspicuously absent; utterly disinterested in anything or anybody other than myself; providing no air cover or back-up whatsoever.

Hands-on: 1. Thoroughly involved in every aspect of a project. 2. Anal, obsessive, infuriating micro-manager; permanently convinced that they are the only person on the planet competent enough to do anything; purveyors of the time-honoured phrase *"If you want something done, do it yourself"*, usually accompanied by a large sigh or raising of the eyebrows to the heavens.

Handbags, dancing around the: 1. Not getting to the point. 2. Consistently dodging the issue to the point of blind ignorance; refusal to accept the facts; flagrant self-denial.

Hard decisions: 1. Decisions. 2. Easy decisions a child could make, made pathetically complex by politics, incompetence and self-aggrandizement.

Hard-wired: 1. Permanently wired into a computer. 2. Preternaturally inclined to do precisely what the boss says, regardless of common sense, personal safety or the more balanced opinion of colleagues. (*see Brown-nosing*)

Harnessing synergies: 1. Making several things work together properly. 2. A futile attempt to post-rationalize a ragbag of initiatives as having some kind of coherent rationale; cynical ploy to charge customers over the odds, or more than once for the same product or service. (*see Synergy*)

Hatchet, bury the: 1. Agree to stop arguing. 2. Pretend to stop arguing, while simultaneously continuing to bad-mouth and discredit a rival. (*see Back stabbing*)

Hate sponge: 1. Source, or subject of, all negative comment. 2. Lightning conductor for everything bad in a company; rotten apple; invidious presence; spiteful gossip; weasel; goblin; troll; poison-penned anonymous contributor to online feedback forums; ne'er-do-well; vituperative venom source; bad penny; single-handedly responsible for low company morale; force of darkness; constant subject of amazement due to uncanny ability to escape the chop whenever there is a round of redundancies, probably down to possessing incriminatory evidence about the Chief Executive.

Headcount: 1. Number of people in room, department or company. 2. Highly volatile statistic that could change in an instant; random number; seemingly ever-decreasing quantity; number of staff that the Finance Director can instantly compute as a payroll cost; target list of people to be fired. (*see ABC session; Axe, face the; Phone list, go down the*)

Head honcho: 1. Person in charge; top dog. 2. Curiously Hispanic-tinged seniority reference; shades of drug baron hierarchy with mildly sinister overtones; Spaniard running organization, as is increasingly common in Britain. (*see Big cheese; Fromage, grand; Heavy hitter; Player, big*)

Head of the valley syndrome: 1. Phenomenon to do with source of a river, perhaps; source of something generally. 2. Vague sweeping reference to something somewhere else (origin obscure); irrelevant and meaningless geographical observation inappropriately applied in a business context. (*see Blue yonder*)

Head off at the pass: 1. Stop before it goes wrong, or happens at all. 2. Nostalgic Cowboys and Indians reference, usually drawn from a childhood spent watching too many John Wayne films; mild military analogy invoked when it would be easier simply to say *"I'm going to stop that"*. (*see Nip in the bud; Rabbit, cutting the legs off the _____ to fit it in the hutch; Roots, take the plant up by the; Wagon, the Indians have surrounded the*)

Head office, I'm from _____ and I'm here to help: 1. *"I'm in charge – can I help at all?"* 2. *"I'm in charge – what the f**k are you playing at?"*; head office is deeply concerned about your performance: I'm a power-wielding xenophobe and I've jetted in to sort this out. (*see Big cheese; Black swan; Conference call; Management by walking about; Paper cup, here's a _____, there's a tidal wave coming; Stick that, some American is going to jet in and tell you exactly where to*)

Heads down: 1. Several crania crouched low; concentrate hard on desk work; avoid eye contact. 2. Hide from all possible blame or responsibility; pretend to be hard at work when in fact nothing is happening, as in *"We need to keep our heads down on this one, Steve"*. (*see Heads up*)

Heads up: 1. Update; collective lifting of crania. 2. Vital information, as in *"Thanks for the heads up on this one, Brian"*; curious reference to head position as indicator of ability to assimilate news or pay attention; dire warning, as in *"I need to give you a heads up on tomorrow's meeting, Jane"*. (*see Beans, spill the; Face time; Face-to-face; Heads down; Help and guidance; Interface; Loop, out of the, keep in the; One-to-one*)

Hearts and minds, winning: 1. Appealing both to feelings and logic, or limbic brain and neocortex. 2. Horribly overused phrase to describe anyone paying attention at all; suggestion of linkage between brain and coronary apparatus. (*see Gut feel; Information needs; Look and feel; Needs and wants*)

Heat, take the: 1. Be blamed and receive the appropriate punishment; warm up. 2. Get it right in the neck; full frontal assault, mental or physical; massive bawling out, often in front of colleagues; humiliation; be dismissed. (*see High jump, in for the; Scapegoat, make a _____ out of*)

Heavy hitter: 1. Powerful striker of a baseball; senior person. 2. Senior person hired at great expense, as in *"We need to invest in a heavy hitter like Jenkins"*; lightweight hitter with over-inflated reputation; puffball; narcissist; show-off; physically overweight board member, having over-indulged on company expense account. (*see Big cheese; Chairman; Fromage, grand; Head honcho; Player, big*)

Heavy lifting, do the: 1. Difficult work, by crane or person. 2. Assertion that the hard work has already been done, as in *"We've already done the heavy lifting on this one, Nigel"*; sudden realization that no one has done any work at all on a project, as in *"Why the f**k hasn't anyone done the heavy lifting on this project?!"* (*see Shift, put in a*)

Heavyweight: 1. Weighty; senior. 2. Obese; fat; overly large; obsessed with biscuits, especially in meetings; constantly eating; focal point of all office cake consumption; Bernadette from accounts. (*see Doorstepped*)

Hedge our bets: 1. Back both sides; refuse to commit. 2. Fudge; obfuscate; be vague; refuse to recommend or take a position; mealy-mouthed; non-committal; obsequious fawning in two directions at once; act like a civil servant (*see Brown-nosing; Obfuscation; Play the percentages*)

Helicopter view: 1. Bird's-eye view; overview; full picture. 2. Another in the significant lexicon of the visually confused; constantly fluctuating between far away and close up; delusions of aeronautical prowess; boyhood aspirations of becoming a pilot; utterly bereft of any understanding about what the view is indeed like from a helicopter; phrase usually used by someone who has never been in such a craft. (*see Big picture; Closer look, stand back and take a; Deep dive; Holistic; No stone unturned; Witch-hunt*)

Hell in a handcart, we're all going to: 1. It's all going wrong; we're about to be found out. 2. Awful sensation of *"Oh shit, they're on to us"*; sweeping declaration about state of the nation or company, as in *"Project Ballbag is a complete shambles – we're all going to hell in a handcart"*. (*see Flight path*)

Help and guidance: 1. Assistance or training. 2. Hindrance and obstruction; tiresome micromanagement; under observation in case someone cocks it up, as in *"I want you to give Veronica some help and guidance on this one"*; direct instruction with no deviation allowed; mandatory. (*see Heads up*)

Herding cats: 1. Gathering together of felines. 2. Unfeasible metaphorical task; something that cannot be done, or is nigh on impossible; exasperated cry of person trying to organize a large meeting, as in *"Getting the Board together is like herding cats!"* (*see Diarize; Locked into*)

Here-and-now-ness: 1. Immediacy; contemporaneity. 2. Nasty pseudo-noun twisted into an adjective; arbitrary addition of -ness suffix to any word or phrase in sight; desperate realization that now is all that matters, having spent far too long staring blankly at the future without actually doing anything. (*see Frontofmindness; Going forward; Must-have; Worklessness*)

Herring, chasing a different: 1. Pursuing a fish of a different kind. 2. Aquatic analogy gone AWOL; loose grasp of piscatorial basics; extraordinary ability to distinguish between two different types of soft-finned teleost fish – a skill beyond most of us. (*see AWOL, go; Bark into the wind, up the wrong tree; Fish up a tree, he looks like a; Sprat to catch a mackerel*)

Hierarchy: 1. System of people or things in a graded order. 2. Ability to pull rank; nasty seniority ladder often leading to competent staff being summarily overruled by less competent bosses. (*see Dotted line; Matrix; Non-hierarchical; Organogram; Pecking order; Pull rank; Viper's nest*)

High flier: 1. Overachieving executive. 2. Yet another pseudo-military aeronautical term; inference that humble office workers somehow have the skill and bravery of jet pilots; hints of altitude and speed, much loved by land-based slow people; low flier; slowcoach; laggard; slothful individual who tries something racy only to crash and burn horribly.

High ground; take the moral _____: 1. Superior position. 2. Hugely arrogant stance; intrinsic self-belief; hubris; *"cock of the roost"* mentality; engage in intense bout of narcissism; thumb nose at plebs. (*see Premium; Rise above it*)

High jump, in for the: 1. Athletic contestant specializing in levitation. 2. In deep trouble; due for a massive bollocking; liable to be fired imminently; being set up as a scapegoat; done up like a kipper by devious colleague. (*see Heat, take the; Scapegoat, make a _____ out of; Team, take one for the*)

High profile: 1. Very visible; noteworthy. 2. Horribly exposed; destined to take one for the team; project or person constantly talked about, with variable consequences; not high profile at all, but described as such. (*see Hype; Parapet, heads above the, keep our head below the; Team, take one for the*)

High risk: 1. Very likely to go wrong. 2. To be avoided at all costs; foolhardy; very dangerous indeed, for both individual and company; disastrous; only one possible outcome: failure. (*see Crash and burn; Wheels coming off*)

Hints and tips: 1. Advice and suggestions on how to do something. 2. Patronizing *"how to"* ideas designed for children; so-called *"step-by-step"* guides claiming to be with you *"every step of the way"*; selling techniques disguised as impartial advice; nudges to purchase; inspired by the pseudoscience of behavioural economics. (*see Advisorial; Behavioural economics; FAQs; Practical advice; Shell-like, a word in your*)

Histogram: 1. Pictorial representation of data. 2. Work of graphic fiction; Lego-like series of tower blocks depicting the square root of nothing; impenetrable skyscraper-style skyline of sales figures; irreversible sales decline shown in stark relief. (*see Bar chart*)

Hit the ground running: 1. Strike terra firma whilst on the move. 2. Macho military phrase redolent of paratroopers landing and breaking into a sprint in one uninterrupted movement; apparent ability to begin something immediately, without any training or direction; vain attempt to plug gaps in staffing or service, as in *"Dave will hit the ground running as soon as he arrives"*. (*see Rubber hits the road, when the; Seamless*)

Holding our nerve: 1. Sticking to a decision when it looks like a bad one. 2. Unpleasant sinking feeling denoting a very bad move; knowledge of imminent disaster; flying in the face of all sensible advice; stubbornness; pig-headedness.

Honours even: 1. Equal on both sides. 2. We got our revenge.

Hoist with one's own petard: 1. Undone by one's own actions, from the old French word for explosives used to breach walls or doors. 2. So stupid as to destroy one's own prospects of success without any assistance from a third party; monumentally dim; incapable of knowing when to stop; prone to self-immolation. (*see Enablement; Foot, shoot oneself in the; Kamikaze; Mountain to climb; Own goal, spectacular; Platform, eat one's own*)

Holistic: 1. Working as one. 2. Overworked adjective suggesting that the sum is greater than the parts, as offered up by Gestalt theory; thinly-veiled effort to claim that this sub-standard piece of crap will be absolutely fine when viewed *"in the round"*; pretence at understanding the complete picture. (*see Big picture; Helicopter view*)

Holy Grail: 1. Chalice, supposedly used by Jesus. 2. Chimeric outcome, never to be achieved; ideal; nirvana; dream situation; job you will never get; woman you will never sleep with, such as Julia on reception.

Hook to hang our hat on: 1. Useful repository for headgear. 2. Reflected glory from something far superior to ours; vicarious benefit; so-called *"piggyback"* effort to improve poor position. (*see Piggyback*)

Hoops, jump through: 1. Have to prove a series of points. 2. Humiliating initiation process for new recruits; pointless sequence of redrafts of presentation or document only to end up making exactly the same point; tiresome approval process; endless round of budget justifications.

Hopper, pour into the: 1. Fuel, feed or otherwise top up supply. 2. Agricultural metaphor much loved by new business executives, as in *"We need to pour more leads into the new business hopper guys!"*; spurious grain-related theme, redolent of hour glasses, funnels and other tapering sales prospect diagrams. (*see Baseline; Leaky bucket; Pipeline, in the*)

Horizon, above the, change the, below the, small ripple on the: 1. Place where sky appears to meet land or sea. 2. Imaginary baseline; ever-shifting basis; semblance of vanishing point where none truly exists; God-like claim to be able to defy physics, as in *"Guys, we need to change the horizon on this one"*. (*see Baseline; Blue yonder*)

Horse, flogging a dead: 1. Continuing to hit equine after vital signs have stopped. 2. Persisting with a lost cause; insisting on carrying on with same approach even though it isn't working; failure to learn from new information; beating up hapless colleague; trying to secure pay rise for umpteenth time. (*see All over bar the shouting; Fat lady, it's not over till the _____ sings; Seal, stabbing a _____ with a banana*)

Hospital pass: 1. Receiving handover (of ball or project) resulting in need of medical attention. 2. Appalling and cowardly act of delegation; classic enactment of blame culture; slick manoeuvre to avoid all responsibility; project handover or apparently comprehensive briefing that singularly fails to reveal any of the associated pitfalls. (*see Ask, big; Blame culture; Bombs, box of; Buck, pass the; Catching a falling knife; Drop the ball; Micromanaging; Out of office message; Poisoned chalice; Riot act, read the; Wash our hands of it*)

Hot desking: 1. Being able to work at any desk, any time. 2. Abject failure of company to provide enough desks; total absence of appropriate office furniture; loose aggregation of bean bags and second-hand chairs bought in a car boot sale; kitchen table powwow. (*see Powwow; Soft area*)

Hot lead: 1. Contact very likely to result in business. 2. Dead end; random phone number; clapped out data provided by a direct marketing agency, including many so-called *"deads and gone aways"*; bloke the Managing Director met in a bar last night; lap dancer called Suki, who might know the Chairman of a potential customer as reliable as Enron. (*see Chuggers; Cold calling*)

Hot potato: 1. High temperature vegetable; tricky-to-handle issue. 2. Subject that must never, ever be raised; CEO's ex-wife; CEO's mistress; CEO's sexual proclivities; mysterious item found in company kitchen microwave.

Howler, strategic: 1. Dreadful error of judgment in business planning. 2. Horrible logic disconnect; abject failure to connect A to B intellectually; synapse jump from A to H with no apparent explanation; eccentric ramblings of so-called *"brand strategist"*; blatant lie; patently incorrect approach dressed up as a firm recommendation; utter f**k up.

Huddle: 1. Small team gathering. 2. Embarrassing man cuddle; so-called team meeting; gay *"metrosexual"* hug, usually causing intense mental discomfort, and often requiring subsequent therapy; ill-advised clench with Sylvia over the photocopier, usually resulting in disciplinary action. (*see Soft area*)

Human resources: 1. People, viewed as a commodity; department in charge of same. 2. Retirement department for people fed up with doing the frontline job; roving gang of ladies called Veronica and Beverley who are good at the touchy-feely stuff; ferocious hit squad fronted by Bernadette, equipped with an all-encompassing brief to *"decruit"*; brown-nosing mouthpiece of CEO, whose remit is to fire anyone or everyone on demand; curious, dusty function located somewhere in the basement, next to maintenance; non-existent department, usurped by power-crazy Managing Director who hires and fires at will. (*see Decruit; Touchy-feely*)

Human wind tunnel: 1. Person unable to stop talking. 2. Individual inordinately keen on the sound of their own voice; Chairman; Sales Director; Jeanette from the legal department; crashing bore; incessant monologue of inane drivel; person delivering same; perpetual word dumper; consummate purveyor of verbal diarrhoea. (*see Breathes through his arse; Chairman; Dialogue; Fire hydrant, trying to drink from a; Word dump*)

Hungry, are they _____ enough: 1. Has this individual eaten recently?; Is this individual sufficiently keen? 2. Can I work this employee like a dog?; can this person be pushed to within an inch of their life? (*see Driven*)

Hymn sheet, singing from the same: 1. Intoning the same song as someone else; doing the same thing; seeing eye to eye. 2. Doing utterly different things; disagreeing entirely; not remotely in line with policy or view of company or colleague; categorically not aligned; off brief; out of sync; out of tune; in fundamental disagreement. (*see Align, aligned; Ducks in a row, get our; FIFO (2); Loose cannon; Off message; Off-piste; Realignment; Wavelength, on the same, not on the same; Wildebeest in a row, has the lion got his*)

Hype: 1. Exaggerated publicity or sales promotion. 2. Excessive hysteria about humdrum product; unjustified hoo-ha; so-called *"buzz"*, noise, clutter or general static; PR brouhaha; here today, gone tomorrow; song and dance; bells and whistles. (*see All-singing, all-dancing; Bells and whistles; Buzz; High profile; Pull out all the stops; Push the boat out*)

Ii

Iconic: 1. Like an icon; highly distinctive and memorable. 2. Fractionally better than all the other dross surrounding it; not that impressive at all really, but good for morale. *(see Idea, big)*

Idea, big: 1. An idea. 2. A small, perfectly ordinary idea described as a big one to make the originator feel more important. *(see Bad idea, there's no such thing as a; Iconic; Initiatives; Innovation, innovative, innovatively)*

If you can't beat 'em, join 'em: 1. If you are losing, join forces with whoever is winning. 2. If you are being outmanoeuvred by lowdown, dirty tactics, then start using them yourself.

iGod: 1. Self-appointed technological guru who believes they are omniscient. 2. Tiresome IT bod who condescends all other staff on the grounds that they *"don't get the Internet"*; skateboarding, bobble hat-wearing scruff ball called Mike, who commands an extortionate salary because no one understands what he does, including the people that hired him. *(see Digital native)*

Impact (vb.), impacting: 1. To have an impact or bearing on. 2. An unforeseen domino effect, in which one seemingly trivial action brings down the whole pack of cards with unpleasant consequences.

Impact, high, low: 1. High impact means somebody noticed. 2. Low impact means nobody did, so you wasted your time. *(see Plug-in impact)*

Impactful: 1. Having impact. 2. Vastly over-used faux-adjective to suggest making any sort of impression, as though making little or no impression would be preferable. *(see Choiceful; Insightful; Meaningful)*

Implement: 1. To carry out. 2. To take orders blindly from an uncaring boss without having a clue as to why.

Implementation, strategic: 1. Doing things. 2. A futile attempt to make doing things sound more important than it actually is.

Impossible, nothing is: 1. We genuinely believe we can do anything. 2. Patently untrue mantra given that time travel, unaided flight, the firing of mind bullets and a vast array of other dreams clearly remain out of the reach of humans; massively patronizing cri de coeur much loved by motivational therapists and desperate call centre managers, as in *"Impossible is two letters too long guys!"* (*see Asking a duck to bark; BHAG; Can do attitude; Failure is not an option; Greatest imaginable challenge; Unthinkable, think the*)

In a nutshell: 1. In just a few words. 2. In many words, typically a 20-minute corridor verbal download that you weren't expecting.

In cahoots: 1. In collusion. 2. Horribly intertwined in a shady way, via nepotism, favouritism or outright bribery.

Incentive, staff: 1. Potential prize for a job well done. 2. Suggestion of a potential prize that will never be forthcoming; chimera; wishful thinking. (*see Carrot, big, _____ and stick*)

Incentivize: 1. Provide an incentive. 2. Repulsive Americanism once again needlessly turning a noun into a verb, a process doubtless referred to as *"verbizing"*. (*see Carrot, big, _____ and stick; -ize*)

Influencer, influence the: 1. Affect the opinion of someone influential. 2. Phrase much loved in the PR industry; hopeful notion that a celebrity or opinion-former can be swayed, usually with cash; repetitive statement that is a staple of self-styled *"brand strategists"*, as in *"Of course what we need to do here to champion brand success is to influence the influencer"* ; sage nods typically follow such a remark even though nobody has a clue what to do as a result.

Information needs: 1. What must be known. 2. Strange suggestion that people somehow "need" data. (*see Hearts and minds, winning; Needs and wants*)

In for the long haul: 1. Around for the long term. 2. Earnest pledge of commitment suggesting constancy where there is none, as in *"Don't worry Roger, you have my personal word we're in for the long haul"*; immediate withdrawal at the first sign of trouble; short-termist; fly-by-night; churn and burn. (*see Churn and burn; Leaky bucket; Long term; Marathon not a sprint, it's a*)

Initiatives: 1. Ideas or actions showing some enterprise. 2. What decent employees should be doing all day as a matter of course; standard behaviour dressed up as somehow special; sub-standard behaviour treated the same way; lame ideas; below par tat. (*see Idea, big; Innovation*)

In it to win it: 1. Necessity of being present in order to stand a chance of succeeding. 2. Trite, nursery rhyme-like aphorism that is tiresomely self-evident; patronizing exhortation to overworked sales staff, as in *"Come on guys, you've got to be in it to win it!"*; annoying statement of the bleeding obvious, pointing out that a competitor needs to compete in order to achieve something, which even the dimmest person already knows. (*see Milestones*)

Innovation, innovative, innovatively: 1. Something new. 2. Nastily over-used word to describe any half-baked idea; one half of the classic tautological howler *"new innovation"* (literal meaning: *"new new thing"*); old idea hastily pulled out of a dusty bottom drawer; random thought in the shower; re-hash of previously-rejected proposal. (*see Idea, big; Initiatives; Mission statement; Values*)

Input, inputs: 1. Something put into something else; suggestion; data entry. 2. Pseudo-technical twaddle referring to anyone saying anything at all, as in *"I'd really value your input on this one, Wayne"*; baffling suggestion of scientific rigour where there is none, as in *"Once we've got all the inputs we'll make a decision guys"*. (*see Insights; Obvious, a firm grasp of the; Outputs*)

In respect of: 1. Relating to. 2. Thoroughly pointless modifier. (*see In terms of; In the context of*)

Insights: 1. Things we have learned, or now understand. 2. Massive unexpected developments; things we had no knowledge of before at all; Road to Damascus-style revelations; blinding flashes of the patently obvious; patronizing summing up of extended awayday diatribe, as in *"I'd like to thank Keith for his valuable insights there"*. (*see Input, inputs; Obvious, a firm grasp of the; Valuable*)

Insightful: 1. Full of insight. 2. Horrible bastard son of insight; another in a long line of words with -ful placed at the end to generate a lazy adjective that invariably adds nothing to understanding, as in *"Thanks for your highly insightful comment, Bernard."* (*see Choiceful; Impactful; Meaningful*)

Insperience: 1. Experience happening indoors. 2. Dreadful elision of the words *"inside"* and *"experience"*, coined by trite futurologists to point out that many people these days are quite capable of enjoying themselves in their own home, as though this were a major surprise.

Inspirational: 1. Full of inspiration. 2. Not remotely inspiring; monumentally dull; dreary and predictable, as in *"Thanks for that inspirational address, Mr Chairman"*.

Integrate, integral, integration: 1. Join together; absorb. 2. Desperate attempt to join the unjoinable; ragbag of disparate junk that will never fit together in a million years; not remotely integral. (*see Merger; Mix, the right, the wrong; Vertical market, _____ integration*)

Intelligent, if you were any less _____, I'd have to water you once a day: 1. You are as stupid as a plant. 2. You are too dim to work here; horticultural insult reserved for the most mentally challenged employees. (*see Bandwidth, he doesn't have the; Follow, do you; Mental furniture; Obvious, a firm grasp of the; Psychic RAM; Shilling, not the full*)

Interface: 1. Point where two things come together or interact. 2. Literally, *"between the face"*; chronically over-used way to describe even the most basic of interactions, as in user interface; at its worst as a verb, as in *"We need to interface with Malcolm on Project Stepladder"*. (*see Face time; Face-to-face; Heads up; One-to-one*)

Internal communications: 1. Informing one's own staff. 2. Total radio silence; smokescreen; complete absence of any information whatsoever; pack of lies; set of diversionary tactics; propaganda; earnest announcement, as in *"As the new CEO I can categorically confirm that there will be no redundancies"*, followed immediately by a swingeing round of redundancies. (*see Motivational posters; Swingeing cuts*)

Internalize: 1. Consider from a personal perspective. 2. Take personally; resent entirely; stew over; rake over in one's mind again and again; generate a personal head of steam; fume; quietly smoulder, then erupt the following day with unseemly outburst to boss; fester on an issue and subsequently over-state the case in public, usually leading to disciplinary action or outright dismissal.

Interpersonal skills: 1. Ability to deal successfully with others. 2. Abject failure to deal successfully with others, as in *"With respect Dave, you're a f**king idiot"*.

In terms of: 1. Relating to. 2. Utterly pointless modifier that merely confirms that the person speaking has not made it clear what they are referring to in the first place; mindless repetition of something already known, as in *"This is the best phone on the market, in terms of phones"*. (*see In respect of; In the context of*)

In the bag: 1. Agreed; signed and sealed. 2. Not a certainty at all; absolutely not in the bag; wishful thinking; pie in the sky; evidence of testosterone-fuelled hubris on return from new business meeting, as in *"Great news guys, it's in the bag!"* (*see Done deal; Pipeline, in the; Seals, left them clapping like*)

In the context of: 1. Relating to. 2. Thoroughly pointless modifier. (*see In respect of; In terms of*)

In the same boat: 1. Experiencing similar circumstances. 2. Misleading nautical reference with two entirely different meanings: (a) I'll succeed or fail with you because we are genuine equals or (b) I'm making it sound as though we're in this together because it's good for morale but at the first hint of trouble I'll be off; patently untrue matey reference, as in *"We're all in the same boat on this one, Steve"*. (*see Blame culture; Rock the boat, don't; Rowing in the same boat; direction*)

-ize: 1. Action-based suffix. 2. One of the most pervasive and undisputed kings of the bullshit world; near-omnipresent in almost any business meeting or document; disgraceful weapon in gradual erosion of English language. (*see Diarize, Incentivize, Internalize, Maximize, Optimize, Prioritize, Productize; Professionalize; Utilize; -wise*)

Issue, key: 1. Important matter. 2. Totally unimportant matter; trivia; part of a tiresome long list, as in *"There are 17 key issues here"*; quite unrelated to keys in any way. (*see Key criteria; Key learnings*)

Issues, I have _____ with that: 1. I don't agree with you. 2. That's utter bollocks and you know it; if you try to enact that I'll have you fired/resign on principle; I don't agree, but I haven't a clue why; I am too stupid to articulate my reservations with your proposal; I have issues with myself. (*see Buy-in; Green light; Greenlit; Problem, I don't have a _____ with that; Redlit; Unhappy, I'm not _____ with*)

Jj

Jargon: 1. Specialized vocabulary concerned with a particular subject or industry. 2. Pretentious twaddle intentionally designed to confuse, obfuscate and make the speaker seem more intelligent, usually with precisely the opposite effect.

Jazz Hands: 1. All style and no content. 2. Soup this presentation up immediately because it is essentially content-free (*see Zee, we've covered everything from A to; Full Monty, the; Turd, polishing a; Wow factor*)

Jigsaw, final piece of the: 1. The last piece of the puzzle. 2. Final recruit to a team, meaning that the boss won't have to do a stroke of work from now on.

Jobsworth: 1. Someone who invokes the precise letter of the law to do the absolute minimum amount of work without being summarily dismissed. 2. The entire civil service workforce of the United Kingdom, France, Spain and Italy. (*see Adminsitrivia; Bread and butter; Bureaucracy; Closure; Forth Road Bridge, like painting the; Panjandrum; Process; Risk-averse; Spaghetti junction; Target manager; Vin ordinaire; Viper's nest*)

Joined-up thinking: 1. A selection of ideas that make sense together. 2. Trite phrase to hoodwink anyone who will listen into believing that a random set of thoughts have some coherence, when they patently don't. (*see Connectivity; Seamless; Segue*)

Joining the dots: 1. Working out the relationship between several facts. 2. Extended bout of head scratching in a vain attempt to make sense of some impenetrable waffle uttered by the Chief Executive, who is doubtless convinced that he has found El Dorado, Shangri-La or the Promised Land.

Journey, customer: 1. Sales or service process experienced by the customer in which the brand purports to *"delight them every step of the way"*. 2. Infuriating sequence of hard-sell encounters, cross-selling attempts, failed deliveries, automated call centre frustrations, surly staff conversations and ball-breakingly annoying set of interactions leading to increased medical bills and, on occasion, suicide.

Jump start: 1. Effort to get something underway. 2. Last-ditch attempt to resuscitate a hopeless case. (*see Horse, flogging a dead; Kickstart; Last chance saloon, drinking at the*)

Jungle out there, it's a: 1. Our market is rather nasty. 2. It's certainly not a jungle out there, unless stated by a Brazilian in the Amazon – more likely it is a car park in Basingstoke filled with identical silver saloons, or a bleak industrial estate capable of draining all sense of hope from even the most optimistic of salesmen. (*see Battleground; Environment, business, challenging; Out there*)

JFDI: 1. Just F**king Do It. 2. I am a power-crazed autocrat who will brook no discussion and is undoubtedly in the right.

Kk

Kamikaze: 1. Suicidal Japanese pilot. 2. Crazed executive with a not dissimilar death wish; hellbent on destruction, of company, self or colleagues, in no particular order; a dangerous idiot, to be avoided at all costs. *(see Crash and burn; Foot, shoot oneself in the; Grasp the nettle; Hoist with one's own petard; Pacesetter; Platform, eat one's own; Right arm, give your _____ for:)*

Keep it dark: 1. Don't tell a soul. 2. Bury it immediately – it's illegal and we'll go to prison if we're caught. *(see Broad brush; Gloss over; Mum, keep; Ps and Qs, mind your)*

Keeling over like flies: 1. Almost everyone is off sick. 2. The boss has driven them like a pack of dogs for months, and they can't take it any more.

Key criteria, indicators, influencers, people, priorities: Criteria, indicators, influencers, issues, people, priorities – none of them are key at all. *(see Criteria, key; Drivers; issue, key)*

Key learnings: There is no definition for this – learning is knowledge gained by study. There is no such thing as a key learning, nor several of them, unless it means learning how to use a key *(see Learnings)*.

Kickstart: 1. Prompt immediate action. 2. Realize with horror that a critical project has been thoroughly mismanaged, and you are in for the chop; immediately start scanning the corridors for someone to take the fall. *(see Blame culture, Jump start)*

Kidology: 1. The art of bluffing or deception, usually in harmless jest. 2. Blatant lies to hurt, deceive or commit a full-blown crime. *(see Fiscal juggling)*

Killer whale: 1. Orca; large aquatic mammal. 2. Ludicrous expression referring to online offers that generate large volumes – a whale is large, and a killer whale even bigger. *(see Off the scale; Whaling)*

Kill the competition: 1. Be a commercial success, at the expense of competitors. 2. Macho exhortation designed to motivate sales force; ever-recurring use of the military metaphor; suggestion that death is somehow acceptable in the normal course of business; ridiculous notion that annihilation of all other companies in the category will be beneficial; blinkered hatred of rival company, only to defect to said competitor only a few months later for a higher salary.

Kimono, open the: 1. Reveal a little of the inner workings. 2. Disgracefully sexist remark perpetrated by sweaty businessmen in Terylene suits to imply that business is somehow like sex. (*see Collars and cuffs, I bet the _____ don't match; Get into bed with; Matching luggage; Playtex strategy*)

KISS: 1. Keep It Simple Stupid; a term originally coined by designer Kelly Johnson at the Lockheed Skunk Works. 2. Trite acronym trotted out by poorly educated Sales Directors who are usually both simple and stupid; rapid attempt to clarify something one doesn't understand, but without wishing to admit it; failure to comprehend, followed by offensive-defensive tactic, as in *"Enough of the technical mumbo-jumbo Robert, it's clearly a case of KISS here"*.

Kitchen sink: 1. Water-bearing receptacle in culinary area. 2. The full works; everything; the lot; the whole shoot, with absolutely no editing, as in *"They've really thrown the kitchen sink at this"*. (*see Death by PowerPoint; Full Monty; the; Pull out all the stops; Up the ante*)

Knee-jerk reaction: 1. Involuntary reflex action of knee joint, usually generated by neurologists testing muscular responses. 2. Tit-for-tat return strike; petty eye-for-an-eye act of revenge; puerile determination to get one's own back; vicious counter strike when spited. (*see Knock-on effect; Tent, standing outside the _____ pissing in*)

Knitting, stick to the: 1. Continue to do what one is best at, coined by Peters and Waterman in their 1982 book *In Search of Excellence*. 2. Plangent plea to resist temptation to diversify, as in *"For f**k's sake stop fiddling about at the margins!"*; counterintuitive idea that doing what you've always done is just fine – an alien concept for all macho CEOs. (*see Competencies, core; Core; Loose-tight properties*)

Knock spots off: 1. Win emphatically. 2. Curious nose-thumbing statement often enjoyed by gloating winners, as in *"We knocked spots off the competition guys!"*; of unclear origin, possibly suggesting a leopard or cheetah being reduced to a neutral hue, as though that were some sort of benefit.

Knock-on effect: 1. Thing happening as a result of something else. 2. Nasty unexpected reaction; totally unforeseen consequence; abject failure to anticipate (usually entirely predictable) sequence of events. (*see Knee-jerk reaction*)

Know-how: 1. Knowledge; expertise. 2. Inference that knowledge or experience can take on the cachet of voodoo or black magic; suggestion of mysterious intangible mojo. (*see Knowledge management, transfer; Talent, war on*)

Know it when I see it, I don't know what I want but I'll _____: 1. I don't know what I want but can you help me work it out? 2. I don't know what I want and I never will, even when I do see it; frustrating stance that is the bane of all exasperated advertising executives trying to work out what their clients really want. (*see Needs and wants; Open-ended; Straw man*)

Knowledge management, transfer: 1. Control, or handing over of, wisdom. 2. Catastrophic inability to control or hand over any wisdom at all; brain drain; complete loss of expertise when one intelligent person leaves the company; collapse of all IT functions when Dave leaves; haphazard filing system that passes on no knowledge whatsoever. (*see Know-how; Talent, war on*)

KPIs: 1. Key performance indicators, usually poor. 2. Trumped up metrics rolled out either to demonstrate that a target has been hit and thus a self-satisfying bonus triggered, or to prove that a member of staff should be fired for incompetence; almost never key. (*see Benchmarking, category, industry; Markers, put some _____ down; Metrics; Milestones: Success, what does _____ look like?*)

LI

Ladder it up: 1. Make it look bigger and more impressive. 2. Take something distinctly average and try to make it seem bigger and impressive, to no avail. *(see Putting lipstick on a pig; Ramp up; Ratchet up; Turd, polishing a)*

Lamb, sacrificial: 1. Scapegoat. 2. Hapless individual who takes the blame for an entire department or company when there has been a colossal cockup, even if they were clearly nothing to do with it, on holiday or on secondment at the time. *(see Fall on your sword: Spear, fall on one's; Team, take one for the)*

Land, we need to _____ this one: 1. We need to win this contract. 2. For once, can we please win? Our new business track record is woeful. *(see Failure is not an option)*

Landmark: 1. A recognizable feature. 2. Any port in a storm that will give us our bearings, since we don't have a clue what we are doing. *(see Grasping at fog; Milestones)*

Large, giving it: 1. Boasting. 2. Indulging in braggadocious behaviour to disguise basic lack of talent and competence. *(see Braggadocious behaviour)*

Last chance saloon, drinking at the: 1. On a final warning. 2. About to be fired, probably this afternoon. *(see Coals, walk on hot; Line in the sand, draw a; Riding the razor blade)*

Late breaking gay: 1. Person who changes sexual preference later in life, usually male. 2. Mid-forties man, commonly of suspiciously louche disposition, who announces unexpectedly that he *"prefers Martin"*; colleague demonstrating unnerving wardrobe relaunch after sabbatical in Costa Rica; Rupert on reception, recently seen sporting a newly-acquired 5 o'clock shadow look. *(see Mid-life crisis)*

Lateral thinking; 1. A way of solving problems by unorthodox and apparently illogical means. 2. Idiotic and foolhardy random thought that bears no relation to the matter in hand and has absolutely no chance of helping. (*see Bad idea, there's no such thing as a; Conceptual thinking*)

Launch: 1. The bit at the beginning; take off. 2. Damp squib; flop; embarrassing failure; best-kept secret. (*see Flagpole, run it up the _____ and see who salutes; Growth trajectory, personal, explosive*)

Lay off: 1. Fire. 2. Dismiss. (*see Decruit; Dejob; Downsize*)

Lead from the front: 1. Set a good example and take total responsibility. 2. Set a dreadful example based on hubris and an inflated sense of self-importance. (*see A-team, this calls for the; Cavalry over the hill; Eleventh hour, at the*)

Leader, category, market, thought: 1. The product or service that sells the most. 2. The product or service that doesn't sell the most, but would desperately love to; persistent *"reframing"* of leadership concept in order to make it appear as though you are number one, such as *"brand leader, premium category"*, when it is only in fact a small brand; so-called *"thought leader"* being the spurious idea that if you are not the leader you can think like one, as though that might help. (*see Thought leadership*)

Leading: 1. In front; ahead. 2. Invariably used to describe something that is not leading, but would like to be.

Leading edge: 1. Sharp corner of blade or surface such as a table; advanced. 2. Hackneyed catch-all term for any old crap that needs pepping up, as in *"Our leading edge products are the envy of our competitors"*. (*see Bleeding edge; Cutting edge; Next-generation; Pioneering*)

Leaky bucket: 1. Sub-standard water receptacle. 2. Woeful ability to retain customers; condemning evidence of sustained appalling customer service; losing business as fast as it can be won; incessant turnover of customer base; lamentably low quality performance. (*see Black hole, disappeared into a; Churn and burn; Hopper, pour into the; In for the long haul; Pipeline, in the*)

Leap of faith: 1. Pledge or decision based on little or no evidence. 2. Absolute shot in the dark; pure guesswork; finger in the air stuff; whim; blind optimism; foolhardy decision-making; flying in the face of all known information; commercial insanity.

Learn the ropes: 1. To gain a thorough understanding of a sphere of activity. 2. Work out what on earth one's job involves; receive no brief at all; endure hopelessly inadequate farce of a *"handover"*; sit through painful induction programme; learn on the job (aka. make it up as you go along); fly by the seat of one's pants.

Learning curve, steep, vertical: 1. Amount of increased understanding, of variable speed and quantity. 2. Disastrous geometrical collision of straight and curved lines wreaking havoc in the business world, as in *"We have a steep learning curve on that one, Stephanie."*; euphemism for *"We f**ked it up completely but don't tell anyone"*. (*see Experiential curve; Growth trajectory, personal, explosive*)

Learning opportunity: 1. Chance to find out something. 2. Abject failure to listen; head-in-sand approach to paying attention; faux-humble word pairing suggesting some form of progress or improvement; panic-stricken scramble to acquire even the most basic of starter information; ABC approach to new subject; widespread ignorance, with little hope of enlightenment, ever. (*see Learnings; Lessons*)

Learnings: 1. More than one piece of knowledge acquired. 2. Grim plural of active verb, suggesting intellectual progress on all fronts where usually there is precious little, as in *"It's time we accumulated our learnings on Project Earwig everybody"*. (*see Experiential curve; Key learnings; Learning opportunity, setback*)

Left field, from: 1. Out of nowhere; emanating from a grassy area not on one's right hand side. 2. Another in the seemingly ubiquitous baseball lexicon; totally unexpected; a real turn up for the books; unnerving development leading to dismissal. (*see Sucker punch*)

Left hand, not knowing what the right is for, _____ and second left hand: 1. Lack of coordination between departments or individuals. 2. Total chaos; Armageddon; anarchy; risible failure to communicate even the simplest of information; uncoordinated; random; haphazard; fundamentally disorganized. (*see Reinventing the wheel; Right arm, give your _____ for*)

Legs, it's got: 1. This animal or person has the ability to stand up or walk; this project has long-term potential. 2. There's an outside chance this idea might work; it's rubbish – it'll never work; it's the best we've got even though it's a no-hoper; flimsy attempt to introduce the athletic metaphor to business; vague allusion to sprint versus marathon aphorism; hint of endurance, where normally none is warranted; putdown when confronted with lame idea, as in *"It's a decent enough idea Patrick, but has it got legs?"* (*see Bench, has this got; Real estate, how much _____ does this have; Success, what does _____ look like?*)

Lessons: 1. Teaching occasions. 2. Often *"hard-learned"*; utter cockups; fundamental failure in product or service delivery; nightmare scenarios; abject collapse of infrastructure; closure of company; outright shutdown. (*see Learning opportunity*)

Let go: 1. Allow to leave; force to leave. 2. Deceitful five letters designed to make dismissal sound acceptable, as in *"We had to let Doug go"*. (*see Metrics*)

Let's not go there: 1. Let's not discuss it. 2. We can discuss it, but you won't like it; if you insist on pursuing this I'm going to humiliate you in front of everyone that matters, or blame you outright. (*see Blame culture; Scapegoat, make a _____ of*)

Level playing field: 1. Non-sloping sports venue; a fair chance for all contestants. 2. Quaint notion that many sports venues are on a hill, thus providing an advantage to the side playing downhill; failure to spot that all sports involve a change of ends precisely to make matters fair; pathetic use of sporting metaphor to allude to bias or lack of fair play, as in *"We didn't win the business but it wasn't a level playing field"*; basic sour grapes. (*see Failure is not an option; Unfair advantage*)

Leverage: 1. Ability to move something with a lever. 2. Horrible and near-omnipresent noun or verb; false notion that business is anything whatsoever to do with physics; suggestion of power and influence; last bastion of cliché-ridden presenter in full bullshit mode, as in *"We really need to leverage our assets on this one, Steve"*. (*see Competitive advantage, edge*)

Lifestyle: 1. Way of life to which one aspires or is accustomed. 2. Lazy catch-all for anything remotely aspirational, as in *"This is clearly a lifestyle brand"*; over-used and quite pointless word.

LIFO: 1. Last In First Out, usually applied to tasks in in-tray or email in-box. 2. Swift and clinical firing policy in which the most recently hired are the first to go; failure to cope with in-box, dealing only with most recent requests and ignoring the rest. (*see ABC session; FIFO; Phone list, go down the*)

Lift up a rock: 1. Raise geological specimen to see what is underneath; investigate. 2. Find out what is really going on, almost always with unpleasant consequences; recoil in horror on discovering the unadulterated truth; unveil corruption on an unprecedented scale. (*see Drains up, have the; Flush out; Look, take a long hard; Root-and-branch review; Witch-hunt*)

Light bulb experience: 1. Moment when inspiration strikes. 2. Complete failure to generate any decent thoughts at all; bereft of initiative; false suggestion at brainstorm that a breakthrough has been achieved, when none has. (*see Aha moment; Brainstorm; FMF*)

Line in the sand, draw a: 1. Beach related message or artwork; agree not to mention something uncomfortable again. 2. Final warning; uneasy truce after significant bust up; last chance; pretence at moving on, usually followed by a trail of vindictive bullying. (*see Last chance saloon, drinking at the; Mum, keep*)

Line manager: 1. Person to whom you report. 2. Person who has no clue who you are or what you do, but is nevertheless in charge of your career development. (*see Appraisal, one degree; Appraisal 360 degree; Performance review*)

Lips, read my: 1. Pay careful attention to what I am saying. 2. I'm going to say this only once: if you cock things up again you'll be fired; favourite staple of hectoring Sales Directors, as in *"Read my lips Mervin, Project Puddle will never see the light of day while I'm around"*. (*see DILLIGAF; Enlighten me; Follow, do you; Respect, with*)

Literally: 1. In a literal manner. 2. Pointless and inaccurate hyperbole as in *"It was literally an eye-opener"*. (*see Absolutely; At the end of the day; Basically; Frankly; Real teeth, our campaign needs to have _____*)

Lock and load, let's: 1. Get ready for action. 2. Tired military metaphor borrowed from a range of overly macho Hollywood war films; ludicrous idea that preparing for a business meeting is somehow akin to going into battle; even worse if the expression is accompanied by a hand action mimicking a cocked gun or slotting an imaginary bullet into the breach. (*see Rock and roll, let's*)

Locked into: 1. Immovable; fixed. 2. Something that simply cannot be shifted from the diary of an important person, as in *"Brian's locked into 11.30 but 1 o'clock is when we're hitting it"*. (*see Diarize; Herding cats*)

Long tail, the: 1. Extended set of niches or small components of a market, rather than the big volume hits, coined by Chris Anderson in the book of the same name. 2. Poorly understood and often misused term referring to anything that's rather longer than expected; often deployed by so-called *"brand strategists"* with a knowing nod, as in *"Of course, Veronica, this is a classic example of a long tail"*, without really knowing what one involves. (*see Contiguous niches; Coterminous; Niche, carve out a, market _____*)

Long-term: 1. Consistently committed for a long period of time. 2. Nowhere to be found; gone; absent; not there; done a runner; vamoosed; pulled out; scarpered; reneged comprehensively; naffed off; set in train and then moved jobs; bailed out completely. (*see In for the long haul*)

Look, take a long hard: 1. Comprehensive search or analysis. 2. Unwelcome post-mortem; thorough interrogation, usually unearthing something rotten; inquest; uncomfortable period of soul searching, normally after a spectacular cockup, such as a disastrous product launch. (*see Lift up a rock; Pathologist's interest; Root-and-branch review; Witch-hunt*)

Look and feel: 1. How something appears or comes across. 2. Omnipresent pat phrase deployed by clichéd designers everywhere, as in *"Guys, we need to make the look and feel consistent across all consumer touchpoints"*. (*see Hearts and minds, winning; Rebrand; Touchpoints*)

Loop, out of the, keep in the: 1. Informed, or not. 2. Weird idea that information is circular, thereby generating some kind of circuit; misinformation; gossip; deliberate exclusion from same in order to disadvantage or humiliate; covert operations-style lingo, as in *"Thanks for keeping me in the loop there, Gordon"*. (*see Beans, spill the; Chinese whispers; Heads up*)

Loose cannon: 1. Dangerously unsecured armament. 2. Appallingly indiscreet member of staff; Chairman after two glasses of claret; complete liability; inclined to say something completely inappropriate at precisely the wrong moment. (*see Arse, up your own; Bull in a china shop; Off message; Off-piste*)

Loose-tight properties: 1. Seemingly contradictory characteristics of a successful company, first propounded by Peters and Waterman in their 1982 book *In Search of Excellence*. 2. Improbable and very-hard-to-pull-off blend of not giving a damn on the one hand and constantly meddling on the other. (*see Closer look, stand back and take a; Competencies; Control freak; Knitting, stick to the; Micromanaging*)

Lose-lose: 1. Whatever we do we'll fail. 2. Mindless repetition of the word lose, with no increase in meaning; most commonly deployed as a *"situation"*, as in *"As far as I can see Mary, this is a lose-lose situation"*; statement of the blindingly obvious. (*see SNAFU; Win-win*)

Low-hanging fruit, go for the: 1. Do the easy stuff. 2. Do the easy stuff first and see if you can get away with it; avoid hard work at all costs; skive; take path of least resistance; cut corners; exploit. (*see Wins, quick, easy, there are no easy*)

Low risk: 1. Not dangerous. 2. Highly dangerous, but not packaged as such, as with almost all financial investments.

Loyalty, beyond reason, customer, staff, team: 1. Sustained patronage or goodwill. 2. Self-deluding nonsense suggesting that staff or customers are truly enthralled with every aspect of management or product range; messianic, cult-like qualities attributed to workaday items such as cleaning products or the mundane business of just turning up at the office. (*see Delighting customers*)

Machiavellian: 1. Cunning, amoral and opportunist. 2. Acting like an utter shit with no regard for others – it's me, me, me and the rest can go hang. *(Shit creek, up _____ without a paddle)*

Magic ingredient, there is no: 1. This is quite difficult. 2. We haven't got a bloody clue how to sort this out. *(see Easy answers, there are no; Quick fix, there is no; Silver bullet, there is no; X factor)*

Make a difference: 1. Make a significant contribution. 2. Make no difference whatsoever, as in *"Steve, I want you to really make a difference on Project Woodlouse"*.

Make it happen: 1. Make it happen. 2. Fail to make it happen after being blocked at every turn by obstructive colleagues, unreliable suppliers and a fundamental lack of skill and charisma.

Manager: 1. Someone who manages. 2. Someone who utterly fails to manage anything whatsoever; incompetent bureaucrat. *(see Administrivia; Bread and butter; Bureaucracy; Jobsworth; Panjandrum; Target manager)*

Management by walking about: 1. Inclusive management style based on regular interaction with staff. 2. Chief Executive with a massively annoying tendency to turn up unannounced, make some unhelpful observations, derail a project and then disappear just as quickly. *(see Head office, I'm from _____ and I'm here to help)*

Managing downwards, upwards, sideways: 1. Managing a subordinate, boss or equal-ranking colleague. 2. Floundering around in all directions, bullying direct reports, fawning to management and knifing rivals at every opportunity. *(see Back stabbing; Blame culture; Brown-nosing)*

Managing change, expectations: 1. Reassuring colleagues when things are changing so that they don't get any nasty surprises. 2. Deliberately introducing a package full of said nasty surprises in order to increase status and pay.

Man up: 1. Increase virility or masculinity levels; mature; grow up. 2. Take some responsibility for the first time in your life; make a decision for once; get on with it; ditch metrosexual wishy-washy stance and deliver to required level at last; knuckle down. (*see Grow a pair*)

Map, on the: 1. Recognized by anyone who needs to know. 2. Totally obscure and unheard of, as in *"It's time to get this brand on the map"*, precisely because at the moment it's nowhere; peculiar cartographical reference implying sense of direction where usually there is none; vocabulary loosely lifted from outward bound course or distant boy scout memories; not registered at all; totally unnoticed by anyone except the most zealous devotee.

Marathon not a sprint, it's a: 1. This will take a long time so don't rush it. 2. Exasperated plea from Managing Director to try a more thoughtful approach, even though he probably set the punitive monthly targets himself; delusion by same that he is somehow similar to the best Olympic coaches; athletics metaphor misapplied; thinly-disguised attempt to appear *"strategic"* in a meeting by proposing a more orderly method to solving the problem. (*see Closer look, stand back and take a; In for the long haul; Methodology*)

Marching orders, get your: 1. Be fired. 2. Be fired emphatically, on the spot; be escorted from building by security; be defenestrated (*advertising industry in particular*). (*see Bombshell; Bullet, get the; Defenestrate, defenestration; Dejob; Destaff; Out, I want him/her; Swingeing cuts*)

Marker buoy, let's stick a _____ on that: 1. Let's come back to that point. 2. Bizarre faux-nautical observation attributing marine qualities to a point made in conversation; possible over-use of drugs by the person saying this; hints of some kind of fantastic hallucination in which all conversations are oceans, and the comments made are represented by life buoys; maritime mash-up of massive proportions. (*see Mental lay-by; Ringfence; Tangent, returning to the*)

Markers, put some _____ down: 1. Outline clearly. 2. Wreak trail of havoc; enumerate erratic history of financial performance; recalibrate; change criteria to create semblance of improved position; fabricate previous targets to imply success; plot points on a graph to invent a shape where none exists. (*see Benchmarking; Fiscal juggling; KPIs; Metrics; Milestones*)

Market-leading: 1. The number one product or service. 2. Delusional catch-all rarely used by true market leaders; aspirational hot air spouted by all market followers; also-ran; has-been; piss-poor; dog; generic wibble desperately grasping for quality. (*see Challenger brand; Thought leadership; World class*)

Market share: 1. Proportion of sales in relation to competitors. 2. Ever-shifting percentage that can be recast in multiple ways to suit the ends of the owner of the data; market share is very low=*"I need more budget"*; market share is very high=*"I want a pay rise"*.

Marketing: 1. Publicity and communication designed to increase sales. 2. Strange alchemy purporting to increase sales, but frequently unproven; advertising puffery; ability to talk theoretically about *"the brand"* without taking any practical responsibility for the tangible aspects of a business; smoke and mirrors; snake oil salesman's favourite preserve. (*see Architecture, brand _____, business _____; Brand onion, pillars, pyramid, values; Positioning; Smoke and mirrors job*)

Marketing guru: 1. Expert in communication. 2. Self-styled expert in communication, in order to procure publishing contract or public speaking fees; hints of Indian mysticism, or request to visit one's own personal ashram; occasionally mistyped as the embarrassing *"marketing gnu"*, suggesting a particularly savvy wildebeest; at its worst when uttered by a person describing themselves, as in *"Pleased to meet you, I'm a marketing guru"*. (*see Brand strategist; Entrepreneur; Positioning*)

Mark-up: 1. Surcharge on base price in order to generate a profit. 2. Near-infinite additional charge in order to fleece customer; favourite domain of so-called *"luxury goods"*, safe in the knowledge that their clients are loaded and indiscriminate; strange notion that paying more is actually better – a phenomenon only true of vainglorious show-offs.

Marriage made in heaven: 1. Perfect match. 2. Doomed to failure, like many marriages; divorce fodder; victims of relationship fatigue; awkward pairing; glib referral to rosy relations in honeymoon phase, followed by acrimonious dust-up. (*see Halcyon days; Rose-tinted*)

Massage the numbers: 1. Rearrange finances or statistics to create a different conclusion. 2. Deceptive, often downright illegal, alteration of financial reporting information in order to generate an entirely different outcome, usually favourable; slight of hand; legerdemain; malfeasance; contemptible twisting of reporting line to create a better picture, often resulting in company closure or personal imprisonment. (*see Bottom line; Cook the books; Crunch the numbers; Fiscal juggling; Negative growth, profit; Obfuscation; Smoke and mirrors job*)

Match fit: 1. Ready for action; in good condition. 2. Sporting metaphor applied to anything from a person to a team, division, presentation or a whole company; training analogy run rampant, suggesting that knackered and over-worked staff are in some way finely-tuned athletes, when a quick glance at their physical condition would suggest otherwise; shades of winning the cup or playing in the Premier League; usually applied to thoroughly corpulent and out of shape executives. (*see Purpose, fit for; Rock and roll, let's*)

Matching luggage: 1. Items looking, or appearing to be, the same; part of a set. 2. Frantic appeal for a ragbag of ideas or products to look as though they are part of the same suite or range, when they are categorically not; dissimilar, unrelated thoughts; cri de coeur from enthusiastic Product Manager, as in *"We need to make sure we have matching luggage on this one guys!"*; sexist speculation about whether a woman's bra and panties are of the same material. (*see Collars and cuffs, I bet the _____ don't match; FULLAB; Kimono, open the; Playtex strategy*)

Matrix: 1. Latticework; enclosed environment; connective tissue. 2. Hazardous labyrinth of working relationships that requires impeccable navigation in order to avoid humiliation or dismissal; viper's nest; snake's honeymoon; bear trap; minefield of politics and hierarchy. (*see Dotted line; Hierarchy; Organogram; Non-hierarchical; Pecking order; Pull rank; Snakepit; Snake's Honeymoon; Viper's nest*)

Maxed out: 1. At full speed or capacity. 2. US air force lingo hijacked by oppressed executives usually working in far less glamorous fields such as baby food, pharmaceuticals or feminine hygiene; attempt to fob off request to take on extra work , as in *"I'd love to help, Marion, but I'm all maxed out this week as it is"*. (*see Crash and burn; Essay crisis; Needle, moving the; Needle, pushing the; Participation; Pushing the envelope; Pyramided out; Wheels coming off*)

Maximize: 1. Make the most of. 2. Squeeze even more juice out of an already empty vessel; invariably referring to potential, as in *"We need to maximize the potential of Project Dog Bowl, Bernard"*. (*see –ize; Potential*)

MBA: 1. Master of Business Administration. 2. Dreary, time-consuming and very costly learning programme; last-ditch effort by mature businessman to make up for abject squandering of university years; near-endless stream of semi-fictitious case studies that can rarely be applied to the real world; excuse to avoid the monotony of the day job. (*see Sabbatical*)

Meaningful: 1. Full of meaning. 2. Utterly bereft of meaning, as in *"We need a meaningful solution here, Veronica"*. (*see Choiceful, Dialogue; Impactful; Insightful*)

Mechanics: 1. People who fix machines; the nuts and bolts of a programme. 2. Crass attempt to liken the flabby and diffuse world of business with precision engineering; much loved in wishy-washy areas such as marketing and advertising, as in *"Gemma is now going to walk us through the mechanics of the campaign"*. (*see Vehicle*)

Mediocracy: 1. Organization in which mediocrity is the norm. 2. Relentlessly average as standard; bland; ordinary; humdrum; workaday; quite unremarkable; qualities often displayed by companies claiming to have lots of *"drive"* and *"passion"*. (*see Challenger brand; Drive; Gynocracy; Passion, passionate; Run-of-the-mill; Vin ordinaire*)

Meetings: 1. Gatherings, ostensibly with the purpose of discussing or deciding something important. 2. Gargantuan waste of time; superb smokescreen for appearing busy when in fact the participants are merely holding court, eating biscuits, falling asleep or pretending to listen when in fact checking their personal emails. (*see BlackBerry prayer; Death by PowerPoint; Moi presentation; Open door policy*)

Mega: 1. Really big. 2. Claimed to be really big in order to make the claimer appear to be so; not that big really; unrealistic aspiration or plain exaggeration, as in *"Project Bugbear is going to be really mega guys!"* (*see Gangbusters, it's going; Meta; Monster, it's a*)

Mental furniture: 1. Brainpower; intelligence. 2. Near-complete lack of gumption, as in *"Darren just hasn't got the mental furniture for this"*; partial DIY component to thought-processing capability; common sense; straightforward expertise or competence. (*see Bandwidth, he doesn't have the; Intelligent, if you were any less _____, I'd have to water you once a day; Obvious, a firm grasp of the; Psychic RAM; Shilling, not the full*)

Mental lay-by: 1. Daydream; thought cul-de-sac. 2. Near-permanent frame of mind in meetings; off with the fairies; looking out of the window; hypnagogic dream state; half asleep; fantasizing about Julie from accounts; reverie, often broken by an unwanted question from other meeting attendee. (*see Marker buoy, Let's stick a _____ on that; Meetings; Tangent, returning to the*)

Merger: 1. Joining of two companies or departments. 2. Unsuccessful joining of same; coming together of disparate parties resulting in no discernible benefit; warfare; bitter hatred between rivals; takeover; triumphant, self-serving manoeuvre orchestrated by Board keen to realize their share options. (*see Apples with apples, not comparing; Assimilation; Integrate, integral, integration; Mix, the right, the wrong; Pay through the nose*)

Messenger, don't shoot the: 1. Don't blame the person who delivers the bad news. 2. On the contrary, blame the person comprehensively; emphatically attach news to bearer; shout *"Oh my God!"* and run to the toilet in tears; nasty precursor to appalling revelation, as in *"Don't shoot the messenger but Stephanie says they're shutting the whole department down"*.

Meta: 1. Vast; overarching. 2. Four letters cunningly deployed to make something sound unfathomably large; much loved by data planners, as in *"I propose we do a meta analysis of this data set, Roger"*. (*see Mega*)

Methodology: 1. Method. 2. Transparent attempt to lend intellectual credence to something far less important by adding the suffix -ology; way of doing something; approach; how it is going to get done; pseudo-academic line of enquiry, as in *"What's our methodology on Project Earwax, Sebastian?"* (*see Marathon not a sprint, it's a; Strategy, strategize*)

Metrics: 1. Measurement criteria. 2. Futile and time-consuming effort at measuring the unmeasurable; pointless data set that will never be looked at again; amorphous headings used to fire staff for apparently poor performance, as in *"I'm sorry, Doug, but the management metrics clearly show that your work is below par, so regretfully we have to let you go"*. (*see Benchmarking; KPIs; Landmark; Let go; Markers, put some _____ down*)

Micromanaging: 1. Checking every tiny detail; breathing down a subordinate's neck. 2. Infuriating inability to allow perfectly competent executive to get on with a task; misguided belief that only you can do something properly; characteristic consistent with control freaks unhappy leaving their *"comfort zone"*; meddling; fiddling unnecessarily; making pointless tweaks to the work of others that have no bearing at all on the content or outcome; hovering; loitering at a colleague's desk; constantly asking whether the report requested for Friday will indeed be ready on time, to which the reply is invariably *"Yes it will be, so long as you f**k off and let me get on with it"*. (*see Autonomy; Buck, pass the; Comfort zone, out of one's; Control freak; Loose-tight properties; Non-judgmental*)

Mid-life crisis: 1. Near-total breakdown in confidence, usually experienced in one's forties. 2. Bizarre hormonal change leading to erratic and frankly embarrassing behaviour traits; ill-judged series of *"personal relaunch"* decisions, which may include injudicious new haircut, a complete wardrobe change, purchase of sports car, motorbike or skateboard; appearance at highly unsuitable events such as office rave only for the secretaries; change of sexuality; purchase of ear stud or sudden sporting of inappropriate tattoo; wholesale introduction of gymnasium-based routine, complete with Day-Glo Lycra ensemble; utter loss of respect and integrity; loss of wife; gain of pitying looks from own children; all the above, often leading to dismissal for being too weird after a string of unfavourable staff complaints. (*see Ballistic, go; Bandwagoneering; Basket case; Box of frogs, mad as a; Bundle, one stick short of a; Late breaking gay; Picnic, one sandwich short of a; Postal, go; Pram, to throw one's toys out of*)

Milestones: 1. Road markers indicating mile-length distances; moment or recognition of a significant achievement. 2. Serious attempt to herald progress where usually there is precious little; suggestion of forward motion; triumphant production of tangible but invariably cheap memento of success, such as a plaque, hastily printed certificate or plastic trophy emblazoned with *"Brain surgeon of the month"*, or *"Waxer of the Year"*; misty-eyed intonation much loved by Chairmen, as in *"I am convinced we will look back on Project Jellybean as a significant milestone in the company's history"*. (*see Benchmarking; In it to win it; KPIs; Landmark; Markers, put some _____ down; Metrics*)

Minefield, complete, tiptoeing through a: 1. Area of ground strewn with lethal explosives. 2. Political nightmare, best avoided. (*see Bombs, box of*)

Minister for fun: 1. Member of staff charged with keeping morale high. 2. Self-appointed office wag; wearer of bad ties and purveyor of unfunny jokes and non-PC remarks; twat; court jester; organizer of frequently unpopular social events, such as karaoke; horrible job description devised by companies with lousy products and low pay, along with either non-existent or inhumane HR policy; brief to keep staff happy with no budget or resources other than an arsenal of cheap knob gags. (*see Catalyst; Dress to impress; Emotional intelligence; Empathy; Poisoned chalice*)

Mission critical: 1. Vital to the task. 2. Not at all vital, merely claiming to be so; suggesting that the task in hand is somehow as important as a space rocket flight. (*see DNA*)

Mission statement: 1. Declaration of what a company does, or intends to do, or stands for. 2. Hackneyed bundle of weasel words and cliché; wishful thinking checklist of desired characteristics, most of which will never materialize; formulaic tick box of attributes usually including *"world class"*, *"exceeding customer expectations"*, *"innovative"*, *"passionate"* and other such drivel, none of it accurate. (*see Expectations, exceeding, failing to achieve, living up to, managing, meeting; Innovation, innovative, innovatively; Passion, passionate; Values; Vision, visioning; Voodoo, corporate; World-beating, -changing; World class*)

Mix, the right, the wrong: 1. Blend, hopefully correct. 2. Oil and water; nasty clash of interests, usually due to inappropriate casting. (*see Apples with apples, not comparing; Assimilation; Casting; Integrate, integral, integration; Merger*)

Mode: 1. Style; way of doing. 2. Rather annoying word merely specifying what someone is up to, as in *"He's in new business mode at the moment"*, or *"Jenny's in presentation mode this week"*; invariably unnecessary.

Module: 1. Component part; capsule or piece. 2. Strange way to denote the elements of a training programme, such as *"Derek's just completing module two of our People's Champion Induction Course"*.

Moi presentation: 1. Speech or presentation entirely for the benefit of the person making it. 2. Colossal showboating; pointless tirade whose sole purpose is to make the speaker appear rather brilliant; grandstand bravura performance, but with no tangible outcome or application; hot air; piffle; expedient drivel where silence would have been more productive. (*see BlackBerry prayer; Death by PowerPoint; Meetings*)

Momentum: 1. Impetus. 2. Manifestation of the business world's obsession with pace; effort; forward motion suddenly requested on seemingly already dead tasks, as in *"We need some serious momentum on Project Birdbath, Brian"*. (*see Going forward*)

Mondayize: 1. Contrived verb for moving a statutory holiday to the nearest Monday in order to secure a long weekend, originated in New Zealand. 2. Push to next week in the hope something will have changed; start the week in style, probably with a formulaic and depressing status meeting. (*see -ize*)

Monetize: 1. Make money from. 2. Repugnant financial verb coined by so-called digital natives, as in *"We need to work out how to monetize content here, Alex"*; statement of something monumentally self-evident – that business activities should indeed make some money, unlike most social media, hence the urgent request to *"monetize"*. (*see Democratize; Digital native; -ize; Productize*)

Money for old rope: 1. Easy cash. 2. Stacks of income for doing sod all; outrageous margins on premium products just because rich show-offs don't know the true value of anything; fleece; swindle; hoodwink; con; embezzle. (*see Pay through the nose; Premium*)

Monitoring: 1. Keeping an eye on. 2. Posher word for basic research, allowing self-appointed *"monitoring"* company to charge a great deal more. (*see Guardian, brand*)

Monster, it's a: 1. It's big and/or very scary. 2. This presentation is far too long; this project is so unwieldy it will never succeed; this Sales Director is horribly overweight; this budget is bloated because the CEO thinks it's a winner. (*see Gangbusters, it's going; Mega; Meta*)

Moon, barking at the, over the, through the: 1. Mad, elated or both simultaneously. 2. Baffling lunar reference, possibly rooted in lunacy itself; not the full shilling. (*see AWOL, go; Ballistic, go; Box of frogs, mad as a; Plot, lose the; Postal, go; Pram, to throw one's toys out of; Rails, gone off the; Sandwich, one _____ short of a picnic; Shilling, not the full*)

More than one way to skin a cat, there's: 1. There are a number of techniques for removing the epidermis of a feline. 2. We can approach this a number of ways, and frankly I haven't a clue which is the best, despite being in charge; redundant throwaway line much loved by dim sales managers in idea sessions.

Motivation, lack of, team: 1. Desire to do something, individual or collective; 2. Lack of desire to do something, individual or collective; boredom; ennui; listlessness; depression; oh what's the bloody point?; word only used when motivation is an issue, such as in badly-run companies with no money and a bad staff record, as in *"Come on guys, we need something motivational for the troops!"* (Team, there's no I in; Troops, the)

Motivational posters: 1. Notices on company wall designed to enthuse workforce. 2. Pat half-jokes that are in themselves the butt of much staff cynicism and, in some cases, outright abuse; homespun versions include the hardy perennial *"You don't have to be mad to work here but it helps!"*; company-generated efforts invariably depict Lord Kitchener doctored to feature the Managing Director's face declaring *"Your company needs you!"*, or a highly contrived mantra that no one understands, such as *"Aptitude+Attitude=Altitude!"*; typically found taped to the wall next to a furred up old kettle or in the wash and scrub up area next to the fire evacuation procedure; best avoided. (*see Internal communications*)

Mountain out of a molehill, make a: 1. Generate a big issue out of nothing much. 2. Completely overdo it; brew up vast head of steam; lose the plot; fail to cope; stack problem upon problem until the task is apparently insurmountable, when in fact it is perfectly straightforward; delay simple task and thereby make worse, such as fail to do expenses or timesheets for a year and then complain it will take the whole weekend.

Mountain to climb: 1. Large rock structure that needs ascending; difficult task. 2. Often part two of a project or series of presentations, such as the second half of a football match; usually preceded by sorry under-performance and therefore almost always of one's own making, as in *"Since we shot ourselves in the foot in round one now we have a mountain to climb"*. (*see Foot, shoot oneself in the; Hoist with one's own petard; Own goal, spectacular*)

Movers and shakers: 1. People with power and influence, possibly from a 19th-century poem by Arthur O'Shaughnessy. 2. All Board directors; customers in significant purchasing positions; members of procurement function; young buck on the up; Chief Executive's personal assistant, often referred to as *"the gatekeeper"*; Chairman's wife, often the one genuinely in charge of strategic direction; receptionist or security guard, who usually know more about the company than all the rest put together. (*see Chairman's wife*)

Multicultural: 1. Relating to, or involving, several cultures. 2. Lazy adjective used to suggest diversity of any kind, as in *"As you can see we're a pretty multicultural bunch here, Victoria"*, usually pointing to an all-Caucasian work force. (*see Broad church; Diversity*)

Multitasking: 1. Doing many things, usually at the same time. 2. Claiming to do many things at once, and failing to complete any of them; making a grandiose start on all fronts, with no discernible delivery of anything in particular; taking on far too much and underachieving as a result; making the schoolboy error of claiming to be good at multitasking, as in *"Hi, I'm a brilliant multitasker!"*, and then being given far too much to do. (*see Entrepreneur; Paper cup, here's a _____, there's a tidal wave coming*)

Multiskill: 1. To train employees to do a number of different tasks. 2. To claim to train employees to do a number of different tasks, not do so, and yet still ask them to do a number of different tasks; to woefully under-equip; to leave high and dry; to work like a dog with no relevant training. (*see Paper cup, here's a _____, there's a tidal wave coming*)

Mum, keep: 1. Say nothing, as in mum's the word (14th century, believed to be suggestive of closed lips). 2. Say nothing on pain of death; under no circumstances mention what's gone on or you'll be fired; deploy utmost secrecy; obfuscate; cover up; throw a veil over; refuse to reveal inner workings, especially of true pricing; demonstrate opacity; refuse to be transparent, normally whilst claiming to be so. (*see Gloss over; Keep it dark; Line in the sand, draw a; Obfuscation; Ps and Qs, mind your*)

Musical chairs: 1. Party game; any situation involving a number of people in a series of interrelated changes. 2. Similarly childish manoeuvres at the top of any company, such as putting the Production Director in charge of marketing when he knows absolutely nothing about it; arbitrary shuffling of sales force to create the illusion of improvement; bizarre merry-go-round of CEOs in which a failure from one company is suddenly hailed as the saviour of another, despite widespread knowledge of their incompetence; job swap; career carousel; March madness.

Must, this is a: 1. We have to do it, or have it. 2. I'd like to prevail with my bias immediately, albeit in the absence of any sensible knowledge of the subject; instinct and opinion must win out over the facts; my hunch is better than yours; forget time-consuming research and investigation, let's just crack on with it. (*see Gut feel; Must-have; Pants, fly by the seat of our*)

Must-have: 1. Vital; absolutely required. 2. Irritating adjective originally pioneered by style magazine journalists intent on telling people what they *"must have"*, as though it's any of their concern; absolutely not needed at all; froufrou; flash in the pan; ephemeral; here today, gone tomorrow. (*see Here-and-now-ness; Must, this is a; Tipping point, the*)

Mustard, cut the, that's _____ that is: 1. (It has) come up to expectations. 2. That's really clinched it; we're on fire; we're brilliant; that's great; triumphant expression of apparent achievement, often before calamitous fall. (*see Bee's knees, it's the; Dog's bollocks*)

Nn

Nail it: 1. Hammer a nail into something; get it right, usually first time. 2. Generate a trite sound bite that creates the impression of clarity and decisive action, whilst in truth there is none whatsoever; much loved by politicians, but also true of shyster Chief Executives.

Nailing a jelly to the wall, trying to: 1. Attempting an impossible task. 2. Using jelly to do something for which it was not intended; trying to use tools that will never do the job, however insane the job is; hammering away with an inappropriate approach, too dim to realize that pausing for reflection could be more productive. (*see Banana, stabbing a seal with a; Grasping at fog*)

Name and shame: 1. Find the culprit and let everybody know who they are. 2. Realize it's actually your fault, and then frantically generate a trumped-up case to incriminate someone else. (*see Backlash; Back stabbing; Blame culture; Front stabbing; Witch-hunt*)

Nationwide: 1. All over the country. 2. London plus a bit, but we couldn't afford anything else and we don't want to be accused of being Southern Softies. (*see Pan-global; -European*)

Natural order of things, don't upset the: 1. Don't do anything disruptive. 2. I love the status quo because it means I am in charge, so don't change a thing or you'll be fired. (*see Apple cart, don't upset the*)

Navel gazing: 1. Looking distractedly at one's belly button; being overly introspective. 2. Obsessively inward-looking; blindly hell-bent on one's own category, as in narrow-minded recruitment ads that demand previous experience of the sector, without realizing this will simply perpetuate the current stasis. (*see Black swan; Forward-looking; Futureproof; Go round the houses; Natural order of things, don't upset the; Planning; Research*)

Neck of the woods: 1. A particular part of the woods, and certainly nothing to do with the neck. 2. Arcane and highly specific area that you are not supposed to know about, usually shrouded in cringe-worthy jargon in order to obfuscate. (*see Jargon; Need to know; Obfuscation*)

Need to know basis: 1. Literal meaning: you or I need to know something. 2. We are treating this on a *"need to know"* basis, and you don't need to know because we are covering up something very nasty indeed. (*see Access to information*)

Needle, moving the: 1. Making something happen; going faster than before. 2. Full-throttle, balls-to-wall, cock-of-roost, unadulterated machismo; this expression has everything that testosterone-fuelled Sales Directors require, including suggestions of fighter pilots, racing cars, speed and power; a veritable classic for pumping up the troops, as in *"We really need to move the needle on this one guys!"* (*see Crash and burn; Maxed out: Needle, pushing the; Pushing the envelope; Troops; Wheels coming off*)

Needle, pushing the: 1. Moving at excessive speed; about to explode. 2. An even heavier duty version of moving the needle; in this example it has been pushed as far as it can go, with dangerous consequences; running hot; overheating; about to blow a gasket; massively over-doing it, usually due to hubris or too much coffee; losing it on the chicane; careening perilously close to edge; crashing imminently. (*see Crash and burn; Maxed out; Needle, moving the; Pushing the envelope; Wheels coming off*)

Needs and wants: 1. What someone wants or needs. 2. Fairly mindless distinction between what someone needs and what they want; rather arrogant assumption that you know better, as in *"Aha – that's what they say they want, but is it what they really need?"*; lazy and condescending catch-all phrase to describe hypothetical mood of a target audience, much loved by so-called *"brand strategists"*, as in *"Now Michael, let's drill down into the sub-segments to look in detail at their needs and wants".* (*see Brand strategist; Drill down; Hearts and minds, winning; Know it when I see it, I don't know what I want but I'll _____; Open-ended*)

Negative growth, profit: 1. No profit or growth; decline in same. 2. Egregious weasel phrase for attempting to disguise backward motion, significant failure or outright loss; abject inability to use plain language; hubristic assumption that no one else is smart enough to spot the pathetic attempt at a cover-up. (*see Dead cat bounce; Downsize; Entering a new plateau; Flatline; Massage the numbers; Quantitative easing; SNAFU; Worklessness*)

Nero syndrome: 1. Failure to acknowledge the unpleasant truth, named after the Roman emperor who played the fiddle whilst watching Rome burn. 2. Ego-driven refusal to face the facts; head-in-sand attitude to bad news; Enron-like denial; outright lying; blinkered obduracy, much evidenced by Sales Director who simply will not accept that it's all going wrong. (*see Coffee, wake up and smell the; Dick-swinging; Empire building; Wheels coming off*)

Net net: 1. Remaining after everything is considered; conclusive. 2. Truly exasperating six letters in which three are quite obviously redundant; phrase much loved by pompous management consultants, as in *"Of course, net net this will go gangbusters at the end of the day"*; flip line usually delivered after a long and drawn out debate, whilst leaning back in one's chair and assuming the air of a business sage; confirmatory flourish offered by finance people after intense scrutiny from a colleague who doesn't trust the numbers, as in *"Yes Colin, net net, when all is considered, that is indeed the margin"*. (*see At the end of the day; Gangbusters, it's going; Net out*)

Net out: 1. Conclude; arrive; decide. 2. Variation on *"net net"*, morphed into an active verb, as in *"Where do you net out on this one, Luke?"*; mealy-mouthed alternative for asking or telling someone straight, perhaps along the lines of *"What do you think?"* (*see Net net*)

Network: 1. Make social or business connection with people; series of online connections. 2. Over-used word for meeting lots of people, often for exploitative purposes, but without admitting as such; similarly over-used in an online context, as in *"Mary has a network to die for – she has 2,000 LinkedIn connections, 10,000 followers on Twitter and a highly popular blog"*.

Next-generation: 1. New. 2. Silly word pairing that does little to inform; curious idea that business ideas or products give birth to the "next generation" in the way that humans and animals do; hints of evolution and Darwinism; suggestion that the latest product is de facto better than the one before – a notion not supported by history. (*see Bleeding edge; Cutting edge; Leading edge; Pioneering*)

Next level, take it to the: 1. Improve; make better; up the ante. 2. Crass piece of machismo perpetrated mainly by males who have spent far too long playing computer games; suggestion that increasing effort or productivity in business is something like playing Tomb Raider; weird idea that business has *"levels"* at all; euphemism for pulling one's finger out, as in *"We really need to take this to the next level, Steve"*.

Niche, carve out a, market _____: 1. Find a gap in the market; relating to or aimed at a small specialized group. 2. Tired way of describing who is likely to buy your product or service; use of niche to suggest premium; use of niche to suggest significantly big; general confusion all round with regard to how large a niche actually is; occasional suggestion that many niches can be linked together to create something altogether bigger, and therefore presumably mass market; as such, not niche at all. (*see Across the board, right; Contiguous niches; Coterminous; Long tail, the*)

Nightmare, utter: 1. Terrifying or deeply distressing dream. 2. Something going badly wrong in waking hours; meltdown; chronic failure of everything that matters; career-threatening development. (*see Crash and burn; Ongoing; Wheels coming off*)

Nip in the bud: 1. Check or destroy the growth of. 2. Chop off at the knees; head off at the pass; stop forthwith; cease; desist; prevent from developing; identify as dangerous and take immediate and evasive action; intervene early, as in *"I think we need to nip this one in the bud, Jeremy"*. (*see Head off at the pass; Rabbit, cutting the legs off the _____ to fit it in the hutch; Roots, take the plant up by the*)

No-brainer: 1. Decision that is a foregone conclusion; requiring no thought. 2. Decision that probably does require more thought; hasty default for small-minded executives who may indeed have no brain; impetuous decision, often regretted later, as in *"It's a no-brainer guys!"*, followed by spectacular failure of product or service.

Non-core: 1. Not related to the main point; irrelevant. 2. Superfluous piffle; all the stuff that people and companies do all day when really they shouldn't be; displacement tactics; prevarication; nothing to do with the main point; peripheral in the extreme; marginal; fundamentally off brief; absolutely not the crucial issue; Chairman's speech. (*see Core; Knitting, stick to the; NPD; Principle, core*)

Non-exec: 1. Non-Executive Director. 2. Old bloke who used to work in the industry and is fairly out of touch; primary duties include swanning into quarterly meetings, failing to grasp the working reality, dispensing a few bon mots, failing to write anything down, then buggering off, leaving the business in precisely the same position it was in beforehand. (*see Consigliere; Consultant*)

Non-hierarchical: 1. Everyone on the same level; not prone to issuing orders or pulling rank. 2. Deceptive modern concept to describe ultra-hip new ways of working, much loved by executives favouring a *"casual"* working environment; excuse to wear relaxed office attire badly; contradictory management style suggesting involvement of staff opinion, only to over-rule it comprehensively when it doesn't tally with the views of the Board; faux-consultative stance, as in *"We're all partners in this, Gordon – it's totally non-hierarchical"*, followed by an autocratic and unilateral decision. (*see Dotted line; Hierarchy; Matrix; Organogram; Pecking order; Pull rank*)

Non-judgmental: 1. Not inclined to take a view on other people. 2. Very inclined to take a view on other people; insidious criticism; constantly sniping; convinced that the other person isn't as good as you; nitpicking, as in *"I'm non-judgmental, Adrian, but this work is sub-standard"*. (*see Micromanaging*)

Non-verbal: 1. Not using words. 2. Truly baffling phrase usually married with communication, as in *"His non-verbal communication skills are sub-optimal"*; bizarre idea that non-verbal communication is indeed a possibility in the world, sign language excluded; failure to acknowledge that both speech and writing include verbs; source of general confusion, as in *"He came into my office and congratulated me verbally"*. (*see Communication, lack of; Sub-optimal; Talking out loud*)

No-quibble guarantee: 1. Customer protection charter with no loopholes. 2. Lengthy treatise purporting to provide same, but with no intention of doing so; significant latitude in which to wriggle out of paying refund or compensation; document the length of *War and Peace*, riddled with ambiguity and room for manoeuvre; chapter and verse full of escape clauses; comprehensive attempt to abdicate or avoid responsibility of any kind. (*see Chapter and verse*)

No stone unturned: 1. Every rock now facing upward; nothing left uninvestigated. 2. Phrase much loved by politicians and business people desperate to suggest that their efforts will be comprehensive; most commonly used when things have gone spectacularly wrong and someone has been rumbled, as in *"Our investigation will leave no stone unturned"*. (*see Drains up, have the; Flush out; Lift up a rock; Root-and-branch review; Witch-hunt*)

Nought percent: 1. Nothing. 2. Outrageous attempt to imply quantity where there is none at all; spurious introduction of percentage element when everyone knows that nought percent of nothing is nothing; often used to forge a desperate connection with growth, as in *"Growth will be nought percent next year"*.

NPD: 1. New Product Development. 2. All-embracing descriptor for people fiddling about aimlessly; last bastion of fruitless brainstorming sessions; increasingly frantic attempt to generate more sales when all existing products have stalled. (*see Brainstorm; Non-core*)

Nuclear, go: 1. Adopt fission-based energy approach. 2. Explode in a fit of rage; lose it completely; bawl out colleague; fail to see the funny side of things; defenestrate pot plant, or employee. (*see AWOL, go: Ballistic, go; Defenestrate; Mid-life crisis; Moon, barking at the, over the, through the; Plot, lose the; Postal, go; Radar, off; Rails, gone off the*)

Number, do a _____ on: 1. Convince someone of your point of view. 2. Do up like a kipper; stitch up; prevail over; lean on; bully; overwhelm; send the boys in; beat up.

Numbers, the: 1. Statistics. 2. Any spreadsheet with figures on it; entire set of company accounts; profit and loss estimate; annual budget. (*see Cook the books; Crunch the numbers; Fiscal juggling; Massage the numbers*)

Nut, sledgehammer to crack a: 1. Excessive power for the job in hand. 2. Completely over the top; machismo gone mad; testosterone flowing over; totally unnecessary resources for the task; overkill; too much firepower; display of force. (*see Bazooka after a fly, we're not going to send a; Feet, to dive in with both*)

Nutcracker: 1. Implement used to break open nuts. 2. Vicious female boss determined to *"crack nuts"*; verbal cousin of, but completely unrelated to, the Nutcracker Suite; neither suite nor sweet, in fact, downright bitter. (*see Ballbreaker; Gynocracy; Rottweiler*)

Obfuscation: 1. Deliberately making something obscure or difficult to understand. 2. An egregious lie or cover-up; frantic fudging of the truth to disguise incompetence or outright crime. (*see Access to information; Bollocks, talking; Broad brush; Bullshit; Hedge our bets; Keep it dark; Mum, keep; Off the top of my head; Prevaricate; Talking out loud; Techno-babble; Waffle; Word dump*)

Object, defeating the: 1. Having the opposite of the desired effect; negating what you set out to do. 2. Suicidal act of self-destruction; woeful ability to set out to do one thing, and then immediately do the other. (*see Foot, shoot oneself in the; Platform, eat one's own*)

Objectives: 1. Things you want to do. 2. Appalling ragbag of poorly thought-through stuff, usually cut and paste without thought into a so-called brief and handed to someone else to unravel. (*see Aims; BHAG; Buck, pass the; Target, hit the _____, miss the point, miss the _____ left right and centre, moving*)

Obvious, a firm grasp of the: 1. Ability to understand something quite simple. 2. Utterly thick, as in *"Simon has a firm grasp of the obvious"*, usually meaning that he doesn't, or that it's the only thing he ever will grasp. (*see Bandwidth, he doesn't have the; Input, inputs; Insights; Intelligent, if you were any less _____, I'd have to water you once a day; Mental furniture; Psychic RAM; Shilling, not the full*)

Office, the: 1. A place of work. 2. A place that in truth performs a social function, where hungover employees gather to discuss football results and Coronation Street. (*see Water cooler conversation*)

Office bike: 1. Environmentally friendly mode of transport thoughtfully provided by one's employer. 2. Emma from accounts who will shag anyone for a small Martini. (*see Office party; Soft area*)

Office party: 1. Grand annual celebration of the year's achievements, including a triumphant speech by the Chairman. 2. Rampant bacchanalian orgy at which everyone calls their boss an arsehole, tries it on with Emma from accounts (regardless of whether they are male or female), and throws up on the way home, usually in some form of public transport. (*see Autopilot; Chairman; Christmas party; Compatible, not; Go the whole hog; Office bike; Snakepit*)

Office politics: 1. Rational discourse between colleagues concerning the relative merits of the country's politicians. 2. Naked posturing and allocation of blame. (*see Back stabbing; Blame culture; Front stabbing*)

Offline, take it: 1. Something not done online. 2. I refuse to discuss this now because I can't think of a decent response on the spot, so I am resorting to the first awful Americanism I can think of to buy some time. (*see Clicks and mortar; Obfuscation; Ringfence*)

Off message: 1. Saying the incorrect thing, or not what was originally intended. 2. Saying what you really mean, despite clear instructions from the boss to toe the party line, usually resulting in dismissal. (*see Decruit; Dejob; Off-piste; On message; Realignment*)

Off-piste: 1. Relating to skiing on virgin snow outside the regular runs. 2. Horribly off brief; out of line; touting unauthorized view; a liability. (*see Ducks in a row, get our; Hymn sheet, singing from the same; Loose cannon; Off message; Realignment; Wildebeest in a row, has the lion got his*)

Off ramps: 1. Gone wrong. 2. Bizarre automotive analogy suggestive of a daredevil attempt or circus act; notion that something was going up a ramp, and has now fallen off. (*see On-rails experience; On ramps; Wheels coming off*)

Off-site: 1. A meeting happening somewhere other than the office. 2. Usually unsuccessful effort to change the mood by leaving the stifling environment of the office; posh hotel hired in vain attempt to lift morale; golf venue favoured by Chairman; opportunity to wear disastrous "casual" clothes in front of colleagues; location of horrendous piss-up in hotel bar, leading to a series of indiscretions; Room 27, scene of Malcolm being caught in flagrante delicto with Sylvia from HR; origin of a series of staff dismissals. (*see Autopilot; Awayday; Bad idea, there's no such thing as a; Brainstorm; Executive retreat; Flip chart; Workshop*)

Off the scale: 1. Much better, or possibly much worse, than anticipated. 2. I have no language at all to describe what I am witnessing; unprecedented; unexpected; beyond all current experience. (*see Killer whale; Whaling*)

Off the top of my head: 1. Something has just fallen from my cranium, such as a hat, or my wig. 2. I haven't a clue what I'm talking about, so I'll just spout any twaddle I can think of and hope that nobody notices because they are all doing the same thing. (*see Bullshit; Talking out loud; Waffle; Word dump*)

On a roll: 1. In a good flow of work; so excited that I just can't stop. 2. I am in the staff canteen and I truly have just sat on a cheese roll.

Ongoing: 1. Happening now. 2. An appalling saga that simply won't end; endless nightmare; incapable of finishing a project or meeting due to lack of skill or decisiveness. (*see Meetings; Nightmare, utter*)

On message: 1. Saying the correct thing, or what was originally intended. 2. Parroting the company line by rote, whilst simultaneously failing to say what you really mean. (*see Off message; Yes man*)

On-rails experience: 1. Interface on a mobile device that is easy to use in a clear and linear way. 2. Piece of utter gobbledegook from the online world, spouted by self-appointed digital natives; curious train-based notion somehow likening the orientation of rolling stock with fiddling about with a mobile phone; as close as it comes to defying definition. (*see Digital native; Free-roaming experience; Off ramps; On ramps; User experience*)

On ramps: 1. Going according to plan. 2. Still on a ramp, as originally initiated, for reasons unknown. (*see Off ramps; On-rails experience; Wheels coming off*)

One fell swoop, in: 1. Done in a single action. 2. Hastily; rashly; in a draconian fashion, often referring to the sacking of large swathes of the work force. (*see At a stroke; Dejob*)

One-stop shop: 1. Venue where you can buy everything you want in one place. 2. Rather glib phrase now in common parlance when companies are trying to suggest that they can cater for your every need; flagrant attempt to hoover up as much income as possible for the least amount of effort; thinly-veiled effort to have just one place of work, thus saving on any other premises; pretence at jack-of-all-trades capability, where usually none exists.

One-to-one: 1. In person, two people talking to each other. 2. Quite baffling expression of two people having a conversation, as though that were a complicated concept to grasp; reinvented as a *"one-to-one"*, presumably in the hope that the re-expression clarifies the numbers involved, for those of us too dim to understand. (*see B2B; B2C; Cherry pick; Face time; Face-to-face; Heads up; Interface*)

One-to-many: 1. One person or company addressing many people. 2. Dreadful bastard son of *"one-to-one"*; needless distinction between an individual and their likelihood of communicating with more than one person; unhelpful jargon often found in communications briefs, as in *"This is essentially a one-to-many communications challenge"*. (*see B2B; B2C; One-to-one*)

One-upmanship: 1. The art of achieving advantage over others, often by slightly unscrupulous means. 2. Naked ambition; legerdemain; slight of hand; deviousness; preparedness to throw all colleagues to the lions in order to advance one's own position; complete lack of morals; selfishness; desire to win at all costs; propensity to gloat uncontrollably when winning or getting one's own way; smugness.

Open: 1. Receptive to new ideas; unprejudiced. 2. Part of a modern suite of words aimed at conveying transparency, particularly in matters of finance; suggestion that the business is not *"closed"* or secretive, when it usually is; up for grabs;

up for anything; relaxed about revealing inner workings, as in *"We are open to suggestions"*, aka. we have no ideas at all so do please come up with something. (*see Open door policy; Openness; Transparency*)

Open door policy: 1. You can drop by any time; we have removed all the doors from the office. 2. Phrase much loved by touchy-feely bosses, as in *"Come and see me with your issues any time, Justin – I operate an open door policy"*; closed door policy in which any attempt to *"drop by"* unannounced will be met with fierce resistance from a Rottweiler of a personal assistant; comprehensive blocking out of the diary; perpetual unavailability on account of *"being in a meeting"* all the time. (*see Open; Openness; Meetings; Rottweiler; Touchy-feely; Transparency*)

Open-ended: 1. Without definite limits. 2. Infinite; truly never-ending; disastrously over-running; something urgently requiring clarity, as in *"Of course this is an open-ended brief, Ralph"*; hopelessly unclear; beyond vague; near-impossible to get a handle on. (*see Know it when I see it, I don't know what I want but I'll _____; Needs and wants*)

Open-heart surgery, it's not: 1. This is nothing to do with surgical repair of the heart; it's not very complicated. 2. Rather dismissive way of saying that something is dead easy, when it may or may not be; used in a variety of circumstances, but most commonly when a frustrated but poorly-informed senior executive is trying to get some forward motion on a project; invariably followed by the embarrassing realization that the task is indeed quite complicated, albeit probably not as much as open-heart surgery. (*see Brain surgery, it's not; Real teeth, our campaign needs to have _____; Rocket science, it's not*)

Openness: 1. Propensity to be open. 2. Susceptibility to outside influence; open-mindedness; pretence at having these qualities, but with no intention of doing anything other than what you wanted in the first place – a trait common in Chief Executives. (*see Open; Open door policy; Transparency*)

Opportunity: 1. Chance to do something. 2. Complete rebranding of the word *"problem"*, probably borrowed from a quote attributed to the author Dorye Roettger: *"There are no problems – only opportunities to be creative"*. (*see Ask, big; Challenges; Poisoned chalice; SWOT analysis*)

Optimal: 1. Another word for optimum; the best possible result, even if it involves compromise. 2. Interesting word that effectively tries to make the most of a bad job by adding an optimistic feel to a state of affairs that usually isn't; the best we can do, all things considered; not really optimal at all – more of a fudge; cracks papered over; not that good; distinctly average; whatever we could knock up in the time; patchy. (*see Bugs, iron out the; Crafting, it needs a bit of; Drawing board, back to the; Satisficing; Sub-optimal*)

Optimize: 1. Take full advantage of; make better; be as efficient as possible. 2. Exploit to the full; squeeze every last drop out of; frantically try to improve; bring up to scratch, if that's possible; scrabble to meet basic entry criteria. (*see –ize; Optimal; Sub-optimal*)

Options, explore the: 1. Consider all the possibilities. 2. Look urgently for an alternative, as in *"F**king hell, is this all we've got?!"*; mildly pejorative expression suggestion that colleague has not really done their homework properly, as in *"I seriously think we need to look at all the options, Bernard"*; hastily search for other possibilities; panic; generate a head of steam; be all of a fluster.

-oriented: 1. Suffix meaning designed for, directed towards, motivated by or concerned with. 2. Trying to suggest direction or some sort of centre of gravity where usually there is none; a close cousin of -centred and -centric; almost invariably redundant and should probably be stripped out of every document or presentation in which it appears. (*see -centred, -centric; -driven; -focused, people-, goal-; Goal-oriented*)

Orchestra model: 1. System in which the boss sets direction and an expert team get on with executing it. 2. Polar opposite of what happens in most companies, due to (a) a boss who is incapable of setting a clear direction and leaving the staff alone or (b) insufficiently skilled staff. (*see Conductor's baton, wave the; Pull out all the stops*)

Organogram: 1. Variously spelt organigram or orgnagram, a diagram of how a company is organized. 2. Impenetrable tangle of reporting lines signifying bugger all; wiring diagram gone haywire; snake's honeymoon; horribly misleading latticework of inter-relationships designed to make everyone think they are more senior than everyone else; originator of the dreaded dotted line – source of tremendous confusion and tension, as in *"I am very much my own man, but I have a dotted line in to Brian"*. (*see Dotted line; Hierarchy; Matrix; Non-hierarchical; Pecking order; Pull rank; Snake's honeymoon; Viper's nest*)

Out, I want him/her: 1. I want them fired. 2. I have no particular reason but they have to go; my ego has got the better of me and I feel threatened; he/she appears more competent than me and I can't have that; get them out, before I'm exposed; call HR immediately and trump up some justification for getting them out. (*see Marching orders, get your*)

Out of office message: 1. Automatically generated email response pointing out that the intended recipient is not there. 2. Brilliant smokescreen for being away when one is patently not; frequently abbreviated to OOO, which adds a frisson of emotion to matters; often accompanied by a throwaway line such as *"In my absence do contact Gay or Rebecca on extension 3875"*. (*see Hospital pass*)

Outcomes, negative, positive: 1. Things that happen as a result of something else, for better or worse. 2. Thoroughly unexpected developments; unforeseen consequences; stuff you really never meant to happen; dreadful fallout; wishy-washy list at the end of brainstorm suggesting what really should happen, when none of the attendees has the slightest inclination to do any of them. (*see Action, actioned, actioning; Bandwagon, jumping on the negative _____ ,positive _____ ; Brainstorm; Outputs: Success, what does _____ look like?*)

Outputs: 1. Things that happen, usually as a result of some inputs. 2. Flabby plural noun to denote something that needs to be done; even worse as a verb, as in *"Can* *you output this one please, Marjorie?"*; huge checklist of trivia, none of which has any bearing on the main point; mad ramblings of boss converted into irrelevant action. (*see Action, actioned; Delivery of outputs; Input, inputs*)

Outsmart: 1. Outwit rival using intellect. 2. Outwit rival using nefarious means, cheating, deception, rank, forces of darkness or pure violence.

Outsourcing: 1. Process of buying in services rather than conducting them in the company; literally, sourcing from outside. 2. Smokescreen for screwing supplier costs and charging a higher mark-up without doing any of the work; excuse to reduce own workforce significantly, reducing the original company to a soulless administrative shell.

Out there: 1. Somewhere away from here, such as outside this building, town or country. 2. Consummate piece of bullshit added to any sentence to create spurious impression of scale, as in *"There are lots of opportunities out there, Paul"*; invariably used without any thought as to where *"there"* is; general impression that *"there"* is vast, scary, intrepid, somehow pioneering or dangerous; nebulous and fictitious catch-all for a place that no one can ever define; in short, total bollocks. (*see Environment, business, challenging; Jungle, it's a _____ out there; Space*)

Over a barrel: 1. In a compromising position; powerless. 2. Completely boxed into a corner; nowhere to run or hide; uncomfortably exposed; caged; with no choice at all; damned if you do, damned if you don't; a daily occurrence in most job descriptions. (*see Cocks on the block*)

Over-arching: 1. Forming an arch over; all-encompassing. 2. Perfectly reasonable word in the right context, as in when something is genuinely forming an arch over something else; more commonly used by self-appointed *"brand strategists"* to create some sort of tangible basis for an ethereal concept. (*see Architecture, brand _____, business _____; Brand strategist; Foundations, lay the, firm, shaky; Umbrella*)

Overview: 1. A general survey. 2. Monumentally vague sweeping statement or eye-wateringly-long report that concludes nothing at all. (*see Closer look, stand back and take a*)

Ownership, take _____ of: 1. Take responsibility for. 2. Shirk; duck the issue; delegate immediately; claim credit if it goes right; hide if it goes wrong; pretend to add to list of tasks and ignore completely; use as fodder to impress boss and then shove in a drawer; bury; stifle at birth; add to status report and then go to the pub.

Own goal, spectacular: 1. High profile scoring of goal for the opposition. 2. Blatantly counter-productive move; demonstration of gross incompetence; public display of stupidity, usually born out of hubris or pride. (*see Foot, shoot oneself in the; Hoist with one's own petard; Mountain to climb; Platform, eat one's own; Shafted down the river, yourself; Tent, standing outside the _____ pissing in*)

Pp

Ps and Qs, mind your: 1. Be careful to behave properly or use the correct language. 2. Say nothing that will incriminate you; say nothing for fear of revealing incompetence or indolence. (*see Gloss over; Keep it dark; Mum, keep*)

Pacesetter: 1. The frontrunner who sets the pace. 2. Foolhardy first mover in any market. (*see Kamikaze; First mover advantage*)

Package: 1. Parcel or box with something in it. 2. Hotchpotch of ill-conceived ideas hastily lashed together to create the semblance of coherence. (*see Raft of ideas, proposals, respondents; World class*)

Pan-global, -European: 1. Across the world, or Europe. 2. Dick-swinging over-claim designed to make a project or company seem bigger than it really is; test market in Tyne Tees hyped beyond all reasonable levels of expectation. (*see Across the board, right; APAC; EMEA; Nationwide; World class*)

Panjandrum: 1. A pompous self-important official. 2. Utter twat who delights in reciting the company policy on anything, whilst failing to lift a finger to help on the grounds that it's *"More than my job's worth mate"*. (*see Administrivia; Bread and butter; Bureaucracy; Compliance; Manager; Process; Target manager; Timesheets; Vis-à-vis*)

Pants down, caught with our: 1. Caught on the hop. 2. Caught in flagrante delicto with Julia from HR, or Gary from the post room. (*see Drop our trousers*)

Pants, fly by the seat of our: 1. Make it up as we go along. 2. Business as usual. (*see Adhocracy; Gut feel; Must, this is a; SNAFU*)

Paper cup, here's a _____, there's a tidal wave coming: 1. Something very nasty is on its way, and here is something quite inadequate to help you deal with it. 2. Classic approach to hanging an individual out to dry, much loved by sweaty Sales

Directors from the *"school of hard knocks"*; implication that torture is somehow character building; woeful under-equipping of staff for scale of task in hand; line often delivered with a knowing wink and a patronizing arm round the shoulder, as though it's a favour; apparent rite of passage, as in *"There's a tidal wave coming David – here's a paper cup, I'm sure you'll cope"*. (*see Eastern front, this is the like the* _____ *when the bullets didn't turn up; Head office, I'm from* _____ *and I'm here to help; Multitasking; Multiskill; Titanic, rearranging the deckchairs on the*)

Papering over the cracks: 1. Patching up a bad job. 2. Business as usual. (*see Pants, fly by the seat of our; Turd, polishing a*)

Paradigm shift: 1. Radical change in beliefs or theory, coined by US science philosopher T. S. Kuhn (1922-1996). 2. Precisely the same old shit we've always done; no real change at all; minor difference pathetically trumpeted as a brave new dawn. (*see Sea change; Step change*)

Parapet, heads above the, keep our head below the: 1. Take responsibility for something, or don't. 2. Pathetic and entirely inaccurate military analogy that fails miserably to convey the insignificance of almost any action – above or below, it makes no difference whatsoever. (*see High profile; Stand up and be counted; Trenches, in the*)

Park it: 1. Manoeuvre a vehicle into a stationary position. 2. Shut up; say nothing; bury that toxic bit of information immediately in case we're found out. (*see Offline, take it; Ringfence; STFU; SUMO*)

Participation: 1. Joining in. 2. Frequently meaning the opposite; exclusion; being kept in the dark; cover-up for not involving someone, as in *"Make sure we have Gordon's participation on Project Peabrain, Dorothy"*; cynical scheme to overload someone's in-tray by insisting on their *"participation"* in every single project you can think of; cause colleague to collapse due to over-participation. (*see Maxed out*)

Partners: 1. Allies; companions. 2. Desperate and rarely successful attempt by suppliers to command an equal footing with their customers; often wrapped up in the soft language of bonding, as in *"We are delighted to be strategic partners"*, when in fact the company receives a daily whipping and simply does what it's told. (*see Bonding, team; Proactive; Reactive; Strategic alliance; 60:50 relationship, this is the perfect*)

Party, bring to the: 1. Contribute. 2. Oddly childish idea based on kindergarten tradition of always bringing a balloon or present to a birthday celebration; shades of whoopee cushions, streamers and paper hats; possible requirement to attend meeting with cake for all, as in *"If we're going to involve Sharon in Project Wetwipe, I want to know exactly what she's going to bring to the party"*; sometimes used in a broader company sense when considering whether to hire someone, as though their appeal would increase if they had an imaginary friend or a puppy.

Pass the baton: 1. Hand something over, such as a project, as in a relay race. 2. Consummately fail to do precisely that; bugger off with no further comment; leave company, along with a calamitous collection of half-finished projects;

nightmare trail of unintelligible paperwork, or none at all; create the illusion of a comprehensive briefing, when it is anything but; mislead; misdirect; provide no direction at all; obfuscate; delegate hastily with no regard for successor. (*see Buck, pass the; Drop the ball; Hospital pass; Obfuscate*)

Passion, passionate: 1. Keen; enthusiastic; ardently affectionate. 2. Ubiquitous piece of wibble vainly attempting to verify that the company and its staff will be dedicated, relentlessly supportive and there at any second of the day; rather seedy implication that there will be some sort of sexual relations between customer and supplier, as though that would be a benefit; almost invariably over-claim, as in *"As you can tell, at Babcock, Bored and Bandycoot, we are passionate about the ball bearing market"*. (*see Always on; Authenticity; Constantly striving; Expectations, exceeding; Mission statement; Sun, the _____ never sets at; 24/7/365; Values*)

Pathologist's interest: 1. Concerned posthumously, as in a post mortem. 2. Macabre reference to forensically raking over a dead project, or possibly colleague (medical profession only); outside chance of a desire to learn and improve matters next time, but more likely a need to gloat and laugh generally at the trail of incompetence that will almost certainly be uncovered; delight in watching a project unravel; voyeur's interest, for the sole purpose of saying *"I told you so"*. (*see Eastern front, this is the like the _____ when the bullets didn't turn up; Forensic, send it down to the boys in; Look, take a long hard; Paper cup, here's a _____, there's a tidal wave coming; Pulse, check the, finger on the; Titanic, rearranging the deckchairs on the; Tits up, it's all gone*)

Paving the way: 1. Laying down flagstones to make the route easier; smoothing the passage of something. 2. Greasing the wheels; putting in the spadework; trying to make something a foregone conclusion; making all the decisions before the meeting even happens, as is common practice in Japan, thereby derailing all insignificant (and oblivious) colleagues. (*see Done deal*)

Pay through the nose: 1. Pay an exorbitant price. 2. Significantly over-pay, or fleece a client into doing so; much loved practice of companies peddling so-called *"premium"* brands, aka. cheap tat dressed up as expensive and flogged to undiscerning show-offs who don't know any better; phrase often associated with self-obsessed Chief Executives who think nothing of shelling out inordinate amounts on acquiring another company to boost the value of their shares, as in *"Anthony did the deal but he certainly paid through the nose for it"*. (*see Merger; Money for old rope; Premium*)

PDQ: 1. Pretty Damn Quick(ly). 2. Ridiculously fast; now, if not sooner; by yesterday; annoying and rather sanctimonious acronym typically deployed by bosses with one of two unfortunate characteristics: (a) chronic disorganization, as in *"I've sat on this for weeks and now it's screamingly urgent"* or (b) a dismal inability to say no, as in *"I've had an extremely unreasonable request from a client but I haven't got the balls to talk them out of it so you'll have to do it"*. (*see ASAP; Buck, pass the; ETA*)

Pear-shaped, it's all gone: 1. It's gone badly wrong. 2. Fruit-themed analogy of unknown origin, suggesting somewhat that the design of a pear is in some way undesirable, although no one has ever ventured to suggest why that might be;

possible allusion to the sagging figure of an older woman (unverified); severity ranges from a mildly derogatory horticultural reference to an expression of extreme dismay, spanning from *"This has gone a bit wrong"* to *"Everything's f**ked and I'm being fired this afternoon"*. (*see AWOL, go; Tits up, it's all gone*)

Pecking order: 1. Seniority sequence. 2. Vindictive chain of bullying, drawn from the avian world, but true of almost every tribe, including those containing humans; starting from the top, the CEO bollocks the MD, who bollocks the nearest director, who finds a subordinate to blame, who delegates responsibility to the hapless bastard who ultimately gets fired. (*see Dotted line; Hierarchy; Matrix; Non-hierarchical; Organogram; Pull rank; Snake's honeymoon*)

Penetration: 1. The ability or power to penetrate. 2. Seedy, semi-sexual description of the degree to which something has an effect; much loved by those in advertising and media, as in *"This campaign will deliver 100% penetration of the target audience"* – a remark likely to get most other people thrown into jail.

Penthouse, furnishing the: 1. Doing all the nice stuff before the grunt work is done. 2. Partial architectural reference to the fact that in most companies the Board resides on the top floor, well away from the hoi polloi; suggestion that senior people always concentrate on the so-called *"big picture"* so as to avoid doing any actual work, as in *"He's busy furnishing the penthouse and we haven't even laid the foundations yet"*. (*see Foundations, lay the, firm, shaky; Grunt work*)

Percent, give a hundred and ten: 1. Deliver, probably overly so. 2. Mathematically impossible twaddle originating from the world of football and now all-pervasive in business, particularly sales; purveyors of this classic appear unaware of how stupid it makes them sound; staple of sweaty, Terylene-suited Sales Directors at the annual sales conference, as in *"I need you to give 110% to Project Beanstalk guys!"* – an exhortation usually followed by the playing of motivational music such as Pink Floyd's Money, Tina Turner's Simply the Best or S.U.C.C.E.S.S. by Holly Johnson.

Performance review: 1. Assessment of capability; meeting to discuss same. 2. Cursory glance at one's achievements and activities, usually poorly informed; meeting with someone who barely knows who you are or what you do, a role often called "line manager"; annual meeting that is crucial to you but that is postponed at short notice on several occasions and sometimes never happens at all; sham. (*see Appraisal, one degree; Appraisal, 360 degree; Line manager*)

Permanently reducing prices: 1. Lowering the cost of something all the time. 2. Idiotic marketing claim that is mathematically impossible; ludicrous suggestion that the price will continue to drop even past the point of being free – in other words, they'll have to pay you.

Permission marketing: 1. Marketing that checks that an individual or company is happy to be marketed to before embarking on it; a phrase coined by author Seth Godin in his book of the same name. 2. Somewhat self-deluding notion that many people love to be *"marketed to"*; laudable idea to ask people first, but often wrapped up in deceptive clothes, such as tick boxes, opt-out clauses and terms and conditions; in certain cases, marketing without consent.

Peter Principle, the: 1. Principle that in a hierarchy every employee tends to rise to his level of incompetence, coined by Peter and Hull in the book of the same name, in 1969. 2. Although the book was a spoof, it sent shock waves through the business world, which realized with horror that it was true; suggestion that all senior people are merely in transit out of the organization, having themselves reached their level of incompetence. (*see 80/20 rule*)

Phone list, go down the: 1. Scan list of company employees. 2. Scan list of employees with the express purpose of getting rid of a large quantity of them; hold *"ABC"* session in which all employees are graded and all the C grades disposed of; cull; prune; destaff. (*see ABC session; Axe, face the; Decruit; Dejob; Destaff; Headcount; LIFO*)

Picnic, one sandwich short of a: 1. Somewhat light on foodstuff for an outdoor meal. 2. Not very smart; thick; slow off the mark; useless; a hindrance to the team. (*see AWOL, go; Basket case; Box of frogs, mad as a; Bundle, one stick short of a; Gene pool, swimming in the shallow end of the*)

Pie chart: 1. Circular diagram with segments denoting quantities. 2. Widely abused way of presenting information, often offering a car crash of colour, three-dimensional graphics and hard-to-read appended figures; deliberate way of disguising the fact that the figures are not very good, or not even interesting enough to warrant a chart at all.

Pigeonhole: 1. Small compartment for papers and letters; to classify in a rigid manner. 2. Application of irrational bias, fuelled by a range of misguided emotions including sexism, racism, jealousy and xenophobia; uncanny ability to stereotype everyone to fit one's own world view.

Piggyback: 1. To ride on someone's shoulders; as an addition to something else. 2. Transparent attempt to bundle two things together, such as workload, responsibility or budget; try to get two things for the price of one; gain cover by joining in with something else; engineer potential scapegoat in case it all goes wrong. (*see Air cover; Hook to hang our hat on; Scapegoat, make a _____ out of*)

Pig's ear: 1. Something badly or clumsily done; 2. Botched job; cockup; piss-poor attempt, as in *"Bloody hell Kev, you've really made a pig's ear out of this one"*. (*see Cockup*)

Pilot (vb.): 1. To guide or steer. 2. Give semblance of direction and then abdicate all responsibility, leaving subordinates high and dry; pseudo aeronautical term to suggest confidence, competence and skill at speed – characteristics perennially lacking in managers from Buenos Aires to Bolton.

Pitch: 1. Word with over 40 different meanings, but most commonly in business, a sales presentation. 2. Pack of lies; elaborate web of fabrication that bears absolutely no relation to the working reality if lucky enough to win the business; farrago of half-truths and empty promises; piffle; hot air; not worth the paper it's written on; fiction.

Pioneering: 1. Exploratory, truly innovative, genuinely new. 2. Over-worked adjective to suggest ingenuity, usually applied to thoroughly workaday stuff. (*see Bleeding edge; Cutting edge; Leading edge; Next-generation*)

Pipeline, in the: 1. Coming soon. 2. Wishful thinking; not really ever likely to occur; improbable; included in a status report to add extra bulk, as when cold-calling agencies report back to their clients; not a cat in hell's chance of seeing the light of day; blocked; baulked; grounded; tightly wedged in and never likely to budge. (*see Done deal; Hopper, pour into the; In the bag; Leaky bucket*)

Pivot: 1. Reorient business direction to improve product or income. 2. Embark on a massive U-turn after significantly cocking it up; much-loved so-called entrepreneur's term for changing tack after embarking on a dead duck. (*see Coming or going, he doesn't know if he's; Evolving to meet customer demand; Tweak; U-Turn*)

Planning: 1. Working out how to do something; discipline or department intended to do the same. 2. Interminable phase of navel gazing from which some products, or indeed whole companies, never emerge; extended excuse to do the square root of sod all, and yet remain under the comfortable banner of *"strategy"*. (*see Go round the houses; Navel gazing; Research; Strategy, Strategize*)

Plate spinning: 1. Fine art of rotating multiple items of crockery on poles, for reasons best known to those doing it. 2. Having far too much on the go at the same time, with any one element likely to crash at any moment; unfeasible balancing act that will inevitably go wrong; accident waiting to happen; imminent crash or collision. (*see Ball juggling; Balls in the air, on the block, to the wall; Crash and burn; Python, wrestling with a*)

Platform, online, sales, user: 1. Base on which to do something, such as offer technology or interact with customers. 2. Increasingly over-used word, seemingly applied to everything from railway stations to websites. (*see Burning platform; Platform, eat one's own; Platform, exceed the*)

Platform, eat one's own: 1. Destroy one's own source of business. 2. Rather eccentric idea of eating an inedible thing, in this case probably made of wood or metal; sales platform notion arguably taken a step too far; cannibalistic instinct possibly over-applied, to the point of killing customer base; short-sighted and inadvisable short-term approach to aggressive sales, thereby putting future customers off for life. (*see Bazooka after a fly, we're not going to send a; Foot, shoot oneself in the; Hoist with one's own petard; Kamikaze; Object, defeating the; Own goal, spectacular*)

Platform, exceed the: 1. Topple over; spill over designated boundary. 2. Completely overshoot; run hot; lose the plot; blow it; overdo it comprehensively; over-cook; blow a gasket; drop; explode in all directions; fail to control; run amok; overstep brief, with unpleasant consequences. (*see Bazooka after a fly, we're not going to send a; Drop a Ricket; Feet, to dive in with both; Nut, sledgehammer to crack a*)

Play hardball: 1. Act in a ruthless or uncompromising way. 2. Be macho; take no nonsense; make it clear you are the king of the castle; refuse to back down, ever; be quite sure that you are right, always.

Play out of our skins: 1. Do better than we usually do. 2. Pull off quite a surprise; over-achieve for once; perform to the most of our potential; a rare state of affairs.

Play the percentages: 1. Bet a little here, a little there. 2. Cover every angle; fail or refuse to commit one way or the other; play one side off against the other; divide and conquer. (*see Hedge our bets*)

Player, big: 1. Tall or corpulent competitor; influential individual. 2. Narcissistic puffball; over-paid CEO with a reputation for failing spectacularly and generating big personal payoffs; someone who hobnobs with celebrities; tax avoider, or quite possibly evader; sometimes used to refer to an entire company that acts in approximately the same way, and is probably the subject of a major court case at any given moment. (*see Big cheese; Chairman; Fromage, grand; Head honcho; Heavy hitter*)

Playing away: 1. Having a meeting at someone else's office; in league with the competition. 2. Indulging in industrial espionage; married, but nevertheless sleeping with Tracy from production.

Playtex strategy: 1. To lift and separate two elements of the plan, named after the bra advertising in the sixties and seventies suggesting the same effect for breasts. 2. Another in the large lexicon of semi-sexist, usually sweaty and greasy, Sales Directors who haven't been laid for years; a close cousin of the *"A car is like a beautiful woman Steve"* school of sales, this phrase likens a strategy to mammary glands, but only for tenuous reasons. (*see Collars and cuffs, I bet the _____ don't match; Get into bed with; Kimono, open the; Matching luggage*)

Plot, lose the: 1. Mislay running order for theatrical production. 2. Miss the point entirely; veer off disastrously; go nuts; lose sense of humour as well as job; go loopy, thereby alienating family, spouse and friends. (*see AWOL, go; Ballistic, go; Box of frogs, mad as a; bundle, one stick short of a; Gene pool, swimming in the shallow end of the; Mid-life crisis; Moon, barking at the, over the, through the; Picnic, one sandwich short of a; Postal, go; Pram, to throw one's toys out of the; Radar, off the; Rails, gone off the*)

Plug-in impact: 1. Immediate effect. 2. Strangely electrical allusion to making a difference; shades of jump starting, or hitting something with a charged current; daft phrase for potential effectiveness of an advertising campaign. (*see Impact, high, low*)

Poisoned chalice: 1. Seemingly attractive drink containing a nasty surprise; apparently good brief that isn't. 2. Semi-medieval or biblical reference referring to ornate goblet purporting to have been used by the messiah and containing an elixir giving eternal life; task presented in glowing terms by boss or colleague when it is nothing of the sort. (*see Ask, big; Bombs, box of; Hospital pass; Minister for fun; Opportunity*)

Portfolio: 1. Art bag; collection of works. 2. Arty word to suggest a breadth of skills or achievements; oeuvre; portmanteau collection of stuff; client list, often falsified or out of date.

Positioning: 1. Position; point of view. 2. Form of words laboured over for months by so-called *"brand strategists"*; nitpicking between clusters of generic adjectives; brand maps, onions, pyramids and so on, claiming to *"capture the essence"* of a brand. (*see Architecture, brand _____, business _____; Brand onion, pillars, pyramid, values; Foundations, lay the, firm, shaky; Marketing; Marketing guru; Overarching; Smoke and mirrors job; Value proposition, judgments*)

Postal, go: 1. Flip completely; walk out, never to return. 2. Go off the deep end; go walkabout; believe oneself to be a tree; take unexplained trip to Bournemouth to feed the seagulls; stare at the sea for weeks; sell all worldly possessions and live in a tent by the A24; refuse to cut nails ever again; start playing the sitar in meetings; reach just inside the door of Board meeting and turn the lights on and off repeatedly whilst leering through the glass from outside and going la-la-la; start supporting Stenhousemuir football club when living in Aldershot and with no previous connection to the area. (*see Alarm bells, set the _____ ringing; Arse in alligators, up to my; AWOL, go; Ballistic, go; Basket case; Box of frogs, mad as a; Bundle, one stick short of a; Gene pool, swimming in the shallow end of the; Midlife crisis; Moon, barking at the, over the, through the; Picnic, one sandwich short of a; Plot, lose the; Pram, to throw one's toys out of the; Radar, off; Rails, gone off the; Riot act, read the*)

Potential: 1. What can be achieved. 2. Polite word for all the things an individual could in theory do, but never has; wish list of unfulfilled promise; gap between claimed performance and reality; uncomfortable shortfall between CV and working truth; ethereal chimera that may never be realized; dream. (*see Maximize*)

Pound of flesh: 1. Required amount or contribution. 2. Grizzly butcher-cum-anatomical reference; visions of sausage meat or a slab in a mortuary; macabre idea that cash or effort should yield a dollop of dermis in return, as in *"I'm going to make sure Dennis gives me his pound of flesh for this one"*.

Powder dry, keep one's: 1. Hold some power in reserve; not mention or reveal something yet; musketeer's necessity, otherwise ignition will not occur. 2. Fail to reveal; deliberately conceal; withhold information in order to compromise a colleague; hold back crucial news to gain an advantage; play cards close to chest.

Power breakfast, lunch, nap: 1. Fast and virile approach to eating or sleeping. 2. Daft notion that if you're really important you simply haven't got the time to do anything for long, when in reality you should have been able to delegate everything and therefore generate plenty of time for eating or sleeping at length; essential sham based on the assumption that if you are busy you must be important, when the opposite should apply; concept effectively invented by people who rather like food and sleep.

Powwow: 1. Talk, conference or meeting; North American First Nations ceremony. 2. Huddle where people get together and make it look as though they have something important to discuss; covert gathering; intense gossip session in which all company members, except those present, are right royally slagged off; international awayday at which nothing is decided at all, but a lot of golf is played; management meeting at which staff are graded and selected for firing.

(see ABC session; Axe, face the; Destaff; Headcount; LIFO; Phone list, go down the; Water cooler conversation)

Practical advice: 1. Helpful suggestions that can be applied effectively in reality. 2. Pointless theory that cannot ever be applied; condescending lectures from companies to customers on how to do or not do things that are blatantly obvious, such as *"This coffee may contain hot water"*, or *"To open door, turn handle"*; conversely, hugely unhelpful information such as the instructions to build a flat-packed desk; academic's trope, as in *"Ah yes, it works in practice, but does it work in theory?"* (see Advisorial; FAQs; Hints and tips; Shell-like, a word in your)

Pragmatic: 1. Practical. 2. Unprofessionally expedient, as in *"I think we're going to need a pragmatic approach on this one Derek"*; cutting corners, flying in the face of all thoroughness.

Pram, to throw one's toys out of the: 1. Child's propensity to eject entertainment devices from their bespoke transport vehicle. 2. Lose the plot completely (adult); behave extremely immaturely; throw a wobbly; embark on embarrassing paddy in the office; seethe with anger; lick the windows; snap at imaginary flies; climb the walls; reveal what everyone else already knew – that you have the maturity level of a two-year-old. (see AWOL, go; Ballistic, go; Big match temperament; Box of frogs, mad as a; Bundle, one stick short of a; Gene pool, swimming in the shallow end of the; Mid-life crisis; Moon, barking at the, over the, through the; Picnic, one sandwich short of a; Plot, lose the; Postal, go; Radar, off; Rails, gone off the; Riot act, read the)

Pre-emptive strike: 1. Doing something before someone else does. 2. Smashing someone straight in the face just because you think they might do it to you first, usually leading to dismissal; rushing a product launch out of the door half-cock, based on the paranoid assumption that the competition is about to do the same; criticism of colleague sent to HR immediately before they file the same complaint about you; submission of resignation letter five minutes before a meeting in which you know you are going to be fired. (see First mover advantage; First past the post; Retaliation, get your _____ in first)

Prejudice: 1. Opinion already held and now immovable; bias or dislike. 2. Obnoxious quality prevalent in those who think they know it all; narrow-mindedness; views of Chairman's wife. (see Chairman's wife)

Premium: 1. Worth paying more for than the standard version. 2. Categorically not worth paying more for; a puffed up product with a trumped up margin; cock-and-bull notion invented by greedy companies and corroborated by show-off rich people; brash; showy; myth that *"premium"* people buy *"premium"* products – clearly not true in the case of premium lager. (see Commoditized; Enhance, enhancement; Gold-plated; High ground, take the moral _____; Money for old rope; Pay through the nose; Prestige)

Pressure, face the, handle the, under severe: 1. State of being pressed, usually uncomfortable. 2. Apparently near-permanent state of affairs for every member of staff; non-physical, purely mental condition, but nonetheless very real to those experiencing it; too much going on, coupled with an inability to cope with it all. (*see AWOL, go; Ballistic, go; Box of frogs, mad as a; Bundle, one stick short of a; Gene pool, swimming in the shallow end of the; Mid-life crisis; Moon, barking at the, over the, through the; Picnic, one sandwich short of a; Plot, lose the; Postal, go; Radar, off; Rails, gone off the*)

Prestige: 1. High status achieved through success, influence or wealth. 2. Ability to gloat at everyone else, especially the hoi polloi; greasy adjective used to describe so-called premium brands, as in *"There's no doubting this is a prestige offering, Rupert"*. (*see Commoditized; Enhance, enhancement; Gold-plated; High ground, take the moral ____; Money for old rope; Pay through the nose; Premium*)

Prevaricate: 1. Speak or act evasively with intent to deceive. 2. Daily activity at work. (*see Obfuscation*)

Principle, core: 1. Central tenet. 2. Strongly-held belief spouted loudly and then roundly ignored when it comes to the filthy money, as in *"These are my principles but if you don't like them I have others"* (*see Core; Non-core*)

Prioritize: 1. Give priority to. 2. Do in any order that springs to mind; verb much loved by people who badly want to convey the impression that they are highly organized, when they almost certainly are not, as in *"I'll prioritize that immediately, Bernard"*, invariably followed by complete failure to give any priority to the matter at all; euphemism for putting something to the bottom of the pile or ignoring it all together. (*see -ize*)

Proactive: 1. Tending to initiate rather than react. 2. Omnipresent adjective in advertising and PR agencies, as in *"We pride ourselves on taking a proactive approach"*, as though a passive or reactive one would be more appealing; pretty much redundant word, and a close contender for worst bull of the lot, along with *"going forward"*. (*see Going forward; Reactive*)

Problem, I don't have a _____ with that: 1. It's fine by me. 2. Hugely annoying reverse phraseology meaning it's alright as far as I am concerned; laced with a nasty, power-tripping twist, just reminding you that I could have a problem with this if I wanted to, but this time I'm being nice about it. (*see Buy-in; Green light; Greenlit; Issues , I have _____ with that; Redlit; Unhappy, I'm not _____ with*)

Process: 1. Method for doing something. 2. Whatever we fancy doing today; random assortment of actions that bear little relation to each other; assorted stuff; much loved by people who have no imagination and must therefore fall back on *"process"*. (*see Adminsitrivia; Bureaucracy; Jobsworth; Panjandrum; Target manager*)

Product: 1. Item produced by a company with a view to selling for a profit. 2. Term bandied around for any old tat that gets produced, including intangible things such as services. (*see Productize*)

Productize: 1. Turn something into a product. 2. Repellent faux verb denoting *"We desperately need to start making money out of this"*; process classically involving drawing a diagram that explains in kindergarten fashion how something gets done; most commonly used by frantic executives in industries that never make much money, or none; a stalwart of so-called *"digital natives"* who love farting about on the Web but can rarely explain how to get paid, citing the old adage that *"information wants to be free"*. (*see Democratize; Digital native; -ize; Monetize; Product*)

Productivity: 1. Amount of product generated. 2. Much abused word hinting at, but not necessarily accurately reflecting, the amount of stuff being made or generated; apparent measure of output, albeit eminently capable of being reported in a highly misleading way; sum total of what a business or country does, which may not amount to much in some cases.

Professionalize: 1. Make more professional. 2. Here we go again – another attempt to –ize something, in this case, professionalism; fundamental contradiction, given that amateurs are not professionals, and vice versa; strong whiff of charade, inasmuch as a company or executive is either professional or they are not – any effort to *"professionalize"* probably indicates a cover-up, or at the very least shoddy behaviour up until now. (*see -ize*)

Profile, raise the: 1. Make more noticeable. 2. Make anyone notice at all; much loved clarion call for PR agencies, particularly with crap brands or Z list so-called celebrities. (*see Z list celebrity*)

Project X: 1. Code name for a task. 2. Hilarious notion that giving something a project name will prevent anyone else from finding out what it really is, particularly the competition; superb opportunity to choose a risible name for whatever nonsense one has been asked to work on, as in Project Slug, Wibble, or Hatstand; unintended playground for amusement months later, as in *"Project Gazelle will take three years"*.

Promise, brand, broken: 1. Claim to live up to, or renege on. 2. Trail of disappointments based on a perpetual sequence of bombast and failure; brand promises something and is found wanting – repeat ad infinitum. (*see Brand strategist; Foundations, lay the; Guardian, brand ; Guidelines, brand, corporate; Positioning*)

Promotion: 1. Job elevation; price reduction or other incentive to buy. 2. Twice as much work with exactly the same pay; a new posh title with no material effect on job quality or pay; desperate attempt to persuade someone to buy something when all else has failed; vague suggestion of riches to come, as in *"If you crack this you'll almost certainly be up for promotion, Darren"*.

Proof of concept: 1. Verification that the idea will work. 2. More twaddle from our friends the management consultants, as in *"Before we give this the green light, Nigel, are we sure we have proof of concept?"*; perfectly valid idea of testing something first, bastardized into a phrase that makes it sound as though (a) there's a method to achieve it and (b) the whole thing is as scientific as a rocket launch or finding a cure for cancer. (*see Acid test; Blue touch paper, light the; Purpose, fit for; Success, what does _____ look like?*)

Provenance: 1. Proof of authenticity or origin. 2. Cynical rewriting of history, or naked invention of it, to suggest that a brand has *"authenticity"*; pack of lies, such as *"forged in the crucible of time"* or *"hand-stitched by aborigines"*, when in fact the product was made in Runcorn. (*see Authenticity*)

Proximity: 1. Closeness to. 1. Over-used word for anything that needs to be shown to be related to something else, such as *"These product credentials clearly demonstrate the proximity of the two brands, Robert"*.

PRP: 1. Performance-Related Pay; remuneration that goes up, or possibly down, depending on how well things go. 2. Brilliant device invented by procurement departments to pay less for everything; performance criteria are cunningly designed to ensure no bonus is ever payable; even worse, some contracts demand a refund for poor performance, thereby guaranteeing the supplier will make a loss before they even start work.

Psychic RAM: 1. Ability to remember or absorb mental stimuli; combination of Random Access Memory from the world of semiconductor storage capacity, with a twist. 2. Idiotic collision of the mental and physical worlds; stupid idea that the brain's ability can be likened to the storage capacity of a computer, as in *"Hey guys, you're using up too much of my psychic RAM!"* (*see Bandwidth, he doesn't have the; Intelligent, if you were any less ¬_____, I'd have to water you once a day; Mental furniture; Obvious, firm grasp of the; Picnic, one sandwich short of a _____; Shilling, not the full*)

Pull out all the stops: 1. Use every available resource. 2. Church organ-style full throttle phrase; go gung ho; go the whole hog; deploy everything, regardless of suitability for the task; overdo it; over deliver; work on all fronts to retrieve situation. (*see All-singing, all-dancing; Conductor's baton, wave the; Go the whole hog; Gung ho; Kitchen sink; Orchestra model; Push the boat out*)

Pull rank: 1. Over-rule by citing greater seniority. 2. Create semblance of collaboration and then apply personal bias anyway; intervene and humiliate subordinate; decide on a whim with no suitable evidence; revert to playground approach to decision-making, as in *"My conker is bigger than yours!"* (*see Gut feel; Hierarchy; Matrix; Organogram; Pecking order*)

Pull the levers: 1. Manipulate handles, for reasons various. 2. Play puppeteer; pull strings; lead a merry dance; try everything in the hope that something works; throw as much stuff at the wall as possible in the hope that something sticks.

Pull your finger out: 1. Remove digit from an unspecified place. 2. Get on with; make an effort for once; put on a sudden burst of sustained endeavour in order to save the day or get the job done, usually after doing nothing for months; finally attempt to work out what one's job truly involves, rather than just sitting around reading the occasional email. (*see Engender*)

Pulse, check the, finger on the: 1. Measure the mood of something; be in tune with what's happening. 2. See if elderly colleague is still alive; establish whether any colleague is awake during phenomenally boring meeting; forensically examine the workings of an entire company to see if there's any life in it at all. (*see Forensic, send it down to the boys in; Pathologist's interest*)

Punch above our weight: 1. Hit harder than a boxer of that size should; do better than expected. 2. Stolen from the boxing world and it's gradation of fighters by weight to determine fairness of a contest; further confirmation of the business world's obsession with sporting competition; suggestion that a company or team are somehow akin to a prize fighter, oiled and ready for action; whiffs of the underdog, as the lesser equipped company heroically beats a bigger rival; David and Goliath re-enacted in Basingstoke to secure a contract for heat pumps, or something rather less glamorous than a fair maiden or a kingdom. (*see Sucker punch*)

Purpose, fit for: 1. Capable of doing the job. 2. Utterly pointless phrase querying whether the subject in question will do the job, as in *"I can see the spec Brian, but is this product fit for purpose?"*; another gem from the sleazy world of management consultancy, where such phrases are invented for the dual purpose of patronizing clients and charging more. (*see Acid test; Match fit; Proof of concept; Success, what does _____ look like?*)

Pushback (n.): 1. Response or feedback, usually proffering the opposite view. 2. Euphemism for outright disagreement combined with the likelihood that one side won't mention it at all; weasel word formed by a rather pointless elision of push and back, in order to generate a new phenomenon – wait for it – the notion of pushing back; mealy-mouthed smokescreen for not having the courage to come to the point and say what you really mean, as in *"I really think you need to provide some pushback to Adrian on this one"*; in short, any response at all that disagrees with what's been said, usually by a more senior person. (*see Feedback; Quality feedback*)

Push the boat out: 1. Launch something; throw more effort at something than is strictly necessary. 2. Go over the top; overdo it; add a little gloss to something that is essentially workaday; make a song and dance about it; throw everything at it. (*see All-singing, all-dancing; Fat man in the canoe; Go the extra mile; Go the whole hog; Hype; In the same boat; Pull out all the stops; Rock the boat, don't*)

Pushing the envelope: 1. Move a piece of stationery across the table; push the boundaries of what is possible, from the aeronautics jargon referring to graphs of aircraft tolerance. 2. Another cracker from the kit box of oleaginous executives who wished they had become a Top Gun pilot but never had the skill; notional envelope used to denote Mach number or speed ratio a pilot or plane can endure before passing out or self-destructing; ludicrously applied to the world of business, populated as it is by flabby, Terylene-suited men slumped in warehouses, rather than an elite squad of finely-tuned pilots. (*see Crash and burn; Flying unstable; Maxed out; Needle, moving the; Needle, pushing the; Wheels coming off*)

Put to bed: 1. Tuck a young child in at night, and possibly read them a story; finish the job. 2. Rather odd phrase denoting completion of a task; shades of a nostalgic longing for childhood, perhaps with a Freudian hint of fond memories of one's mother; slight suggestion that since night-time is reminiscent of the end of the day, it somehow represents the conclusion of something. (*see At the end of the day; End of play*)

Putting lipstick on a pig: 1. Applying cosmetics to a porcine beast, presumably to make it look better. 2. Frantically try to make something appear better than it is, usually to no avail; futile cover up effort. (*see GIGO; Jazz hands; Rebrand; RIRO; SISO; Turd, polishing a*)

Pyramided out: 1. At full stretch; unable to cope or take on any more. 2. Truly bizarre and wildly off-the-point expression suggesting that someone is all over the place, presumably pulled in a minimum of three directions; conversion of this thought into a piece of twisted geometry, only to end up with a trumped-up verb, to *"pyramid out"*, or be *"pyramided out"*. (*see Maxed out; Triangulate*)

Python, wrestling with a: 1. Grappling with the largest snake in the world. 2. Trying to cope with a very tricky problem, and probably failing; being attacked on all fronts, as though by many slippery tentacles; dealing with many departments, none of them cooperative; scrabbling to draw multiple components together and make them work; any task in the civil service. (*see Balls in the air, on the block, to the wall; Ball juggling; Plate spinning; Snakepit; Snake's honeymoon; Viper's nest*)

Quality assurance mechanism: 1. System designed to ensure decent quality. 2. Load of guff intended to disguise a lack of quality, such as *"the customer is always right"*, or *"exceeding your expectations"*.

Qualitative: 1. Relating to quality. 2. Biased views and irrational preferences displayed by Marketing Directors the world over; flying in the face of the numbers; doing a *"gut feel"* or going on a hunch. (*see Gut feel; Pants, fly by the seat of our*)

Quality feedback: 1. Accurate comment on the performance of a product or person. 2. Massive bawling out from one's boss about shoddy workmanship, absenteeism, incompetence, poor attitude and range of other defects. (*see Feedback; Pushback; Riot act, read the*)

Quantifiable: 1. Measurable, countable. 2. Unquantifiable; lies and damn statistics; bewildering pie charts containing misleading averages to obscure the true picture. (*see Crunch the numbers*)

Quantitative easing: 1. Reducing pressure on the numbers. 2. Distorting the numbers so they look nicer and everyone can convince themselves that everything is okay. (*see Crunch the numbers; Downsize; Fiscal juggling; Negative growth, profit*)

Quarter, one, two, three, four: 1. Three months. 2. Arbitrary division of the calendar year into pointless chunks to make it easier for mentally-challenged Finance Directors to understand what is going on; time-wasting excuse for Department Heads to *"look at the figures this quarter"* instead of doing any real work; predictable annual landmark on which the CEO cancels the training budget he approved only two months before. (*see Above and beyond; Fiscal juggling; Tertial*)

Question, million dollar, $64,000: 1. The one question which, if properly answered, will allow some progress to be made. 2. A perfectly pedestrian line of enquiry that should have been looked at as a matter of course, now blown out of all proportion into the golden solution. (*see Silver bullet, there is no*)

Questions, ask the hard: 1. Ask some perfectly normal questions. 2. Say what everyone else is thinking but dare not mention – that the project is a pup and the CEO is a tosser. (*see Team, take one for the*)

Quick fix, there is no: 1. This is going to take a long time and needs to be done properly. 2. We've skimmed this for too long and now it's completely buggered – we'll either have to start again from scratch or give up completely. (*see Easy answers, there are no; Magic ingredient, there is no; Silver bullet, there is no*)

Rr

Rabbit, cutting the legs off the _____ to fit it in the hutch: 1. Changing something just so that it falls in line with another, with unfortunate consequences. 2. Blindly destroying something perfectly fine in order to make it succumb to some other arbitrary construct. (*see Nip in the bud; Roots, take the plant up by the _____ to see how it's growing*)

Rabbit, let the dog see the, let the _____ see the trees: 1. Make the reward evident. 2. Crass animal-cum-hunting metaphor that means next to nothing; standard incentive-based nonsense spouted by Sales Directors, mainly in Basingstoke.

Radar, off the, under the: 1. Visible or not visible, depending on preference and circumstances. 2. Part of a seemingly never-ending suite of pseudo-military metaphors that make businessmen feel more virile, even if they work in the feminine hygiene category. (*see AWOL, go; Ballistic, go; Box of frogs, mad as a; Bundle, one stick short of a; Gene pool, swimming in the shallow end of the; Mid-life crisis; Moon, barking at the, over the, through the; Picnic, one sandwich short of a; Plot, lose the; Pram, to throw one's toys out of; Rails, gone off the*)

Raft of ideas, proposals, respondents: 1. Some ideas, proposals or respondents. 2. Disparate gaggle of half-baked and semi-witless suggestions knocked up in the cab on the way to the meeting; certainly not presented on a raft, and probably not even near water at all. (*see Package; Tranche*)

Rails, gone off the: 1. No longer on track. 2. Gone totally doolally; flipped; wigged out; lost it. (*see AWOL, go; Ballistic, go; Come a cropper; Moon, barking at the, over the, through the; Plot, lose the; Postal, go; Pram, to throw one's toys out of the; Radar, off*)

Ramp up: 1. Push something up a ramp, probably a car. 2. Make bigger; exaggerate; over-claim; over-hype. (*see Ladder it up, Ratchet*)

Range, product, _____ extension: 1. Goods for sale, sometimes new. 2. We are likening the goods we offer to the great expanse of the American Midwest – a vast range of goods and services to cater for your every conceivable need, now available in Guatemalan honey flavour.

Ratchet up: 1. Tighten with a mechanic's tool. 2. Grasp vainly at automotive vocabulary in a futile attempt to make a flimsy programme seem more macho; much loved by Sales Managers in Birmingham, particularly in the bathroom fittings category. (*see Ladder it up, Ramp up*)

Rationale: 1. Line of argument to explain direction of thinking. 2. Total flimflam and post-rationalization made up on the spot to justify woolly thinking or sub-standard crap. (*see Bullshit*)

Reactive: 1. Only acting in response to something else. 2. Bone idle, and incapable of original thought. (*see Proactive*)

Real estate, how much _____ does this have: 1. How much lasting value does this idea have? 2. Daft American question trying to compare the long-term price of something with the property market; another in a long line of asinine semi-rhetorical lines of enquiry, such as *"What does success look like?"*; unanswerable, inasmuch as the question is nonsense. (*see Bench, has this got; Legs, it's got; Success, what does _____ look like?*)

Real teeth, our campaign needs to have _____: 1. Our communications effort needs to be effective; dental structures are crucial to our efforts. 2. Another in a long line of medical metaphors applied to business; mindless application of the word *"real"*, when patently the teeth in question will not be the real thing; implication that most of the time the campaigns embarked upon do not have any teeth, in any sense of the word. (*see Literally; Open-heart surgery, it's not*)

Realignment: 1. Instance of restoring or changing to a previous or different position. 2. Issue of a direct order to do what you're told or f**k off, as in *"We need some serious realignment here, Geoff"*; use of the reasonably soft word *"align"* as a surrogate for full agreement; alignment thus becomes a seemingly inoffensive word for toeing the party line whether you like it or not; in extreme cases, realignment can include the wholesale firing of anyone who chooses not to *"realign"*. (*see Align, aligned; Ducks in a row, get our; FIFO (2); Hymn sheet, singing from the same; Off message; Off-piste; Wildebeest in a row, has the lion got his*)

Reality check: 1. Occasion to consider a matter realistically or honestly. 2. Moment that seldom occurs in business due to too much haste or downright stupidity; sometimes used in pseudo-rigorous way by glib managers, as in *"I'm broadly in agreement, but I think we need to take a reality check here, Sebastian"*, and often accompanied by a broad sweep of the hand or a thoughtful tug of the beard.

Re-baselining: 1. Changing the baseline, or basis of measurement. 2. Shocking collision of baseball terminology, measurement criteria and egregious fiddling of the numbers; different way of saying that we don't like what the figures are saying so we'll change the way we portray them; typically, choosing a different vertical scale, converting currency, shortening or lengthening the time period being analyzed, or re-calibrating in any way that will make things appear different; obfuscating. (*see Baseline; Fiscal juggling; Obfuscation*)

Rebrand: 1. Change name of product, or significantly overhaul the manner in which it is portrayed. 2. Reach the stage where a knackered old product or service is so reviled by customers that it can't go on; spend a fortune talking to self-appointed *"brand strategists"* to ascertain what on earth can be done; spend a fortune on *"focus groups"*, only to find out what you already knew – that people hate it; scour the globe for another way of presenting the same old tat; choose a new name, or invent one entirely from random paper cuttings or pieces of Latin loosely stitched together to suggest authenticity; sit back and wait for results; revert to original name the following week after public outcry of sham and cover up; leave company in disgrace. (*see Authenticity; Brand strategist; Focus group; Look and feel; Putting lipstick on a pig; Redeploy; Redesign; Re-engineer; Repackage; Reposition; Re-purpose; Restructure; Turd, polishing a*)

Recruitment: 1. The hiring of personnel. 2. Time-consuming and futile charade involving interviews, character profiling, psychometric testing and the gathering of fictitious references – candidates are often said to be *"pursuing other options"* three months later. (*see Card, red; Decruit*)

Redeploy: 1. Use somewhere else. 2. Fire. (*see Rebrand; Redesign; Re-engineer; Repackage; Reposition; Re-purpose; Restructure*)

Redesign: 1. Change of specification. 2. Start again; go right back to the beginning; rip up original plan; acknowledge terminal flaw in current version. (*see Drawing board, back to the; Rebrand; Redeploy; Re-engineer; Repackage; Reposition; Re-purpose; Restructure*)

Redlit: 1. Subject to a stop signal; not happening. 2. Repellent past tense of red light, joined together and turned into an adjective, signifying a project on hold or going nowhere. (*see Green light; Greenlit; Issues , I have _____ with that; Problem, I don't have a _____ with that; Unhappy, I'm not _____ with that*)

Redundancy: 1. Superfluous to requirements in job. 2. Close cousin of being fired, but with slightly different phraseology; helpful catch-all for employers keen to get rid of a large number of people; excessive proliferation or superfluity; too many people doing the same stuff; too many products doing the same thing; too much of everything, leading to significant pruning.

Re-engineer: 1. Restructure a company or part of its operations; generate a new version of a machine. 2. Part of a suite of words with the re- prefix designating changing something because it just isn't working. (*see Rebrand; Redeploy; Redesign; Repackage; Reposition; Re-purpose*)

Reinventing the wheel: 1. Creating something that has already been done somewhere else. 2. Omnipresent phrase for a monumental waste of time; colossal duplication of work; one department doing something identical to the next department; two colleagues doing the same; abject failure to communicate, resulting either in doubling up or having to repeat the whole thing; exasperated cry from Managing Director, as in *"For f**k's sake guys, we're not reinventing the wheel here!"* (*see Left hand, not knowing what the right is for, _____ and second left hand; Wheels coming off*)

Repackage: (*see Rebrand; Redeploy; Redesign; Re-engineer; Reposition; Re-purpose; Restructure*)

Reposition: (*see Rebrand; Redeploy; Redesign; Re-engineer; Repackage; Re-purpose; Restructure*)

Re-purpose: (*see Rebrand; Redeploy; Redesign; Re-engineer; Repackage; Reposition; Restructure*)

Research: 1. Systematic investigation to establish facts or principles. 2. Seemingly endless process of trying to find out what on earth is going on; starting from scratch when knowing sod all about a subject; playing catch up; wading through mountains of data in the futile hope of finding something enlightening; revisiting the same idea again and again, with little progress; sitting through interminable debriefs; posing a huge set of bland questions and receiving a similar quantity of equally dull answers; gathering vast quantities of information and then not knowing what to do with it. (*see Go round the houses; Navel gazing; Planning*)

Respect, with: 1. Pay attention, I'm about to disagree with you. 2. Two very dangerous words presaging a flaming row, as in *"With respect Michael, you're talking bollocks"*. (*see Enlighten me; Follow, do you; Lips, read my; Teach your grandmother to suck eggs, don't, would never, would you; Warts and all*)

Rest on our laurels: 1. Be satisfied with past achievements and cease to try any more. 2. Standard state for pompous, arrogant organizations; trite component of any Chairman's statement, as in *"This has been an exceptional year of achievement but be assured we will not rest on our laurels"*; announcement frequently followed by catastrophic collapse of share price due to resting on laurels.

Restructure: (*see Rebrand; Redeploy; Redesign; Re-engineer; Repackage; Reposition; Re-purpose*)

Results-driven: 1. Motivated by the outcome. 2. Completely pointless phrase, as helpful and informative as a human who is oxygen-driven or a car that is fuel-driven; as ever, this piece of nonsense fails to register that if someone is doing something then they are more likely than not going to be interested in what happens as a result of their efforts; much loved by recruitment consultants as a crass way of describing a person who will probably get the job done, as in *"Julian is a results-driven individual who will undoubtedly add value to any organization"*. (*see -centred, -driven; -centric; -focused, people-, goal-; –oriented; Task-oriented; Value-add, value-added*)

Retaliation, get your _____ in first: 1. Do something before it gets done to you. 2. Fantastically circular idea that someone can predict when someone else is going to take revenge on them, even before anyone does anything; hilarious notion that getting your own back is a good thing to do in the business world;

hints of battleground vengeance, vindictive action and an overall eye-for-an-eye mentality; interesting idea that an all-out brawl in the office would be beneficial, even when no one knows why. (*see First mover advantage; First past the post; Pre-emptive strike; Rise above it*)

Reverse gear: 1. Going backwards. 2. Hasty retreat; sudden change of heart; manoeuvre similar to Italians in Second World War; spectacular U-turn; total policy change, often disguised as a small adjustment. (*see Evolving to meet customer demand; Tweak; U-Turn*)

Ride, bumpy, along for the, roughshod over: 1. Journey of varying types – uneven, free or at the expense of others. 2. Highly adaptable suite of phrases to suit many needs; preparatory briefing suggesting hard times to come, as in *"Hang on tight guys, we're in for a bumpy ride!"*; plaintive remark related to not just making up the numbers, as in *"We're not just along for the ride here, guys!"*; defiant comment on interference from unwanted colleagues or other departments, as in *"If they think they can ride over us roughshod, they've got another thing coming".* (*see Handrails, hold the; Last chance saloon, drinking at the; Saddle, cycling with no*)

Riding the razor blade: 1. Caught in an uncomfortable position. 2. A truly eye-watering image for either sex, implying lacerated genitals at the slightest wrong move; visions of careening down the banister only to come a cropper near the end; gung ho behaviour often followed by a nasty ending; living unnervingly close to the edge; sailing close to the wind; risking everything; cavalier attitude to personal and career safety. (*see Coals, walk on hot; Handrails, hold the; Last chance saloon, drinking at the; Rock and a hard place, caught between a; Saddle, cycling with no; Wind, sailing close to the*)

Right arm, give your _____ for: 1. Make significant sacrifices to gain something; be prepared to do almost anything. 2. Extreme personal gesture to get something done; as severe as loosing a limb or possibly sawing it off oneself; serious desire to get something; obsession; irrational objective that cannot be shifted; near-insane death wish. (*see Kamikaze; Left hand, not knowing what the right is for*)

Right-size (vb.): 1. Make the right size; make something fit. 2. Silly way of pointing out that if something is going to work or fit properly then it needs to be the right size; unnecessarily turned into a verb.

Ringfence (vb.): 1. Put a fence around something; cordon something off. 2. Annoying phrase that allows someone to point out that they don't want to talk about something now and would rather deal with it later, as in *"It's a fair point, Mary, but let's ringfence it and take it offline"*; delaying or stalling tactic, dressed up as modern parlance; evasion. (*see Marker buoy, let's stick a _____ on that; Offline, take it*)

Riot act, read the: 1. Warn or reprimand seriously, originally from the 1715 English statute stating that people committing a riot had to disperse within an hour of the reading of the act by a magistrate. 2. Bawl out comprehensively, frequently in front of colleagues for maximum humiliation; tear off a strip; go ballistic; go crimson with rage. (*see Appraisal, one degree; Ballistic, go; Postal, go; Pram, to throw one's toys out of the; Quality feedback*)

RIRO: 1. Rubbish In Rubbish Out. 2. Simple principle that if you start with crap, then you'll probably finish with it – the moral being to use good ingredients. (*see GIGO; Putting lipstick on a pig; SISO; Turd, polishing a*)

Rise above it: 1. Don't let it bother you, usually of adverse conditions. 2. Suggestion of some kind of elevation, probably not physical; find a higher plane; don't retaliate; don't get involved. (*see High ground, take the moral _____; Retaliation, get your _____ in first*)

Risk-averse: 1. Not prone to taking any chances. 2. Inherently conservative; weak-willed; unadventurous; lily-livered; scared; not likely to do anything that might cause any trouble; ineffective; possibly not worth having around; a bit useless; not helping much; preferring to stay at one's desk rather than get up and do something. (*see Jobsworth*)

Risk management: 1. Discipline claiming to be able to manage risk. 2. Not a cat in hell's chance of managing anything, given that the future is unpredictable and events are so often random. (*see Black swan*)

Roadmap: 1. Cartographical device to find out where you are going. 2. Irritating way of suggesting that a company or project has some direction; attempt to attach geographical substance to an amorphous concept; part of the extensive arsenal of all rhetorical question askers when trying to appear organized or authoritative, as in *"Thanks for the detailed rundown, Nigel, but what is the roadmap for Project Begonia?"*

Robust: 1. Strong; hardy. 2. Odious adjective when misused, most commonly when referring to numerical information, as in *"How robust is this data, Geoff?"*

Rock and a hard place, caught between a: 1. On the horns of a dilemma. 2. In a nasty situation, with all choices being unsatisfactory; state of affairs intentionally generated by a colleague to humiliate you, or self-generated due to naivety or incompetence. (*see Riding the razor blade*)

Rock and roll, let's: 1. Let's go; let's make a start. 2. Hilarious attempt by middle-aged, corpulent or bald executives to appear like rock stars; stealing vernacular from a more sexy industry imbues them with a sense of youth and vigour, whilst their colleagues observe them with all the disdain of watching their Dad dance at a disco. (*see Lock and load, let's; Match fit*)

Rock the boat, don't: 1. Don't upset anything or anyone; don't make a fuss. 2. Say nothing; we know it's all wrong but the Chief Executive thought it up so don't complain; we know it's rubbish but it's the best we've got; I invented this and am not prepared to admit that it's poor; I'm your boss so shut up and get on with it. (*see Fat man in the canoe; In the same boat; Mum, keep; Push the boat out; Rowing in the same boat, direction; SUMO*)

Rocket science, it's not: 1. It's not very complicated. 2. I haven't a clue what rocket science is, but I want to use a patronizing phrase that highlights my superior intelligence; much loved by poorly educated sales managers struggling to appear intellectual; frequently applied to issues that are in fact quite complex; it may not be rocket science but it may well be beyond the understanding of your tiny brain. (*see Brain surgery, it's not; Open-heart surgery, it's not*)

ROI: 1. Return On Investment – almost never proven. 2. Acronym usually deployed by industries that have real difficulty in proving that they generate any return on investment at all, such as advertising and PR; intended to add some heft to otherwise flimsy projects with little financial rationale; also used as a humiliation device when a decision is required on whether a project is going ahead or not, as in *"I can see the business case for Project Madras, Gerald, but can we really prove the ROI?"* (*see Effectiveness*)

Roll-out: 1. Full launch of something that was previously only a test or in pilot phase. 2. Much abused word pairing designed to give a bit of clout to something otherwise quite functional, such as making a product launch occur; shades of royalty, as in rolling out the red carpet, which presumably lends a monarchic flavour to humdrum projects; hints of national, and sometimes international, domination, as in rolling out across the nation, as though on some kind of glamorous tour; shades of grandeur, as in *"Victoria, could you drop by with the roll-out plans for project Tiny Tim this afternoon please?"*

Root-and-branch review: 1. Survey conducted on a large scale and without discrimination. 2. Colossal witch-hunt to find someone to blame for monumental cockup; process that sometimes alights on one individual who is then ceremonially fired, or an entire department, who are then humiliated and subject to ridicule by all concerned; semblance of a thorough investigation but with absolutely no intention of changing anything at all. (*see Deep dive; Drains up, have the; Lift up a rock; Look, take a long hard; No stone unturned; Roots, take the plant up by the; Witch-hunt*)

Roots, take the plant up by the _____ to see how it's growing. 1. Break something that was perfectly fine by fiddling with it. 2. Marvellous horticultural metaphor involving the destruction of a perfectly healthy plant by pulling it up to see how it works; tremendous parallels in business, mainly from the *"If it ain't broke, don't fix it"* school; salutary lesson to micromanagers intent on meddling with anything they can get their hands on, often with unfortunate results. (*see Micromanaging; Rabbit, cutting the legs off the _____ to fit it in the hutch*)

Rose-tinted: 1. Excessively optimistic. 2. Charming adjective usually used to describe those with an overly favourable view of the past, or a rather naïve perspective on the current position; sometimes used in dismissive fashion, as in *"I think you need to take off your rose-tinted glasses here, Nigel"*. (*see Halcyon days; Marriage made in heaven*)

Rottweiler: 1. Breed of large German dog with a reputation for toughness. 2. Hard-as-nails operator; ballbreakingly tough executive; character who always believes they are right and simply will not back down; frequently narrow-minded and blinkered bully who treads all over subordinates without a care. (*see Ballbreaker; Ferret on amphetamines; Nutcracker; Open door policy*)

Rowing in the same boat, direction: 1. Pulling together and aiming at the same goal. 2. Athletic-cum-aquatic phrase exhorting everyone to work as a team; usually rolled out when people are patently not working as a team; exasperated comment on bitter in-fighting, back stabbing, front stabbing and all-out internecine warfare between colleagues; plea to squabbling executives, as in *"Come on guys, we're all rowing in the same boat here!"* (*see Back stabbing; Bus, who's driving the; Fat man in the canoe; Front stabbing; In the same boat; Push the boat; Rock the boat, don't; Train, who's driving the; Wavelength, on the same, not on the same*)

RTFM: 1. Read The F**king Manual. 2. You have clearly had no basic training in the use of this equipment and lied at interview. (*see CV; FOFO; SOP*)

Rubber hits the road, when the: 1. When things really start happening. 2. Rather curious automotive reference implying somehow that before anything happens the rubber is not on the road; unclear position of rubber up till that point; suggestion of a car being dropped suddenly from a height; semi-macho racing driver reference, as in *"We need to be firing on all six when the rubber hits the road, guys!"* (*see Firing on all six, on all cylinders; Hit the ground running*)

Rubber stamp: 1. Approve without challenging. 2. Implication that there will be no trouble getting something approved – not always a wise assumption; on the nod; passed without difficulty; blessed from on high without question. (*see Run it past*)

Rule of thumb: 1. Rough and practical approach based on experience. 2. Pure guesswork, with no basis in fact or experience at all; finger-in-the-air stuff.

Rules of engagement: 1. Code by which two sides will abide when coming together, sometimes in war. 2. Apparent set of principles that everyone roundly ignores; chaos or free-for-all; trite question asked by ill-informed person trying to catch up in a meeting, as in *"Just remind me, Julian, what are the rules of engagement here?"* (*see Unfair advantage*)

Run it past: 1. Ask for someone's opinion. 2. Politically astute consultation to see if something is likely to meet with approval or not; canny effort to save enormous amounts of wasted effort by establishing whether an idea is effectively dead in the water before it starts; experienced nod to the way things work round here, as in *"I think we better run it past Norman before we proceed"*. (*see Buy-in; Rubber stamp*)

Run-of-the-mill: 1. Ordinary; average. 2. Relentlessly undistinguished colleague or product; boring; bland; dull; dreary; not worth having around; beige. (*see Mediocracy; Vin ordinaire*)

Runway, on the: 1. Ready to take off. 2. Aeronautical reference to suggest potency; power in reserve; visions of jets about to take off; revving engines, clearance awaited; Top Gun-style remark that makes sales executives feel particularly virile, as in *"It's great to have Project Catflap on the runway at last, Graham"*.

Russian roulette: 1. Game of chance in which each player spins the cylinder of a revolver loaded with only one cartridge, and presses the trigger when pointing it at his own head. 2. Any act which, if repeated, is likely to have disastrous consequences; precisely what many companies and individuals do – repeat the same hazardous approach again and again, in the vain hope that something will work out better next time; abject failure to learn from experience; glib comment on risk taking, as in *"I'm simply not going to play Russian roulette with you on this one, Kate"*.

Ss

Sabbatical: 1. Period of leave granted to staff or academics, usually after seven years of service. 2. Mad, drug-fuelled excursion round the globe under the approximate guise of charity fundraising. *(see MBA)*

Sacred cow: 1. A person, institution or custom beyond criticism. 2. Subject matter absolutely out of bounds due to the extreme entrenched views of the Chairman, or his wife – usually based on fanaticism, elitism, sexism, chauvinism or some equally undesirable trait. (*see Aunt Sally*)

Saddle, cycling with no: 1. Proceeding without the appropriate equipment. 2. Eye-watering analogy to portray the lonesome act of being woefully under-equipped, whether of resource, technology or intellect, for the job in hand. (*see Hand rails, hold the; Last chance saloon, drinking at the; Riding the razor blade*)

Sanity check: 1. Period of brief reflection to see if common sense has prevailed. 2. Horrible moment of realization that common sense has certainly not prevailed, usually occurring moments before a crucial presentation or product launch.

Satisficing: 1. Curious elision of *"satisfy"* and *"suffice"* coined by American professor of computer science and psychology Herbert Simon to describe the manner in which people do just enough research before buying products. 2. Dreadful compromise brought about by chronic lack of resources and talent. (*see Optimal; Sub-optimal*)

Scalable: 1. Capable of being made bigger; capable of being climbed (a wall, for example). 2. Tragic Americanism designed to make hard-pressed managers feel they are on course for world domination. (*see Upscale; World class*)

Scapegoat, make a _____ out of: 1. Single out for blame. 2. Cynically select an individual or department who had nothing at all to do with the disaster that has just occurred; spend inordinate amounts of time and energy putting a case together that proves it was all their fault; report to Managing Director with comprehensive dossier, saying you're very sorry but the truth had to be revealed and you felt it was your duty. (*see Heat, take the; High jump, in for the; Let's not go there; Piggyback; Team, take one for the; Witch-hunt*)

Scenario, best-case, nightmare, worst-case: 1. A summary of the plot of a play; a predicted sequence of events. 2. Situation, almost always disastrous; prediction, almost always wrong. (*see Armageddon plan; Doomsday scenario*)

Scope, scope out: 1. Work out what to do. 2. Spread out vast amounts of paper on the boardroom table in a desperate attempt to make sense of it all, often resulting in resignation or dismissal; alternatively, resort to an impenetrable last-ditch diagram that is so convoluted that no one else will admit they don't understand it. (*see Last chance saloon, drinking at the*)

Scorched earth policy: 1. Warfare policy of removing absolutely everything to do with the enemy, usually by fire. 2. Wanton slash and burn approach deployed by Kamikaze managers, often in high churn businesses such as telecommunications – there are rarely any survivors. (*see Armageddon plan; Doomsday scenario; Efficiency drive; Kamikaze*)

Scraping the barrel: 1. Using one's last or weakest resource. 2. Winging it; just getting by; gathering anyone in the company who could possibly join in, including the tea lady; presenting the most useless material ever; thin, cliché-ridden proposal; not a cat in hell's chance of winning. (*see Ambulance chasing; Bottom feeding*)

Scratch my back and I'll scratch yours: 1. Do something helpful for me and I'll reciprocate. 2. Mantra much loved by corrupt executives on the take in disgraceful incestuous arrangements that are entirely for their own benefit. (*see Get into bed with; Kimono, open the*)

Screw it, let's do it: 1. What the hell, let's get on with it; a philosophy espoused by Richard Branson in the book of the same name. 2. Reckless, cavalier approach adopted by unscrupulous salesmen in order to hit this month's target.

Screwed: 1. Fastened by a screw; had sex with; in an awkward position. 2. Fired; destroyed; humiliated; incapable of redeeming self-esteem or employment. (*see Shit creek, up _____ without a paddle*)

Sea change: 1. A seemingly magical change, originally coined by Shakespeare in *The Tempest*. 2. Pray desperately for a total change of fortune, such as increased sales or salary. (*see Paradigm shift; Step change*)

Seagull manager: 1. Manager who flaps around a lot, makes a big noise and dumps on everyone from a great height. 2. 90% of all managers.

Seals, left them clapping like: 1. Elicited a delighted reaction from an audience. 2. Vainglorious report from a sales meeting, almost always over optimistic; hubristic analysis of chances of winning, rarely correct; inflated self opinion manifested in a belief that one is a superb presenter and really rather brilliant. (*see Beavers, defending it like; Done deal; In the bag*)

Seamless: 1. Continuous or flowing. 2. Ubiquitous word now applied to anything that needs to look as though it hangs together; almost certainly used in connection with things that patently do not hang together, but must be made to appear so if the company is to have any chance of success. (*see Connectivity; End-to-end; Hit the ground running; Joined-up thinking; Solutions, end-to-end*)

Search and destroy: 1. Track someone down and eliminate them. 2. Aggressive approach to *"killing"* the competition much loved by macho executives; similar approach to identifying scapegoats who can be blamed for any failing, so long as it is clear that the fault is not yours. (*see Take no prisoners*)

Segue: 1. To proceed from one section to another without a break, usually in music, from the Italian seguire, to follow. 2. Egregious way to suggest everything working beautifully together, used both as a verb and a noun; hilariously, frequently spelt *"segway"* by those stretched to the limits of their linguistic capabilities when trying to be just a bit too smart for their own good. (*see Connectivity; Joined-up thinking; Seamless; Tranche; Vis-à-vis*)

Set in stone: 1. Fixed. 2. Not really fixed at all; shades of Excalibur and Arthurian tales; often used in the reverse, as in *"Of course, Nigel, these proposals aren't completely set in stone"*.

Setback: 1. Something that has gone wrong, usually causing delay. 2. We're absolutely f**ked; it's all over; that's the end of it; surrogate for admitting that it'll never happen; much loved by Chairmen when discovering an utter disaster, as in *"We have suffered a setback but we remain determined to launch Project Vortex as soon as circumstances allow"*. (*see Fat lady, it's not over until the _____ sings; Learnings*)

Shafted down the river, yourself: 1. Done oneself a disservice. 2. Superb collision of aquatic and sexual-cum-spear-wielding imagery to engineer a state of affairs where a person (gender unspecified) has managed to *"shaft themselves"*, for reasons unknown. (*see Appraisal, one degree; Appraisal 360 degree; Foot, shoot oneself in the; Own goal, spectacular; Shit creek, up _____ without a paddle*)

Share and air: 1. Show what you've been doing and discuss it with colleagues. 2. Showboat; gloat that your stuff is better than theirs; gerrymander judging criteria so that all your material wins in-house awards. (*see Show and tell*)

Shark, keep moving like a, waiting for the sharks to circle: 1. Maintain forward motion, or be surrounded by aggressive competitors. 2. Macho, or perhaps mako, notion that to be a success in business you always have to be doing something, when in fact most studies show that consistency is more effective; phrase based completely incorrectly on the belief that sharks need to keep swimming in order to breathe, which is errant nonsense, as demonstrated by the nurse shark which remains stationary for sustained periods; sense of panic as though surrounded by bloodthirsty carnivores. (*see Wagon, the Indians have surrounded the*)

Shell-like, a word in your: 1. I'd like a private word with you. 2. You're really in the shit this time; something has gone spectacularly wrong, and all fingers point to you being the culprit. (*see Advisorial; Hints and tips*)

Shift, put in a: 1. Work hard; pull one's weight. 2. Mark of respect; acknowledgment that team member has really contributed. (*see Heavy lifting, do the*)

Shilling, not the full: 1. Less than the required amount; not all there. 2. Totally batty; prone to garrulous outbursts of drivel at all the wrong times; overly loquacious; an embarrassment; can't be taken anywhere; not clever; a liability. (*see Bandwidth, he doesn't have the; Intelligent, if you were any less _____, I'd have to water you once a day; Mental furniture; Moon, barking at the, over the, through the; Obvious, a firm grasp of the; Psychic RAM; Picnic, one sandwich short of a _____*)

Shit creek, up _____ without a paddle: 1. In a hopeless position. 2. Deep in the brown stuff; absolutely knackered; with no hope of reprieve; state of affairs that can be self-inflicted or due to Machiavellian behaviour by a colleague, or several of them. (*see Machiavellian; Screwed; Shafted down the river, yourself*)

Shit hits the fan, when the: 1. The moment when it all goes wrong. 2. Charming image of excrement being thrown at an air cooling device, only to find that it is catapulted all round the office; images of fair proportions of it ending up on you, and certainly all over your desk; mildly-threatening rebuke, as in *"Bloody hell, Steve, thanks to you the shit has really hit the fan"*. (*see Air cover*)

Show and tell: 1. Demonstrate and explain to colleagues the nature of your work. 2. Twee lunchtime sessions designed to improve team bonding; hapless staff are tempted by the promise of free cheap sandwiches, and always accept due to chronically low pay and lack of foodstuffs in the fridge at home; thinly-veiled showboating session in which the organizer gets to explain how clever their work is and how brilliant they are. (*see Bonding, team; Share and air*)

Showcase (vb.): 1. To show. 2. Redundant verb that merely makes the perfectly adequate verb *"to show"* four letters longer, with no gain in understanding; when something has been shown, it may have been part of a showcase, or perhaps even put in one.

Show the door: 1. Point out the features of a hinged dividing panel; fire. 2. Quaint way of saying that someone has been asked to leave; non-specific with regard to where the said person is leaving; has come to mean leaving the building, for good; part of a range of options for exiting the office. (*see Defenestrate, defenestration*)

Sidetracked on all fronts: 1. Not concentrating on anything specific. 2. Spatially-challenged phrase to denote utter confusion; comprehensive ability to be distracted; butterfly mind; daydreamer; self-styled creative type who refuses to knuckle down under the pretext that they are *"thinking"*.

Silos, working in: 1. Conducting one's business affairs from inside a silage storage container. 2. Daft pseudo-agricultural term to signal that everyone is doing their own thing and not talking to each other – standard practice in most companies;

even worse as a verb or adjective, as in *"We don't want to silo the Accounts Department"* or *"Production has really become siloed, don't you think, Jane?"*

Silver bullet, there is no: 1. There is not one simple and effective answer. 2. Truly bizarre idea that if one did have a silver bullet it would help in some way; shades of the wild west or perhaps an assassin's brief for a hit; all-round bafflement that such a ballistic item cannot be found, as though there really should be plenty of them in an office environment. (*see Easy answers, there are no; Magic ingredient, there is no; Question, million dollar, $64,000; Quick fix, there is no; Smoking gun*)

Silver lining, every cloud has a: 1. Fanciful idea that this desperate or unhappy situation may lead to something better. 2. Misleading blind optimism that is rarely justified in companies that continue to limp along from one crisis to another.

SISO: 1. Shit In Shit Out. 2. Wise and eternally verified notion that if you put poor data or other effort into something, the result will be just as bad as the crap it always was. (*see GIGO; Putting lipstick on a pig; RIRO; Turd, polishing a*)

Situation: 1. State of affairs; circumstance. 2. Sorely abused word added to pretty much any sentence you can imagine, with no discernible improvement in understanding; no-win situation; global situation; anything situation; cornerstone word for any meaningless wibble, as in *"Well clearly, Graham, as you see, this is where this area fronts up this situation"*. (*see Solutions, end-to-end; Space*)

60:50 relationship, this is the perfect: 1. This relationship is imbalanced. 2. Superbly exasperated expression of being set upon in a lopsided partnership that is supposed to be equal. (*see Partners*)

Skeleton staff: 1. The fewest number possible to do what needs to be done. 2. An even lower number; not enough people at all; hard-pressed workforce in dire need of rest and more resources; underfed and losing weight fast, possibly on the verge of becoming genuinely skeletal.

Skeletons in the cupboard: 1. Nasty information about the past that could return to cause trouble. 2. The history of every company in the world, and their directors. (*see Smoking gun; Sucker punch*)

Skill set: 1. Capabilities. 2. Stupid pairing of words that reduces a person's talents to something sounding like a primary school pencil case.

Skin in the game, they need to have some: 1. We would like them to have a vested interest. 2. Truly a crown prince among the candidates for worst piece of drivel in the world, this phrase really takes the biscuit; apparently based on the frankly mind-boggling principle that one might embark on a game that involves flaying oneself in some way, or perhaps gluing a part of your epidermis to another person; even better, the person making this ludicrous request clearly believes this would be a perfectly reasonable thing to ask someone to do; chuck-across-the-room dreadful.

Slam dunk: 1 Scoring shot in basketball in which a player jumps up and forces the ball down through the basket. 2. Fast and completely conclusive result, unless claimed by a self-deluded salesman returning from a meeting and wanting to sound impressive, in which case it could be anything but. (*see Done deal*)

Small stuff, don't sweat the: 1. Don't worry about the detail. 2. Glib imprimatur from lax boss giving subordinate carte blanche to ignore all the practical stuff; invariably leads to the client asking for more detail, or failing to award the business on the grounds that it was *"all too big picture"*.

Smoke and mirrors job: 1. An illusion. 2. Any pitch by an advertising agency; work of fiction; things that will almost certainly not come to pass; spectacular feat of storytelling. (*see Behavioural economics; Ether, float into; lost in the; Marketing; Transparency*)

Smoking gun: 1. Proof that a killing occurred only recently; evidence of wrongdoing. 2. Lethal material locked in the Chairman's safe, or that of a journalist with a point to prove. (*see Silver bullet, there is no; Skeletons in the cupboard*)

SNAFU: 1. Situation Normal, All Fucked Up. 2. The standard state of affairs is that nothing works; Royal Air Force acronym generated as a pat response when the Captain asks for a status report; nothing functions properly, but what's new? (*see Armageddon plan; Fear; FUBB; Lose-lose; Negative growth, profit; Pants, fly by the seat of our*)

Snake oil salesman: 1. Disreputable salesperson offering a cure-all for every need. 2. Account Executive in advertising or public relations. (*see Balanced scorecard; Vin ordinaire*)

Snakepit: 1. Depression containing serpents. 2. Open plan office; vicious collection of rivals and desperadoes intent on killing each other; gaggle of secretaries surrounding Chairman in a cordoned-off area at office party. (*see Office party; Python, wrestling with a; Viper's nest*)

Snake's honeymoon: 1. Tangle of wires; complex intertwining of issues. 2. Chaos on all fronts; IT nightmare often found under desk with too many computers; vivid analogy for company or individual with far too much going on; diary car crash; impossible overlap of timelines on several projects that will undoubtedly lead to disaster. (*see Action list; Framework, operating, over-arching; Matrix; Organogram; Pecking order; Pull rank; Python, wrestling with a; Touchpoints; Viper's nest*)

Socialize: 1. Get on with people. 2. Fail to get on with people, but smile anyway. (*see Commoditize; Diarize; Democratize; Monetize*)

Soft area: 1. Trendy collection of bean bags and curious furniture quite unlike anything else in the office. 2. Location of lunchtime detritus, such as old crispy bit of Pot Noodle, found unnervingly down the side of a lime green sofa; scene of inappropriate gossip after the boss has left; venue for occasional snog after Friday drinks; designer showcase that rapidly becomes grubby and dog-eared, rather like the office bike. (*see Bean bags; Breakout groups; Come on people; Hot desking; Huddle; Office bike*)

Solus: 1. Alone; separate. 2. Truly odd word meaning just the one; often used to describe just one execution in advertising, as in *"Okay so we haven't got the budget for several posters, Darren, so we'll just crack this one out solus"*.

Solutions, end-to-end: 1. Totally pointless addition to almost any word, as in painting solutions (painters), marketing solutions (marketing) and even food solutions (food); often end-to-end, as in *"seamless"*; now parent of the awful bastard son *"solutionism"* – spawn of the devil if there was any. (*see Seamless; Situation; Space*)

SOP: 1. Standard operating procedure. 2. How we normally do it round here; semblance of process that may or may not be written down; if written, it is expected to be followed to the letter; if not written, staff are expected to know anyway; sometimes called culture, although no one can ever define what that is. (*see Building the plane as we fly it; Culture, company; Fly by the seat of one's pants; RTFM; SNAFU*)

Space: 1. Area or market. 2. Pathetic new use of a perfectly good word, as in *"We want to be leaders in the technology space"*.; as redundant as *"situation"*, *"solution"*, and *"out there"*. (*see Out there; Situation; Solutions, end-to-end*)

Space cadet: 1. Idiot. 2. Vacant colleague.

Spaghetti junction: 1. Motorway interchange with many underpasses and over-passes; nickname of Gravelly Hill Interchange in Birmingham. 2. Absolute pandemonium in the work place; Brownian motion; briefs and projects flying everywhere without any control; utterly bereft of process; Jobsworth's idea of hell; carnage; abject absence of procedure; free-for-all; business as usual in an advertising agency. (*see Jobsworth*)

Spanish archer, he got the. 1. He was fired. 2. Euphemism for being fired, based on one of the worst puns ever, as in *"He got El Bow"*, a pidgin-Spanish version of *"He got the elbow"*, hence El Bow, the Spanish Archer; truly dreadful.

Spear, fall on one's: 1. Impale oneself; resign on a technicality. 2. Make a mistake and have to go; be forced to go as an example to others; have to leave because the Chairman cocked up but he wants to stay; act as scapegoat. (*see Fall on your sword; Lamb, sacrificial; Scapegoat, make a _____ out of*)

Spondulix: 1. Slang for money, of unknown origin. 2. Another word used to make the perfectly ordinary deployment of a budget sound more exotic, as in *"We're spending serious spondulix on Project Bedpan you know, Derek"*. (*see Wonga*)

Spots, stripes or a bit of turbo: 1. Any of a range of options. 2. General confusion based on a vague brief, as in *"I don't know what you want – spots, stripes or a bit of turbo?"* (*see Turbo-charge*)

Sprat to catch a mackerel: 1. Use a small incentive or loss leader to land a bigger prize. 2. Discount so heavily that you don't have any chance at all of making a profit; bend over and take it; ensure the company will go bust within the year;

misjudge and mismanage; fundamentally underestimate size of task and cost accordingly. (*see BOHICA; Drop our trousers; Herring, chasing a different*)

Square the circle: 1. Attempt the impossible, based on the insoluble mathematical problem of constructing a square with exactly the same area as a given circle. 2. Conundrum faced by managers of failing businesses every day; conjurer's trick that can't be pulled off in the real world; Catch-22. (*see Box, think outside the, try and put a _____ round that one; Catch-22*)

Squeeze the lemon in both directions and drive the swine to market: 1. Meaning unknown, despite extensive research. 2. Comprehensive gobbledegook mixing three metaphors, combining fruit with livestock and trying to make a point at the same time; genuinely staggering.

Stacked, completely: 1. Piled high comprehensively. 2. Incapable of taking on any more work; not coping; snowed under; stuffed; under the cosh; on the verge of a breakdown; in need of medical assistance, both mental and physical. (*see Back-to-back; Cocks on the block; Under siege; Wall-to-wall*)

Stakeholder: 1. Person or company with shares in an organization, or some other kind of vested interest. 2. Horribly abused word for any Tom, Dick or Harry who wants to have a say; particularly abhorrent when manacled to another word, as in stakeholder interests, stakeholder values or stakeholder issues; the phrase *"increasing stakeholder value"* invariably means the opposite, or is a smokescreen for increasing value only for the company directors. (*see Engage, engaged, engagement; VC; War chest*)

Stand up and be counted: 1. Take responsibility. 2. Take responsibility, for once in your life; get it in the neck; reap what you sow; endure the consequences of one's actions. (*see Parapet, heads above the, keep our head below the*)

Static: 1. Transmission interference. 2. Similar confusing noise made by Chairman. (*see Background noise; Blue-sky thinking; Communication, lack of, plan, skills; Waffle; White noise*)

Status report: 1. Regular report explaining state of play on a range of jobs. 2. Utterly pointless tome that no one bothers to read; copied in to scores of uninterested parties around the world; time-wasting activity that takes a hapless junior executive the whole of Friday every week to produce; ragbag of meaningless updates from around the company; work of fiction only fit for burning.

Step change: 1. Significant change or improvement. 2. Very rare in business, in fact almost never seen, despite management claims in annual reports. (*see Paradigm shift; Sea change*)

Stick that, some American is going to jet in and tell you exactly where to: 1. You may well be over-ruled by a foreign executive. 2. Frank admission that one's boss in New York holds all the strings; slap on the wrist for Managing Director of regional office when the big guns arrive in town. (*see Head office, I'm from _____ and I'm here to help; Where the sun don't shine, shove it*)

STFU: 1. Shut The Fuck Up. 2. Stop talking immediately. (*see Park it; SUMO; Word dump*)

Still heading west: 1. Restless. 2. Reference to pioneers who arrived in California but still wanted to keep travelling; *"never satisfied"* quality desired by some organizations looking for a bit of pep to spice up otherwise limp workforce. (*see Head off at the pass; Wagon, the Indians have surrounded the*)

Strategy, strategize: 1. What you intend to do. 2. Broad canvas for endless wibbling about what you intend to do, wrapped up in arcane phraseology, reams of diagrams, trite statements, research debriefs and countless meetings; favoured domain of the indecisive. (*see Big picture; Brand strategist; Game Plan; Go round the houses; Methodology; Planning; Research; Wall-to-wall*)

Strategic alliance: 1. Mutual agreement between two companies. 2. Agreement between two companies who will later screw each other and end up in court, both claiming the other reneged on the deal. (*see Bonding, team; Partners*)

Straw man: 1. Outline or example for discussion that will never be enacted. 2. Pointless proposal that takes the same time to prepare as a proper proposal, but which will never be executed; utter waste of time dumped on you by your boss to pad out a meeting; much loved by bosses who recite the disgraceful mantra *"I don't know what I want but I'll know it when I see it"*. (*see Aunt Sally; Know it when I see it, I don't know what I want but I'll _____*)

Stretch target: 1. Number that is bigger than the real target. 2. Increased target produced under pressure from aggressive Finance Director; figure that will never be achieved in a million years; arbitrary addition of 20% to any realistic number supplied by the person who knows the nature of the work best; annoying line of interrogation in sales meetings, as in *"Yes, William, I can see the spreadsheet, but what's your stretch target?"* (*see Flexible, flexibility; Target, hit the _____, miss the point, miss the _____ left right and centre, moving; Target manager*)

Style Nazi: 1. Person who insists on an immaculate office environment. 2. Politically incorrect descriptor of fastidious individual who spends their entire time wandering around the office tidying up and criticizing the habits of others, thereby earning the sobriquet of Little Hitler, or similar; precise, vain individual whom no one particularly likes, but can't afford their designer clothes or interminable purchasing of the latest gadgets.

Sub-optimal: 1. Not good enough. 2. Woolly hyphenated word to say *"This is a bit crap"*. (*see Bugs, iron out the; Drawing board, back to the; Crafting, it needs a bit of; Non-verbal; Optimal; Satisficing; Under-performance*)

Success, what does _____ look like?: 1. How will we know if we have achieved anything? 2. Absolutely disgraceful rhetorical question that has crept into the language in the last few years; truly banal, inasmuch as success doesn't look like anything at all, being an abstract concept; flip query to team in session to suggest some sort of measurement will be needed, and aren't I jolly clever for being the one to point it out; errant twaddle of the first order. (*see Bench, has this got; KPIs;*

Legs, it's got; Outcomes, positive, negative; Outputs; Proof of concept; Purpose, fit for; Real estate, how much _____ does this have)

Sucker punch: 1. Sudden, unexpected knockout blow. 2. Swift development that ruins a product or business, catching the management completely unawares; scandal; sexual revelations in the boardroom. (*see Double whammy; Left field, from; Punch above our weight; Skeletons in the cupboard*)

SUMO: 1. Shut Up, Move On. 2. Get over it; stop whining. (*see Coming from, where I'm; Park it; Rock the boat, don't; STFU*)

Sun, the _____ never sets at: 1. We are always open for business. 2. Dreadful never-ending promise to attend to a customer's every need, as in *"The sun never sets at Sunshine Desserts"*; impossible-to-deliver claim; world domination theme. (*see Always on; Constantly striving; Expectations, exceeding; Global, globalization, globally; Passion; 24/7/365; Work-life balance*)

Swingeing cuts: 1. Punishing, severe reduction in budgets or staff levels. 2. The grim reaper arrives at your office, swinging his scythe; scenes akin to satanic mills and purgatory; depression all round; marching orders for everyone. (*see Across the board, right; Draconian; Internal communications; Marching orders, get your*)

SWOT analysis: 1. Strengths, weaknesses, opportunities, threats; analysis usually made before taking a product to market. 2. Flawed exercise that no one ever completes properly because they don't have the humility and realism to declare the weaknesses and threats properly; such meetings then become peppered with self-deluding narrative such as *"Of course there are no threats, Robin, only opportunities"*, or the truly derogatory: *"There are no threats, Caroline, only challenges"*. (*see Challenges; Opportunity*)

Synergy, synergies, synergize: 1. Acting together. 2. Lazy catch-all for anything lumped together in an amorphous blob; often used for components that have no relationship at all; horrible as a plural (*"We are looking for serious synergies here, Mervin"*), and even worse as a verb, as in *"We are looking to synergize our offer with yours, Malcolm"*. (*see Harnessing synergies*)

Tt

Ts and Cs: 1. Terms and Conditions: 2. Slack abbreviation for all the technical detail that could derail the entire deal; contract; modus operandi; process and pricing structure; basis for making a whopping loss after the euphoria of winning the business has died down.

Table, bring to the: 1. Carry towards a piece of furniture on which items can be set. 2. Overly serious phrase for someone contributing something to a discussion, as in *"Are you sure we need Jeremy in the meeting? What's he going to bring to the table?"*

Tail wagging the dog: 1. Unlikely scenario of a canine being vibrated to and fro by its own appendage; something less important influencing a greater component. 2. Queasy realization that all the wrong priorities are being pursued; feeling of being taken to the cleaners by a lesser power; underdog beating the professionals; tiny detail confusing the main point; usually couched as a question, as in *"Surely this a case of the tail wagging the dog, Roger?"*

Take on board: 1. Absorb; pay attention to; take into consideration. 2. Rather highfaluting quasi-nautical term to let someone know that you acknowledge their point; partial suggestion that the person in question is captain of a ship and has a considerable crew at their disposal; suggestions of luggage or ballast, inasmuch as taking something on board would presumably involve a crane or an embarkation ticket at the very least; broad brush phrase for hearing something but having absolutely no intention of doing anything about it, as in *"That's fine, Mr Chairman, I've taken all your points on board"*.

Take no prisoners: 1. Be uncompromising and determined in one's actions. 2. Blame everybody and destroy everything; dismantle projects and departments willy-nilly; utter annihilation caused by macho gung ho behaviour in the office; hellbent on retribution; barnstorming bravura performance by power-crazy

Managing Director determined to find a scapegoat; slash and burn, and hang the consequences. (*see Search and destroy*)

Talent, war on: 1. Sustained effort to find high quality staff. 2. Baffling phrase reminiscent of political or military campaigns such as the War on Terror or War on Drugs; comprehensive failure by all parties to realize that it is physically impossible to wage war on a concept, be it an inclination to blow people up, distribute illicit narcotics or be a skilled practitioner in the workplace; an additional flaw in the notion becomes apparent upon noticing the use of the word *"on"* rather than *"for"*, rather suggesting that companies would like to engage in battle with the very people whose skills they covet. (*see Know-how; Knowledge management, transfer*)

Talk the talk, walk the walk: 1. Make your actions match your words. 2. Trite rhyming axiom for delivering what you claim you will; presumably born of intense frustration with the large number of people who don't; often directed at those who waffle interminably but never do anything, or entire companies who do the same, as in *"Forget all the bluster, Rod, if you're going to talk the talk you'll need to walk the walk"*.

Talking out loud: 1. Saying something audible. 2. Tautological twaddle that fails to spot that talking intrinsically involves making some kind of noise in order to be effective; staple phrase of dimwits incapable of formulating a point of view before opening their mouths, as in *"I'm just talking out loud here, Joe."* (*see Bullshit; Non-verbal; Off the top of my head; Word dump*)

Tangent, returning to the: 1. Discussing once again something that was irrelevant in the first place. 2. Approach much favoured by wafflers who are incapable of sticking to the point; not content with having veered off the subject in the first place, they then insist on coming back to off brief material again and again; deeply irritating for all present. (*see Marker buoy, Let's stick a _____ on that; Mental lay-by*)

Target, hit the _____, miss the point, miss the _____ left right and centre, moving: 1. Achieve an objective, fail to do so or change it entirely. 2. An obsession for almost everyone in business – the need to hit a target – although almost no one explains why this might be important; arbitrary figure or deadline chosen by the Chief Executive for the hell of it, or to increase the value of his own personal share portfolio. (*see Aims; BHAG; Objectives; Stretch target; Target manager*)

Target (vb.): 1. Aim at or for something. 2. Nasty bastardized verb, now almost ubiquitous in any marketing or media discussion; lazy catch-all dressed in action-oriented clothes, as in *"We need to target 20-35 year olds without alienating teenagers and pensioners"*. (*see Demographic; Stretch target; Target, hit the _____, miss the point, miss the _____ left right and centre, moving; Target manager*)

Target manager: 1. Person whose job description is to ensure that other people hit their targets. 2. Truly bizarre governmental creation; idea that hitting an arbitrary figure will somehow make the quality better; loathsome individual who is the subject of intense ridicule; focal point of concerted attempts to play the system, as in seeming to hit a target when the working reality is horribly different; pointless process of hitting the target whilst comprehensively missing the point. (*see Administrivia; Bread and butter; Bureaucracy; Jobsworth; Panjandrum; Process; Target, hit the _____, miss the point, miss the _____ left right and centre, moving; Vin ordinaire*)

Task-oriented: 1. Concerned with a job. 2. Completely redundant descriptor that for some reason feels the need to highlight that someone is concerned with getting the job done; begs the question "Why are you bothering to point this out?"; linked implication that some people do not concentrate on the matter in hand; at its worst when used as a headhunter's fawning piece of praise, as in *"Gordon is a task-oriented operator who would be a tremendous asset to the company"*. (*see Results-driven*)

Teach your grandmother to suck eggs, don't, would never, would you: 1. Try to tell somebody something they already know. 2. Preach; showboat; hold court; pontificate; drone on; state the bleeding obvious; repeat oneself; waffle; patronize; condescend; assume everyone is a dullard except for you. (*see Enlighten me; Follow, do you; Respect, with*)

Team, take one for the: 1. Selfless personal sacrifice in the interests of the greater good. 2. Flagrant brown-nosing in the desperate hope of peer recognition or promotion; be nominated as a scapegoat and dismissed immediately. (*see Above and beyond; Anonymise; Ask, big; Brown-nosing; Can, carry the; Flag up; High jump, in for the; Lamb, sacrificial; Scapegoat, make a _____ out of*)

Team, there's no I in _____: 1 Axiom suggesting that teamwork cannot function properly if ego is involved. 2. Tired mantra much loved by HR personnel; deployed whenever someone wants to humiliate a certain individual, or spitefully squash an example of personal individuality; commonly followed by the addition of the person's name and a patronizing raising of the eyebrows, as in *"There's no I in team, Bernard"*. (*see Motivation, lack of, team; Troops, the*)

Techno-babble: 1. Unintelligible technical talk. 2. Impenetrable nonsense spouted by the IT department. (*see Obfuscation*)

Teflon: 1. Trademark name for polytetrafluoroethylene, used for nonstick cooking vessels; person to whom nothing bad sticks. 2. Annoying colleague who gets up to all sorts of nefarious deeds but never gets caught; bright-eyed favourite who always gets the credit; hugely annoying person and source of much office envy.

Teleconference: 1. Conversation on the phone between more than two people. 2. Hilarious opportunity to muck about or do sod all; includes amusing rigmarole involving narrating passwords to a robot, as though the conversation were so hush-hush it requires security; chance to pick fluff out of one's navel and drop in the odd obtuse remark such as *"That'll never fly, Brian"*; extended breather in which you can catch up on your personal emails. (*see Videoconference; Webinar*)

Tent, standing outside the _____ pissing in: 1. Urinating into camping apparatus; ruining one's own chances. 2. Hilarious, mildly scatological imagery denoting someone who keeps sabotaging everyone's best efforts; self-destruct mode; death wish; corollary of standing inside the tent and pissing out –

presumably a more hygienic state of affairs; theme for exasperated intonation, as in *"Oh for God's sake, Barry, just for once can't you stand inside the tent and piss out?"* (see Knee-jerk reaction; Own goal, spectacular)

Tent pole: 1. Long and slender piece of wood or metal for holding up camping equipment. 2. Stupid word pairing to describe any spike in sales as depicted on a graph; even more stupid when applied to a non-graphical item, as in *"Do you think this campaign is going to tent pole, Roger?"*

Tertial: 1. A four-month period. 2. Perverse way of dividing up a financial year into three tertials rather than four quarters; fun technique for annoying Finance Directors in sister companies or other countries, particularly France and the USA, who then have to convert all the numbers back to quarters so they can compare like with like. (see Fiscal juggling)

That's what this is called: 1. Needless repetition of the name of something. 2. Hugely irritating tautological trait much loved by dimwitted executives, as in *"That's called quality, that's what this is called"*.

There by the grace of God go I: 1. That could have been me. 2. Pseudo-religious admission that one has got away with it; commonly used when observing an equally-qualified colleague being hauled over the coals or given the boot.

Things, bigger and better: 1. Hypothetical place where ambitious people go when they leave. 2. Euphemism for admitting that the person leaving was far better than the company; mealy-mouthed admission that the company is crap at retaining staff, due to low morale, lousy products and bad pay; staple of all-staff memo explaining why someone has gone, as in *"Graham has moved on to bigger and better things"*, but without wanting to say what.

Think do: 1. If you think of something, do it immediately. 2. Good advice for all procrastinators; get on with it.

Think-tank: 1. Group of specialists convened by a business to undertake intensive study of a problem. 2. Any random gang of hapless attendees charged with sorting out something that has gone badly wrong. (see Brainstorm)

Thought leadership: 1. Idea that if you don't have the resources to be the true market leader, you can at least have ideas befitting one. 2. Weasel phrase much loved by also-rans, has-beens and no-hopers; charming idea that if you're not number one, you can nevertheless think you are and somehow all will be fine. (see Challenger brand; Leader, category, market, thought; Market-leading; World class)

Tick all the boxes: 1. Fulfill all desired criteria. 2. Phrase which should in theory convey complete satisfaction, but which in reality rarely does; often used in the negative by earnest procurement types, as in *"I'm afraid you didn't win the business because you failed to tick all the boxes"*.

Time-poor, time-rich: 1. Having plenty of time, or not enough. 2. Modern pairing of phrases to describe use and availability of time; loosely based on the "time is money" concept by equating poverty or wealth to the number of available hours in a day; often coupled with other -rich/-poor criteria, as in *"This audience is information-rich and time-poor"*; lingo much used by media types and self-appointed *"brand strategists"*. (*see Brand strategist*)

Timesheets: 1. Record of number of hours spent on a particular task or client. 2. The bane of staff the world over; subject of doleful comments around the office about needless administration; worst enemy of procrastinators who fail to fill them in for months and then complain it will take them all weekend to catch up. (*see Administrivia; Panjandrum; Vis-à-vis*)

Tin, does what it says on the: 1. A product or person that does what it claims it will. 2. Rare occurrence in the over-hyped world of marketing; a pleasant surprise to encounter the unadulterated truth for once; usually attributed to Ronseal, which uses it as their strapline.

Tipping point, the: 1. Moment at which a phenomenon or craze *"tips"*, moving from little-known to highly popular, coined by Malcolm Gladwell in the book of the same name. 2. Widely abused term to be found most frequently in the political and PR worlds; hard to articulate, let alone generate; a notion that is as rare as hen's teeth. (*see Must-have*)

Tissue session: 1. Meeting at which rough concepts are discussed. 2. Touchy-feely expression which is a close cousin of the *"chemistry"* meeting; dangerous opportunity for a client to write their own ads in front of the ad agency who should be doing it themselves; classic chance for a committee to design a camel by taking elements from several campaign ideas and nail them all together in an unholy mess.

Titanic, rearranging the deckchairs on the: 1. Futile tinkering when the ship is already sinking. 2. Macabre metaphor for marginal manoeuvres when all is doomed. (*see Eastern front, this is the like the _____ when the bullets didn't turn up; Paper cup, here's a _____, there's a tidal wave coming; Pathologist's interest*)

Tits up, it's all gone: 1. Breasts now pointing skywards. 2. A close cousin of belly up, it appears all is not well when parts of the anatomy point to the heavens; possible allusion to being on one's back on a mortuary slab. (*see Pathologist's interest; Pear-shaped, it's all gone*)

TLC: 1. Tender loving care. 2. Trite acronym denoting showing even a modicum of sympathy in a business context; often used in a condescending way by thoughtless managers, as in *"Given the fact that Julie has just lost her father, I think we should give her a little TLC"*.

Ton of bricks, subtle as a: 1. As heavy-handed as a large quantity of rubble. 2. With all the finesse of a gung ho Sales Director careening into a meeting unprepared, calling the client a wanker and thundering out again. (*see Gung ho*)

Ton of bricks, you can see through that like a: 1. Totally obvious. 2. Not visible or obvious at all; hideous metaphor collision in which construction material is strangely confused with glass; effectively indecipherable.

Tools, management, unique: 1. Systems that help business owners and managers understand what is happening, almost never unique. 2. A continuing obsession with construction instruments in a vain attempt to suggest precision and craftsmanship where there is precious little. (*see Collateral; Crafting, it needs a bit of; Woodwork, spanners in the, spanners jumping out of the*)

Topline: 1. Very sketchy summary. 2. Very sketchy summary open to massive misinterpretation; seeds of regular confusion as everyone gets the wrong end of the stick; originated by impatient managers desperate to hear the results but unable to wait for a detailed report; hugely misunderstood in a financial context, where the topline is nastily juxtaposed with the bottom line; the topline figure may be relatively healthy, whilst the bottom line may reveal a whopping loss; occasionally customized into the odious *"top topline"*, which is presumably so brief that it reveals absolutely nothing. (*see Bottom line*)

Top of mind: 1. In someone's thoughts, ideally all the time. 2. Nirvana for all marketers and advertisers, who desire this as a permanent state for their brands; presumably similar to the frame of mind of an obsessed lover who thinks of nothing other than their new love all day, as though that were likely for a brand of teabag; little reference to bottom of mind, thus raising the tacit assumption that the brain somehow organizes thoughts by physical height.

TQM: 1. Total Quality Management. 2. The apparently revolutionary idea that controlling quality should not be left to a quality controller, but should be the responsibility of everyone involved; pioneered by the very efficient Japanese in the sixties; blindingly obvious piece of management consultancy twaddle that even your grandmother could have told you.

Touch base: 1. Arrive in time at a baseball base to prove you are not out; say hello; update. 2. More sports verbiage, with businessmen all over the world now *"touching base"* regularly, even though they have probably never played the game, and possibly never even seen a match; slightly flip reference to staying in touch, often deployed when gathering papers together and finishing a meeting, as in *"Okay, Malcolm, we can touch base on Project Bugle later"*. (*see Baseline; Re-baselining*)

Touchpoints: 1. Number of occasions, or different media, used by brands and customers to interact. 2. Rather silly modern word invented to cope with proliferating media channels; unnecessary in an age when television, press, radio, cinema and posters was all there was; now the hub for unintelligible spider diagrams showing hundreds of interactions and purporting to be able to control them all, even though consumers do what the hell they want regardless. (*see Look and feel; Snake's honeymoon*)

Touchy-feely: 1. Sensitive; aware of emotions. 2. Mildly derogatory hyphenated adjective to poke fun at those in companies who deal with the soft stuff, typically the not-remotely-softly-named Human Resources; a regular stomping ground for hard-nosed sales people, deriding the appraisal process and raising their eyebrows to the heavens, as in *"I suppose when we review Marcus we'll have to do some of the touchy-feely stuff"*. (*see Bonding, team; Emotional intelligence; Human resources; Open door policy*)

Traction, gain, give it: 1. The act of drawing or pulling; being pulled; adhesive friction between a wheel and its surface. 2. Idiotic contemporary phrase denoting gaining any foothold whatsoever; most commonly applied to ethereal concepts such as campaigns and ideas, which palpably can never gain traction with anything, being intangible; shades of county fairs and traction engines, being slow and lumbering, like most ideas that people want to "gain traction"; consummate nonsense.

Trailblaze: 1. Cut a path through the jungle; pioneer in a particular field. 2. Epic-sounding verb almost always used by a shrinking violet who barely left Basingstoke; not trailblazing at all, in fact probably rather ordinary; typically deployed to add a touch of flair to something really dull, as in *"Colin, I'm convinced that the new XL variant of our panty pads range will trailblaze the market"*. (*see Vin ordinaire*)

Train, who's driving the: 1. Is this an automated transport vehicle or operated by a person?; Who's in charge here? 2. Classically used when there is total chaos and it is apparent that no one is setting direction at all. (*see Bus, who's driving the; Rowing in the same boat, direction*)

Tramlines: 1. Lines on which electrically driven public transport vehicles run. 2. Constraints; parameters; any kind of direction at all would be helpful frankly; often uttered by exasperated executives given no brief whatsoever, as in *"Dave has told me to progress Project Ringpull, but he hasn't given me any tramlines at all"*. (*see Guidelines; brand, corporate*)

Tranche: 1. Portion or installment, especially of a loan or share issue, from the French word for slice. 2. Supercilious way of saying *"a piece"*; unfortunate and generally unwanted spill over from the financial world, with our old culprits the management consultants very much at fault too; another classic in the lexicon of averagely-educated executives who never passed O-level French but are determined to add a whiff of Gallic flair to proceedings. (*see Raft, of ideas, proposals, respondents; Segue; Vis-à-vis*)

Transparency: 1. Openness. 2. Modern obsession with *"being transparent"*, without having any intention of shedding light on what the company gets up to at all; closed shop; secret order; shady dealings behind the scenes; smokescreen; so-called *"Corporate Social Responsibility"* charter with no meat and no action. (*see CSR; Open; Open door policy; Openness; Smoke and mirrors job*)

Trawl for it: 1. Rummage deeply for an item, such as a particular chart in a presentation of over a hundred. 2. Scrabble to find information in an unholy mess; make reference to a point buried somewhere and be conspicuously unable to find it; attempt similar exercise on one's own chaotic desk; regret mentioning the point in the first place.

Trenches, in the: 1. Doing the dirty work. 2. Another from the over-worked military school that tries to imply that business is akin to warfare; under the cosh; doing all the work while others are swanning around. (*see Parapet, heads above the, keep our head below the; Troops, the*)

Triangulate: 1. Form of trigonometry that measures lengths, lines and angles. 2. Ludicrous verb created for the sole purpose of describing three people meeting, as in *"You, me and Derek need to triangulate on this later"*. (*see Dialogue; Pyramided out*)

Troops, the: 1. The people who do the work. 2. Over-worked and underpaid workforce, often referred to dismissively by management as though they were some sort of military battalion. (*see Motivation, lack of, team; Parapet, heads above the, keep our head below the; Team, there's no I in; Trenches, in the*)

Trousers, still in short: 1. Still immature or inexperienced. 2. Throwaway phrase normally used to denigrate a trainee or less senior colleague; frequently uttered by people who are themselves pretty naïve but wish to cover up the fact by pointing out that someone else is a no-hoper.

Tub thumping: 1. Making a racket. 2. Making a racket, often for no reason at all; clarion call hammered out by oppressed Chief Executive with hapless and disinterested workforce; blast of invective delivered by Sales Director whose team is underperforming horribly; physical destruction of boardroom table when stridently making a point and somewhat over-doing it. (*see Bang the drum*)

Turbo-charge: 1. To inject extra energy or pace into an engine or an activity. 2. Classic macho word pairing redolent of racetracks, the Grand Prix, thundering down the motorway in a sports car, picking up women, and so much more; only ever used by people who haven't had a shag for years, typically Terylene-suited salesmen from Bolton. (*see -driven; Spots, stripes or a bit of turbo*)

Turd, polishing a: 1. Attempting to smarten up excreta; futile exercise to make something fundamentally bad look marginally better. 2. Profoundly frustrating process of being told to improve something when it's effectively dead in the water; mildly scatological imagery reminiscent of having one's hands deeply in the doo-doo whilst simultaneously having to put on a brave face and pretend everything is alright. (*see Destigmatize; GIGO; Jazz hands; Ladder it up; Putting lipstick on a pig; Rebrand; RIRO; SISO*)

Turf wars: 1. Battles between different factions in business. 2. Outright warfare, most commonly between departments vying for their slice of the budget, but sometimes between rival companies pitching for their share of a contract; blatant disregard for professional etiquette; underhand tactics; occasional violence in car parks when emotions run too high. (*see Collaboration*)

Tweak: 1. Tiny adjustment. 2. Monumental U-turn. (*see Coming or going, he doesn't know if he's; Evolving to meet customer demand; Pivot; Reverse gear; Turd, polishing a; U-turn*)

20/20 hindsight: 1. Brilliantly accurate when it comes to what has already happened. 2. Hugely annoying trait of many politicians and business folk who appear fantastically lucid and well-informed after the event; as helpful as saying *"I wouldn't have done that if I were you"*.

24/7/365: 1. Permanently open or available. 2. Aggravating numerical sequence depicting hours, days and months; spawn of the Internet age in which nothing ever closes; excuse for companies to make their people work all hours. (*see Always on; Amber, treat every _____ as red; Constantly striving; Expectations, exceeding, failing to achieve, living up to, managing, meeting*)

Two-faced: 1. Deceitful; insincere; hypocritical. 2. Janus-like, as in the Roman god often depicted on doors looking in opposite directions, depicting looking back to the old and forward to the new – hence the month of January; utterly untrustworthy; unreliable; slimy boss who talks a good game and then does something completely different; crowd-pleaser who says yes to everything and then does nothing.

Typo: 1. Typographical error. 2. Every third word in a press release; woeful grammatical skills displayed in the majority of business paperwork.

Uu

Umbilical cord, cut the: 1. Sever all ties. 2. Deny all knowledge of; abdicate all responsibility; bail out; do a runner; leave hanging; hang out to dry; hide in cowardly fashion; be thoroughly attached to, and then disappear without trace; announcement of severing a relationship, as in *"I think we're going to have to cut the umbilical cord on this one, Veronica"*.

Umbrella (vb.): 1. Rain protection apparatus; over-arching cover. 2. Peculiar verb to denote overall protection; since migrated into a strangely active verb, as in *"We need to umbrella these proposals, Derek"*; approximately meaning to draw together under one theme. (*see Over-arching*)

Unbundling: 1. Process of disaggregation. 2. Dismantling into component parts; going back to basics; unraveling a product or service that was always far too complicated; realizing that something was massively confusing and needs to be simplified. (*see Granular, let's get*)

Under siege: 1. Surrounded by the enemy. 2. Surrounded by the enemy at work; snowed under; stacked; coming in from all sides; short of food and getting weaker by the minute; comprehensively outvoted by colleagues; in a minority of one. (*see Balls in the air, on the block, to the wall; Stacked, completely; Wagon, the Indians have surrounded the; Wall-to-wall*)

Underperformance: 1. Sub-standard showing. 2. Mealy-mouthed word to highlight that things have not gone well; attachment of under- prefix to a word that normally suggests a decent result, as in a performance. (*see Sub-optimal*)

Unfair advantage: 1. Improved success, through nefarious means. 2. Frankly bizarre phrase suggesting that winning can be achieved by cheating or somehow bending the rules, as though that were acceptable in business; a notion that raises the question as to whether a fair advantage would be equally acceptable; nonsensical request to staff, as in *"We need to generate an unfair advantage on* *this one guys!" (see Failure is not an option; Forces of darkness, deploy the; Level playing field; Rules of engagement)*

Unhappy, I'm not _____ with that: 1. I am happy with that. 2. Crass use of a double negative to stress that you are perfectly fine with something; mini-bullying phraseology that reminds the other person that you could be unhappy if you wanted to; reassertion of authority by pointing out that you could veto this if you had a mind to; part of an arsenal of similar phrases in the power mind games lexicon. (*see Buy-in; Green light; Greenlit; Issues , I have _____ with that; Problem, I don't have a _____ with that; Redlit*)

Unquantifiable: 1. Incapable of being measured. 2. A perfectly good adjective if used to describe something that truly cannot be measured; more often used inappropriately to exaggerate when something can in fact be measured, as in *"This offer is whaling so much it's unquantifiable!" (see Quantifiable; Whaling)*

Unthinkable, think the: 1. Have an original idea. 2. Absolutely pathetic piece of contradictory twaddle that ignores the fact that if something is unthinkable then it cannot be thought; truly ridiculous request often heard at brainstorms, as in *"I need us to think the unthinkable here guys!" (see BHAG; Brainstorm; Failure is not an option; Greatest imaginable challenge; Impossible, nothing is)*

Up for it: 1. Ready for the challenge. 2. Rather macho statement of preparedness; hints of a call to arms; keen; enthusiastic; full of spunk and energy; fist-clenching and tub-thumping; braced for action.

Upscale: 1. Make bigger; more expensive. 2. Aggravating use of up- as a prefix, when *"scale up"* would be more suitable; interchangeable as a verb or an adjective as in *"This needs to be more upscale, Bill,"* as well as *"We need to upscale this, Amanda"*; strong chance that neither of these phrases means anything much at all; make bigger; increase willy size, for no apparent reason. (*see Scalable; Upsizing; Upskill*)

Upside: 1. Advantage; the pro to the con; the bit where things go right. 2. Likely benefit; the good bit, usually offset by an unwanted bad bit; rough and ready measurement system, as in *"That's the upside, Steve, but what's the downside?"(see Downside)*

Upsizing: 1. Making bigger. 2. More machismo based on scale. (*see Upscale; Upskill; Upweight*)

Upskill: 1. Hire more people who can do the job properly; train existing staff to be better at what they do. 2. More up- prefix twaddle, suggesting a northerly direction for skills; euphemism for pointing out that the current workforce is crap and can't do the work effectively; stupid word to convey the need for more capable people. (*see Upscale; Upsizing; Upweight*)

USP: 1. Unique Selling Point. 2. Utterly generic point, which may or may not lead to sales; lazy acronym much used in advertising to pinpoint the reason why a customer might possibly buy a product; desperate scramble for uniqueness, invariably resulting in the usual old claims, such as *"washes whiter"*; hackneyed cliché that rarely motivates.

Up the ante: 1. Increase gambling stake; increase risks or considerations involved in taking an action or reaching a conclusion. 2. Throw everything at it to call the other person's bluff; gamble on a large scale; chuck in the kitchen sink; petulantly bet on a winning outcome by deploying every possible resource at the same time; macho power play, as in *"I think we need to up the ante on this one, Malcolm"*. (*see Kitchen sink*)

Up-to-the-minute: 1. Latest. 2. Probably out of date; somewhat tired; lacklustre; old; obsolescent.

User experience: 1. What a customer has to go through when using a product or service. 2. Catalogue of frustration; phrase much loved by so-called *"brand strategists"* and digital natives, especially in connection with mobile devices and Internet products. (*see Brand strategist; Digital native; Free-roaming experience; On-rails experience*)

Utilize: 1. Use. 2. Pointless longer version of the verb to use.

U-turn: 1. Complete reversal of stance. 2. Embarrassing turnaround frequently propagated by roguish politicians and indecisive companies; visions of hurtling down the road in one direction, slamming on the brakes and suddenly turning round to head the other way; total change of mind, for reasons often left unexplained; bare-faced lying, often refusing to admit a change of direction at all; self-deluding insistence that nothing has changed at all, and that it is simply business as usual, when everyone else can see the about turn. (*see Coming or going, he doesn't know if he's; Evolving to meet customer demand; Pivot; Reverse gear; Tweak*)

Upweight: 1. Make more weighty. 2. Yet another pointless up- prefix culprit. (*see Upscale; Upsizing; Upskill*)

Vv

Valuable: 1. Of value. 2. Often not of any value at all, as in *"Thanks for those valuable insights, Mr Chairman"*. (*see Insights; Value-add, Value-added*)

Value-add, value-added: 1. Addition of value. 2. Deeply annoying piece of management consultancy jargon; variously used as a noun, as in *"What's the value-add here, Geoff?"*, and as an adjective, as in *"This is a value-added proposition, Martin, as you can clearly see"*; based on the counterintuitive notion that anyone worth their salt would attempt to add no value at all. (*see Results-driven*)

Value chain: 1. Bundles of activities, described by original proponent Michael Porter as building blocks, that design, market, deliver and support a product. 2. Massively misinterpreted management tool that few people really understand, including possibly the author; MBA concept that allows for the generation of significant amounts of hot air, as in *"Of course, Derek, we need to examine the value chain in detail"*, when no one really knows what it is. (*see Value creation*)

Value creation: 1. The art of building a company that is actually worth something. 2. Ponderous and seemingly never-ending academic debate about what the true value of a company really is; variously measured via stockmarket value, balance sheet, expectation of future performance, cash in the bank or the Chairman's wife's middle name; pointless hypothetical figure based on fabricated evidence. (*see Chairman's wife; Value chain*)

Value proposition, judgments: 1. Statement that has some worth; decisions based on a set of principles. 2. Nothing of the sort; cliché-ridden piece of piffle using the same old words, and interchangeable between products the world over; flabby set of platitudes that no one cares much about and has no intention of emulating; nothing to do with value, more likely long-winded pontification about this and that in order to fill a space on the boardroom wall. (*see Positioning; Vision, visioning*)

Valued customer: 1. Someone buying our product that we care about. 2. Someone buying our product that we couldn't give a toss about, so long as we've got their money; fawning, oleaginous phrase beginning a sales letter, as in *"Valued customer, you'll recall you bought a sofa from us last year and we are writing to let you know that the no-stain guarantee we flogged you under duress has now expired"*. (*see Expectations, exceeding, failing to achieve, living up to, managing, meeting*)

Values: 1. Principles a company holds dear. 2. Rambling set of adjectives defining a perfect world that no one can hope to live up to; typically containing a description of the perfect partner, as in passionate, innovative, and world class. (*see Change drivers; Innovation, innovative, innovatively; Mission statement; Passion, passionate; Vision, visioning; World class*)

Variable (n.): 1. Item that can vary. 2. Catch-all word for any component of anything, as in *"So what variables are we actually dealing with here, Fiona?"*; hints of mathematical rigour where there is none whatsoever, as in the correct meaning of having a range of possible values; variable indeed, as in very vague.

VC: 1. Venture Capitalist. 2. Shady organizations and individuals who lend money with a smile and then demand it back at an inconvenient moment whilst holding a large firearm; greasy posh blokes with braces and a penchant for leaning back in chairs and holding court; windbags; usurers. (*see Stakeholder; War chest*)

Vehicle: 1. Conveyance for transportation, taking various forms. 2. A word now strangely usurped to denote almost anything in business, particularly intangible items such as plans and frameworks; suggestion of solidity where there may be none, as in *"Which communications vehicle are we using in this campaign, Rupert?"* (*see Mechanics*)

Vertical market, _____ integration: 1. A specific market; merging two businesses that are at different levels of production. 2. Overly posh phrase for two companies getting together because they each need what the other has; completion of a previously patchy service; *"vertical market"* adds a particularly pointless dimension to what should otherwise simply be a market, especially when abbreviated to *"verticals"*, as in *"Charlie, can you give me a rundown on the verticals in the telecoms market please?"* (*see Integrate, integral, integration*)

Video conference: 1. Discussion in which each attendee is visible to the other via a video screen. 2. Hilarious method of non-communication; opportunity to investigate nasal hair of boss in remote city; chance for office wags to hide just out of screen and suddenly dive in with a remark, thus scaring the pants off unwitting colleagues in far-off countries. (*see Teleconference; Webinar*)

Vin ordinaire: 1. Standard but not very exciting table wine. 2. A distinctly average kind of person; dull; beige; wan; bland; mediocre; Colin in accounts; civil servant. (*see Balanced scorecard; Jobsworth; Mediocracy; Run-of-the-mill; Snake oil salesman; Target manager; Trailblaze; Vis-à-vis*)

Viper's nest: 1. Home of many poisonous snakes. 2. Certain departments traditionally housing gossips, feckless layabouts, and ne'er-do-wells; spiteful gathering of vituperate pessimists, hellbent on slagging off everything and everybody; occasionally embodied in just one person, such as Bernadette from HR; hot bed of bad blood, negative rumour and poor morale. (*see Hierarchy; Matrix; Organagram; Python, wrestling with a; Snakepit; Snake's honeymoon*)

Vis-à-vis: 1. In relation to; regarding (from the French face to face). 2. Ultra smug way of saying *"in relation to"* or *"regarding"*; risible attempt to add a dash of Gallic flair to proceedings, or suggest an education rather more elevated than is truly the case; usually perpetrated by panjandrums, as in *"Stephen, I need to talk to you vis-à-vis your timesheets"*. (*see Panjandrum; Segue; Timesheets; Tranche; Vin ordinaire*)

Vision, visioning: 1. Ability to see; dream of how things could be. 2. Over-blown statement of what a company wants to do, now turned into a labour-consuming process and imbued with all the qualities of black magic; puffery; nothing much at all; series of staid platitudes nailed to boardroom wall or tired-looking reception area; even worse, turned into a horrible verb, as in *"Darren, when you've finished visioning we'll take it to the Board"*. (*see Change drivers; Mission statement; Value proposition, judgments: Values; Voodoo, corporate*)

Voice mail: 1. Electronic system for leaving a message. 2. Perfect way to delegate and do a runner; arch coward's way of breaking bad news without doing it in person. (*see BCC; CC; Email*)

Voodoo, corporate: 1. The spirit of a company. 2. Daft ethereal phrase along the lines of defining someone's *"mojo"*; shades of black magic or casting of spells, as though that were standard practice in conventional business; hard-to-bottle essence; strident Chief Executive's character directly reflected in a petrified bunch of subservient employees. (*see Forces of darkness, deploy the; Mission statement; Vision, visioning*)

Waffle: 1. Combination of words that amount to very little. 2. Piffle; static; white noise; nonsense; twaddle; wibble; hot air; bullshit; most of the contents of this dictionary. *(see Bullshit; Doughnut rather than the hole, it would be wise to concentrate on the; Drive it home; Obfuscation; Off the top of my head; Static; Talking out loud; White noise; Word dump)*

Wagon, the Indians have surrounded the: 1. The game is up. 2. Evocative cowboys and Indians imagery as American First Nation personnel beset some hapless pioneers, possibly on their way to California; visions of tomahawks flying and Davy Crockett-style acts of derring-do; in other words, quite unlike any office you have ever seen. *(see Head off at the pass; Shark, keep moving like a, waiting for the sharks to circle; Still heading west; Under siege)*

Wake up and smell the coffee: 1. Stop sleeping and inhale the scent of roasting Arabica beans; pay attention. 2. American phrase imploring someone to stop daydreaming and realize the true extent of what's going on; usually deployed on very naive individuals, as in *"Oh come on David, when are you going to wake up and smell the coffee?!"*

Walking wounded: 1. Damaged but not dead. 2. Severely battered staff, usually after a horrible setback such as a round of redundancies or the loss of a major contract.

Wall-to-wall: 1. Carpeting that covers the entire floor; a room so full of goods it's almost impossible to move; desk in a similar state. 2. Over-worked with little hope of reprieve; snowed under; not coping; unable to say no to requests to do even more; possibly micromanaging. *(see Back-to-back; Micromanaging; Stacked, completely; Strategy, strategize; Under siege)*

War chest: 1. Box full of kit ready for battle; cash stockpile ready to be used for acquisition. 2. Macho stash amassed to embark upon world domination plan; VC contribution gathered for same purpose; springboard to massive payday for a privileged few; no cash at all, merely borrowings to facilitate all the above using someone else's money. (*see Stakeholder; VC*)

Warts and all: 1. With all blemishes evident. 2. Frequently shocking revelation of the true state of affairs in a company; nasty picture, with no holds barred; frank analysis of doomed set-up; precursor to news you really don't want to hear, as in *"OK Keith, I'm now going to give you the full picture, warts and all"*. (*see Drains up, have the; Respect, with*)

Wash our hands of it: 1. Take no further part, nor responsibility. 2. Do a runner; bail out; pretend we never were involved; pass the buck; hand over, regardless of stage reached; pay a forfeit just to be shot of something. (*see Buck, pass the; Hospital pass*)

Wash its face: 1. Pay its own way; break even. 2. Curious ablution reference to describe a project or budget reconciliation, as in *"I'm happy to proceed with Project Sideboard, so long as it washes its face"*.

Watch the boards light up: 1. Hope to observe a positive reaction. 2. Asinine expression drawn from the world of telecommunications, in which lights appear on a switchboard when callers connect; shades of some mad villain surveying a child-like model of an empire, with lights denoting various outposts; fairground drama mirroring the rather more mundane process of customers buying some product; overly macho enthusiasm for something relatively humdrum, as in *"Of course, Barbara, as soon as we launch the new barbeque flavour we can really watch the boards light up"*. (*see Flagpole, run it up the _____ and see who salutes*)

Watchout, I've picked out a: 1. I have identified something we need to keep an eye on. 2. Deeply aggravating conversion of the two words *"watch"* and *"out"* into a one-word noun; hints of danger and imminent peril when in fact people are just sitting in a room staring at some fairly boring data; overly histrionic intervention in a meeting, as in *"Hang on guys, I've just picked out a watchout from the Tyne Tees figures"*.

Watch this space: 1. Keep an eye open because something is going to happen. 2. Obtuse way of saying things are moving pretty rapidly and you'd better be sufficiently on-the-ball to keep up; much loved by project managers working on something mind-numbingly dull who wish to convince themselves that their work is actually rather dynamic; implication of being in-the-know when you're not, as in *"I can't reveal all the details yet, Martin, but what I can say is, watch this space"*.

Water cooler conversation: 1. Chat with a colleague when collecting a thirst-quenching beverage. 2. Phenomenal opportunity to gossip indiscreetly and waste vast amounts of time; exchange of views concerning football results, what was on the television last night and how hot the temp on reception is; relating of unfortunate drinking stories, as in *"You'll never believe it, but Colin over-shot on the shandy and threw up on Victoria's briefcase"*. (*see Office, the; Powwow*)

Wavelength, on the same, not on the same: 1. Listening to the same radio station; in tune generally, or not. 2. Broad theme for a complete communication breakdown; collapse of relations; propensity to take a call from the Mumbai office, or ignore it completely; internecine refusal to help colleague; spite; obduracy; total failure to agree. (*see Ducks in a row, get our; Hymn sheet, singing from the same; Rowing in the same boat, direction; Wildebeest in a row, has the lion got his*)

Webinar: 1. Seminar held on the web. 2. Theoretically helpful medium for discussing information online, but much abused; forum for a succession of idiotic questions that must be endured by large numbers of better-informed individuals; opportunity to daydream and count the number of nasal hairs sported by the presenter. (*see Teleconference; Videoconference*)

Whaling: 1. Killing large marine mammals; an online offer that is selling in much higher quantities than normal. 2. Monumentally banal American expression for offer that is *"going off the scale"*; highly inappropriate allusion to the death of one our most impressive beasts, applied to the rather less important world of social media; even more tragic in office patter, as in *"I see that the 2 for 1 cinema tickets offer is really whaling, Chris"*. (*see Killer whale; Off the scale; Unquantifiable*)

Wheels coming off: 1. Falling apart; about to crash; not going well. 2. Everything going wrong; on the verge of collision, or total annihilation; spectacularly shit; badly handled; incompetence in action; project about to be terminated due to lack of professionalism; company in the same position. (*see Crash and burn; High risk; Maxed out; Needle, moving the; Needle, pushing the; Nero syndrome; On ramps; Off ramps; Pushing the envelope; Nightmare, utter; Reinventing the wheel*)

When the chips are down: 1. When the gambling is about to begin; when it comes to the crunch. 2. Macho betting phrase that tries to lend a little frisson of danger to the most boring of subjects, such as the pet care and personal hygiene markets; perpetuation of the ridiculous notion that shifting air conditioners from a warehouse in Purley is somehow as glamourous as playing James Bond in Casino Royale. (*see When the going gets tough, the tough get going*)

When the going gets tough, the tough get going. 1. When things are difficult, decent people come to the fore and take responsibility. 2. The polar opposite of what happens in most companies; when the going gets tough, most senior executives are nowhere to be seen, often having gone on holiday deliberately to avoid criticism; flip parroting of clichéd Billy Ocean song title as a pathetic motivational speech by hackneyed Sales Directors, as in *"Well, Sebastian, when the going gets tough, the tough get going!"* (*see When the chips are down*)

Where the sun don't shine, shove it: 1. Stick it up your arse! 2. Profane rejoinder conveying complete disdain for the request and the requester; approximate translation: *"If you seriously expect me to do that, you can f**k right off!"* (*see Brown-nosing; Stick that, some American is going to jet in and tell you exactly where to*)

White elephant: 1. Elaborate venture that proves useless. 2. The majority of all projects undertaken by companies. (*see Elephant in the room; Wild-goose chase*)

White noise: 1. Electrical sound with a wide continuous range. 2. General racket from which no helpful sound can be discerned; boardroom discussion about car parking spaces or share allocation; Annual General Meeting at which disgruntled shareholders are rioting in response to invidious Director's pay awards; gaggle of secretaries in local bar drinking Martinis and talking bollocks at high pitch; Chairman's speech. (*see Background noise; Blue-sky thinking; Communications, lack of, plan, skills; Static; Waffle; Word dump*)

Wild-goose chase: 1. Absurd or pointless pursuit of something unattainable. 2. The majority of a company's activities every year; dead end; blind alley; cul-de-sac; directionless effort; waste of time for everybody; chimera; vain hope; Managing Director's doomed cause célèbre; ship of fools, bound for nowhere. (*see Goal posts, move the; White elephant; WOMBAT*)

Wildebeest in a row, has the lion got his: 1. Do we agree on this? 2: Staggeringly ridiculous wildlife reference suggesting a decent working knowledge of the savannah, whilst simultaneously revealing colossal ignorance of same; quaint implication that the King of the Beasts would do what comes naturally to every apex predator, that is to say line up his prey in a neat row before embarking on an attack. (*see Beavers, defending it like; Ducks in a row, get our; Hymn sheet, singing from the same; Loose cannon; Off message; Off-piste; Realignment; Wavelength, on the same, not on the same*)

Win or lose, we're in with a chance: 1. Contradictory nonsense probably attempting to convey that it's not over until it's over. 2. Utter bollocks, inasmuch as if you have won or lost then you have indeed won or lost, and are therefore no longer in with a chance, since the element of chance has now been comprehensively removed. (*see Fat lady, it's not over until the _____ sings; Winners and losers, there are always*)

Win-win: 1. Advantageous or successful in more than one way; both sides can benefit. 2. Irritating word pairing from our persistent culprits the management consultants; patronizing ruse to suggest that this is not just one victory, but two or more; hoodwinking idea that no one actually loses; deep joy, we all win!; smug aside in meeting, usually accompanied by a knowing wink, as in *"This looks very much to me like a win-win, Geoff!"* (*see Lose-lose; Wins, quick, easy, there are no easy*)

Wind, sailing close to the: 1. At full tilt and in danger of capsizing. 2. Travelling perilously fast; careening; losing it on the chicane; over-cooking it; at full throttle and most likely to crash and burn. (*see Crash and burn; Flying unstable; Riding the razor blade*)

Window of opportunity: 1. Chance to do something. 2. Peculiar imagery suggesting that a chance to do something is somehow akin to a pane of glass or aperture to look through; shades of voyeurism, as in peeping through a window to sneak a glance of something salacious, such as the Chairman shagging the new receptionist over the boardroom table.

Windsurfing in peanut butter: 1. Attempting something nigh on impossible. 2. Brilliantly inventive vision of tackling an unachievable task, but valiantly so; invokes the retort *"Smooth or crunchy?"*

Winners and losers, there are always: 1. Someone will win and someone won't. 2. Comprehensively self-evident platitude much loved by small-minded and obtuse salesmen; totally pointless waste of anyone's time, as though some earth-shattering insight has suddenly been revealed; trite twaddle spouted by office bore, as in *"Of course, Jane, there are always winners and losers"*. (*see Win or lose, we're in with a chance*)

Wins, quick, easy, there are no easy: 1. We can succeed fast; there is no way to succeed fast. 2. Glib throwaway hinting at prior knowledge or implying experience where there may be nothing more than guesswork; mildly hectoring tone, as in *"Of course there are no easy wins in this market, Sally"*. (*See Low-hanging fruit, go for the; Win-win*)

WIP: 1. Work in progress. 2. Euphemism for it hasn't been done. (*see Development; Flatline*)

-wise: 1. Relating to whatever precedes this. 2. Horribly over-worked suffix stuck on to the end of pretty much any word people can get hold of when they haven't expressed themselves clearly, including hardy perennials such as company-wise, control-wise, country-wise, product-wise, market-wise and many more; not wise at all, in fact, rather ignorant. (*see –ize*)

Witch-hunt: 1. Rigorous campaign to round up or expose dissenters on the pretext of safeguarding the safety of the community. 2. Comprehensive search for someone to blame; no expense spared in finding a culprit, having deployed no funds so far in helping to make something a success; vindictive finger pointing; accusatory activity; methodical search for a scapegoat, followed by public humiliation or dismissal. (*see Backlash; Blame culture; Deep dive; Lift up a rock; Look, take a long hard; No stone unturned; Root-and-branch review; Scapegoat, make a _____ out of*)

Within our gift: 1. In our power. 2. Dismissive phrase usually trotted out when something can't be done, or when someone wants to abdicate responsibility for doing something helpful; pompous, rather archaic way of saying I don't have the authority to do that, as in *"I'd love to give you a pay rise, Julian, but it is simply not within my gift"*.

WOMBAT: 1. Waste of Money, Bandwidth and Time. 2. Financially futile, not worth the mental effort nor the hours needed to do it; pointless; suicidal; baseless; any project that should never have been commissioned. (*see Bandwidth, he doesn't have the; White elephant; Wild-goose chase*)

Wonga: 1. Informal term for money, possibly from the Romany word for coal, wongar. 2. Term much loved by people who want to make budgets sound more impressive, as in *"We're spending serious wonga on this product launch, Nigel"*. (*see Spondulix*)

Woodwork, spanners in the, spanners jumping out of the: 1. Unexpected problems arising. 2. Strange collision of carpentry and mechanical tools; no justification as to why spanners might be relevant to woodwork at all; worse still, suggestion that they might reside inside the woodwork – a physical impossibility; even more ludicrous, suggestion that they might jump of their own accord; overall, outright gobbledegook. (*see Crafting, it needs a bit of; Tools, management, unique*)

Wood, can't see the _____ for the trees: 1. Unable to see the overall picture due to too much detail, or unable to see the specifics due to too much vagueness. 2. Near-permanent state of affairs whenever anyone in business is staring at data; inability to understand what on earth is going on. (*see Closer look, stand back and take a*)

Woods, not out of the _____ yet: 1. We are not yet in the clear. 2. Ominous warning of complacency or celebrating too early; suggestion of getting away with something, or not being rumbled; common in companies that are skimming it or flying by the seat of their pants. (*see Fly by the seat of one's pants*)

Word dump: 1. Spontaneous outburst of verbiage enacted in front of someone else. 2. Nasty trait of people who can't think for themselves; sudden pouring out of half-baked drivel, perpetrated on hapless colleague on the way to the toilet; verbal diarrhoea ejaculated without warning. (*see Bounce ideas off; Brain dump; Criteria, key; Data dump; Drive it home; Enlighten me; Human wind tunnel; STFU; Waffle; White noise*)

Word of mouse: 1. Information disseminated on the Internet. 2. Dismaying word play turning word of mouth into its online cousin.

Word on the street: 1. Opinion generally held. 2. Hip, down-with-the-kids saying used by executives who want to show that they are in touch with a customer base or group of colleagues; phrase usually used by nouveau riche executives who have rarely left their gated community, let alone listened to anything on the street.

Work cut out for us, we've got our: 1. We have a lot to do. 2. We have too much to do and we'll never make it in time.

Worklessness: 1. Unemployment. 2. Truly disgraceful replacement for the word *"unemployment"*; odious avoidance of the plain fact that someone has no work; cowardly twisting of words to skirt round the truth; deliberate inclusion of the word *"work"* in order to suggest that there is some. (*see Frontofmindness; Here-and-now-ness; Negative growth, profit*)

Work-life balance: 1. Sensible ratio of work and free time. 2. Complete inability to achieve any balance between the two at all; chronic over-work, comprehensively encouraged by one's employer for no particular tangible benefit; exploitation; slave labour; abject failure to see partner or family for weeks on end; obsession with projects that any other person would find dull and unimportant; all night work for sustained periods, followed by lengthy absence through illness; vacillating horribly between two extremes; lack of balance. (*see Always on; Constantly striving; Expectations, exceeding; Sun, the _____ never sets at; 24/7/365*)

Workshop (vb.): 1, To conduct a meeting, usually to come up with some ideas. 2. Unsatisfactory verb that covers a multitude of sins; almost certainly nothing whatsoever to do with a workshop in the artisan or craft skills sense; random collection of unsuitable people idly toying with an apparently important business issue; group of international colleagues exchanging banter and achieving f**k-all; marathon consumption of biscuits and coffee, at someone else's expense; humiliation by smug facilitator; horrible participation in childish *"team bonding"* exercises, to no discernible end; futile solution to almost every business challenge, as in *"I think we need to workshop this one, Shaun"*. (*see Awayday; Brainstorm; Executive retreat; Off-site*)

Workshy: 1. Not inclined to work. 2. The majority of employees in the world.

World-beating, -changing: 1. The best there is; revolutionary. 2. Truly breathtaking piece of arrogant twaddle; suggestion that a project or product can change the world, or beat everyone else; arrogance on a staggering scale, even judging by the appalling standards of macho businessmen in the highest echelons of an enormous company; pompous, elitist hubris of the lowest order; rank self-aggrandisement; words to be avoided at all costs in company reports and mission statements. (*see Mission statement; World class*)

World class: 1. As good as any comparable product or service in the world. 2. Almost certainly nothing of the sort; decidedly average; impossible to measure, since no satisfactory metric of *"world class"* has ever been developed. (*see Challenger brand; Market-leading; Mission statement; Scalable; Thought leadership; World-beating, -changing*)

Wow factor: 1. An element of a proposal or product that evokes the reaction *"Wow!"* 2. Derisory piece of histrionics designed to distract the audience from the fact that the proposal has no substance, or that the product is distinctly sub-standard. (*see FMF; Jazz hands; X factor*)

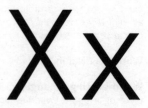

X factor: 1. Mysterious ingredient that makes something brilliant. 2. Disastrous television programme that provides a national platform for contestants to humiliate themselves in front of the largest possible audience. *(see FMF; Magic ingredient, there is no; Wow factor)*

Yy

Y2K: 1. The year 2000. 2. Pointless mnemonic deployed at the start of the millennium by smug executives in a futile attempt to sound impressive.

Yes man: 1. A male who always says yes. 2. Obsequious and fawning subordinate of either sex who has no opinion of their own and so always does what they are told, regardless of the consequences. *(see Brown-nosing; On message)*

Zz

Zee, we've covered everything from A to: 1. We have thought of everything. 2. We've done sod all, but are claiming that we have been hard at work; we are gratuitously using the American Zee rather than the English Zed to let you know we are thoroughly in tune with our friends across the pond. *(see A-Z; Chapter and verse; Full Monty, the)*

Z list celebrity: 1. Barely-known person. 2. Unknown person wanting to be known. *(see Profile, raise the)*

Zone, in the: 1. In contention; in the running; concentrating properly. 2. Frankly nowhere, but grasping yet another phrase from American sport to suggest that we are on the case. *(see Ballpark figure; Cover all the bases)*

ABOUT THE AUTHOR

Kevin Duncan is a business adviser, marketing expert, motivational speaker and author. After 20 years in advertising, he has spent the last 13 as an independent troubleshooter, advising companies on how to change their businesses for the better, via change management programmes, non-exec work or better pitching.

For 30 years he has collected the material in this book, and done his best to avoid using any of it, except in jest.

Contact the author:
kevinduncan@expertadvice.co.uk
expertadviceonline.com

Add your own examples and stay posted at **bulldictionary.com**

BEYOND
THE WRITTEN WORD

Authors who speak to you face to face.

Discover LID Speakers, a service that enables businesses to have direct and interactive contact with the best ideas brought to their own sector by the most outstanding creators of business thinking.

- A network specialising in business speakers, making it easy to find the most suitable candidates.

- A website with full details and videos, so you know exactly who you're hiring.

- A forum packed with ideas and suggestions about the most interesting and cutting-edge issues.

- A place where you can make direct contact with the best in international speakers.

- The only speakers' bureau backed up by the expertise of an established business book publisher.